D1256579

*Financing the Athenian Fleet*

# Financing the Athenian Fleet

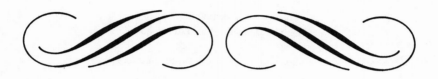

## Public Taxation and
## Social Relations

### Vincent Gabrielsen

The Johns Hopkins University Press
*Baltimore and London*

© 1994 THE JOHNS HOPKINS UNIVERSITY PRESS
All rights reserved. Published 1994
Printed in the United States of America on acid-free paper
03  02  01  00  99  98  97  96  95  94    5  4  3  2  1

The Johns Hopkins University Press
2715 North Charles Street
Baltimore, Maryland 21218-4319
The Johns Hopkins Press Ltd., London

Library of Congress Cataloging-in-Publication Data
will be found at the end of this book.
A catalog record for this book is available
from the British Library.

ISBN 0-8018-4692-7

*To Kirsten and Andreas*

# Contents

Preface    xi
Abbreviations    xiii

*Introduction*    I
    Concepts and Aims    3
    Sources    13

PART I ∼ THE ESTABLISHMENT OF THE INSTITUTION

ONE *The Origin of the Trierarchy*    19
    The Naukrariai and the Athenian Fleet    19
    Early Naval Organization    24
    The Establishment of the Trierarchy    26

PART II ∼ QUALIFICATIONS FOR THE TRIERARCHY

TWO *Qualifications by Wealth*    43
    The Liturgical Census Theory    45
    Visible and Invisible Wealth    53
    The Role of Inheritance    60

THREE *Appointment*    68
    Preselection of Nominees    68
    Formal Appointment    73

The Length of Service    78
The Allocation of Ships    80

FOUR *Exemption*                                                          85
Regular Exemption    85
The Antidosis    91
The Hiring Out of Trierarchies    95

PART III ~ FINANCIAL RESPONSIBILITIES

FIVE *The Crew*                                                         105
The Recruitment of Crews    105
Pay and Provisioning    110
Funding the Fleet    114
Logistics and the Cost of Service    118

SIX *The Ship*                                                         126
The Hulls    126
The Condition of Hulls    129
Shipbuilding    131
The Replacement of Hulls by Trierarchs    136
The Cost of a Hull    139
The Significance of Compensatory Payments    142

SEVEN *Equipment*                                                      146
Shortages    146
Misappropriation of Equipment by Officials    149
Misappropriation of Equipment by Trierarchs    153
The Recovery of Naval Debts    157
The Treatment of Defaulters    162

PART IV ~ INSTITUTIONAL TRANSFORMATION

EIGHT *The Reforms*                                                    173
The Syntrierarchy    173
Periandros's Reform    182
Voluntary Naval Contributions    199
Demosthenes' Reform of 340    207
The Sociopolitical Profile    213

Epilogue   218
Appendix: Standard Equipment   227
Notes   229
Bibliography   273
Index   293

# Preface

The costs of keeping substantial fleets afloat and the fiscal systems developed by maritime states in order to finance naval activity are important issues for historians interested in the social and economic changes undergone by major naval powers. This study attempts to describe the system of fleet finance employed in classical Athens; it originates from my belief that a fresh and thorough treatment of the subject has long been needed. Neither the overall picture I draw nor the individual conclusions on which that picture is based can lay a claim to finality or absolute completeness. If this work stimulates debate and further research, it will have accomplished its primary goal.

Passages quoted from Greek texts are given in English translation. For most ancient authors, I have used (often in slightly adapted form) the translations of the Loeb Classical Library. Major Greek terms appear in italicized transliteration at their first use, and are briefly explained in the text and notes. With the names of places and people, I have been slightly, and deliberately, inconsistent. Corinth, Cyprus, and Crete, I feel, are most familiar in that form, but I see little point in Anglicizing Korkyra, Knidos, or Koresos. Herodotos, Aischylos, and Dionysos should be recognizable to the reader as Herodotus, Aeschylus, and Dionysus, but it might not be obvious to some that Thoukydides is the well-known historian Thucydides.

This study would not have been possible without the unsparing support of several institutions, friends, and colleagues. Foremost among my obligations are those to the University of Copenhagen, the Danish Council for the Humanities, and the Carlsberg Foundation, from which I have received generous scholarship grants. In 1989, I was a Visiting Fellow at Wolfson College, Cambridge, and had the opportunity to enjoy the hospitable environment and useful facilities of that institution. No less welcoming and helpful have been Dr. D. Peppa-Delmousou, former Director of the Epigraphical Museum in Athens, and her staff. The patience and kind assistance of the staff of the Odense University Library are gratefully acknowledged. My colleagues in the departments of classics and history at the University of Copenhagen have been a constant source of inspiration, encouragement, and good counsel. I am deeply indebted to them all, but special thanks are due to Mogens Herman Hansen and Jens Erik Skydsgaard, who tirelessly and uncompromisingly offered me guidance. My gratitude to Signe Isager of the University of Odense is immense. She has followed the progress of my work with admirable patience, and her characteristically gentle but clear criticisms made me rethink and refine my arguments. Many others have been liberal with their time and help. John S. Morrison has, with unfailing enthusiasm, shared with me his expert knowledge of the history of the trieres. Drafts were read by Robert W. Wallace and David L. Silverman, with whom I had profitable discussions about naval matters. The reader for the Johns Hopkins University Press saved me from many errors and offered insightful suggestions. My debt to this anonymous colleague is considerable.

Eric Halpern and his associates at the Press embraced this project with enthusiasm, concern, and cooperation; I truly appreciate their professionalism. Jane Lincoln Taylor's editing efficiently clarified my prose and helped eliminate inconsistencies. I, however, carry sole responsibility for the contents of this book.

# Abbreviations

Ancient authors and titles are cited in accordance with the standard abbreviations in the *Oxford Classical Dictionary* (2d ed., 1970). Titles of periodicals are abbreviated according to the system of *L'année philologique*.

## Books

| | |
|---|---|
| *AFD* | B. D. Meritt. *Athenian Financial Documents of the Fifth Century.* University of Michigan Studies, Humanistic Series, no. 27. Ann Arbor, 1932. |
| Amit *AS* | M. Amit. *Athens and the Sea: A Study in Athenian Sea-Power.* Collection Latomus, no. 74. Brussels and Berchem, Belgium, 1965. |
| *APF* | J. K. Davies. *Athenian Propertied Families, 600–300 B.C.* Oxford, 1971. |
| *ATL* | B. D. Meritt, H. T. Wade-Gery, and M. F. McGregor. *The Athenian Tribute Lists.* 4 vols. Cambridge, Mass., 1939–53. |
| Beauchet *Droit privé* | L. Beauchet. *Histoire du droit privé de la république athénienne.* 4 vols. Paris, 1897. |
| Behrend *Pachturkunden* | D. Behrend. *Attische Pachturkunden: Ein Beitrag zur Beschreibung der μίσθωσις nach den griechischen Inschriften.* Vestigia, no. 12. Munich, 1970. |
| Beloch *GG* | J. K. Beloch. *Griechische Geschichte.* 2d ed. 4 vols. in 8. Strasbourg, Berlin, and Leipzig, 1912–27. |

| | |
|---|---|
| Brillant "Trierarchia" | M. Brillant. "Trierarchia, Trierarchus." In Daremberg-Saglio (1912), 5:442–65. |
| Busolt-Swoboda *GS* | G. Busolt, rev. H. Swoboda. *Griechische Staatskunde*. 2 vols. Munich, 1920–26. |
| Casson *SSAW* | L. Casson. *Ships and Seamanship in the Ancient World*. Princeton, N.J., 1971. |
| Daremberg-Saglio | C. Daremberg and E. Saglio, eds. *Dictionnaire des antiquités grecques et romaines d'après les textes et les monuments*. 5 vols. Paris, 1877–1919. |
| Davies *Wealth* | J. K. Davies. *Wealth and the Power of Wealth in Classical Athens*. Salem, N.H., 1981. |
| Develin *AO* | R. Develin. *Athenian Officials, 684–321 B.C.* Cambridge, 1989. |
| *FAC* | J. M. Edmonds, ed. *The Fragments of Attic Comedy*. 3 vols. Leiden, 1957–61. |
| *FGrH* | F. Jacoby, ed. *Die Fragmente der griechischen Historiker*. 3 parts in 15 vols. Berlin and Leiden, 1923–58. |
| *GOS* | J. S. Morrison and R. T. Williams. *Greek Oared Ships, 900–323 B.C.* Cambridge, 1968. |
| *GSW* | W. K. Pritchett. *The Greek State at War*. 5 vols. Berkeley and Los Angeles, 1971–91. |
| Harrison *LA* | A. R. W. Harrison. *The Law of Athens*. 2 vols. Oxford, 1968–71. |
| *HCT* | A. W. Gomme, A. Andrewes, and K. J. Dover. *A Historical Commentary on Thucydides*. 5 vols. Oxford, 1945–81. |
| Hommel "Naukraria" | H. Hommel. "Naukraria, Naukraros." In *RE* 16.2 (1935), cols. 1938–52. |
| *IG* | *Inscriptiones Graecae*. Berlin, 1873–. |
| Jordan *AN* | B. Jordan. *The Athenian Navy in the Classical Period: A Study of Athenian Naval Administration and Military Organization in the Fifth and Fourth Centuries B.C.* University of California Publications, Classical Studies, no. 13. Berkeley and Los Angeles, 1975. |
| Kahrstedt *Forschungen* | U. Kahrstedt. *Forschungen zur Geschichte des ausgehenden V. und des IV. Jahrhunderts*. Berlin, 1910. |
| Kahrstedt *Staatsgebiet* | U. Kahrstedt. *Staatsgebiet und Staatsangehörige in Athen*. Studien zum öffentlichen Recht Athens, no. 1. Stuttgart and Berlin, 1934. |
| Kolbe *Re navali* | W. Kolbe. *De Atheniensium re navali questiones selectae*. Tübingen, 1899. |

| | |
|---|---|
| Labarbe<br>*Loi navale* | J. Labarbe. *La loi navale de Thémistocle.* Paris, 1957. |
| Lipsius *AR* | J. H. Lipsius. *Das attische Recht und Rechtsverfahren.* Leipzig, 1905–15. Reprint (3 vols. in 1). Darmstadt, 1966. |
| LSJ | H. G. Liddell, R. Scott, and H. S. Jones, eds. *A Greek-English Lexicon.* 9th ed. Oxford, 1973. |
| Macan<br>*Herodotus* | R. W. Macan. *Herodotus: The Fourth, Fifth, and Sixth Books.* 2 vols. London, 1895. |
| | ————. *Herodotus: The Seventh, Eighth, and Ninth Books.* 2 vols. London, 1908. |
| Martin<br>"Naukraria" | A. Martin. "Naukraria." In Daremberg-Saglio (1907), 4:3–7. |
| ML | R. Meiggs and D. M. Lewis, eds. *A Selection of Greek Historical Inscriptions to the End of the Fifth Century B.C.* 2d ed. Oxford, 1988. |
| *RE* | A. Pauly, G. Wissowa, and W. Kroll, eds. *Real-Encyclopädie der klassischen Altertumswissenschaft.* Stuttgart, 1894–. |
| Rhodes *AB* | P. J. Rhodes. *The Athenian Boule.* Oxford, 1972. |
| Rhodes<br>*Commentary* | P. J. Rhodes. *A Commentary on the Aristotelian "Athenaion Politeia."* Oxford, 1981. |
| Schaefer<br>*Demosthenes* | A. Schaefer. *Demosthenes und seine Zeit.* 2d ed. 3 vols. Leipzig, 1885–87. |
| *SEG* | *Supplementum Epigraphicum Graecum.* Leiden, 1923–. |
| *SIG* | W. Dittenberger, ed. *Sylloge Inscriptionum Graecarum.* 3d ed. 4 vols. Leipzig, 1915–24. |
| *Staatsh.* | A. Boeckh. *Die Staatshaushaltung der Athener.* Berlin, 1817. 2d ed. 2 vols. Berlin, 1851. 3d ed., rev. M. Fränkel. 2 vols. Berlin, 1886. |
| Strasburger<br>"Trierarchie" | H. Strasburger. "Trierarchie." In *RE* 7.A1 (1939), cols. 106–16. |
| Thumser<br>*De civium* | V. Thumser. *De civium Atheniensium muneribus eorumque immunitate.* Vienna, 1880. |
| Tod | M. N. Tod, ed. *A Selection of Greek Historical Inscriptions.* Vol. 2, *From 403 to 323 B.C.* Oxford, 1948. |
| *TrGF* | S. Radt, ed. *Tragicorum Graecorum Fragmenta.* Vol. 3. Göttingen, 1985. |
| *Urkunden* | A. Boeckh. *Urkunden über das Seewesen des attischen Staates.* Berlin, 1840. |
| Wyse | W. Wyse. *The Speeches of Isaeus.* Cambridge, 1904. |

## Periodicals

| | |
|---|---|
| *AA* | Archäologischer Anzeiger |
| *AAntHung* | Acta antiqua academiae scientiarum Hungaricae |
| *AC* | L'antiquité classique |
| *AD* | Archaiologikon deltion |
| *ADAW* | Abhandlungen der deutschen Akademie der Wissenschaften zu Berlin |
| *AE* | Archaiologikē ephēmeris |
| *AFLPer* | Annali della facoltà di lettere e filosofia, Università di Perugia |
| *AJA* | American Journal of Archaeology |
| *AJAH* | American Journal of Ancient History |
| *AJPh* | American Journal of Philology |
| *AM* | Mitteilungen des deutschen archäologischen Instituts, athenische Abteilung |
| *AncW* | Ancient World |
| *ASAA* | Annuario della scuola archeologica di Atene e delle missioni italiane in Oriente |
| *AU* | Der altsprachliche Unterricht |
| *BCH* | Bulletin de correspondance hellénique |
| *BSA* | Annual of the British School at Athens |
| *CEA* | Cahiers des études anciennes |
| *CJ* | Classical Journal |
| *C&M* | Classica et mediaevalia |
| *CPh* | Classical Philology |
| *CQ* | Classical Quarterly |
| *CR* | Classical Review |
| *CSCA* | California Studies in Classical Antiquity |
| *CW* | Classical World |
| *DHA* | Dialogues d'histoire ancienne |
| *EHR* | Economic History Review |
| *G&R* | Greece and Rome |
| *GRBS* | Greek, Roman, and Byzantine Studies |
| *HSPh* | Harvard Studies in Classical Philology |
| *HThR* | Harvard Theological Review |
| *IHR* | International History Review |
| *IJNA* | International Journal of Nautical Archaeology and Underwater Exploration |
| *JEA* | Journal of Egyptian Archaeology |
| *JHS* | Journal of Hellenic Studies |
| *JKP* | Jahrbücher für klassische Philologie |

| | |
|---|---|
| *JŒAI* | *Jahreshefte des österreichischen archäologischen Instituts* |
| *JWG* | *Jahrbuch für Wirtschaftsgeschichte* |
| *LCM* | *Liverpool Classical Monthly* |
| *MAI* | *Mémoires de l'Académie des inscriptions et belles lettres* |
| *MGR* | *Miscellanea greca e romana* |
| *MM* | *Mariner's Mirror* |
| *QUCC* | *Quaderni urbinati di cultura classica* |
| *RA* | *Revue archéologique* |
| *REG* | *Revue des études grecques* |
| *RhM* | *Rheinisches Museum* |
| *SBAW* | *Sitzungsberichte der Bayerischen Akademie der Wissenschaften, philosophisch-historische Abteilung* |
| *SO* | *Symbolae Osloenses* |
| *TAPhA* | *Transactions and Proceedings of the American Philological Association* |
| *WS* | *Wiener Studien* |
| *ZPE* | *Zeitschrift für Papyrologie und Epigraphik* |

*Financing the Athenian Fleet*

# Introduction

In his account of the naval engagement between the Greek and Persian fleets at Artemision in 481/0, Herodotos sums up the achievements of the Greek side this way: "Of the Greeks on that day the Athenians bore themselves best . . . of the Athenians, Kleinias son of Alkibiades distinguished himself campaigning with two hundred men, whom he provided from his own means, and on his own ship."[1] Herodotos's note is too brief to do more than arouse curiosity about Kleinias's person and conduct. Its implications, however, are significant enough fully to justify a recent characterization of it as "invaluable evidence for the history of the Athenian navy."[2] My concern here is not with the navy as such, however, but with the closely related subjects of the classical Athenian trierarchy and naval finance.

As the number of men—two hundred—suggests, Kleinias's ship, described by Herodotos simply as a *naus,* was properly a *triērēs.*[3] Therefore Kleinias must have formally held command of that ship in his capacity as trierarch (captain of a trieres). But he was a trierarch of a kind fundamentally different from that of most other commanders of the fleet. While the majority of these were in charge of ships and crews supplied by the state, Kleinias participated with his own trieres and crew. A clue about the stature of Kleinias—not only his social status but also his prowess—can perhaps be found in a similar instance, also reported by Herodotos, concerning Philippos son of Boutakides, from Kroton, who, in circa 510, joined the forces of the Spartan Dorieus on his own trieres and with a crew he provided at his own expense. "This Philippos," remarks Herodotos instructively, "was an Olympic victor and the goodliest [*kallistos*] Greek of his day."[4]

No example identical to that of Kleinias ever appears in accounts from the fifth and fourth centuries B.C., and, to be sure, its deviation from what must have been the prevailing practice in 481/0 stood out clearly enough for Herodotos, later on, to find it worthy of mention. We owe him gratitude for putting on record perhaps the last representative of a class that, by the beginning of the fifth century B.C., was becoming virtually obsolete: that of wealthy aristocrats who by means of glorious deeds and munificent contributions in war were observing a paramount moral obligation that was inextricably bound up with, and dictated by, their social and political status. Certainly others came to succeed them, but these were a different breed, living in a different social and political environment.

Some 150 years after Kleinias, similarly large public outlays were made by Konon Anaphlystios, the son of the well-known fourth-century general (*strategos*) Timotheos and grandson of the victor of Knidos (394). Konon, too, was a trierarch with a remarkably active career that can be followed closely through a number of years. From circa 342/1 to 325/4 he had been in charge of no fewer than eleven different ships, either alone or jointly with one or more colleagues. The naval records show him to have paid outstanding debts incurred from these services amounting to the considerable sum of 34,923 drachmas. But this turns out to be a mere fraction of his total expenditure, as it covers only his liability for replacing ships' equipment and compensating for damaged or lost hulls, all of which debts were discharged after the termination of service. If his running expenditures on each trierarchy are added (and 3,000 drachmas apiece would be a reasonable estimate), then his total outlays on known trierarchies rise to 67,923 drachmas.[5]

Konon's munificent outlays, too, were made toward fulfilling the important obligation to perform trierarchies. This obligation, however, was imposed by the solemn and perspicuous letter of the law—indeed, not just any law, but that of the fully developed Athenian democracy. Because this was a different political and institutional setting, with a passion for publication and openness as well as a demand for accountability, a fairly detailed record of Konon's services and expenditures exists.

Kleinias and in some measure Konon are fairly atypical and possibly extreme examples of their time: each acted as a commander on a trieres, but while the former was predominantly a captain of a warship, the latter was more of a taxpayer. Yet this is precisely my reason for choosing to open the present study by introducing them side by side. Their differences and atypicality shed light on the complex history of the classical Athenian trierarchy from the time of its emergence as a component of sociopolitical status through its vigorous transformation into the mature liturgical institution into which it was molded by fifth- and fourth-century democratic legislation.

## Concepts and Aims

A reexamination of the trierarchy needs little justification. No full-scale study of the institution has been undertaken since the appearance of August Boeckh's fundamental *Urkunden über das Seewesen des attischen Staates* in 1840, later incorporated into his *Die Staatshaushaltung der Athener*. Subsequent contributions are of limited scope and deviate little, if at all, from the views originally developed by Boeckh. Apart from the standard entries in the lexica, scholarly interest in the trierarchy is concentrated in three areas. The first, and by far the most traditional, is the history of the Athenian navy (W. Kolbe; J. S. Morrison and R. T. Williams; M. Amit; B. Jordan). The second is economic (A. Andreades), fiscal (R. Thomsen; P. Brun), or political history (G. Busolt and H. Swoboda; A. H. M. Jones). The third, and perhaps the least transparent of all, is that of commentaries on fourth-century oratory—for example, Isaeus (W. Wyse), Demosthenes (A. Schaefer; U. Kirchhoff), and particularly the epigraphic groundwork laid by the (re)edition of naval inscriptions, including the now enormous volume of literature on the Themistokles decree.

In terms of a formal and general description of the institution, surprisingly few (and mostly minor) issues have been subject to controversy. Almost everyone agrees that the trierarchy was instituted by Themistokles in 483/2 to succeed its precursor institution, the *naukrariai;* this view was elaborated in detail in 1957 by J. Labarbe in *La loi navale de Thémistocle*. From the last decade of the fifth century onward the fiscal character of the trierarchy was expanded at the expense of its military character, and this process accelerated after the mid-fourth century. Until then, A. Andreades and others claimed, the financial burdens of a trierarch were simply a consequence of his position as commander of a warship.[6] A singular exception to the consensus, however, is the recent and still ongoing debate about the organization and function of the trierarchy after the introduction of the *symmories* (groups into which trierarchs were arranged) in the mid-fourth century.[7]

Lack of an up-to-date and full account of the trierarchy also means neglect of an important—though, at the same time, daunting—body of material that constituted the primary foundation of Boeckh's exposition: the inscriptions known as the naval records. By means of his admirable mastery of that material Boeckh was able to disclose the many and various facets of the trierarchy. However, in the intervening 150 years that corpus of evidence has been revised and to a modest degree augmented, while fresh inscriptional evidence about and new insights into Athenian history in general have emerged. On a more practical level, the recent reconstruction and sea trials of a single trieres replica have led to a better understanding of the enormous infrastructure and funds that were needed to operate and maintain a fleet. In short, although some of what Boeckh said is still valid, many of his conclusions cannot stand unchallenged today. Furthermore, a fresh analysis of the naval records using a different approach to the subject can shed new light not only on the institution itself but also on the social, political, and ideological mechanisms of which it was part.

My purpose is thus twofold. I shall attempt to map out the origin, function, and evolution of the trierarchy, focusing on its prime but continually changing importance to naval finance and, therefore, on the gradually changing role of its members, the wealthiest Athenians, during the course of the fifth and fourth centuries. And in so doing I shall be concerned with what I consider to be equally a desideratum: the presentation, interpretation, and commentary (but not reedition) of a body of evidence that has remained largely unexploited: the naval records.

The term *trierarch* designates an officer occupying a distinct rank in the military establishment. The Greek *triērarchos* is a compound of *triērēs,* the name of a particular type of warship, and *archos,* "commander"; hence *trierarchy* (Greek: *triērarchia*) for the service performed by the commander of a warship. However, although certain intrinsic features of his office brought the trierarch into approximate alignment with other military officers such as, for instance, the *taxiarchos, phylarchos,* and *hipparchos*

(Arist. *Pol.* 1322b2–6), different features distinguished him from these officers in a profound way.

The most potent feature is that his military tenure was at the same time a liturgy (and frequently the most onerous at that), which, in turn, means that the supreme criterion for holding the position was possession of wealth. Granted, the generals, although not liturgists, were legally required to be men of substance. But while with the generalship, just as with some higher financial offices tied to property qualifications (treasurers: *Ath. Pol.* 8.1), the law either was not strictly enforced or was largely ignored,[8] with the trierarchy wealth possession remained an invariable, principal criterion. To comprehend why the trierarch enjoyed this unique status, one must look briefly at some crucial aspects of ancient naval warfare.

In his introduction to Vice Admiral W. L. Rodgers's *Greek and Roman Naval Warfare*, John Basset Moore stresses the universal validity of naval-war doctrine from the time of Themistokles to modern times by citing Sir Walter Raleigh's maxim: "Whosoever commands the sea, commands the trade of the world; whosoever commands the trade of the world, commands the riches of the world and consequently the world itself." That Athens's control of the seas aimed primarily at the protection and expansion of its commercial interests was one of Rodgers's main theses.[9]

Notwithstanding the conspicuous (and successful) efforts of Athens to become a consummate naval power, to an Athenian, or to any Greek, these statements, carrying the unmistakable ring of the Mahanian "sea-power" orthodoxy,[10] would have sounded like wishful thinking—not because the concepts of "naval strength" and "sea power" (*thalassokratia*) were unknown, but because "control of the seas," in the above sense, was virtually impossible to achieve. Naval power, to be sure, was recognized as a decisive political instrument: "Sea power is indeed a great thing," says Thucydides (1.143.5), the historian of the Peloponnesian War and a participant in it as a commander, and there is every reason to trust his judgment. But naval warfare in antiquity, and well beyond, remained an altogether different kind of activity from that of modern times.[11]

This was mainly due to the peculiar characteristics of the warship. In the classical period, naval powers were engaged in a fierce competition to augment their fleets by acquisition or construction of the then technically preeminent and universally used man-of-war, the galley trieres. Though slight variations in design did exist, it tended to be a long (about 37 m) and slender (about 6 m wide at the beam) craft with a crew of two hundred. Two sails supplemented the motive power generated by 170 oarsmen, tightly accommodated in three fore-to-aft levels within the hull. With the entire crew aboard there remained hardly enough space to take any substantial amount of food and water; additional weight meant sacrificing the vessel's lightness for speed. Speed and maneuverability were crucial, yet it was no less crucial to keep the crew well fed and watered.

The trieres' tactical capabilities as an offensive vessel were clearly recognized, but so were its limitations. The combined effects of the ship's structural design, its sizable complement, and not least its almost exclusive reliance on human muscle to produce mechanical energy for propulsion limited greatly its operation in both space and time. The result was a large degree of dependence on coastal bases close to the scene of action. Tactically and strategically, therefore, the main issue was access to and control of vital bases. A corollary to this was that most operations were not purely naval but amphibious in nature. Dominion of the seaboard adjacent to bases (and within the ship's radius of action) could be exercised only by means of the constant presence of an efficient, adequately prepared, and fully manned fleet. Control of the seas as such, however, hardly seems possible. Naval power and supremacy could only be maintained by continuous and intense naval activity, even if that meant defiance of impediments to navigation during the winter months.

In effect, naval warfare posed persistent requirements for resources that, by ancient standards, were immense. Funds, manpower, and timber thus came to be the three most precious items to any classical Greek polis with naval aspirations. Indeed, they were so much in demand that a good portion of the period's diplomatic and economic history can be written in terms of those who had and those who needed any one or all of these resources. The construction and maintenance of the ships were costly enterprises. The logistic demands arising from the peculiarities of naval warfare were no less burdensome. Few, if any, state treasuries had the ability to fund such projects entirely on their own. The operation of triereis fleets required a solid fiscal infrastructure. To find this Athens (and perhaps other states) had to turn to the liturgy system:[12] each commander of a warship was asked to perform a *leitourgia*.

Compounded of the elements "public" and "work," this term came to signify "work for the people," hence "a service rendered to the state." By definition, the term *lēitourgia* encompasses the idea, deep-rooted in antiquuity and in later periods, that wealthy individuals had an obligation to expend part of their wealth and time on some service to the community. The ethical and ideological matrix of which the liturgies were part dates from the time of the earliest written records in Greek, the Homeric poems. In these and other works of the preclassical period, benefactory services to the community are presented as the prerogative of a class of men distinguished by high birth, wealth, and military valor. Possession of these qualities, but above all their overt and successful demonstration, particularly in war exploits, confirmed the excellence (*aretē*) of a man's deeds, and conferred on him the highest title of moral commendation, *agathos;* this in turn gave an individual a strong claim against society. This pattern of behavior, then, was solidly founded on a traditional ethic that democratic Athens perpetuated and successively cultivated for political as well as fiscal purposes.[13]

In the fifth and fourth centuries B.C., wealthy citizens and metics carried an obligation to perform civic liturgies at the national or deme level: the *choregy* (financing of dramatic choruses), *gymnasiarchy* (supervision of athletic contests), *hestiaseis* (provision of public banquets), *architheoria* (leadership of a sacred embassy), *arrhephoria* (organization of a procession), and a few more.[14] In addition, citizens were required to discharge the military liturgies, the *proeisphora* (the obligation to pay the war tax, *eisphora,* in advance), and the trierarchy (the duty to serve as commander of a warship and to defray part of the cost accruing from that service).

The Athenian liturgy system in the classical period was firmly attached to democracy—an attachment emphasized by the reorganization undergone by the whole system shortly after Athens's departure from democratic rule.[15] Oligarchic ideology sat uneasily with the liturgical demands imposed on men of affluence: Aristotle advised the attachment of liturgies to magistracies under oligarchy (*Pol.* 1321a31–42), while his pupil Theophrastos made his oligarchic character lament the obligations under which his class was suffering by asking "When shall we cease to be victims of these liturgies and trierarchies?" (*Char.* 26.6). In the Hellenistic period the general tendency was for an assimilation of liturgies to magistracies.[16] But if the liturgy system had a political character, it had a political and social function as well,[17] and therefore can be used as a reasonably reliable guide to the position—and even transformation—of the economic elite in democratic Athens; that in this context the trierarchy occupies a special place is illuminated in part by the comparison between Kleinias son of Alkibiades and Konon son of Timotheos. The history of the Athenian trierarchy, in short, is also part of the history of the Athenian propertied class.

In almost any discussion of Athenian public or private life, mention is made of the obligation imposed on wealthy citizens to perform expensive trierarchies and of the social or political benefits (expected or actually gained) by trierarchs. But some crucial issues still need to be clarified. How expensive were these services? Were they, as is frequently claimed, always equally oppressive or burdensome to all? What conditioned the magnitude of expenditure and, by extension, how much truth is there in the belief that the duty, throughout the fifth century and for part of the fourth, remained predominantly a military one? Even more important, what were the sociopolitical and legal control mechanisms regulating the frequency and efficacy of trierarchic contributions? An examination of the institution now makes it possible to add some flesh to the bare bones and to modify previous sweeping statements about the financial oppressiveness of the system and about its deployment by rich Athenians as a secure means of gaining popular support. The embodiment of both option and compulsion in the trierarchic obligation gave the institution its characteristic savor. Right at the heart of all these issues lies the important question of the attitude of democracy toward the wealthy citizens, or the liturgical class.

Boeckh's stand on this question is a guarded pessimism: the financial burdens of the trierarchy were not necessarily oppressive, although application of unfair principles of distribution and abuse of the system led to the impoverishment of the rich.[18] The views of Andreades are much less guarded (and balanced): out of shortsightedness and greed the crowd (his favored synonym for demos in the Greek edition of his book) took pleasure in the oppression of the wealthy, who were utterly ruined by the burdens of the trierarchy and other liturgies. Such a thinly disguised confiscatory tendency was detrimental to the national wealth, and finally caused the destruction of the state.[19]

Manifestations of the oppressive nature of liturgical obligations (for example, the dissatisfaction expressed by Theophrastos's oligarchic character) loom large in contemporary opinion. The morbid remark of a comic poet that the trierarch hangs himself in despair (Antiphanes fr. 204, apud Ath. 3.103F) is echoed with undiminished force in the complaints and grievances of others. "Athens," Isokrates claimed in 355 (8.128), "is rife with lamentations. For some are driven to rehearse and bewail amongst themselves their poverty and privation while others deplore the multitude of duties enjoined upon them by the state—the liturgies and all the nuisances connected with the symmories and with exchanges of property [*antidoseis*]; for these are so annoying that those who have the means find life more burdensome than those who are continually in want." Similar sentiments had been aired previously, in the early 420s, by an oligarchic pamphleteer (Ps.-Xen. *Ath. Pol.* 1.13): the choregies, gymnasiarchies, and trierarchies provide entertainment and profit for the people, but all expenses connected with these duties are paid by the wealthy. "At least the people think themselves worthy of taking money for singing, running, dancing, and sailing in ships, so that they become wealthy and the wealthy poorer."

However, their biases apart, these testimonies hardly tell the whole truth. Not surprisingly, a shrewd remark, which at once pierces through the arguments sustaining such complaints and shows that rich Athenians had the ability to eschew trierarchic service and keep their wealth to themselves, comes from Aristophanes. In the interchange that takes place among Aischylos, Euripides, and Dionysos in the play *The Frogs* (405), Aischylos is made to say to Euripides: "Your kings in tatters and rags you dressed, / and brought them on, a beggarly show, / To move, forsooth, our pity and ruth." Asked by Euripides: "And what was the harm, I should like to know," Aischylos explains: "No more will a wealthy citizen now / equip for the state a galley of war [*triērarchein*]. / He wraps his limbs in tatters and rags, / and whines *he is poor, too poor by far*"; to which Dionysos adds: "But under his rags he is wearing a vest, / as woolly and soft as a man could wish. / Let him gull the state, and he's off to the mart; / an eager, extravagant buyer of fish" (1063–68). Concealment of wealth, as I will argue below, was widely practiced in the fourth century and perhaps also in the fifth.

A much more convenient and balanced point of departure, therefore, is J. K. Davies' thesis that in the fourth century the possession of wealth still constituted a real but limited basis of power that could be used to gain influence in public life: property owners might attempt to affect adversely the execution of public policy by minimizing their contributions (otherwise of a considerable magnitude) to the national revenue. Or they might deploy their wealth via energetic ambition and ostentatious expenditure as a claim to forensic and political gratitude (*charis*), or as evidence of ability and willingness to meet the responsibilities of the higher military offices. Charis, in short, had become an intrinsic part of the institutional setting of the liturgies.[20]

An analysis of the trierarchy may help qualify and expand Davies' thesis. It is true that trierarchic expenditure in particular seems to have been publicly recognized as one of the qualities most deserving of charis,[21] and to such a degree that in order to achieve it some trierarchs would spend much more than they were legally obliged to spend.[22] Defending himself against a charge of having embezzled public money (thus running the risk of forfeiting his property), the speaker of Lysias 21 mentions the many and sumptuous liturgies he had performed within the short period of eight years (including service as trierarch in seven consecutive years), and stresses that, had he chosen to limit his services to the letter of the law, he would not have spent a quarter of what he did spend (1–5). What he expected to receive in return is spelled out later in the speech (11–13), where he says to the jurors:

After so many dangers encountered in your defense, and after all the good services that I have rendered to the state, I now request, not a boon for my reward, as others do, but that I be not deprived of my own property; for I consider it a disgrace to you also, to take it both with my will and against my will. I do not mind so much having to lose my possessions; but I could not put up with an outrage, and the impression that it must produce on those who shirk the liturgies—that while I get no credit for what I have spent on you, they prove to have been rightly advised in giving up to you no part of their own property . . . you ought, therefore, to see the surest revenue for the state in the fortunes of those who are willing to perform the liturgies.

Voluntarism was at a premium, unwillingness to discharge trierarchies the object of public disdain. Time and again speeches in law courts mention individuals enumerating their trierarchic expenditures with a view to justifying their wealth and as proof that they had most prudently and willingly administered their wealth in the interest of the community.[23] The appeal to charis was occasionally translated into a concrete appeal by the wealthy litigant to be allowed to retain his wealth.[24] In that sense, performance of trierarchies was an indispensable means by which to defend and preserve one's economic position. Indeed, alongside the incentive of honorific rewards this was an essential force at work in optionally undertaken trierarchies and other liturgies.

The speaker of Lysias 21 claimed that he did not mind losing his property; but of course he did mind, very much so, for he hurried to defend it, warning the jurors at the same time that if it were taken away from him the loss would be equally great to the state: "So, if you are well advised, you will take as great care of our property as of your own personal possessions, knowing that you will be able to avail yourselves of all that we have, as you were in the past . . . whereas, if you impoverish me, you will wrong yourselves besides" (13–14). The point he seems to be making is that he depends on the goodwill of the state just as much as the state depends on his cooperation in making his wealth available for public use. A claim by this or any other wealthy litigant to lenient treatment by a law court proceeded from the widely acknowledged notion that an owner of great property made certain demands on democratic ideology and practice, which at the same time demanded certain things of him.

But that said, one should perhaps abstain from envisaging rich Athenians as perpetually and frantically engaged in public generosity simply in order to defend their property or to avert the hostile intentions of the demos;[25] nor is there good evidence for the frequently made assumption that the tangible rewards claimants hoped to receive in return for such deeds were always or automatically bestowed on them.

Given that redistribution of property never occupied a significant part in Athenian democratic thought and practice—resources were obtained through the enforcement of fiscal-distributive mechanisms—the state had an equally great interest in the preservation and goodwill of its primary object of taxation. Its interest was economic *and* political: economic, because any abuse would lead to declining cooperation on the part of property owners, or even worse to exhaustion of their financial potential; political, because unlimited fiscal demands would be bound to cause social unrest or even *stasis* (civic strife). Both of these are implicit in Aristotle's cautionary remark that democracies ought to let wealth remain in private hands—an idea consonant with the prevailing belief in Athens and elsewhere[26]—and to limit expenditure by its owners on liturgies that are of *no real use* to the public (*Pol.* 1309a14–20; cf. 1305a4–5). In previous passages he had mentioned oligarchic revolts prompted by fiscal burdens in five states (1304b20–1305a7), the one in Rhodes having been started by financially hard-pressed trierarchs; this is one of the main causes given by Thucydides for the oligarchic coup in Athens in 411 (8.47.2–48; 63.4).[27]

The relationship between the state and the trierarch-liturgists was one of reciprocity and interdependence.[28] Not all aspects of the institution bear directly on this issue. But enough of them do for some of the arguments in the following chapters to be concerned with illustrations of how attempts were made to keep that relationship balanced, and of the variety of mechanisms employed by the state in order to preserve, while maintaining its control over, a vital object of taxation. Substantiation of that thesis is, on the theoretical level, among the central concerns of the present study.

A word must be said about the chronological limits of what I have called the classical period. Even though the year 483/2 is an indisputable upper limit, supported by Athens's decision at that date to initiate a large shipbuilding program, by far the best-documented period, not least epigraphically, is the fourth century. Some, but not all, of my conclusions may safely be extrapolated to apply to the fifth century. Thus "classical" is to some degree a misnomer. The lower limit must necessarily be the year of the latest extant document belonging to an important dossier of inscriptions, the naval record of 323/2, which also coincides with the year of Athens's greatest naval defeat, at Abydos and off Amorgos, and, less neatly, with the abolition of the liturgy system at some date between 317/6 and 307/6.

I offer a synchronic account of the institution in the fourth century and then attempt a diachronic account in connection with the major reforms. Part 1 addresses the intriguing question of origin. In part 2 the issues of membership, eligibility, appointment, and exemption are given separate treatment for the purpose of bringing out the interplay of the legal and economic determinants of trierarchic liability. Part 3 delineates the main areas of financial responsibility by assessing, in general terms, the volume of burdens accruing from the maintenance of crews and ships, and gauges the mechanisms of dividing that responsibility between state and trierarchs. Finally, part 4 attempts to reconstruct the most salient features of the trierarchic reforms and to explore the ways in which they helped reshape the institution in the course of the fourth century.

## Sources

Many Attic inscriptions and ancient authors (not least the historians Herodotos and Thucydides), and numerous extant, published speeches of the fourth-century Athenian orators (particularly Demosthenes' orations 14, 47, 50, and 51), shed light on the navy and the trierarchy. Each of these sources poses its own problems, and therefore requires the use of a special technique in order to determine, above all, its credibility. However, here I can conveniently, and (I hope) justifiably, confine discussion to one class of inscriptional evidence that furnishes detailed and firsthand information: the naval records. From the fifth century only three small fragments survive, dated to 435–410.[29] Although quantitatively these are insignificant, their very existence bears testimony to a well-established naval administration in this period.

Considerably more numerous and extensive are the extant fragments from the fourth century, most of which were found during the excavations, in 1834, of a late Roman or Byzantine portico on the south side of the Kantharos harbor in the Piraeus. The first to discover the significance of the inscribed stelai, conveniently reused as water channels connecting a series of basins inside the portico, was Ludwig Ross, then a professor at the University of Athens. His meticulous notes and transcripts were in 1836 placed in the skilled hands of August Boeckh, whose further work resulted in the presentation of the texts with extensive commentary in his *Urkunden*.[30]

The reediting of existing texts and the publication of a few new ones continued, mainly in the pages of the *Athenische Mitteilungen,* by J. Sundwall, W. Kolbe, H. Fränkel, and not least by U. Köhler. Köhler, after careful reexamination of the stelai, later incorporated them as a distinct class in *Inscriptiones Graecae* 2.789–812. J. Kirchner's subsequent republication of the inscriptions as *Inscriptiones Graecae* 2².1604–32 was chiefly based on Köhler's text.[31] More recent work by D. R. Laing (1968) has established the physical characteristics of the stones (owing to the particular purposes of their reuse), the relation between individual fragments, and the opisthographic nature of the inscriptions. However, his promised republication has not yet appeared, and a revision as well as reedition of the texts of *Inscriptiones Graecae* 2 and 2² is urgently needed. Since that task lies well beyond the scope and purpose of the present book, my references will be to the standard editions.

Traditionally, the surviving fragments are assigned to the period 377/6–323/2. These records served two chief purposes: to provide inventories of naval matériel in the dockyards, and to record the day-to-day transactions between naval authorities and trierarchs. They were drawn up by a board of ten officials chosen every year by lot to supervise the three naval bases in the Piraeus (Kantharos, Zea, and Mounichia), the *epimelētai tōn neōriōn* (henceforth dockyard superintendents or officials, or simply epimeletai). Publication of the documents took place at the end of the civic year,[32] within the administrative context of a formal surrender (paradosis) of all naval matters to the incoming officials; when the latter's term expired, they drew up a new record stating what they had received from their predecessors (paralabe) and what they had handed over to their successors.

These are quite difficult documents to assess. Their long, notoriously complicated entries, recorded in a particular bureaucratic shorthand, may test the patience of the specialist. But once the bookkeeping methods and administrative language of the epimeletai are properly understood, their records furnish a wealth of information about juridical, financial, and technical naval matters, as well as a great deal of prosopographical data. The range of historical conclusions one can draw from this material is really (and unhappily) narrower than might have been expected at first, however; the pleasure of having a good part of the navy's "central archive" is somewhat lessened because these documents possess certain chronological and structural limitations.

Viewed as a series of accounts, they fall short of representing evenly the period to which they belong: the few fragments from the 370s and 360s stand in contrast to the richness in volume and detail distinguishing those from the 330s and 320s. Furthermore, what have survived are the *published* accounts of the epimeletai in which their dealings are noted summarily. It is plausible that much more detailed bookkeeping was carried out in other records (of perishable material) for "internal" use (diagrammata).[33] In addition, they are properly "cash accounts" in more than one sense. First, they list only what passed through the hands of the epimeletai. Second, owing to the established practice of official paradosis and paralabe, their contents usually show the situation at the beginning and end of each year; transactions completed in the intervening period may or may not be included in the published documents. Third, defaulting trierarchs are likely to appear more frequently than trierarchs who had promptly discharged their liabilities right after the expiration of their terms. For these reasons, the documents cannot provide a complete picture of naval affairs and administration. This is particularly true of the "total-giving" rubrics, the so-called *arithmos* formulas, to which more attention will be paid below. Such rubrics contain two (apparently contradictory) features: they are all-inclusive, in that they mention as part of the stock ships and equipment that for various reasons were no longer in existence, and they are selective, in that they do not mention ships and equipment that were manifestly in existence and use.

## PART I

*The Establishment of the Institution*

# The Origin of the Trierarchy

As is the case with other Athenian institutions, the origin and early history of the trierarchy are fundamentally important but poorly documented. Hence their particulars remain—and unless entirely fresh evidence comes to view they will continue to remain—not susceptible to sturdy proof. Yet it seems possible and necessary to test the validity of the main hypotheses that have been advanced in this area, and to formulate new ones insofar as these are shown to be consistent both with the existing but limited body of evidence and with the general conceptual framework set out in the Introduction. The question of origin implies treatment of two sets of problems. One is whether or not the trierarchy can justifiably be viewed as the direct (or indirect) successor of the naukrariai, an institution of the sixth century B.C., or perhaps even earlier. Another is the date and circumstances of the inception of the trierarchy itself.

## The Naukrariai and the Athenian Fleet

Prior to the final years of the 480s the Athenian navy was comparatively small. According to Thucydides' reckoning of the early naval powers (1.13–14), Athens's fleet in this early period was dwarfed by those at the disposal of other Greek city-states such as Corinth, Korkyra, and Samos. Moreover, it did not as yet mainly consist of the superior man-of-war

already in use elsewhere, the trieres. For many years it has been widely
believed that the administration and finance of Athenian warships, in the
time before the acquisition of a large fleet by 480, was the responsibility
of the institution known as the naukrariai. The essentials of this view can
be summarized as follows. In the sixth century, and perhaps earlier, there
were forty-eight naukrariai forming subdivisions (twelve to each) of the
old four tribes. Each *naukraria* was presided over by an official, a *prytanes,*
and comprised wealthy citizens, the *naukraroi,* who, by virtue of performing a liturgy, supplied, maintained, and commanded the Athenian
ships and crews. With Kleisthenes' democratic reforms of 508/7 the system was reorganized by increasing the number of naukrariai to fifty and
transferring the duties of the naukraroi to the *demarchs,* the head officials
of the Attic municipalities (demes). But the naval obligations of the institution were retained until Themistokles' institution of the trierarchy in
483/2.[1] Some have proposed an analogy between such a system and the
"wardens of ports" of medieval England who were liable to supply ships
as a tax in kind, or the chartering of private ships by the early modern
French navy.[2]

However, the validity of this prevailing view about the naval duties of
the naukrariai and the existence of the liturgy system before 508/7 can
now be questioned with a force sufficient to suggest that it be abandoned
altogether. A thorough examination of the problem suggests that there is
no firm evidence for the connection between naukrariai and fleet, thus
justifying the earlier verdict of B. Keil: "Wo die Flotte, Keine Spur der
Naukrarien; wo die Naukrarie, Keine Spur die Flotte."[3] A brief review of
the principal sources and arguments that have been adduced in support of
the traditional theory may expose its inadequacies.

(i) On this particular topic the archaeological evidence proves unhelpful. It has been customary to identify the ships depicted on a group of
Athenian vases from the Geometric period (roughly 760–735 B.C.), the
so-called Dipylon group, with those supplied by the naukrariai. But this
is as much a guess (and, indeed, the cause of a circular argument) as is a
similar identification of the trieres depicted on a fifth-century marble
carving, the Lenormant relief, with the sacred ship *Paralos.*[4]

(ii) The earliest extant reference to the naukraroi in the literary
sources is found in Herodotos. However, his account is too brief to provide anything near an adequate description of their specific functions, and
the precise meaning of his words is now debated. In his account of Ky-

lon's attempt to seize power at Athens through an unsuccessful coup (possibly in the period 640/39–621/0), Herodotos writes: "Then he [sc. Kylon] and his men were expelled by the *prytanies* of the naukraroi, who then governed Athens, being held liable to any penalty except death."[5] The most likely rendering of the key words relating to the official powers of the prytanies of the naukraroi (*enemon tote*) seems to be "they governed Athens at that time." Yet any attempt made so far to explain the political or fiscal duties of these officials remains largely speculative,[6] and the puzzling testimony of Herodotos is contradicted (albeit not decisively) by Thucydides, who makes the archons responsible for the expulsion (1.126.8).

(iii) Surely, as *Athenaion Politeia* 8.3 attests, the naukrariai and naukraroi were involved in some sort of financial activity:

And there were four tribes, as before, and four tribal kings. And from each tribe there had been assigned three *trittyes* and twelve naukrariai to each, and over the naukrariai there was established the office [*archē*] of naukraroi, appointed for the levies [*eisphoras:* here in its nontechnical sense, Rhodes *Commentary* 153] and the expenditures that were made; because of which in the laws of Solon, which are no longer in force, the clauses frequently occur, "the naukraroi to collect" and "to spend out of the naukraric fund."

This passage is valuable (in my judgment, the best that exists on the topic) because it gives as its source the obsolete laws, whether of Solonian or other origin.[7] References to these laws were probably found in the book (*Atthis*) of the Attic local historian, Androtion, who mentions payments from the naukraric fund made by other financial officials, the *kolakretai,* in order to cover the traveling expenses of a sacred embassy (*theoria*) to Delphi.[8] Androtion, Hignett suggested ([1952] 48), was possibly also the source of two other clauses, presumably from a law, that mention the naukraroi and naukrariai in an unintelligible context.[9] Very likely, then, the author of the *Athenaion Politeia* had indirect access to reliable documentary material. At 8.3, it clearly presents the naukrariai as a political-administrative entity, and the naukraroi as officials (*archē*) collecting money for, as well as paying out from, the naukraric fund. That their financial dealings included construction and maintenance of warships is, however, an invention of modern scholarship not justified by this passage.[10]

(iv) Nor, emphatically, is the naukrariai-fleet connection directly discernible from another passage of the *Athenaion Politeia* (21.5) dealing with Kleisthenes' reforms of 508/7: "He [sc. Kleisthenes] also appointed demarchs, having the same duties [*epimeleia*] as the former naukraroi, for he put the demes in the place of the naukrariai." The character of the naukrariai as local subdivisions implied here—and explicitly stated by a lexicographer (*Lex. Seg.* 257: "Kolias: an Attic locality . . . it was also a naukraria")—if true, is not incompatible with their status as subdivisions of the tribes (*Ath. Pol.* 8.3). Whether *Athenaion Politeia* 21.5 actually means a complete replacement of the naukrariai by the demes (as postulated by the grossly misleading gloss of Hesychios, s.v. "nauklaroi") is a moot point. What constitutes a real crux, however, are the kinds of duties, or epimeleia, that the demarchs might have taken over from the naukraroi.

(v) Some scholars find the answer to this in a passage from the third book of Kleidemos's *Atthis* (*FGrH* 323: F 8), where it is stated: "After Kleisthenes had created ten tribes in the place of the previous four, it also happened that the Athenians were organized into fifty parts that they called naukrariai, in the same way they now call the hundred divisions symmories." Kleisthenes, it is contended, transferred to the demarchs most of the duties previously performed by the naukraroi, except their naval responsibilities.[11] An identification of "the one hundred parts [*merē*] that are now called symmories" with the trierarchic symmories mentioned in Demosthenes 14.17 (of 354) would, indeed, provide a convenient link between the naukrariai and the fleet. But there are serious obstacles to this.

First, Kleidemos's symmories could be those of the trierarchy only if it were proven that his book dates from the time when the trierarchic symmories were in existence, that is, the second half of the fourth century; even if this were proven (which it cannot be), the simultaneous existence of eisphora symmories would render any identification haphazard.[12] Recent attempts to revive the view that after 358/7 there was only one symmory system will be shown to be unsupported (see pp. 183–90). Second, an association of Kleidemos's "hundred parts" with Demosthenes' proposal of 354 (14.17) to subdivide the existing twenty symmories into a hundred smaller parts will not do, because that proposal was probably never put into effect. An interpretation of Kleidemos's words is further complicated because the number of eisphora symmories is not known. It is, therefore, far from clear which of the two symmory systems Kleidemos had in mind. Moreover, it is impossible to verify his implication of an increase of the naukrariai from forty-eight to fifty (if an increase is what he means), nor does he disclose his grounds for the naukrariai-symmories comparison. The upshot is that Kleidemos's testimony can hardly be used to explain the duties that Kleisthenes transferred from the naukraroi to the demarchs, much less to prove the naval activities of the former.

None of the fifth- and fourth-century sources reviewed thus far offers a satisfactory description of the naukrariai or the duties and mode of recruitment of the naukraroi.[13] Although they seem to have been entrusted with the upkeep of a fund, and for this one must rely on the law clauses quoted in *Athenaion Politeia* 8.3, it has not been proven that the institution or the fund was in any way attached to the navy.

(vi) Such an affinity was only claimed later, by various lexicographers. One of these, the scholar Julius Pollux from the second century A.D., states that "each naukraria supplied two horsemen and one ship" (8.108). However, most of what is said by Pollux (or by his source) on this matter represents purely speculative and improbable accretions to the narrative of *Athenaion Politeia* 8.3 and 21.5 (e.g., he erroneously attributes to the naukraroi the power to decide on the revenues and expenditures of the demes) also characteristic of a variety of versions given by other lexicographers.[14] In particular, the supply of a ship by each naukraria may be an inference based on the assumption that the prefix *nau-* in *naukraros* means "ship"; but does it mean that?

One wonders what was the source (or sources) of another lexicographical description (*Lex. Seg.* 283.20–21) stating that the naukraroi were "those who supplied (or prepared) the ships, performed trierarchies and were under the command of the *polemarch* [one of the nine archons]." Such a direct parallel between naukraroi and trierarchs is highly dubious, since no source contemporary to the naukrariai could possibly have used the term *trierarchy* in its technical sense. So, ultimately, the issue hinges on whether or not the lexicographer was able to consult a contemporary source explicitly linking the naukraroi with the navy; this cannot be confirmed. But a further suspicion remains: that the naukraroi-polemarch connection is the product of an unsupported transposition to earlier times of the historically correct trierarch-*strategoi* connection. In sum, although the possibility that either lexicographer followed closely some other authority or authorities cannot be excluded, it is questionable whether their sources had independent value. For that reason, the naukrariai-navy connection cannot be based solely on these testimonies.

(vii) A chief support for the traditional view, which however has recently been seriously attacked, is F. Solmsen's inference from the nomenclature: *naukraros* is a compound of *nau-* (ship) and *kraros* (head or commander); hence the affiliation of the naukrariai to the navy.[15] An alternative derivation of the *nau-* prefix is proposed by Billingmeier and Sutherland-Dusing (1981), from *nāos* (temple). In their opinion, the word *nāos* is attested in the Attic dialect form *neōs* and the Mycenaean adjective *na-wi-jo,* used to describe bronze,[16] while the various dialect forms for "temple" go back to a proto-Greek *\*naswos* (thematic) or *\*nasu* (athematic). Hence, *na-u-do-mo* (*naudomoi*) in the Pylos tablets (Na 568 and Vn 865.1) are given the rendering "temple-builders" instead of "shipwrights," and the later use of *nau* in the sense "temple" is found attested in the compounds *naokoros* (*neōkoros, nāokoros,* "warden of a temple") and *nauphylax.* The naukraroi, then, were "temple-heads," that is, originally religious-financial officials (probably the oldest treasurers, *tamiai,* of Athens) entrusted with the guardianship of temples and their treasures.

However, this explanation cannot convincingly eliminate the *naus* = ship theory,[17] and is now itself being challenged by yet another alternative: the prefix *nau-* is derived from *naiō,* "I dwell" (*nauein/naiein,* from the root *nas-*), while *kraros* is an old form of *klēros* (lot, piece of land) (LSJ). On this view, *naukrariai* would refer to "every discrete settlement in Attica, perhaps in contradistinction to phratries, which might comprise several discrete settlements."[18]

Three rival theories launched into the academic battleground do not increase our confidence in explanations based on etymology.

## Early Naval Organization

Even though the naukrariai-navy relation is questionable, Athens did have a fleet in the Archaic period. How was it organized and run? No direct evidence exists, but it seems sensible to define the concept "navy" by following U. Kahrstedt's argument that the notion of an entirely state-owned fleet is false.[19] Certain broad but strongly articulated features of early social organization render this a more germane and valid line of approach. Possession of ships by aristocratic families in the Archaic period was not only an effective tool for the military, political, and social preeminence of a whole class, but also the practical means for engagement in economic activity.[20] Success in either field would reward the aspirations of members of noble households for power, wealth, and prestige; and success depended greatly on the possession of naval skills acquired by intensive engagement in the transportation of goods by sea as well as in depredations or regular warfare. In "Athenian Naval Power before Themistocles," Haas (1985) makes a convincing case that the interlocking of these activities was made possible by the standard types of ships then in use.

Before the functional distinction between the merchantman (or the "round" ship) and the specialized warship (represented in its most developed form by the trieres) became complete, other, older kinds of vessels, the *triakontor* and *pentēkontor,* held a dominant position in armed conflict at sea as well as in long-distance transportation of goods. Since especially the latter kind of ship combined the structural characteristics of freight carrier and warship, it could be conveniently used for purposes that, in the period concerned, can hardly be differentiated: sea trade, piracy, and warfare.[21] Discussing the types of ships used by the Greeks in the Trojan expedition, Thucydides remarks that in the early days the Greeks did not have *kataphract* (fenced-in) vessels but vessels "fitted out rather pirate-style in the old-fashioned way" (1.10.4). Piratical activities, Y. Garlan concludes in his seminal study on piracy, are fairly complex phenomena that operated simultaneously at the center and on the fringes of society, both in opposition to and in harmony with the power of the state; they formed, or helped promote, a nexus between economic activity and warfare.[22]

All this suggests a concept of "navy" that is structurally and quantitatively quite different from the "national" navy created later on. The difference lies in the size of the fleet, the types of vessels used, the magnitude of demands for resources, and the scale as well as the sophistication of the framework needed to run the organization. But the most important difference, at least in the present context, is found in the mode of financing naval activity: there was no attachment to a formal, all-embracing network of obligations comparable to the later liturgy system (as the adherents of the naukrariai theory often assume), nor any statutory prescription of who should undertake financial responsibility for the ships and crews. Instead, the system predominantly rested on aristocratic military prowess and generosity, and these were dictated by ethics—above all the pursuit of arete, or excellence—not by law. "*Aretai* that involve no danger," wrote Pindar (*Ol.* 6.9; cf. 10.91), "win no honor either on land or in hollow ships." Still earlier, in the seventh century, the Spartan war-poet Tyrtaios expressed more or less the same idea in even stronger terms: "A man does not become *agathos* in war if he should not hold firm when he sees bloody carnage and thrust at the enemy from close at hand. This is *aretē*" (Tyrt. 12 Bergk). Toil, danger, and expenditure were inseparable from the notion of aristocratic excellence achieved by those able to secure successfully the safety of society with their own armor and ships, and they still had a role to play in the fourth century when armed conflict at sea was sustained by a huge naval system entirely controlled by the state.

A few dim, albeit unmistakable, traces of the old system survived for some time after the introduction of a new one. Kleinias fought against the Persians with excellent valor on his own ship and with his own crew. There can be little doubt that his acquisition of a modern and specialized fighting vessel, the trieres, was a response to the changes in the concept of naval warfare, and others before him had probably responded the same way.[23] Yet no matter the type of ship used, at the core of the conduct of Kleinias and his peers lies the centuries-old tradition of aristocratic ship proprietors, appearing in the guises of warriors, merchants, and pirates. Whether they were called naukraroi or had anything to do with the naukrariai remains unknown.

## The Establishment of the Trierarchy

The date and circumstances of the inception of the trierarchy are largely obscured in the available sources. Only one text, from early Hellenistic times ([Arist.] *Oec.* 2.2.4), would have it that the institution existed before 500 B.C.: it reports the offer made by the tyrant Hippias (527–510) to those expecting to perform trierarchies and other liturgies to commute their service for a moderate sum. Few scholars, if any, will now accept this as historically credible.[24] That the trierarchy was established by Themistokles in 483/2 is, in contrast, a view enjoying almost complete scholarly consensus. But can the extant evidence firmly support this view? Is it true, moreover, as many hold it to be, that from its inception and well into the fifth century the institution had solely or predominantly a military character? Or is one to view its liturgical affiliation, and with it the entire network of naval-fiscal duties, as an aspect with sufficient (and perhaps the greatest) weight from the start? Above all, this issue has political and social-historical significance, but given the absence of direct evidence, it can only be settled indirectly.

The title "trierarch" could have come into use only after the emergence of the trieres, in about the mid-sixth century B.C.[25] However, its establishment as *the* term for the commander of a warship, and with it the founding of the Athenian trierarchy, presupposes at least two things: the existence of a large triereis fleet, and the operation of the liturgy system already in the financial organization of areas other than the navy. A dossier of evidence exists that illuminates with relative clarity the main lines of development in both fields.

## Themistokles' Naval Program

Thucydides ends his list of early maritime powers by saying:

These, then, were the most powerful of the fleets: but it appears that even these, though they were established many generations after the Trojan expedition, employed only a few *triereis,* and were still, like it, equipped with pentekontors and long vessels. A short time before the Persian invasions and the death of Darius . . . , the tyrants of the Sicilian coast and the Corcyraeans acquired *triereis* in large numbers, so that these were the last naval powers of note to be established in Hellas before Xerxes' expedition. The Aeginetans and Athenians, and other such peoples, possessed small fleets, and most of these ships were pentekontors. It was only quite recently that Themistocles persuaded the Athenians when they were at war with the Aeginetans, and when too the Persians were expected, to construct the ships with which they actually fought [at Salamis]. (1.14.1–2; GOS 159–60)

So, put in simple terms, as Thucydides seems to do, the sign of a modern naval power was possession in large numbers of the technically and tactically superior fighting vessel, the trieres. Yet the acquisition of a "national" triereis fleet by Athens would have been a far more spectacular and demanding enterprise than Thucydides (or any other author) imparts to his reader. Given the ancient evidence about the operation of fleets and from modern experiments with a trieres replica, it is possible to specify these demands.

Availability of funds (which is briefly touched on at Thuc. 1.13.1), shipbuilding materials, and technical know-how are just some of the short-term prerequisites for building up a force. Much more important are the long-term requirements accruing from the maintenance and operation of a fleet: (1) uninterrupted access to the sources of supplies (especially timber); (2) permanent harbor and dockyard facilities adequately supplied with equipment and spares in stock and manned by shipwrights and other personnel; (3) an effective administration; (4) quick recruitment of skilled crews for the ships, which now required a complement about four times as large as the complement of the vessels they had superseded, the pentekontors; and last but not least, (5) a steady stream of revenue to enhance the often limited resources of the state treasury. The supposition that an extensive naval infrastructure was established from the outset may lead to a better appreciation of the buildup of the maritime strength of Athens. An attempt to elucidate some of these aspects must begin with discussion of Themistokles' naval program of the 480s.

It is a pity that the state of the evidence about so important a stage in Athenian history—according to one author, "the revolution which transformed the nature and scope of Athenian naval power" (Haas [1985] 46)—is less than ideal. All traditions reporting this event were composed at a later date, some much later. Some comfort comes from their agreement on certain basic points: that Athens acquired a large triereis fleet shortly before the Persian invasion by launching a conspicuous shipbuilding program; that this was made possible by a sudden windfall of revenue from silver mining; and that the program was instigated by Themistokles.[26] One fourth-century source (*Ath. Pol.* 22.7) dates the event to 483/2. Both Herodotos (7.144.1–2) and *Athenaion Politeia* 22.7 mention that originally the surplus money was to be distributed among the citizens—seemingly a recurring procedure.[27]

But this is almost all they agree on. Herodotos claims that the revenue came from the mines of Laureion, that at the ensuing distribution each citizen was to receive ten drachmas, and that owing to Themistokles' intervention the money was eventually spent on construction of 200 ships. *Athenaion Politeia* 22.7 mentions instead the mines at Maroneia, gives the total revenue as one hundred talents, claims that only 100 ships were built, and offers a detailed account of how shipbuilding was financed.[28] Minor details apart (e.g., the source of the mining revenue), two things require further attention: the number of ships envisaged by

Themistokles' program, and more importantly, the implementation of that enterprise.

Labarbe assumes the enactment of two naval laws and the receipt of mining revenues from two unexpected sources, Maroneia and Laureion; each of these, he argues, enabled the Athenians to construct a consignment of 100 ships at the cost of one hundred talents, so that in the years 483/2–481/0, the total number of newly built vessels was 200 (Hdt. 7.144.1–2). But this theory rests on a hazardous harmonization of conflicting testimony.[29] Herodotos and the *Athenaion Politeia* are quite explicit that Themistokles' original scheme envisaged the construction of a total of *either* 200 *or* 100 ships; subsequent accretions to that force (whatever its size) are another matter.[30] A different, and in my view more sound, method employed by some scholars in order to address (though not wholly resolve) the conflict is to take the size of the Athenian fleet in 480 and try to trace various stages of shipbuilding in previous years. Herodotos (8.1.1–2) reports that the Athenian contingent at Artemision numbered 147 ships (including 20 manned by the Chalkidians), while a reserve of 53 ships was later sent as a reinforcement to Salamis (8.14.1)—200 in all. This force, it is contended, consisted of the 50 ships originally possessed by Athens plus 20 purchased from Corinth, of 30 more built before 483/2, and of 100 ships built by Themistokles by 481/0.[31] In this view, the fleet deployed at Salamis had been built up step by step.

There are, admittedly, uncertainties about the number of ships constructed in the intervening years. First, an early force of 50 ships is merely based on a series of assumptions, mainly that each of the fifty (Kleisthenic) naukrariai furnished a ship (*FGrH* 323: F 8 with Poll. 8.108). As argued above, this view should be abandoned; with it must go the 50 ships. Second, whatever the size of this early force, the proportion of triereis in it was too small (Thuc. 1.14.1–2) to have made any significant contribution to the total of 200 ships in 480, the majority of which were triereis. Finally, the conflict between the traditions remains a disturbing one. But having noted these reservations, one should accept the basic point of this latter view: Athenian naval strength in 480 was the result of a gradual buildup over a relatively longer span of time, rather than of a crash program that produced 200 triereis within two years' time. Accordingly, one can conclude provisionally that there is no need to suppose the occurrence of sudden and equally spectacular institutional developments leading to the creation of the trierarchy. The next important item to be addressed is the account in the *Athenaion Politeia* of how that program was implemented and financed.

But Themistokles prevented this [sc. distribution of mining revenue], not saying what use he would make of the money, but recommending that it should be lent to the hundred richest Athenians, each receiving a talent, so that if they should spend it in a satisfactory manner, the state would have the advantage, but if they did not, the state should call in the money from the borrowers. On these terms, the money was put at his disposal, and he used it to get a fleet of a hundred triremes built, each of the hundred borrowers having one ship built, and with which they fought the naval battle at Salamis against the barbarians.

So runs the story of *Athenaion Politeia* 22.7, which admittedly does not lack ingenuity and fills an otherwise displeasing gap in our knowledge. But what is one to make of it? Scholarly opinion is divided. Some accept the credibility of this passage unreservedly, and take it to convey the introduction of the trierarchy. "The ships built in this way," states Amit (*AS* 107), "were state-property and their builders became the Trierarchs." But in fact no source supports the latter part of his conclusion. The interpretation offered by Maridakis is more subtle; he believes (on no good grounds) that the *Athenaion Politeia* gives verbatim the law of Themistokles. It stipulated that the hundred talents should be lent to the hundred richest citizens by way of an arrangement comparable to the Roman *locatio conductio operis* (the undertaking by an individual of the task to complete some work contracted by the authorities) in order to conceal the imposition of a liturgy. Themistokles' real intent was hidden from the public, partly to avoid opposition from the demos (who could not share his foresight about the impending danger from Persia), and partly to bypass the naukrariai.

Furthermore, Maridakis argues, Themistokles' plan has common features with the trierarchy: the triereis are built at public expense, and if one of the richest Athenians receiving a talent does not supply a triereis approved by the state, he is obliged to build another ship at his own expense, in much the same way trierarchs were liable to replace damaged or lost ships. For these reasons Maridakis inferred that the law of 483/2 provided the foundation for establishing the trierarchy.[32]

Others are skeptical about the *Athenaion Politeia*. Burn ([1984] 292 n. 36) calls it a "silly story," and Rhodes (*Commentary* 278) states that it "fails to carry conviction, if only because nothing could be gained by secrecy (and our confidence is lessened by the ascription of similar secrecy to other plans of Themistokles)." It is nevertheless assumed that the story may have a true foundation, that some rich citizens were each made responsible for the building of one ship (ibid.), and that the system of "personal trierarchy" seems to be at least adumbrated in Themistokles' navy bill (Burn [1984] 367).

However, one may reasonably ask how it is possible to challenge the credibility of the main elements in the story of the *Athenaion Politeia* and at the same time single out the part about the rich citizens each assigned to build a ship as deriving from a trustworthy source. Either the whole description is accepted as it stands or it is rejected as nonsense. But to opt for the latter view is not to say that the basic idea it meant to convey is incredible too. I think there is something to recommend the recognition of the common features of Themistokles' plan and the obligations of the trierarchy (most explicitly stated by Maridakis), provided the claim that the hundred richest Athenians were made responsible for building ships is discarded. The key notions are there: wealthy citizens, personal responsibility, fleet finance. Clearly, the concern of the *Athenaion Politeia* is with shipbuilding, not with the trierarchy, which is not mentioned at all. Yet, arguably, in creating an account of how the former was financed, the author could have used and expanded on the financial duties of the very institution established to run and maintain the new fleet. That may be the only true foundation of the story of the *Athenaion Politeia*.

## Institutional Developments

Was Themistokles the founder of the trierarchy in 483/2? One may concede that it is plausible that he was, if one accepts the notion of a sudden and massive naval buildup with the construction of two hundred triereis at a single stroke and at Themistokles' initiative: such a new force, unprecedentedly large and costly, would call for immediate institutional arrangements, both military and financial. But this argument begins to disintegrate if one takes the view that not all the triereis deployed in 480 were built through the Themistoklean crash program. There is much to make the latter a considerably more attractive proposition.

Analysis of the causes behind the decision to expand the influence of Athens at sea is often undertaken either in terms of the need to meet the

Persian threat (foreseen by Themistokles: Thuc. 1.138.3; Plut. *Them.* 4.10), or in terms of the ongoing war with Aigina (Hdt. 7.144.1–2).[33] But while at some stage these considerations would have played an equally important part in the launching of a grand shipbuilding program, the design of an offensive as well as a defensive naval policy seems to have originated at an earlier date. Augmentation and modernization of the fleet were probably under way before 483/2, though presumably at a pace too slow to impress the commentators of the late fifth century (and us) to the same degree as does the program of 483/2. Political events—past or anticipated—demanding participation in armed conflict at sea must have made the Athenians aware of the need to enhance their naval strength.

Again, the sources can only aid in piecing together the crudest of frameworks about the extent and orientation of early Athenian naval aspirations. Early colonizing enterprises, chiefly undertaken in order to secure bases along the corn route to the Hellespont, for example at Sigeion (circa 600), in the Chersonese (from circa 560), and on the islands Imbros and Lemnos (circa 500), did require the deployment of naval forces, not least for maintaining control over these possessions, but little survives to show how well or poorly Athens was in fact equipped for that purpose.[34] More telling is the rivalry (in the late seventh and early sixth centuries) with Megara over the island of Salamis, crucially situated just before the entrance to the Piraeus. Even though it ended with Athenian success in taking possession of the island (ML no. 14), the prolonged conflict hints at the relatively limited means at hand to pursue important naval aims— though one is not obliged to believe the anecdote known to Plutarch (*Sol.* 8–10) that Salamis was won over by an Athenian flotilla of fishing boats and one triakontor.

In 498, a year after the Ionian Greeks had broken out in revolt against Persia, Athens assisted the rebelling cities and islands by sending twenty ships (Hdt. 5.97.3). But after much effort the attempt to repel Persian dominance ended in a signal failure owing to the superiority of the fleet the Persians were able to muster in the crucial naval engagement at Lade (494, by which date Athens had withdrawn). Athenian maritime inadequacy must have been realized after the unsuccessful involvement in the Ionian revolt.

Of greater moment was surely Athens's equally unsuccessful war against Aigina during the early 480s (Hdt. 6.87–93):[35] the Aiginetans had boldly attacked twice, once at Phaleron and on the Attic coast, and again at Sounion (Hdt. 5.81; 6.87), while the Athenians, Herodotos says (6.89), were at the disadvantage of not possessing enough ships to cope with their enemy. Insofar as it was feared later that Aigina might offer itself as a base for the Persian fleet, the threat of a Persian invasion and the pressing conflict with Aigina would have been considered related issues.

The only available figure for Athenian naval strength before 480 is the seventy ships employed by Miltiades in 489 to carry out what in Herodotos's judgment was Miltiades' personal act of vengeance against the Parians (6.132–33). It is unclear whether these ships were all Athens could mobilize. If they were, and provided the twenty vessels procured from Corinth (Hdt. 6.89) were in addition to this force (though this is unconfirmed), the total number of ships in the early 480s would have approximated eighty, when due allowance for losses is made. In any case, the lack of figures from after 489 does not prove that no ships were built in the early 480s. It is attractive to suppose with Burn and others that, although an emergency program was commenced in 483/2, some shipbuilding had been carried out in the preceding years.[36]

Did Themistokles have any involvement in it? The answer is elusive, for little is known about Themistokles' earlier career. Thucydides reports (1.93.3) that he initiated the Piraeus fortification project in an official capacity (*epi tēs ekeinou archēs ēs kat' eniauton Athēnaiois ērxe*), believed to be his archonship of 493/2. Still, one cannot say for certain whether the project was proposed by the archon; it may only have been supervised by him, which led later traditions to credit Themistokles for its inception.[37] It was typical of the Greeks to ascribe a craft or an art or an institution to a single, first inventor (*prōtos heuretēs*), of which a prominent example is the later ascription of the ancestral constitution to Solon.[38] Perhaps the original plan envisaged the exploitation of Piraeus's three natural harbors and the building of shed and dockyard facilities for the ships. Although work was discontinued, then resumed and completed many years later (in 490 Phaleron was still the naval station, *epineion,* of Athens; Hdt. 6.116), these plans at least reflect the initial effort toward a naval buildup.[39]

With or without Themistokles' direct involvement, a naval policy seems to have been adopted earlier than 483/2, and to have included schemes for state-sponsored shipbuilding on a scale reflecting the limited financial resources of Athens. There is an important piece of information on this matter. Herodotos records (6.89) the first known attempt by the state to augment the fleet by purchasing twenty ships—certainly triereis—from a traditional naval power, Corinth. The significance of this step is blurred by what all later traditions saw (not without reason) as a spectacular program initiated in 483/2. Yet seen in its own right, such an accretion to the existing fleet is far from negligible, even though the astonishing price of five drachmas apiece paid by Athens certainly was.

The transaction is noteworthy. First, it suggests the existence of financial impediments to embarking on a large-scale naval buildup: the Corinthians required the nominal price of five drachmas per ship because, by their own law, they were prohibited from making a gift of them; the implication is that Athens had requested a donation. Second, the handsome gesture of the Corinthians may also serve as a warning against the automatic assumption that, when the Athenians did come into possession of funds to acquire many triereis, they were able to conjure up the materials, labor force, and expertise needed for completing such a vast venture in a mere two years' time. (Judging from the building specifications of the trieres replica *Olympias,* the mortise-and-tenon technique used for plank fastening would require some twenty thousand tenons joining together the planks of the hull, and twice as many pegs to hold the tenons in place.)[40] Possibly not all of the hundred or more new vessels had been constructed in Attic shipyards and by Athens. Third, and more signally, this is the earliest known acquisition of ships subsidized by the state. Although no evidence is at hand to prove this point, it is probable that command of such an exclusively "national" force was entrusted to men drawn from a novel and slowly developing institutional setting, the trierarchy proper.

On the whole, it seems likely that the expansion of the fleet of Athens with state-owned triereis was a gradual process, starting slowly and then in 483/2 spurred by the sudden windfall from the silver mines. Consequently, institutional developments leading to the establishment of the trierarchy probably ran parallel to this, and were impelled by the growing need to meet the new and considerably higher demands of a quantitatively and qualitatively different fleet. No specific date can be given for the origin of the trierarchy, nor is there good evidence for its full-fledged emergence through a single enactment proposed by Themistokles. It may well have begun to take form by the mid-480s. A gradual increase in the number of public vessels to be commanded by individuals other than the traditional proprietors of ships began to give shape to a new duty that required a well-defined set of rules; and rules, whether entirely novel or, as seems plausible in this case, modeled on an existing set of habits and ethical values, can only be enforced from within an institution. By 480, when a large fleet had to be manned, funded, and handled, the trierarchy was indispensable.

If the trierarchy was indispensable, can the new institution already have attained its liturgical character at that date? This is both possible and likely. The period under discussion was one of democratic reforms: in 487/6, the lot was introduced for the election of archons and (less certainly) other officials, and by 480 Athens had already experienced the first twenty-seven years of a new political era initiated by Kleisthenes' reforms (508/7), most significantly, the reorganization of the Attic territory and citizenry into new political-administrative units (139 demes and 10 tribes), and creation of the Council of Five Hundred with equal representation of all tribes.[41] In addition to its principal intention, which was to reduce (but not completely eliminate) aristocratic influence, the democratic constitution embodied the requirement that affluent households expend part of their wealth on the city through the fiscal conduits of the liturgy system.

It is possible to plot with some clarity the early stages of development in this latter field. In the 480s the liturgy system, based on the principle that aristocratic munificence should be regulated by law, was hard at work in the area of lyric and dramatic contests at the City Dionysia. The principal evidence is the document (of about 279 B.C.) commonly referred to as *Fasti,*[42] which lists victorious *choregoi* since the beginning of *komoi* in honor of Dionysos. Its first extant entry is for 473/2, but the record began at an earlier year (two, possibly three, of its initial columns are now lost). The most probable date for the introduction and liturgical organization of the festival is 502/1, for dithyramb and tragedy.[43] Capps dated the introduction of comedy into the City Dionysia in 487/6.

So the transference into the liturgical orbit of munificence relating to dramatic performances falls squarely within the period of fundamental democratic reforms; hence it can be safely regarded both as the brainchild of the new political doctrine, on an ideological level, and as the product of democratic fiat, on a practical level. It is possible to conclude, therefore, that in the late 480s the liturgy system had been expanded with the incorporation of the trierarchy.

Unpredictable expenditure, often on a large scale, created a need for a fiscal mechanism to relieve and aid the state treasury by supplying funds quickly and on the spot. A practical, and perhaps ideal, solution was found: placing the ships under the command of individuals capable of acting as financiers. The responsibilities of commandership, in military terms, incorporated and justified a claim to undertake personal financial responsibility for the running and maintenance of the ships. Although the financial aspect of the trierarchy became even more dominant in the fourth century, it was substantially pronounced from the start.

It is doubtful whether ideologically and politically this new arrangement, like the introduction of the liturgy system as a whole, was in such sharp conflict with traditional values and practices that it defied the aristocrats; quite the contrary. Generally speaking, it conveniently maintained and promoted, albeit in modified form, two elements solidly anchored in aristocratic ideology and widely recognized as celebrated avenues to excellence: competitive generosity and military prowess. A gradual naval buildup, and hence an initially modest demand for trierarch-liturgists, may also suggest the absence of motivation for serious political opposition. Perhaps more important, given the existence of antagonism and even convulsion within the higher echelons of society, such an institutional innovation would have had a special appeal to members of the aristocracy who, unlike some of their better-off peers, such as Kleinias, were unable to possess in private the new man-of-war, the trieres, or any warship at all, but who cherished in no less measure an ambition for, and took pride in, munificence, military valor, and the honors bestowed for distinction in both.[44] To this group the trierarchy would have been a welcome innovation.

If I am right in holding that the twenty triereis purchased from Corinth were commanded and financed by trierarch-liturgists, then the 480s can be seen as a time of transition in which alongside the old system of privately owned warships there existed a new system of naval finance and command (at any rate, they coexisted in 480). The latter one, becoming dominant by 480 and ousting its rival completely thereafter, was shaped so as to meet the demands of a slowly growing "national" fleet, and to entice volunteers by offering new terrain in which to win honors through competitive outlay and military distinction. In sum, the economic upper class (or, initially, part of it) needed the new liturgy of the trierarchy just as much as the democratic state needed trierarch-liturgists. The foundations of an interdependent relationship were thereby firmly established.

This conclusion, however, might be rebutted by referring to the Themistokles decree from Troizen. Lines 18–44 of that document contain detailed provisions for the full mobilization and manning of the fleet to meet the Persian advance.[45] My immediate concern is with its provisions concerning trierarchs. The strategoi are ordered to appoint two hundred trierarchs, one to each of the two hundred ships that "have been made ready," beginning on the following day. (The current date is nowhere stated, ll. 18–20; cf. 14.) Then the trierarchs, to be chosen from those who possess land and a house at Athens, who have legitimate issue, and who are not older than fifty, are to be distributed to the ships by lot (*epiklērōsai*, ll. 20–23). In addition, the strategoi shall enlist to each ship ten *epibatai* from those between twenty and thirty years of age, and four archers, and shall also distribute the *hypēresiai* to the ships at the same time as they allocate the trierarchs by lot (ll. 23–27).

Several scholars take the view that originally appointment as a trierarch was predominantly (or solely) a military duty entailing personal service aboard the ship.[46] Themistokles' decree, it is argued (GOS 260), reflects a different organization from that which was prevalent in the later fifth and fourth centuries. Jameson remarks that the requirements for trierarchs—to possess property in Athens as well as legitimate issue and to be able to serve physically (the latter guaranteed by setting the age limit at fifty)—all are qualifications of generals and speakers in the assembly. He concludes, therefore, "In brief, the trierarchs of 480 are closer to *stratēgoi* than they are to trierarchs of later times."[47] But does the Troizen text shed light on all aspects of the trierarchy of 480? Regrettably, it does not.

This is not the place to rehearse the numerous arguments that have been put forth for or against its authenticity.[48] Most would now agree that the text dates from the period between late fourth century (circa 320s) and the early or mid-third century (250s) B.C., and that it is an amalgamation of several decisions relating to different events. According to a recent and convincing view, the compendious decree was inscribed and posted in Troizen in order to glorify Ptolemy II Philadelphus (283–246) by glorifying Athens;[49] a historical document was reconstructed and exhibited publicly for current political purposes. This makes the question of whence its author derived his material unavoidable.

True, Aeschines is reported to have read out, in 348, from the decree of Miltiades, the decree of Themistokles, and the ephebic oath in order to arouse patriotic enthusiasm against Philip (Dem. 19.303). But, as has been shown convincingly by H. Mattingly, only the opening section (ll. 1–18) was known to writers in the late fourth century and the post-Herodotean tradition—"and there is little in these eighteen lines that could not have been built up adroitly by combining Herodotos 7.144 and 8.41"—while the section that is of central importance here (ll. 18–44) is a later addition to the text (Mattingly [1981] 81; cf. Mattingly [1975]).

Hignett, writing before the appearance of the vast literature on the subject, observed that the historical credibility of the same section is damaged by its assumption of a general mobilization and manning of all 200 ships in the early summer of 480 (Hignett [1963] 464–65). Thus it fails to take into account that a substantial number of triereis had already been dispatched to southern Thessaly for the Tempe campaign and had later returned to the Isthmos, where the decision on the Thermopylai-Artemision defense line was taken (Hdt. 7.173–75). The Troizen text reports the Athenian force at Artemision to have been 100 ships; Herodotos (8.1.1–2) says there were 147.[50]

Although I find some of the objections raised by the skeptics to be both weighty and fatal, for my purposes it is enough to note that even those who now defend the authenticity view concede that the Troizen text (based on either literary or documentary material) preserves the main content but not the language of its alleged original.[51] This is a precarious foundation on which to base a reconstruction of the trierarchy of 481/0. And even if any criteria to establish its authenticity were forthcoming, all the Troizen text could depict, beyond its current importance as a source of information about politics in the late fourth and third centuries, would be a single aspect of the working of the trierarchy in a highly exceptional, emergency situation. By its very nature, the Themistokles decree is concerned with the military duties of the trierarchs, not with their financial or liturgical obligations.

This document, then, does not contradict the conclusion that liturgists, predominantly financiers rather than military officers, were needed right from the start to run the fleet. Navigation skills and seafaring abilities in general were an obvious advantage, but apparently never a requirement. Long journeys could usually be carried out with relative ease owing to the favorable climatic and geographic conditions of the eastern Mediterranean.[52] In terms of command and naval adroitness, it was much more demanding to keep battle formation (especially in line abreast) whenever a large fleet was employed as well as to plan and perform the maneuvers required by the tactics of *periplous* and *diekplous* during a direct engagement.[53]

However, the skills required for either of these were possessed by the professional expert on the ship, the helmsman (*kybernētēs*). Crucial decisions during a battle, such as whether to attack or not, were ultimately taken by the trierarch (Hdt. 8.87; 93), the commander of the ship, but often he acted on the advice of his helmsman. When Ps.-Xen. (*Ath. Pol.* 1.2) enumerates the people "who make the city powerful," his list includes only the *kybernētai, keleustai* (boatswains), *pentēkontarchoi* (pursers), *prōratai* (bow officers), and *naupēgoi* (shipwrights)—all belonging to the group of petty officers (*hypēresia*). Mention of trierarchs is reserved by the author until his treatment of the wealthy citizens paying for choruses and athletic contests (1.13); this serves to stress their position relative to the sociopolitical and ideological cleavage he has set about to describe between the "poor" (democracy) and the "rich" (oligarchy).

Similarly, Thucydides (1.143.1) represents Perikles emphasizing the naval resources of Athens in 431 by saying: "We possess citizen *kybernētai* and the rest of the *hypēresia* in greater numbers and better quality than the rest of Greece." It is curious (and telling) that he is silent about trierarchs. In 413 Nikias planned his line of action at Syracuse together with the helmsmen of his fleet; this indicates the importance and competence of these men (but not the insignificance of trierarchs) in naval tactics (Thuc. 7.62.1).[54]

To sum up, although the physical presence of the trierarch remained a requirement for quite a long time, there is no support for the notion that he acted solely (or mostly) as a military commander rather than as a financier. All this cannot (and is not meant to) establish the absence of trierarchs with excellent abilities in both command and seamanship: Herodotos often mentions commanders in action (7.182; 8.93), and occasionally (8.11) singles out an individual of prodigious courage. Also, throughout this period there were competent commanders drawing from past experience as strategoi (Xen. *Hell.* 1.7.5).

But for many the job would have been less demanding because they had an expert in navigation and tactics, the kybernetes, on one side, and a financial expert, the *pentēkontarchos,* on the other side. Ultimately, therefore, what was needed from a trierarch was that he should be a wealthy man.

## PART II

*Qualifications for the Trierarchy*

# Qualifications by Wealth

Apart from their relevance in an inquiry into the function of the institution, each of the aspects relating to qualifications for the trierarchy can elucidate some broader issues. The mode of recruitment and the rules about temporary or permanent exemption from the obligation, to mention only some, witness that while it never entirely lost its military character, the trierarchy was primarily viewed and treated as a fiscal entity. Much of what can be established with at least a tolerable degree of certainty about such topics as the wealth entailing liability (its size and nature), the practical means and administrative procedures used for recruiting new members, the conditions under which men, or properly speaking their estates, could leave the trierarchic class, and so forth, enables us to see how a vital object of taxation was subjected to systematic control and how its potential (financial and numerical) was sought to be maintained at a desirable level. Intertwined with these issues is the question of the particular relationship forged between trierarchs and the state.

"The section of citizens who perform liturgies from their properties," wrote Aristotle (*Pol.* 1291a33–34), "we call the rich." The fundamental truth underlying this statement is that the single most powerful criterion qualifying a man for liturgical, and particularly trierarchic, service was his economic position. This being the case, it is not surprising or fortuitous that, when seen against the background of liturgical obligations, the pervasive dichotomy in Athenian society between "rich" (*plousioi, eu-*

*poroi*) and "poor" (*penētes*) lends itself readily to a meaningful functional definition.[1] The frequency with which a formal and explicit equation is made between the former and the members of the liturgical class, on the one hand, and the repeated stress on the latter's virtual economic inability so as to be distinctly outside that class, on the other hand, is a theme fully explored by Davies (*APF* xx–xxi; *Wealth* 9–14) and need not be reviewed here.

But while the descriptions "rich" and "poor" often prove valuable for their connotation of opposing economic interests in a political context (e.g., Arist. *Pol.* 1279b17–1280a4), they offer no guidance to the amount of wealth constituting the threshold of liturgical liability. Traditionally, the crux of the matter has been to quantify narrowly the liturgical census; this is done by collecting evidence revealing the value of properties that had imposed (or were expected to impose) on their owners the duty to perform liturgies. By way of such quantification, it then becomes possible to locate, on an economic scale, the main segments of Athenian social structure, and in particular the upper class.[2]

The attempts made so far, however, seem more or less to assume both the existence of means by which the total value of properties could be assessed and the credibility of reports on the size of individual fortunes. Moreover, little weight has been given to a qualitative description of various categories of wealth and forms of ownership with direct bearing on the issue of liability. This is regrettable, for, as I will argue in the sections to follow, estates were not always measurable or thoroughly valued, and so their precise worth often remained unknown; and legally, only "visible" wealth made a man eligible for liturgies. These features, putting severe limits to an effective allocation of liturgical obligations, impelled the state to depend largely on the will of property owners themselves to reveal their wealth and to make that wealth available for fiscal purposes. To counterpoise these shortcomings, furthermore, inheritance of property was made a potent factor. Finally, to ensure the constant presence of a sufficient number of trierarchic properties, the number of which may be responsive to economic fluctuations overall, no permanent official registers of those eligible seem to have been used, nor was there any formal economic limit (however broad or narrow) separating liturgical from nonliturgical properties. It is best to begin with treatment of the final point. Because of the broader issues involved here, I shall consider all liturgies together.

## The Liturgical Census Theory

The sources often record individuals whose financial circumstances were either sufficient or insufficient to bear liturgical expenses, but never anything like a clearly defined economic limit. Yet several figures, believed to represent such a limit, have been proposed. The older estimates of two and three talents have now been abandoned in favor of Davies' conclusion (*APF* xxiv): "During the fourth century men whose property was worth less than 3 *tal.* were free from liturgical obligations, while men whose property was over 4 *tal.* were very unlikely to escape such obligations in the long run. The corresponding figures for the fifth century may well have been rather higher, but one cannot say by how much."[3] In spite of Davies' carefully formulated aim, to quantify "fairly narrowly the level of wealth," his three and four talents have since been variously employed as absolute minimums.[4] Recently, Ruschenbusch set the limit at four talents, one thousand drachmas.[5] I propose to examine the evidence adduced by Davies in support of his three-to-four-talent theory by dividing it into three main groups.

(i) The sources listed as nos. i, ii, iii, vi, viii, and ix in *APF* (xxiii–xxiv) can be treated together. These contain information about individual estates whose worth allegedly ranges from less than one talent, two thousand drachmas (Isae. 5.35–36) to over eight talents, two thousand drachmas (Xen. *Oec.* 2.3ff.), and whose owners state explicitly or imply that they have performed liturgies, or are said by others to have done so. However, on closer scrutiny it appears that the actual value of some of these estates remains undisclosed.

Sokrates' estimate of the property owned by Kritoboulos of Alopeke (Xen. *Oec.* 2.3ff.) is probably no more than a guess, and hence unworthy of the significance Davies attaches to it (*APF* 337). Kritoboulos himself does not object to it probably because the composer of the dialogue (Xenophon) wished to drive home his moral point: in spite of his great wealth, Kritoboulos will essentially remain a poor man because of his extravagant lifestyle and because of what Aristotle calls inappropriate lavishness (*Eth. Nic.* 1122a19–1123a). Therefore, all that can be said from this instance is that a man with an estate worth that much could embark on conspicuous consumption and would be expected to discharge liturgies. But it is not possible to relate the amount of eight talents, two thousand drachmas to a liturgical census, any more than one can with the suspect amount that Isokrates (15.156–58) says he possessed two years after he discharged a trierarchy, that is, one thousand staters (which equals three talents, two thousand drachmas or four talents, four thousand drachmas). Nor, finally, can a limit be derived either from the claim that the members of a household worth five talents performed trierarchies (Isae. 7.32, 42), or from Theopompos's misleading assessment of his property at three talents, four thousand drachmas when he insinuated that he performed liturgies (Isae. 11.44, 50).

Not infrequently, part or the whole of a property's worth as stated in the speeches has suffered forensic distortion in one direction or the other. Occasionally, as with Lysias 19, one can unveil the discrepancy between the property's worth as declared by the speaker (61: "If you confiscate our property, you will get less than two talents") and what is more likely to have been nearer the truth (cf. 9 and 59, possibly four talents, four thousand drachmas). But while the speaker's distortions could be exposed by anyone who cared to combine what is said in sections 9, 59, and 61, his claim that he was currently serving as trierarch with a fortune worth less than two talents may have aroused pity only among those of his listeners with no clear recollection of his previous statements. If anything, this instance tells us that it was hoped that such a claim would sound true or, at best, virtuous.

Quite analogous is Menexenos's statement that Dikaiogenes had never undertaken a trierarchy, even though for ten years he received an annual return of one talent, two thousand drachmas as *rentier*, whereas others possessing altogether a fortune worth less than his income performed trierarchies (Isae. 5.35–36). I accept Wyse's view (459–60) that the speaker exaggerates in order to bring out the contrast between Dikaiogenes' flagrancy and the virtue of others: the more other trierarchic fortunes are reduced, the clearer is the picture of Dikaiogenes as at once "rich" (*plousios*) and "extremely knavish" (*ponērotatos*). Davies dismisses this instance as "a gross anomaly, or, more likely, a gross misrepresentation" (*APF* xxiv). It may well be so, but still this source is not devoid of value; the speaker's open exaggeration is in itself a useful piece of information.

Jones wondered whether, if pressed, the speaker would have cited examples of trierarchs owning less than one talent, two thousand drachmas (Jones [1957] 85). More to the point, however, how many of those discharging trierarchies would be willing to admit that they possessed even that much? The answer, to anticipate a point to be made below, is presumably none of them, unless they were forced to, and this is precisely the situation exploited by Menexenos in order to make his extravagant assertions. The real value of this source (and a serious obstacle to the current view) lies not in the statement that some trierarchic fortunes were below three talents, but rather in the illustration it furnishes that a litigant could choose at his convenience whatever quantitative expression served his forensic purposes.

(ii) Isaeus 2.42 (cf. 34–35) and 3.80 (*APF* nos. iv and vii) form another group. In the first, Menekles is said to have been gymnasiarch in the deme from a property worth one talent, five thousand drachmas; in the second, it is said that Pyrrhos's estate of three talents would have compelled him to undertake deme liturgies if he had been married. The value of both is now rejected on two grounds: since these amounts refer to deme liturgies, they tell us nothing about the wealth that carried liability at the national level; the three talents (Isae. 3.80) cannot be made to represent any minimum, but suggest only that the minimum census was higher than this.[6] The second point is fair and calls for no further comment. But one can take issue with the first point because underneath it lie three assumptions: first, that generally deme liturgies were less costly and elaborate than state liturgies; second, that the cost of a liturgy and the census carrying liability to it were interdependent; and therefore, third, there must have existed different censuses for deme and state liturgies. None of these assumptions stands when put to the test.

To begin with, whenever the subject is liturgical liability, our sources speak of liturgies *tout court;* this is also true when the trierarchy is in question. Moreover, a comparison between expenditures on deme liturgies and expenditures on national liturgies is hindered by a problem of method. The few figures available come mostly from the speeches and tend to have an upward bias, mainly because insignificant expenditure, not being dear to the hearts of judges or of the demos, is deliberately (and wisely) suppressed.

The crucial question is not really whether deme liturgies could be less costly, but whether state liturgies (including the one commonly considered the most sumptuous, the trierarchy) were generally, or always, more expensive. In this area there were regulations prescribing two things: the number of liturgies a man was obliged to undertake in a year, and the frequency with which he had to discharge such services in two or more consecutive years. But no legal provisions existed for the size of expenditure involved in a particular liturgy. In fact, the rules regulating this stemmed from a field other than that of law. In the context of agonistic liturgies, the amount of the outlay hinged on a man's eagerness (*prothymia*) and the degree of honorable ambition (*philotimia*) as well as of splendor (*lamprotēs*) he wished to display.

Willingness and ability to undertake expenditure on a large scale, when duly demonstrated, were rewarded with public commendation. Having praised the virtuous conduct of Apollodoros son of Thrasyllos (for being moderate in his private expenditure and dedicating the rest of his fortune to the service of the state by never failing to perform a liturgy), the speaker of Isaeus 7.40 ends by saying: "When he discharged a choregia concerning a boys' chorus, he was victorious in the competition, and the well-known tripod still stands as a memorial of his honourable ambition [philotimia]." Tangible contributions gave tangible returns. Conversely, failure to display liberality in accord with the accepted standards, if exposed, aroused public contempt. Reproaching his adversary Meidias for neglecting to serve the state with his fortune, Demosthenes asks the jurors (21.158): "In what, then, consists his splendor [lamprotes], or what are the liturgies and pompous expenditure of this man?"

So a man had always to consider what was politically and socially acceptable and whether he could afford to limit his outlays to no more and no less than was strictly necessary for discharging a liturgy worth the name. The moral and social motives were equally prominent in the context of the trierarchy, where the size of expenditure depended, in addition, on practical considerations: the length of service, quality of the crew, condition of the ship, and so forth. As admissible evidence for the great eagerness (prothymia) with which he had served the state, Apollodoros son of Pasion rehearsed each item of his lavish trierarchic expenditure ([Dem.] 50.10); shortly thereafter (15), he proudly explained that honorable ambition (philotimia) was his prime motive for choosing to employ excellent but costly oarsmen.

A great part of the fabric into which liturgical spending was woven consisted of traditional aristocratic moral values. The best illustration of this comes from Aristotle's discussion of liberality and munificence in the initial sections of book 4 of his *Nicomachean Ethics*. The liberal man (*eleutherios*) is one who is endowed with the virtue (arete) related to wealth and therefore will use riches best (1120a6–8). Riches are used best when expenditure is serviceable to other people: "And of all virtuous people the liberal are perhaps the most beloved, because they are beneficial to others" (1120a21–23). Magnificence (*megaloprepeia*) consists in suitable expenditure on a large scale. But this greatness of scale is relative since the magnitude of expenditure must always be fitting (*prepousa*) to the occasion, "for the outlays accruing from a trierarchy and from an architheoria are not the same. The suitability of the expenditure therefore is relative to the spender himself and to the occasion or object" (1122a22–25).[7]

In theory and practice, Aristotle's analysis goes on to establish, munificence and particularly "fitting" expenditure exclusively belong to the realm of a distinct social class, the wealthy.

There are . . . those public benefactions which are favourite objects of ambition [*euphilotima*], for instance, the duty . . . of performing choregies splendidly or discharging trierarchies, or even of giving a banquet to the public. But in all these matters, as has been said, the scale of expenditure must be judged with reference to the person spending, that is to his position and resources . . . Hence a poor man [*penēs*] cannot be magnificent, since he has not the means to make a great outlay suitably. (1122b19–27)

While it is doubtful whether anyone other than the philosophers was always so mindful of adjusting the expenditure to the occasion, the guiding principle is provided by a set of ethical rules, not by law, and the decision about how much one would spend (like the decision whether to belong to the liturgical class) was to an appreciable degree optional. Democratic ideology successively cultivated a traditional aristocratic ethic for practical purposes.

At some date in mid-fifth century, Karkinos son of Xenotimos made a dedication to the goddess Athena to commemorate his service as trierarch (Raubitschek [1949] no. 27)—a standing monument to his largess and sense of duty. But not all trierarchs could take pride in having performed their service with distinction, nor were all liturgists victorious enough for their performances to be deemed worthy of commemoration or of such symbolic representations as the tripod displayed by Apollodoros son of Thrasyllos (Isae. 7.40). Some liturgists were unsuccessful, and perhaps deliberately so: they simply avoided spending more than the bare minimum.

Expenditure could vary markedly with individual performances of the same liturgy. The 2,000 drachmas spent by Demosthenes (21.80; 28.17), or the 2,400 drachmas spent by Diogeiton (Lys. 32.14, 26–27), each on a *syntrierarchy,* are beyond comparison with the high costs borne by others. Some opted for sole trierarchies, thus spending much more than those who shared a service with one or more partners. The speaker of Lysias 21 paid an annual average of 5,142 drachmas for seven years' continuous trierarchic service, while the excessive outlays of Apollodoros son of Pasion ([Dem.] 50) compelled him to saddle himself with debt in order to keep a trierarchy of high standard. All in all, within certain limits trierarchs and other liturgists had the power to regulate their expenditure at will.

Despite differences in the amounts spent, in the eyes of the law these men were not really distinguished from one another inasmuch as they all had responded promptly to the state's call to perform their duty (*ta prostattomena*). Voluntary efforts were highly appreciated and often praised, for the simple reason that they constituted the least cumbersome means of mobilizing private wealth for public utility. Those spending lavishly could also hope for, or even stake a claim to, public recognition of their endeavor. Extreme examples apart (Lys. 21.1–5), there is one piece of evidence that makes transparent the difference between what was required by law and what was viewed as socially laudable.

Apollodoros (Pasion's son) made the allegation that his opponent in a lawsuit, Stephanos, although rich enough to give his daughter a dowry of one talent, four thousand drachmas, had never been *choregos* or trierarch, nor had he discharged any other liturgy, even one of the less costly ones ([Dem.] 45.66). This means that Stephanos had the power to keep his wealth virtually unavailable for liturgical purposes; it also shows that the lowest possible voluntary outlay would have fended off some of these accusations. The *eutaxia,* for instance, a liturgy on a national level involving expenditure of fifty or a hundred drachmas, might suffice to that end.[8] However, if a man was thought to possess a substantial fortune (as was said of Stephanos in the source cited above), a eutaxia would hardly help him escape the social embarrassment in which Dikaiogenes found himself because of failure to add any trierarchies to his liturgical record (Isae. 5.35–36). But the picture is not complete without a fine dividing line between the state's dependence on volunteer liturgists and an equally strong dependence of wealthy citizens on liturgies: most significantly, even a lesser outlay represented a prudent investment inasmuch as it would temporarily guard a man against an unpleasant *anti-dosis-* challenge.

The sources do not validate a sharp distinction between the wealth that led to liability for deme and state liturgies. Therefore, although neither the three talents (in Isae. 3.80) nor the one talent, five thousand drachmas (in Isae. 2.42) tell us what the minimum census might have been (nor does any other source), both figures deserve to be counted among the instances expressing the value of properties that were within the liturgical class.

(iii) By far the best information is thought to be furnished by Demosthenes 27.64 (*APF* no. v). Here owners of households originally worth one or two talents are said to have succeeded in doubling and trebling the value of their possessions to two to six talents, and so are called on to perform liturgies. According to the current view, this implies that the owner of an estate of two talents would not be required to perform liturgies, and that the liturgical census was more than two but rather less than six talents.[9] However, one may reasonably ask why Demosthenes did not say just that, instead of using an ambiguous phrasing placing properties of two talents both inside and outside the liturgical class. In my opinion, what this passage actually says is that those most likely to be asked to undertake liturgies were owners of estates worth two to six talents or more, which is what would be expected anyway. That precisely here will have been the proper place to mention a narrower economic limit, if there were any, is quite damaging for the conventional view.

(iv) A final remark. It is often claimed that only properties large enough to bring in substantial returns carried liturgical liability. Only these, it is assumed, could furnish the surplus required for defraying the pertinent expenses. Davies states that to expect a man possessing forty-five hundred drachmas ([Dem.] 42.22) to discharge the most trivial civic liturgy is out of the question; he would need a return of over 15 percent from such a property if he were to have an income equivalent to that of a contemporary skilled worker, that is, seven hundred drachmas, much of which would be required for defraying the expenses of his household.[10] Speaking of trierarchic liability, Brun argues ([1983] 15–18) from attested expenditure in that area that even properties worth five talents (Isae. 7.42) were formally ineligible, unless they yielded a substantial return (capitalized on the basis of the rental value of land in the fourth century, about 8 percent; Isae. 11.42). Expenditure of two thousand drachmas on a mere syntrierarchy required over 3 percent from a ten-talent fortune during a period in which such an estate was expected to bring an income of forty-eight hundred drachmas. Therefore, the aggregate capital (or, according to Brun, *timēma*) incurring liability for the trierarchy was more likely in the vicinity of ten talents.

But this reasoning (though apparently sound) is refuted by a fairly large amount of evidence showing that individuals may have had to raise loans in order to meet liturgical expenditures. Whether or not a house-hold had ready liquid assets was broadly irrelevant to the issue of liability. Indeed, it seems not to have been unusual for a man who was short of cash to hypothecate his property or raise interest-free loans for paying the cost of a service.[11] It suffices to cite the known examples concerning trierarchs. When challenged to an antidosis, Demosthenes had to borrow two thousand drachmas on the security of his estate, without which, he claims (21.80), he would have been unable to discharge the obligation. Apollodoros was forced to hypothecate his property and contract a series of loans for financing his trierarchy ([Dem.] 50). Finally, in 390, Demos son of Pyrilampes had to raise a loan of nineteen hundred drachmas to meet the expenses of his trierarchy (Lys. 19.25–26), and thus avoid the financial embarrassment to which the strategos Timotheos was exposed when he had to borrow seven hundred drachmas from each of the sixty trierarchs of his force in order to pay his crews ([Dem.] 49.11–12). Other evidence showing individuals financially assisting trierarchs unable to meet naval debts is set out in chapter 7.

Taken as a whole, the sources reviewed above either state or imply that properties worth less than one talent, two thousand drachmas, on one end of the scale, and more than eight talents, two thousand drachmas, on the other end, had come or were expected to come into the liturgical class. The certainty with which scholars have sought to estimate nar-rowly the liturgical census is virtually unattainable. Even if the figures could be relied on, the three-to-four-talent interval may only be taken as a convenient average of properties *attested* in the liturgical class, and as such of limited value for inferring what the actual average might have been. While one may reasonably surmise that many liturgical properties were well above the three-talent level, it would be wrong to maintain that others of a net worth of two talents, or perhaps even one talent, automatically became exempt. Besides Isaeus 2.42 and 5.35–36, there is the complaint of a man involved in an antidosis to the effect that it was not easy to live off a property worth forty-five hundred drachmas, which he claimed was the residue of his possessions when his case was heard by a law court ([Dem.] 42.22).[12] Yet the same man ran a considerable risk of having the liturgy of proeisphora imposed on him by a law court in the event the jurors were persuaded that his rival possessed even less than forty-five hundred drachmas.

The wealth bringing a man into the liturgical class was always reckoned in relative terms. This can be attributed to two main considerations. First, changes both in the number of rich Athenians and in the absolute level of private wealth—owing to actual demographic or economic fluctuations, or to "artificial contraction" because property owners hid their wealth—should not have had a negative effect on the number of men needed annually to undertake trierarchies and other liturgies. Second, with a lower limit for wealth entailing liability, prospective shirkers could simply choose to reveal just enough of their wealth to be disqualified from the obligation; without such a limit, however, even the most ardent practitioner of wealth-concealment would find this method quite unrewarding so long as the antidosis procedure was in force.

Paradoxically, but not illogically, therefore, abstention from employing a clear-cut liturgical census may have been one of the means to exercise some control over the liturgical class. But enough has already been said in general terms about concealment of property to invite a more detailed discussion of that practice.

## Visible and Invisible Wealth

It is widely assumed, on a priori grounds, that the volume and value of Athenian properties were generally known (see p. 44). Yet there is good reason now to believe that valuations, in the proper sense, not only never took place but were impracticable. Considering that land, besides being the most stable and secure, politically was the most important form of wealth in that the right to own it was restricted to citizens, one might expect the authorities to have been seriously concerned with systematic registration of owners. However, the absence of official land registers points the other way.[13] True, in one fiscal area, that of the war tax, or eisphora, contributions were levied on the bases of the valuation, or timema, of households. But as de Ste. Croix (1953) has shown, such a timema simply expressed an estate's worth as assessed and declared by the owner himself.[14] More importantly, the timema was never used with the liturgies.

As argued in detail elsewhere (Gabrielsen [1986]), the means of obtaining a reliable picture of a man's economic standing were limited and the opportunities for the individual to prevent such a picture from emerging correspondingly great. To a large extent, this was due to a distinction drawn between two categories of property (not in themselves juridical, though they often appear in a legal context): visible (*phanera*) and invisible (*aphanēs*) property (*ousia*). That distinction, probably existing in the fifth century (Ar. *Ran.* 1063–68), is surely not one between "real" property and "movables," as a lexicographer (Harp., s.v. "aphanes ousia kai phanera") took it to be. Rather, phanera and aphanes reflect different attitudes of owners toward their holdings: to make one's wealth invisible means that, legally or otherwise, it cannot be associated with its owner; conversely, to make wealth visible means that it becomes attributable to, and acknowledgeable by, its owner.[15] In common parlance the former practice was referred to as concealment of wealth (*apokrypsis ousias*). Some evidence exists illustrating a few of the many ways in which either of these could be accomplished. A prime motive was to eschew liturgical service.

(i) Personal effects, and particularly money, were the easiest to convert into invisible property.[16] The deposit of a sum with a bank could be followed by a confidential agreement between owner and banker to the effect that the existence of a part or the whole of that sum should remain a secret.[17] But, since property converted into invisible form in a sense became disowned, there was always a great risk that the owner might be unable to recover his possessions through lack of proof that he really owned what he previously had overtly disclaimed. To find a trustworthy accomplice in dealings of this kind was of the utmost importance. On departing for service, a trierarch left a sum with one Eumathes. When rumors reached Athens that the trierarch had died in the battle fought off Chios in 358, Eumathes made the money visible (*emphanise*) to the family and friends of the deceased and returned it "in a right and honest manner." But by a fortunate chance the trierarch arrived home safely, and the pleasing news about Eumathes' exemplary honesty only enhanced his confidence in him, so the trierarch supplied him with cash when Eumathes established himself as a banker (Isae. fr. 15 [Thalheim]).

For bankers, of course, the opportunities for concealment were great. But equally great was the danger of being publicly harangued for holding invisible wealth. The banker Stephanos found himself in such a plight when Apollodoros son of Pasion attacked him in a law court by saying: "This course of action, involving so great disgrace, he has adopted, men of Athens, with a view to evading his duties to the state and to conceal his wealth, that he may make invisible profits by means of the bank, and never serve as choregos or trierarch, or perform any other of the public duties [sc. liturgies] that befit his station" ([Dem.] 45.66). Unable to adduce direct proof for his accusations (and understandably so, considering the secret nature of these transactions), Apollodoros went on to produce instead an argument that to us would seem quite slender, if not irrelevant: although he has so large an estate that he gave his daughter a dowry of ten thousand drachmas, Stephanos has never performed any liturgy whatever, even the very slightest.

In fact, however, Athenian jurors were expected to accept that argument as both weighty and relevant; the most effective way in which Stephanos or any other man might try to thwart such charges and prove that his holdings were visible consisted in the demonstration of honorable ambition (philotimia) and zeal (prothymia) in performing liturgies. For the same reason, rich Athenians defending themselves in court frequently found it worthwhile to link their liturgies with their commendable decision to keep their holdings unconcealed. But in the same breath they might remind their audience, as a speaker did on behalf of his father, Polystratos, that it was within their power to do otherwise: "Then, when he might well have converted his fortune into invisible property and refused to be useful to you, he preferred that you should have cognizance of it, in order that, even if he chose to play the knave, he could have no chance, but must contribute to the eisphora levies and perform liturgies" (Lys. 20.23). As these and other fourth-century sources illustrate, a nexus had been firmly established between possession of visible or invisible property and willingness or unwillingness to be useful to the state by performing liturgies.[18]

(ii) Although it was more difficult to conceal realty, determined proprietors did not lack the imagination or ability to discover various ways in which to make these possessions invisible also. One could convert realty into cash through sale (*exargyrosis*), and then see to it that no one could keep track of this. However, those opting for this arrangement might have had to face public resentment, especially if the property sold and subsequently squandered had previously enabled its owner to perform trierarchies: to make away with and sell a trierarchic household worth five talents was something deplorable (Isae. 7.42). Land was the basis of wealth, and only its preservation and increase by successive generations could ensure that the expectations of society toward its owners were honored. Dikaiogenes was accused of having disgracefully squandered a large inheritance so that he then pleaded poverty; worse still, he could not justify himself by claiming lavish expenditure on many liturgies (Isae. 5.43, 45).

Expenditure on the city might be accepted as a valid excuse for an otherwise wealthy individual temporarily being in financial straits. "Because of my liturgies and war taxes and my honourable ambition [philotimia] toward you," explains a litigant to the jurors, "some of my furniture is lying in pawn, and some has been sold" ([Dem.] 47.54). This, however, would not always do, for ideally one was expected both to meet his civic obligations and to preserve his property for fiscal purposes. Cautioning the jurors not to be misled by the trierarchies that his opponents are going to cite when pleading for gratitude, a defendant says that

those who while performing liturgies have squandered their own property, bring the state into disrepute instead of rendering her a service. For no man ever yet blamed himself; on the contrary, he declares that the state has taken away his property. But those who zealously (*prothymōs*) perform all the duties you lay upon them, and who by the soberness of their lives in other matters preserve their property, rightly have the better of the others in this respect, that they both have been and will be useful, and also because this service accrues to you from them without reproach. (Dem. 38.26)

But the ideal was one thing; what property owners found most opportune was another, and an alternative means of making realty invisible was to purchase a plot or a house away from one's deme of residence and keep it secret. To accomplish this the owner had to abstain from transactions involving that property (e.g., letting it out; cf. Dem. 28.7), or anything bound to confirm his ownership. For instance, declaration of an estate's timema for eisphora purposes meant making it visible: Pronapes is said to have concealed part of his wealth by underrating his valuation for the war tax, whereas his opponent Apollodoros had converted his entire fortune to visible property, performing liturgies and being among the first to pay *eisphorai* (Isae. 7.39–40).[19] Besides, such declarations revealed the property's value (*IG* 2².2496.25–28).

In sum, any attempt by the authorities to produce accurate assessments was obstructed by the permeable distinction between phanera and aphanes wealth. Not surprisingly, therefore, the only source from which to obtain information about a property's size and worth was the owner himself. The circumstance that what was known of a man's financial standing often was based on rumors or other people's guesses is clearly brought out by the speaker of Lysias 19, who, addressing the jurors, says: "I have been told by my father and other elderly people that you have had similar experiences in the past of being deceived in the fortunes of many men who were supposed to be wealthy while they lived, but whose death showed your belief to be wide of the mark" (45). Clearly, he alludes to a man's will, which may disprove previous guesses but need not disclose the actual holdings of the deceased (Isae. 1.41–42). It is doubtful whether the evidence showing well-off persons in need of liquid assets (especially for discharging a liturgy) always reflects a real shortage of cash, and whether the often insignificant amounts making up the money portion of otherwise enormous properties tell anything near the truth.[20]

Those most likely to know anything about a property (besides the owner) were neighbors and fellow deme members. Local people could keep a watchful eye on outsiders owning land in their district. A document from the deme of Piraeus (*IG* 2².1214.25–26) shows that a man from another deme was required to pay tax in Piraeus because he held property there. In the proeisphora of 362, Apollodoros son of Pasion was made liable to the levy because he was reported to have visible property dispersed in three different demes ([Dem.] 50.8). It is not fortuitous that it was the deme members who (through the councilors) made the report; nor, as is argued by Jones ([1957] 27–28) and others, does the procedure followed in 362 deviate in any way from the normal one.[21]

First, selection of property owners at the deme level is not incompatible with the organization of payers of (pro)eisphora into symmories.[22] Second, the reason Apollodoros does not mention the symmories (which he might be expected to have done, if the normal procedure were followed) could be that in that passage he only describes how he *became* liable to the duty, not how he discharged it. Unless, of course, one endorses Davies' theory (*Wealth* 143–46) that what Apollodoros calls a proeisphora in fact was an exceptional measure designed by Aristophon in order to suspend the right of exemption from the obligation on account of discharging another liturgy at the time. But this theory seems unlikely.[23]

Third, the argument that because of changes in the pattern of residence and because of the increase in invisible property, a previous method of collecting the eisphora in the demes had to be superseded by a nonterritorial arrangement (the symmories),[24] is self-contradictory: fragmentation of estates and increasing conversion of wealth into aphanes would, if anything, render the assistance of local people and authorities indispensable, not superfluous. Fourth, the current view seems to presuppose that it is known what the regular procedure was before 362. The truth is that it is not. In short, the procedure of 362 may have been less exceptional than historians tend to believe. The most appropriate place at which to ascertain who carried liturgical liability on account of possessing phanera ousia was doubtless always the demes with their residents and officials as the primary agents through whom information would pass to the polis authorities. This is important to remember when considering the question of whether the strategoi were able to select personally the men liable to perform trierarchies in a year (see chapter 3).

Legally, what brought a man into the liturgical class was his visible wealth alone, that is, holdings attributable to him. Two examples from Demosthenes' speech against his guardians (28) make this clear. The first, setting out to prove that, contrary to allegations, the Demosthenic household always kept its wealth visible, praises the prodigious Demochares, who "has not concealed his property, but acts as choregos and as trierarch, and performs all the other liturgies, without any fear of such consequences" (28.3). The second is Demosthenes' final plea to the jurors:

If I recover my patrimony through your help, I shall naturally be willing to perform liturgies, being grateful to you for rightfully restoring to me my estate; while this man [sc. his former guardian Aphobos], if you make him the owner of my property, will do nothing of the kind. Do not imagine that he will be willing to perform liturgies for you on behalf of property which he denies having received; rather he will conceal it so as to make it appear that he has avoided these services justly. (28.24)

In language and spirit such utterances strike deep into the vaults of political ideology, with its sympathy for those letting their holdings be visible in the service of the public (Lys. 20.23) and with its overt prejudice against perpetrators of the concealment of wealth for abjectly indulging in something that, as Dinarchos put it sourly, "is surely neither just nor fair nor democratic" (1.70). But in spite of ideological or political censure, the concealment of wealth remained a potent instrument in the hands of property owners for holding their wealth outside the channels of fiscal obligation. With realty things could be complicated: in Aristophanes *Ecclesiazusae* 597–601, Praxagoras's gallant scheme to pool all properties into a common fund with which "to feed and maintain all" is met by Blepyros's bewilderment: "With regard to the land, I can quite understand, / But how, if a man has his money in hand, / Not farms, which you see, and he cannot withhold, / But talents of silver and Darics of gold?" Maneuvering through such difficulties, as the following accusation amply displays, was possible: "for fear of the liturgies to which he would be liable, he sold his possessions . . . a plot in Kephisia, another in Amphitrope, and two workshops at the silver mines" (Aesch. 1.101).

All this, like the absence of a clearly defined liturgical census, serves to underline the state's limited ability to penetrate the massive barrier of wealth-concealment as well as its dependence on volunteer liturgists. Hence the infusion into these services of acclaim and honor, preserving the aristocratic values and commendations, can be seen as an important element in the strategies adopted to countervail the adverse effects of *apokrypsis ousias.* Acclaim for optionally performed services may have been pursued by property owners, as it could be held up whenever a justification of their ownership rights needed to be based on a tangible demonstration that their property had abundantly met the fiscal needs of the community. A defendant advised the jurors thus:

You ought, therefore, to see the surest revenue for the state in the fortunes of those who are willing to perform liturgies. So, if you are well advised, you will take as great care of our property as of your own personal possessions, knowing that you will be able to avail yourselves of all that we have . . . whereas if you impoverish me, you will wrong yourselves besides. (Lys. 21.13–14)

This sounds not merely like a defense but also like a reminder by a man seemingly conscious of the strengths *and* weaknesses inherent in his status as the owner of a substantial fortune. The bonds of dependence worked both ways, and for the most part well enough to ensure the smooth running of the liturgy system. But where the tactics used to entice volunteers failed, enforcement of other, distinctly coercive means did the job; above all, reports of property owners at the deme level and the antidosis helped ensure the ultimate inclusion in the system of those likely to slip through in the first place.

## The Role of Inheritance

A point emerging from the previous discussion is that liturgical liability had become an intrinsic quality, and hence a function, of a man's property. Symbolically and legally, liability and possession of visible wealth, phanera ousia, were inextricably linked by often being used to prove one another. Not unexpectedly, this gave the state a means to surmount with some success any difficulties in recruiting an adequate number of volunteers for the trierarchy. Inheritance came to be a prime determinant for eligibility, and as such deserves more attention than it has usually received in the past.

To exemplify the situation I will take as my point of departure two main types of households functioning as recruiting ground for liturgists. One is the household known for ancestral wealth and liturgical activities. Services performed by its owner committed the descendants, socially and legally, to continue the family's record and reputation. Usually, sons qua heirs were expected, and in some cases obliged, to emulate the liturgical activities of their fathers. Failure to discharge liturgies voluntarily would bring an heir into one or more of the following situations: to be proposed by others; to be faced with a charge of concealing or of having squandered a patrimony that should be used to perform liturgies; and to be challenged to an antidosis. Each of these incorporated the element of coercion applied in various degrees.

Similar requirements had to be met by a household belonging to the *nouveaux riches*. Certain social distinctions do seem to have been drawn between that and a habitually wealthy *oikos* (Arist. *Rh.* 1387a15ff., Dem. 27.64). Still, both were subject to the same rules: inasmuch as newly acquired affluence was visible, the owner would choose, or might be forced, to embark on a liturgical career for most of the reasons stated above. By so doing, he laid the foundation for the careers of successors who were obliged to follow suit, unless of course they tried to disrupt the sequence by resorting to the concealment of wealth. The brothers Diogeiton and Diodotos, for instance, decided to divide between them the invisible part of their inheritance and to possess the visible part in common (Lys. 32.4; cf. Dem. 48.33, 35).

It would seem that up-and-coming metics, especially those possessing *isoteleia* (the right to pay the same taxes as citizens) and *enktēsis gēs kai oikias* (the right to own realty), showed a particular interest in possessing their holdings as visible property, no doubt from political and social motives, and to have been eager to discharge festival liturgies voluntarily and sumptuously. But the evidence on this matter is too poor to support general conclusions, and the trierarchy, it should be remembered, was reserved exclusively for citizens (Dem. 20.18, 20).[25]

Admittedly, the picture I have just drawn cannot help being oversimplified and static. Allowance must be made for variations between the two ends represented by these households at a given time, and within a single household in the long run. Nevertheless, recent prosopographical work confirms the main components of this description. On the a priori (albeit safe) assumption that, according to the rules of inheritance, natural descendants (*ekgonoi*) in most cases were heirs of an estate, the liturgical performances of successive generations, richly documented in Davies' *Athenian Propertied Families,* enable us to draw a number of conclusions.

As Davies' register makes clear, in a large number of instances liturgical services continued with a family branch for more than two generations. Isolated statements in the orators should have prepared us for the notion that heirs automatically became successors (*diadochoi*) of their testator's liturgical liability: "My father died while serving as trierarch," says the speaker of Lysias 19, "and I will try to do what I saw him doing, and raise, by degrees, some little sums for the public services. Thus in practice it continues to be the property ⟨of the state [: Dobree]⟩" (62). Again, at the trial about his patrimony Demosthenes stated: "I as my father's successor [*diadochos*] was to perform liturgies for you" (28.19). It is now possible to argue that these statements carry a wider significance. I will confine my discussion to trierarchic liability, considering possible cases of direct and then of indirect succession.

Direct succession here refers to the direct takeover of a particular service. A probable illustration is offered by the case of Diopeithes Diopeithous Sphettios and Diognetos Diodotou Phlyeus; they were heirs of the trierarchs on *Demokratia Hagnodemou* in 349/8, Diopeithes Sphettios and Diophantos Halaieus. The naval record of 348/7 (*IG* 2².1620) states that the heirs brought joint legal action (*diadikasia*) against the dockyard officials of 349/8, who allegedly had committed some offense. It seems the case was tried by the boule, whose decision, though poorly preserved, is reconstructed as follows: "That Diopeithes Sphettios and Diophantos Halaieus and their heirs, [who have had in their possession] the trieres [Demokrati]a during a voyage in the archonship of [Kalli]machos (349/8), [owe] from De[mokratia] Hagnode[mou]"—items of equipment follow.

Since the record (with the supplements proposed)[26] seems to say that all four individuals had been in charge of the ship during the same voyage, and since Diopeithes the Younger and Diognetos acted as heirs of the original trierarchs, rather than as syntrierarchs with them in their own right, it is likely that Diopeithes the Elder and his colleague Diophantos died while serving (not necessarily on the same occasion), so that their heirs had to take over for the remaining term of service. A similar succession is perhaps suggested by the language of Lysias 19.62 (quoted above): "at this moment, too, I discharge a trierarchy from the residue [sc. of his property]; my father died while serving as trierarch."[27] What this man may be saying is that he had been obliged to succeed his father, who had died just recently while serving as trierarch at the age of seventy (57–58, 60),[28] and this, it should be noted, regardless of his financial standing at the time. In either case, probably, the takeover was compulsory.

The evidence relating to naval debts is an appreciable help in understanding indirect succession. Sometimes the outstanding liabilities of living or deceased trierarchs were shouldered by one or more individuals with no attested legal or kinship ties with the debtor, but these bear a different significance. Far more typical, however, is that debts were posthumously paid by successors or, if still due, entered in the latter's names.[29] Philomelos Paianieus was in 336/5 syntrierarch with Konon Anaphlystios on *Charis Archeneo*. Some time later Philomelos died, and his son and heir, Philippides, took over his father's liability to replace the ship. Thus in two naval records (of 326/5 and 325/4) listing that liability, Philippides is recorded as follows: "Syntrierarch, the heir of Philomelos Paianieus, Philippides Paianieus" (*IG* 2².1628.373–76; 1629.892–95). The use of the term *syntrierarch* is telling.

Like many other heirs, Sostratos Euxitheou Acharneus complied with the letter of the law and took responsibility for the debt of his testator

Demophilos Acharneus; there is nothing unusual in this. But the documents mentioning the debt reveal that although a mere debtor, Sostratos is initially listed in the symmory of his testator as "heir of Demophilos Acharneus" (*IG* 2².1615.96–98), and then, in a subsequent year, in his own right as a full member of that symmory (1616.117–30). It looks as if Sostratos was obliged to enter the trierarchic class in his capacity as heir of a naval debtor, and eventually to obtain full membership.

A slightly different case, though basically implying the same thing, comes from a document (of 336/5–331/0) recording a payment for the trieres *Parrhesia* in the following manner: "On behalf of Derketes Sphettios, Eupeithes Derketou Sphettios and syntrierarchs" (*IG* 2².1624.77–82). This might be an instance in which a son, Eupeithes, served on behalf of his father Derketes.[30] All the same, two things are noteworthy. First, in the official record Eupeithes is given the place usually occupied by the principal trierarch. Second, the formula heading the transactions does not distinguish between "heir-debtors" and "trierarch-debtors," but states: "The following trierarchs made cash payments toward the cost of equipment."

The peculiar appointment of Onetor Onetoros Meliteus (treated in detail in chapter 7) furnishes some further corroboration. It shows that men could attain the appellation "(syn)trierarch" merely by way of undertaking responsibility for a naval debt without actually having themselves performed the service (*IG* 2².1623.144–59; 1629.500–508). One final example is of relevance. Nausikles Klearchou Oiethen is listed in 334/3 as debtor of equipment from *Demokratia Chairestratou*, of which he was in charge in his capacity as strategos (*IG* 2².1623.326–33). Seven years later (in 326/5), Nausikles appears again as owing the same debt, though now as principal trierarch with his son Klearchos as syntrierarch (1628.100–108).[31] Finally, in the following year (325/4), Klearchos alone is recorded as having forwarded a sum toward meeting the debt in his capacity as heir (1629.707–15). Since in 326/5 Klearchos himself was the principal trierarch on another ship (1628.71–78) and perhaps also a syntrierarch on a third one (1628.137–46), his syntrierarchy with his father on *Demokratia* in that year was nominal, postdating the actual trierarchy; its purpose was to assist his father in defraying the debt on a partnership basis, while after the latter's death Klearchos took full responsibility as heir. Once more the use of the term *syntrierarch* in such contexts is noteworthy.

To sum up, the instances of direct and indirect succession highlight the importance of inheritance in obtaining membership in the trierarchic class. But another notable aspect needs to be addressed. Liability for the liturgies and the eisphora was determined on the basis of the financial potential of individual estates; men became immediately liable by virtue of being owners of such estates. It is strictly true that the obligation, first and above all, fell on the legal owner (*kyrios*), usually the father and head of the family. However, *Athenian Propertied Families* documents many instances where the liturgical activity of a son commenced when the father was still alive, while in still other instances, and this is far more important, father and son are attested to have been active simultaneously.

It is possible to explain some of these cases by assuming that sons had set up households of their own so as to perform liturgies in their own right. But not all instances necessarily reflect that situation. There is evidence to encourage the belief that insofar as a household remained undivided, all adult males with an ownership share, including the co-ownership of father and son, became individually liable.

(i) Euktemon Kephisieus and his son Philoktemon possessed their property jointly (Isae. 6.38), at least until Philoktemon predeceased his father (27). It cannot be said with absolute certainty whether their liturgical activities were contemporaneous; but this is perhaps how this statement should be understood: "Euktemon together with his son Philoktemon possessed so large a fortune that both of them were able to undertake the most costly liturgies," which includes the many trierarchies of Philoktemon (6.38).

(ii) That pattern was repeated by another branch of the same family, that of Philoktemon's son-in-law, Phanostratos Kephisieus. It looks as if Phanostratos's seven trierarchies (before 364) were performed by virtue of having Philoktemon's property transferred to him by marriage (*APF* 563–64). Since Isaeus 6.60 says of this family "the fortune of my clients . . . is being spent rather upon the city," Phanostratos and his two sons, Chairestratos and a younger one not named, probably owned their property undivided. The picture given by the magniloquent parade of their liturgical activities is one of an oikos furnishing three liturgists. By 364, Phanostratos had discharged seven trierarchies and all the liturgies; Chairestratos, even though still a young man, had been trierarch, choregos, and gymnasiarch. In addition, they both paid eisphorai as members of the Three Hundred. And whereas previously there were only two of them, now a younger son, having come of age, served as choregos and was listed in the Three Hundred, paying eisphora as a member of that body.

(iii) Nikeratos's three sons inherited a substantial fortune (*APF* no. 10808). Two of the brothers, Eukrates and Diognetos, seem to have owned part of the original inheritance in common and transferred it as such to their own children (the two unnamed sons of Eukrates and their cousin Diomnestos, Lys. 18.21). The third brother, Nikias, had drawn his share out of the inheritance and established an oikos of his own.[32] Therefore, when at the trial for which Lysias 18 was written one of Eukrates' sons stated: "you [sc. the jurors] will receive no less profit from the property than we, the owners, for at this moment Diomnestos, my brother, and I, three of one household, perform trierarchies, and when the state requires money, we pay eisphora contributions from this property" (20–21), he probably meant that all three discharged trierarchies simultaneously as joint owners of one household.

An obvious objection to this is that liturgies performed by more than one member of a household could be optional. That is doubtless true for some but not all cases. One example exists in which membership in the trierarchic class by one member of a household did not prevent the compulsory imposition of a trierarchy on another member. Presumably, Isokrates and his adopted son Aphareus owned their property jointly, at least until 354.[33] By that year they had discharged three trierarchies, two performed by Aphareus in 357 and by 354 ([Dem.] 47.31–32; Isoc. 15.145). However, Aphareus's representation of Isokrates' household (and each of his services should have entitled him to two years' respite) was no obstacle to Megakleides' challenging Isokrates to an antidosis, nor did it spare Isokrates (now over eighty years old) the imposition of a trierarchy.

The material just presented makes credible the view that all joint owners of a household carried individual liability for the trierarchy. This, it may be suspected, was a direct consequence of the principle that, unless it had been divided, a property was owned by any and all joint owners as a whole rather than in portions.[34] Unlike fractional ownership, which enabled a shareholder to enter into transactions affecting his part only, property held in common affected each of its owners in the same manner as if he owned the whole of it alone. An illustration of the complications likely to arise from such a form of ownership is offered by Demosthenes (38).

Nausimachos and Xenopeithes, the sons of Nausikrates, brought legal action in order to recover a debt of thirty *minas* allegedly owed to them by their former guardian, Aristaichmos. But since Aristaichmos was dead, and since his four sons owned their patrimony jointly, each of them was faced with a demand to pay the whole debt separately (the debt being now increased to two talents). Moreover, since Nausimachos and Xeno-peithes, too, owned their patrimony jointly, they sued the four brothers separately so that the total sum demanded from the latter for an original debt of thirty minas eventually turned out to be four talents (38.2ff.)! The extension of the principle to liturgical liability is not hard to imagine, and a lexicographer's claim to the contrary is untrustworthy.[35] These findings go some way toward explaining the presence of a father and son (Strato-kles and Euthydemos Diomeieus, on two occasions, *IG* 2².1612.132–38; 1612.271–78), or of brothers (Onetor and Philonides Meliteus, 1622.656–65) as syntrierarchs on the same ship.

What does all this reveal? First, it suggests that inheritance played a prime role in the transference of trierarchic liability to successors. This seems demonstrable in cases of a direct takeover. If a man died while serving as trierarch, his heir was very likely obliged to take his place, entering the trierarchic class in that capacity and continuing thereafter in his own right. There is a strong impression, moreover, that the financial ability of a successor was kept out of consideration, the idea being that the same, trierarchically viable property had now passed into new hands. Given that a patrimony was distinguished by liturgical pedigree or had been preserved as visible, transference of properties to successors thus embodied the bequest of liability to liturgies, an obligation probably car-ried equally by all joint owners of an estate. Successors wishing to be exempt had no alternative other than to make use of antidosis.

Second, men seemed to enter the trierarchic class as heirs of naval debtors. The extant instances conform to a single pattern: heirs came into the trierarchic class as debtors and then attained full membership in their own right. In this situation, all of a man's heirs were obliged to take over his liabilities, regardless of whether they owned the inheritance in com-mon or had divided it between them; a trierarch's debts were often taken over by two or three successors (e.g., *IG* 2².1627.207–22). Some interest-ing implications follow. For when seen in conjunction with the vast amount of trierarchic debt that dominates the picture of fourth-century naval finances, this magnifies the role of inheritance to an even more forceful means by which to recruit new members than might have been expected. In practice, the state here availed itself of a controlling mechanism enabling it to dispel the worst effects of the concealment of wealth and the dodging of liturgies.

# THREE

# Appointment

## Preselection of Nominees

The ascertainment of property owners liable to perform trierarchies must have taken place in the demes (see chapter 2). An important question that now needs to be clarified is whether in the preselection of nominees the authorities were assisted by centrally kept registers. Specifically, did there exist official and currently revised lists of persons liable for the trierarchy? Most often this is answered in the affirmative (e.g., Jones [1957] 85). A recent exponent of this view, Davies (*Wealth* 24–25), maintains that "lists of trierarchs certainly existed and were continuously kept up to date by the generals. In contrast, no such lists were kept of those liable to agonistic liturgies," a point "demonstrable for the fourth century and which can be safely extrapolated back to the fifth century." Slightly different is the opinion of Rhodes ([1982] 3), who holds that "probably there were lists of men who had served recently, as there were lists of men who had served as hoplites, but . . . there was no complete list of men who were liable"; only "from 357 onwards there was a definite list of men liable for the trierarchy." This question has broader implications for an understanding of the trierarchy, not least because the use of currently updated registers would suggest two things. First, since all persons listed there must have been legally obliged to perform a service, the element of personal choice to undertake trierarchies voluntarily would in practice be nearly nonexistent. Second, trierarchies, especially after 358/7, were discharged by a well-defined, standing group of persons (an occasionally adjusted panel) rather than one assembled afresh every year. What is the evidence for such lists?

To have a well-defined corps of warship commanders, modern practices might lead us to assume, is indeed an indispensable feature of an orderly, organized navy; but once more the evidence points to the inapplicability of this assumption to classical Athens. With the exception of Demosthenes 18.105–6, which makes mention of certain registers, no other traces of such documents are found. So far, their existence has been inferred mainly from the stipulation that after 358/7 trierarchies should be performed by a gross total of twelve hundred men (believed to have formed a clearly defined panel); from the surviving fragments of inscriptions listing persons liable to some duty, the so-called diadikasia documents; and from the sources describing the tasks of the strategoi when appointing trierarchs (e.g., *Ath. Pol.* 61.1 says that the strategos responsible for the symmories "registers trierarchs").

(i) What are the registers (*katalogoi*) mentioned at Demosthenes 18.105–6? In these passages Demosthenes discusses his trierarchic law of 340, which ordered that the financial burdens be distributed among individuals in proportion to their wealth (104). A most important consequence of this, he tells us, was that a person who under the previous legislation could manage to be responsible for only one ship as joint contributor (*synteles*) with fifteen others under the new statute was obligated to be trierarch on two ships.[1] To substantiate his point Demosthenes produces not the law texts themselves but the registers (katalogoi) drawn up in accordance with the obsolete law, and the one currently in force. Certainly, these were lists of trierarchs, but not of those *liable*. To prove his point, Demosthenes had to show the distribution of men to ships under the different laws, which could not possibly appear from a presumed list of those eligible. The only katalogoi able to supply that information were those of trierarchs already appointed to the service and assigned to ships. Indeed, these latter would amply demonstrate what one can now observe indirectly through other documents. A fifth-century list of crews (*IG* 2².1951) attests that two men were cotrierarchs on one ship. Two naval records confirm the point Demosthenes is trying to make: one, from a year before 340, shows seven persons to have been responsible for the trieres *Aglaia Epigenous* (*IG* 2².1622.597–610); another, from a year after Demosthenes' reform, shows that one man, Phrynaios

Athmoneus, served simultaneously as principal trierarch on two ships, and as syntrierarch on a third one, all three sent on a single expedition (1629.91–144).

So the katalogoi, at Demosthenes 18.105–6, were probably lists of names, drawn up by the strategoi, of men designated as trierarchs and assigned to their ships, not permanent lists of men who were liable.[2] In trierarchic contexts, the noun *katalogos* and the verb *katalegein* refer to one of two registers: of all those appointed in a year, or of those designated to a specific expedition. The latter is comparable to the lists of men enrolled for military, especially hoplite, service. Here, as Andrewes observed, the expression "from the catalogue" (*ek tou katalogou*) refers not to the general list of all hoplites, but to the system by which generals made up their own katalogoi for particular expeditions.[3]

(ii) The language of Demosthenes 14.16 (of 354) indicates that the number of persons liable for the trierarchy after 357, twelve hundred, represented a formal *upper* limit: so many men were needed and therefore initially assembled to discharge the service in a year. But the net number of trierarchs in some years, if not every year, seems to have been less than that (by Demosthenes' estimate, only four hundred), and it will hardly be expected to have been invariable. According to Demosthenes, the difference between the number of those needed and those actually available to perform trierarchies arose because certain categories of property owners became exempt from the duty. Since the twelve hundred persons initially selected included among their number (again, on Demosthenes' reckoning) about eight hundred potential or de facto claimants to exemption, one can rule out the supposition that a definite list of men liable was kept after 357; such a list, if it ever existed, should have contained twelve hundred names of persons ready to discharge trierarchies.[4] In addition, while previous trierarchies, by an individual or his family, foreordained eligibility for further services, one can doubt with Rhodes ([1982] 3) that lists of men who had served recently were being systematically employed for such purposes before or after 357.

(iii) Finally, the significance of a group of fragmentary inscriptions, the diadikasia documents. They date from the late 380s to the early 370s and contain lists of names in the formula "B instead of [*anti*] A."[5] The flaws of the older interpretation, that these documents record legal hearings arising from antidosis-challenges for the choregia, proeisphora, and trierarchy, have been exposed by Davies. In his view the *diadikasiai* were held in connection with the preparation of a schedule of one thousand names or units of property (i.e., the body known as the Thousand) that prior to 378/7 were liable for the eisphora.[6] Rhodes ([1982] 13) generally accepts this interpretation, but adds that the "list of the Thousand was a list produced in the 380s of property-owners potentially liable for the trierarchy or for all the liturgies." However, both of these recent views are untenable on several counts.[7]

First, although a distinct body of one thousand was alluded to in the speeches of Lysias (fr. 54) and Isaeus (fr. 33), for their fiscal duties only the word of Harpocration exists. His report may or may not be accurate; the contention that the orators also used a rounded-off figure for the Twelve Hundred (who from 358/7 are associated with the trierarchy) could be Harpocration's own. There are no means, furthermore, by which to connect firmly the Thousand either to the eisphora or to the diadikasia documents. Nor is it certain that the documents (and the legal proceedings to which they refer) were to produce a list of property owners; they may well have been concerned with disputes over payment of public debts.

Another objection is this. The formula used ("B instead of A") surely indicates that these individuals were involved in some dispute. The fragments relating to one year (*IG* $2^2$.1930 and 1931, of 383/2) seem to record 150 disputes,[8] while another (1929, of an unknown year) lists 31 disputes. Even if one concludes that in the 380s as many as circa 200 men were performing trierarchies and about 118 men festival liturgies in a single (Panathenaic) year, the attested number of 150 disputes seems unrealistically high for either the trierarchy or all liturgies. All in all, the exact purpose of the diadikasia documents remains too obscure to permit a positive identification with a trierarchic register.

The search for such documents then yields negative results. But can this be pure coincidence, or is this another elusive sign of the way the institution worked? I am favorably disposed toward exploring the second possibility. Just as the absence of a fixed liturgical census arguably helped ensure some stability in the size of the liturgical class (viz. by allowing the number of property owners needed to remain largely unaffected by overall economic recession), so probably abstention from using lists of those eligible for the trierarchy was motivated by practical considerations. Conceivably, a most important one was preservation of the privilege traditionally enjoyed by property owners to evince patriotic sentiments by asserting their magnanimity and undertaking services at will.

It seems appropriate to postulate a resolute inclination on the part of the economic elite to maintain a certain free play in their display of munificence by opposing the employment of any such lists, and a corresponding concession agreed to by the state with a view, above all, to ward off a deterioration of its relationship with an important fiscal entity. To be sure, trierarchies, like other liturgies, remained to some degree optional, even though it is hard to tell whether genuine volunteers were typical. But be that as it may, the element of voluntarism, enriching trierarchic service with its characteristic ingratiating flavor, is a constant one; and it definitely is at odds with the supposition that liability to the duty was determined by means of centrally kept rosters. Instead of affording better control, such registers would for practical and ideological reasons turn the system into a rigid and far more cumbersome mechanism doomed to malfunction. In chapter 4 I will explore how rich Athenians insisted on exhibiting their voluntarism in liturgical spending also when they enjoyed exemption, and why the extensive use of absentee trierarch-liturgists as commanders of triereis never led to its logical consequence of replacing these financiers with nonliturgist professionals. The interest of the propertied class in preserving voluntarism in this area was a strong one.

An equally permanent feature of the system, however, was compulsion in various degrees. It was possible and, as far as the evidence goes, not unusual at all that some persons were reported by others. I agree with Rhodes ([1982] 4) that, in principle, there were no differences between the trierarchy and other liturgies in this respect. Aristotle (*Rh.* 1399a35ff.) and Andocides (1.132) allude to two instances of such reports, while property owners liable to pay proeisphora in 362 were reported from each deme. The prominent role of the tribes in the area of festival liturgies is completely absent from the trierarchy.[9] Five trittyes-markers (*horoi*) discovered in Piraeus probably indicate no more than that before embarkation citizen crews were assembled and arrayed in the tribal order.[10] Preselection of nominees to the proeisphora and trierarchy is likely to have occurred in the demes. From the gross body of persons selected annually for the navy, only those remaining after exemptions had been granted could be asked to discharge a service.

So men became eligible for the trierarchy in one or more of five ways, each of which contained a greater or lesser degree of option or compulsion.[11] Such a patent admixture becomes perhaps explicable in the face of interests shared by (and hence a relationship of interdependence between) wealthy liturgists and the state. First, an individual might present himself as a volunteer (*ethelontēs*). Often his decision would represent a positive response, partly to a clearly recognized expectation from within the ideological framework and partly to the attraction of honorific rewards. However, social and political pressure stemming from his possession of visible property, or from a commitment to emulate predecessors and family members currently in the liturgical class, or even from anticipation of the need to defend his property ownership (Isae. 7.37–38; Lys. 21.12–13), may be a truer, albeit hidden, motive. Second, after 358/7 men were on certain occasions formally called upon to perform voluntary trierarchies—naval *epidoseis*. Full discussion of this is offered in chapter 8. Here suffice it to note the embodiment in such services too of option and compulsion in equal measure. Third, a person might be reported to the authorities by others. The antidosis-challenge should properly be included in this category. The individual originally enrolled for trierarchic service could obtain a temporary exemption insofar as he proved able to provide another and wealthier man who would take over his duty (see chapter 4). Fourth, it is probable that trierarchic service was bequeathed together with property: men were obliged to succeed their deceased testator either directly, by taking over a particular service, or indirectly, by undertaking responsibility for outstanding naval debts. Finally, compulsion might be enforced within a legal context, notably in the event that a contestant in an antidosis-challenge was deemed by a law court to be wealthier than his adversary.

No registers or absolute economic criteria seem to have been applied, for reasons already discussed. Perhaps the mere notion that an individual was "wealthy" (plousios) or "immensely wealthy" (*plousiōtatos*), although imprecise to us, was in most cases enough for his name to appear, in one of the ways just mentioned, among the nominees of the year. As soon as this was done, the strategoi proceeded to carry out the formal appointment.

## Formal Appointment

The commanders of the sacred ships, *Paralos* and *Salaminia,* bore the distinct title of treasurers, tamiai, and were elected officers; because of their special status, they will be excluded here.[12] With all other trierarchs a common appointment procedure, supervised by the strategoi, was followed. It is commonly assumed, chiefly on the strength of Aristophanes (*Eq.* 912–18, of 424), that the strategoi both selected and designated trierarchs personally; hence they could exercise a good deal of influence on who was to be appointed in a given year. In Aristophanes' play, Paphlagon threatens the sausage-seller by saying: "I'll make you take charge of a warship and have to dig into your coffers. You'll get an old vessel, which you'll never stop spending money on and making repairs to; and I'll contrive to see that you get a sail that's rotten" (tr. Sommerstein [1981]). However, this passage, overexploited by an ancient scholiast and modern scholars alike (e.g., Jordan *AN* 62–63; Davies *Wealth* 24 n. 21), does not (and was not meant to) give an accurate description of the powers of the strategoi, nor does it say that they chose trierarchs personally. It seems best to proceed from a terminological and procedural distinction between selection of those qualifying for the duty, carried out in various ways, and formal designation, carried out by the strategoi. The verb *kathistēmi,* consistently used with trierarchic appointments, as a rule refers to the second situation.[13] If there was an area in which the strategoi may have had a direct influence (and interest), that was the composition of ships and commanders in active squadrons.

Seemingly contradictory evidence has incited controversy about the occasion on which appointments took place. Boeckh believed that formerly they occurred at the beginning of the year, but after 352 just before the dispatch of a fleet. Kolbe held that throughout the period trierarchs were appointed shortly before departure on an expedition. Jordan recognized the shortcomings of each view and proposed a reconciliatory solution: he took the sources adduced by Boeckh to depict regular appointments, those adduced by Kolbe to refer to additional trierarchs needed in time of war to serve on the ships of the reserve.[14] But this seems equally unsatisfactory. The evidence reflects two administratively distinct but perfectly normal situations.

Candidates for the position were selected and designated at the beginning of each year. Around 430, four hundred trierarchs were appointed annually and had their claims to exemption treated at a legal hearing (Ps.-Xen. *Ath. Pol.* 3.4). Since at this time Athens possessed about three hundred ships, then roughly one hundred from the four hundred men would have been exempted. Reporting the decision (431) to set aside every year the best (*exairetoi*) hundred triereis, Thucydides notes also that trierarchs—certainly of an equal number—were appointed to command them

(2.24.2; cf. *HCT* vol. 2, ad loc.). Not all three hundred commanders (and Thucydides' hundred must be included in this number) were simultaneously active on their ships; especially those in charge of exairetoi might remain inactive until ships of that class were sent on a special mission.

Basically the same procedure is attested some eighty years later, in 354. But now twelve hundred property owners were selected every year, of whom about eight hundred usually obtained exemptions on various grounds; those remaining were distributed into symmories for assuming their trierarchic duties (Dem. 14.16; cf. 35.48). In the 320s, appointments had become the responsibility of the strategos supervising the symmories; he "makes lists of trierarchs [*triērarchous katalegei*], deals with their antidoseis and introduces to court cases [*diadikasiai*] concerning them" (*Ath. Pol.* 61.1). Does this mean he was personally involved in their selection? Consider what the same source says (56.3) about the eponymous archon who was responsible for the appointment of choregoi.

In the 320s, the archon appointed (*kathistēsi*), as choregoi for the tragedies (at the Greater Dionysia), three of the richest men from among all Athenians; previously, he had appointed five choregoi for the comedies (at the Lenaia and the Greater Dionysia), but now these were nominated by the tribes (cf. Dem. 20.28, 130; 21.13; 39.7). Given the limited number of men involved, it might be inferred that the archon, prior to the change in procedure, selected choregoi personally. But this cannot be true either about the tribally nominated choregoi (from a year before 348/7), or about a number of other liturgists likewise returned by the tribes and appointed (*kathistasin*) by various officials (Dem. 39.7–8). In such cases, appointment means only "formal designation." The eponymous archon, says *Athenaion Politeia* 56.3, receives the (lists of) choregoi supplied by the tribes, "deals with antidoseis and introduces to court legal hearings [*skēpseis*]" concerning exemptions. The final list of those appointed could be drafted only after the termination of these proceedings.

So the immediate task of the strategos of the symmories was not to select personally all or most of the twelve hundred trierarchs needed in a year, but to enter into a register all nominees who had presented themselves or were proposed by others for service.[15] Given his special sphere of responsibility, the symmories, his list would have specified a man's membership in a particular symmory, a job previously done by the entire board of his colleagues (Dem. 39.8: strategoi register a person in a symmory, *eis symmorian eggraphōsin*). And since membership in a symmory was perennial, appointments would have occurred at the beginning of the year.

A good many of those designated were *nominal* trierarchs. Only men put in command of ships currently in commission assumed active service instantly. Apollodoros could refer to the law stipulating that the newly designated trierarchs should proceed at once to take over the ships from their predecessors serving at sea ([Dem.] 50.66; cf. 50.14–15, 24). Three men so obliged in the beginning of 361/0 were Mnesilochos, Phrasierides (41), and the wily successor to Apollodoros, Polykles. Others remained in the group of nominal trierarchs until their own ships were commissioned. A clear example of this is offered by a decree of 325/4 (*IG* 2².1629.165–271), which authorizes the delivery of ships for the colonizing expedition to the Adriatic and orders the quick dispatch of the force. Lines 178–90 contain instructions to the dockyard superintendents and to trierarchs: "The epimeletai ton neorion shall deliver to the trierarchs the ships and equipment in the manner decreed by the demos; the trierarchs who have been appointed [*tous kathestēkotas*] shall, on their part, bring the ships to the pier in the month of Mounichion before the tenth of that month and shall furnish them in ready condition for the voyage." Subsequent provisions (ll. 199–213) order the *thesmothetai* (six of the nine archons entrusted with the duty to convene the people's court) to empanel *dikasteria* (sections of that court) of 201 jurors so that the strategos of the symmories could introduce to court cases concerning exemptions (*skēpsis* hearings) on 2 and 5 Mounichion.

I take *tous kathestēkotas* (l. 184) to mean "the trierarchs appointed for the occasion," referring to the men called for active service. Since the deadline for skepseis to be held for those claiming exemption was 5 Mounichion (five days before the ships were to be brought to the pier in ready condition), it follows that the penultimate list of trierarchs to sail on that expedition was not known before such hearings had been held. There is nothing in the decree to support Jordan's assumption (*AN* 66–67) that these trierarchs were appointed in addition to those regularly in office. What this document does show is the separate appointment of de facto trierarchs and the staging of legal hearings to be held in connection with exemptions, a situation identical to that to which Demosthenes' strictures (4.36) allude: "But in what pertains to war and its equipment, everything is ill-arranged, ill-managed, ill-defined. Consequently, we wait till we have heard some piece of news, and then we appoint [*kathistamen*] trierarchs, deal with their antidoseis, and contemplate about ways and means of obtaining funds."

On such occasions there were drawn ad hoc lists of commanders in charge of a force. Thrasyllos Leukonoieus, according to Isaeus 7.5, was in the register (katalogos) of trierarchs for the Sicilian expedition (415). With this as background, one may perhaps trust the language of a tradition reporting how Meton the astronomer tried to dodge service as a trierarch on the expedition to Sicily; it says "Meton was also among those listed in the register" (Ael. *VH* 13.12).

At this point one must confront a problematic passage: Demosthenes 39.8. Here Mantitheos, wishing to exemplify the entanglements likely to arise because he and his brother bore the same name, asks: "And in what manner will the strategoi enter our names [*eggrapsousin*], if they are listing [one of us] in a symmory [*eis symmorian eggraphōsin*] or if they are appointing [*kathistōsin*] [one of us] trierarch?" Usually, this is understood as referring to registration into an eisphora symmory and appointment to a trierarchy.[16] But since the symmory system and the trierarchy (not the eisphora) are spoken of in one breath, and given that the chief tasks of the strategoi are to make membership lists of trierarchic symmories and designate active trierarchs, this passage may hint at two different stages of trierarchic appointment: initial registration in a trierarchic symmory at the beginning of the year, and subsequent appointment as de facto trierarch.

Hence, the terms *triērarchia* and *triērarchēma* (and the verb *triērarchein*) often specifically denote service as an active trierarch, and *epitriērarchēma* the prolongation of active service.[17] Consequently, statements to the effect that a man had been appointed trierarch need not mean that he was active throughout the pertinent year. This important qualification must be borne in mind when considering reports on trierarchic expenditure. When the speaker of Lysias 21 claimed that he had been trierarch for seven consecutive years (2, 6), he probably meant that during this period of time he had served active tours of duty of varying lengths.[18]

This system of selecting every year a number of commanders of ships and then assigning current tasks to men from their group seems to have been in force since the second part of the fifth century, and perhaps before. The introduction of the symmories in 358/7 brought only one change in this area: the number of nominal trierarchs was set at twelve hundred men. These were distributed into twenty symmories, and current assignments fell on members of the symmories. Even though the strategoi might have exerted their influence to promote personal preferences (Lys. 29.3), there is no evidence to suggest that they enjoyed extensive influence in the selection of trierarchs. Their tasks seem to have been simple administrative routine: listing nominees, registering antidosis-challenges or claims to exemption, introducing to court legal hearings (diadikasiai/skepseis), and drawing up lists of active trierarchs.

## The Length of Service

Good evidence exists to show that the length of a trierarch's normal term of service was twelve months. The period of exemption for those who either had discharged a liturgy in the previous year or were currently discharging one was one or two archon-years. Also, [Demosthenes] 50 shows that the normal term of Apollodoros's service ran from Hekatombaion 362 to the same month in the next year.[19] However, if at sea at the expiration of his term, he might be asked, or even forced, to serve for an extra period of time until his successor came to take over the ship. Still, even when the successor did arrive, legal ambiguities about the takeover might lead to a further prolongation of active service. The speech ([Dem.] 50) was written for Apollodoros, who had found himself in such a plight: he was nominal trierarch until 24 Metageitnion 362 (4), then active during the remaining ten months of that year (he says he provided pay for his crew for eight months, while his strategos bore that cost for only two months [10, 12]), after which he continued with an extra term (epitrierarchema) in the following year. Since such irregularities added to the unpredictability both of expenditure and of the time during which a man had to neglect his personal business, and since, moreover, they created tensions within the trierarchic class, they deserve discussion.

Prolonged periods of service seem not to have been rare. As new appointments coincided with the season (midsummer) in which a relatively large number of ships were likely to be at sea, successors had to make arrangements for equipment for the ships and often had to travel a long distance before reaching the old trierarchs. In 361, Cawkwell plausibly argues, the Athenian replacements were late partly because of the presence in the Aegean of the ships of Alexander of Pherae, and partly because a substantial number of the fresh trierarchs had hired out their trierarchies.[20] There is really no substance to Apollodoros's insinuations (at [Dem.] 50) that an extra term ran counter to the law. In fact, the legal aftermath of his own extra term (five months and six days) revolved around the issue of cash, not a breach of regulations; he brought charges against his successor Polykles because of the latter's refusal to compensate him for extra expenses. Nor was Apollodoros's extra service exceptional. Most or all other trierarchs in his squadron were in the same situation (33). In Apollodoros's version of his abortive succession by Polykles, three points of a wider significance become apparent.

First, no clear-cut regulations existed about who should bear the extra costs accruing from prolonged service. It looks as if predecessor and successor might come to an understanding about a refund of the former's extra outlays; or a predecessor might eventually recover as much of his additional outlays as he could convince his successor to pay (42). To quarrel stubbornly with one's replacement, as Apollodoros chose to do, would only lead to further delay, or ultimately to a legal battle between the parties—a vicious circle. Polykles' persistent refusal to take over (29–31, 32–37, 39–40, 54–55) was no doubt conditioned by Apollodoros's uncompromising claim to full compensation for his conspicuously extravagant epitrierarchema, which Polykles, understandably enough, was not prepared to accept.

So if a smooth takeover was to occur, trierarchs had a common interest in sharing both gains and losses, and this, I believe, was what happened in most cases. The trierarchy, it appears, should ideally have operated as an efficient but at the same time self-regulating fiscal conglomerate with a minimum of outside intervention; it relied on its members not only to see that the job required from them collectively was done properly but also to settle any differences among them either by mutual consent or, if necessary, by application of force.

Second, the position of predecessors was precarious on several counts. For the takeover to be effective, a successor needed to be assured both of the vessel's seaworthiness and of its being fully manned; to take over an undermanned and unseaworthy ship spelled financial loss as well as risk to life. This being done in the presence of witnesses (usually members of the ship's crew), the successor formally declared his resolution to take charge. (Apollodoros insists that on two occasions he requested Polykles to take charge in the presence of witnesses and while the trieres was fully manned [*plērēs*] [32, 38].) Without the consent of the successor, the old trierarch was under an obligation to continue to perform his usual tasks and to execute the orders of the strategos leading the force. Failure to do so made him liable to imprisonment.[21]

The predecessor, in addition, was compelled to remain on his ship for two further and no less serious reasons. In a normal takeover, the dockyard officials made both predecessors and successors responsible for the ship (IG 2².1612.132–38); without his successor's acknowledgment that he had taken charge (*paradidonai/paralambanein tēn naun,* [Dem.] 50.29, 32, 39, 54–55), the old trierarch alone was held financially accountable.[22] If the trierarch abandoned his ship, he might be charged with desertion and probably be indicted in a *graphē lipotaxiou*.[23] Apollodoros's anxieties concerned both these prospects. He did not conceal this: "so that no one could accuse me of deserting my post or letting my ship be useless to the state" (63); he merely chose to be discreet about it.

Third, it is notable that the strategos commanding the squadron, Timomachos, did not intervene in the dispute between Apollodoros and Polykles. In spite of Apollodoros's insinuations that Timomachos connived at (and even encouraged) Polykles' conduct (43–52), the noninterference of the strategos is consonant with the general view taken by the authorities that, to a large extent, conflicts between trierarchs were private matters.

## The Allocation of Ships

At the beginning of each year, some among the newly appointed trierarchs took charge of the ships currently in commission; others remained temporarily inactive. But how was it decided who should assume active duty and who should not? The answer is furnished by the naval records from the 370s and 360s (IG 2².1604–10). The nucleus of their rubrics are the hulls' name. The name might be immediately followed by the description "old" (*palaia*) or "new" (*kainē*), which refer to different rates (see chapter 6). The next important element is either the name of a trierarch or the term *anepiklērōtos* (unallotted): for example, *Inscriptiones Graecae* 2².1604:

> Delphinia, new. Trierarch Diokles Pitheus. (91)
> Techne, old, unallotted. (20)
> Tragoidia, new, unallotted. (32)

Hulls described as unallotted were those not assigned to any trierarch. The *epiklērōsis* (distribution by lot) was a procedure also widely applied in

Athens within the naval administration: in 357/6, it was used for allocating defaulting trierarchs among debt collectors ([Dem.] 47.21); in 354, Demosthenes (14.18) proposed to divide all triereis into groups and then to distribute each group by lot to the twenty symmories. His language implies that the Athenians were familiar with such a procedure. Indeed, the term *anepiklērōtoi* in the pre-357 records reflects its application, and specifically marks hulls that remained unallotted to trierarchs. In contrast, vessels assigned to trierarchs and that may or may not be in commission are listed with the formula *hull's name + rating + trierarch.*

Since the epimeletai compiled these lists at the end of their tenure, and since some vessels recorded as anepiklerotoi in one year had been under a trierarch in a previous year (e.g., "Aktis, old, unallotted. Euphrantides Hal[——] is [in possession] of *askōmata,*" IG 2².1604.81–82), it follows that hulls of that description had remained unallotted throughout the year. The supposition that they might have been inactive or unassigned to a trierarch only when the epimeletai surrendered their inventories is ruled out by entries noting that an active ship had been hauled up to the dockyards by its trierarch (1604.15), or showing that inactive vessels had a trierarch: "[Ship's name]. Demon Paianieus (trierarch). This ship has a complete set of oars; the remaining wooden equipment has been transferred to [ship's name] on which [someone] is trierarch" (1607.26–27). The term *anepiklērōtos* meant both inactive and without trierarch.[24]

These technical aspects of dockyard administration are important also on another score. Of the approximately one hundred hulls originally listed in *Inscriptiones Graecae* 2².1604, some forty-seven were anepiklerotoi. This means that nearly half the force of Athens could not be deployed because of not being assigned to a trierarch. In *Inscriptiones Graecae* 2².1607 and 1608 (of 373/2), approximately twenty unallotted ships are mentioned. In either case, the actual figures may have been higher, and a similar pattern can be expected to have emerged in most of the remaining (but very fragmentary) records of that period. The ratio of hulls to the number of trierarchs available decided the issue of how many seaworthy ships were to remain unallotted in a year.

It seems likely, therefore, that all vessels, whether in commission or at home at the beginning of the year, were allotted among the newly designated trierarchs. Hence it was decided by lot whether a man should sail right away or remain in the pool of nominal trierarchs.[25] Moreover, groups of cotrierarchs must have been formed before the epiklerosis, because ships had to be allotted among so many units of single trierarchs or syntrierarchs as were present in a year. In [Demosthenes] 50.41, Mne-silochos and Phrasierides are said to have been appointed in the beginning of 361/0 to relieve another pair serving overseas; the implication is that the former knew right after their designation which ship they had to take over. By 357/6, however, the procedure was modified by placing all ships under the care of the symmories instead of allotting them among individ-uals—a change explaining the total absence of anepiklerotos from the records of that period. (See p. 193.)

The naval records are predominantly concerned with de facto trier-archs. Occasionally, however, nominal trierarchs are mentioned with a hull mainly for identification purposes—for example, *Inscriptiones Graecae* 2².1604.87–88: "[Ship's name——Kte]sippos Aixoneus. Amynomene, new. Trierarch Kallibios P[aianieus]." The absence of the words *endei* or *echei* (usually indicating that a ship "lacks" or "has" equipment) cannot be because these hulls already had a complete set of equipment, nor because the trierarchs mentioned used their private instead of public equipment; as a rule, the former fact is recorded with the formula *dokima kai entelē* ("usable and complete"), the latter with *houtoi skeuos ouden elabon* ("these [sc. trierarchs] have received nothing [from the dockyard officials]," *IG* 2².1609.91, 94). Two different (and equally probable) explanations can be suggested: (1) although they had been assigned to trierarchs at the annual epiklerosis, neither of these ships had been commissioned in that year; or (2) when the dockyard superintendents inscribed their record, these ships had not yet returned to the harbor; therefore, the officials could not re-cord any deficiencies in equipment nor who was to be held accountable for them.

(i) Among the rubrics of *Inscriptiones Graecae* 2².1604 is the following: "[Ship's name——]. Trierarch Philostratos Acharneus. This ship is sup-plied with askomata; it lacks shores" (ll. 80–81). A ship being listed as lacking equipment does not automatically warrant the inference that the trierarch named is also the one responsible for it, unless this is explicitly stated, as in lines 91–93: "Delphinia, new. Trierarch Diokles Pitheus. The trierarch withholds askomata. [This ship lacks——] [items of equipment follow]. Diokles is obliged to furnish these items."[26] The first of these entries lists a nominal trierarch assigned to a ship. A subsidiary but im-portant point that these and other entries bring out clearly is the serious shortage of equipment; this is attested both by a statement to the effect that a hull is entirely without equipment, and by the need fully to equip active ships by cannibalizing those temporarily inactive.

(ii) The record of 357/6 (*IG* 2².1611.282–373) lists some triereis sent to the Hellespont under Chares in the previous year;[27] they all were manned with pairs of syntrierarchs. Of the eleven extant or safely restored entries, three have the formula *ship's name* + *syntrierarchs* (e.g., "Polynike, the work of Lysikles. Trierarchs Polyeuktos Lamptreus, Kratinos Erchieus," ll. 286–89). The remaining eight have the formula *ship's name* + *syntrierarchs* + *echousi* ("they withhold," followed by items of equipment; e.g., "Pheme, the work of Hierokles. Trierarchs Alkisthenes Cholargeus, Timokrates ek Kerameon. They withhold wooden equipment," ll. 303–10).

It looks as if the latter eight ships and their trierarchs had returned to Athens when the dockyard superintendents drew up their record (at the end of 357/6), while the former three ships remained in commission. Here "they withhold" means that the pairs of commanders concerned still possessed public equipment after the end of their service, and it is used in the sense "they owe" (otherwise expressed with *opheilousi*).[28] This reconstruction is confirmed by a dedication to Athena (*IG* 2².1953) by trierarchs crowned for their service under Chares in the Hellespont. Of the eight persons attested here, four (possibly five) appear also in the rubrics of the naval record currently discussed (1611). Since the dedication dates from 357/6,[29] the men honored must have returned to Athens before the end of that year, and consequently before the epimeletai inscribed their record; the syntrierarchs on *Hegeso*, Aristokles Eleusinios and Periandros Cholargeus, both crowned in 357/6, are recorded in 1611 with the formula *echousi*. The most obvious inference is that they both had returned to Athens and delivered their hull, but still withheld equipment. On this interpretation, the entries in 1611 without the echousi formula probably list ships still active by the end of 357/6.

The early naval records render it probable that at the beginning of each year all seaworthy hulls were distributed by lot among the newly appointed trierarchs. By way of the epiklerosis each man knew from the outset on which ship he was to serve. Close scrutiny of the records highlights in addition two issues with great impact on fourth-century naval affairs and the trierarchy. One is manpower shortages; the relatively large number of hulls listed as unallotted is an index of a perhaps even greater number of trierarchs lacking in a year, which in turn is indicative of a serious inability to recruit commanders for all serviceable ships. Another is shortages of equipment; in chapter 7, which treats that matter in detail, I argue that a great deal of public equipment not immediately available in the dockyards lay in private hands. These problems seem to be inter-related: a startling leniency toward defaulters, most clearly observable in the period before 357/6, can be seen as the result of a deliberate policy aiming to maintain the goodwill of the trierarchic class and hence to avoid a further aggravation of recruitment difficulties.

This situation seems fairly typical for nearly the whole period covered by the naval records. The wish to cope with shortages in both areas was indeed a motive, perhaps the primary one, for the trierarchic reforms, notably the decisions, in 358/7, to set the number of those annually appointed at twelve hundred property owners, and to introduce the symmories. From then on the allotment of ships among individuals was supplanted by distribution among the symmories, each of which designated hulls to its own members. At about the same time various efforts were made to recover public equipment.

As with almost any other scheme introduced by the state in order to secure a sufficient number of warship commanders, or to control its naval financiers, these efforts had to be designed with due regard to a vital factor: that such measures would not affect adversely the cooperation of the persons toward whom they were directed. A signal consequence of the state's dependence on the trierarchic class was that the real effect of legislative schemes remained limited, with shortages in men and naval equipment persisting as problems fundamentally unsolved.

FOUR

# Exemption

The Athenians viewed the trierarchy as a duty or tax (*telos*); exemption from it was termed *ateleia* and the person exempt was *atelēs*. In this chapter, I discuss the various ways in which an individual might try to obtain a respite: regular exemption or the antidosis. These discussions are followed by treatment of a topic that, although not directly related to exemption proper, reveals how a man could avoid personal service as a trierarch: by the hiring out of trierarchies.

## Regular Exemption

Exemption from the choregy, states *Athenaion Politeia* 56.3, could be claimed on three counts: having previously performed the same liturgy, having just performed any liturgy, or not fulfilling the age criterion, exemplified by the rule (from circa 345) that a choregos for boys' choruses must be over forty years old (cf. Aesch. 1.11). In all three cases, exemption was not granted automatically, but only after a petitioner had his grounds tried and approved at a legal hearing (skepsis or diadikasia). The first rule cannot be valid for the trierarchy. If applied at all, it might relate only to the choregy or perhaps to all other liturgies.[1] Still it is strange that, while many persons boasted of having discharged liturgies continually, no one claimed to have performed the same liturgy twice.

Considerably more is known about the rule that after any liturgy men were entitled to temporary exemption. It was fully acknowledged that liturgists deserved a rest after an often demanding personal involvement and expenditure. With this arrangement the state was also able to promote a practical interest: to maintain the economic ability and enthusiasm of liturgists. The rule was applied to the trierarchy and all other liturgies alike. But while following all other liturgies there was a one-year exemption (Dem. 20.8), after a trierarchy the exemption was for two years. The difference surely testifies to the position of the trierarchy as the most onerous liturgy. Yet definite indications are lacking about when trierarchs attained, and for how long they enjoyed, this special privilege.

Thrasyllos Leukonoieus, it is said at Isaeus 7.38, had served as trierarch "not taking two years off but continuously." The statement need not mean that the two years' respite existed at that time (i.e., before Thrasyllos's death while trierarch in the Sicilian expedition [415–413, (5)]). Nor does the context reveal whether it existed when the speech was delivered (354). Still, this source does not go counter to the supposition that the rule was effective both before 413 and in 354. It is plausible that the period of exemption originally was only one year. If so, extension to two years must have been motivated by an increasing disproportion between the aggregate demands for economic outlay and personal engagement, on the one hand, and the ability or willingness of individuals to meet them in full, on the other. There are good reasons to endorse Rhodes's view ([1982] 3) that the longer exemption with the trierarchy was "a concession made as the burden became too heavy for many men to bear." Provided there is a kernel of truth in the lamentations of an oligarchic pamphleteer to the effect that this burden was indeed felt by some to be particularly heavy around 430 (Ps.-Xen. *Ath. Pol.* 1.13), the period of the initial years of the Peloponnesian War is a likely candidate for such a concession.

Other sources allude to the same rule. In Lysias 19 (of 388 or 387), three years' continuous trierarchic service (possibly in the period 392/1–390/89) is presented as something virtuous (29). Similarly, after having paraded his impressive liturgical record in the period 411/0–404/3, which included seven years' continuous service as trierarch, the speaker of Lysias 21 reminded his listeners that he would not have spent a quarter of the amount he did spend if he had confined his services to what was required by law (1–5). Finally, in Isaeus 5 (of circa 389), Menexenos points out that "our forefathers, who acquired and bequeathed this property, . . . discharged trierarchies without any interval" (41); the liturgical record of this family stretches back to the fifth century (*APF* 145–49).

Certainly, then, the grant of a respite applied also in the fifth century,[2] in the course of which it was probably changed from one year to two, and lived on throughout the fourth century. Various suggestions that it may have been either suspended or reduced to one year again after the introduction of the symmories (358/7) lack both supportive evidence and valid arguments explaining what might have motivated these changes.[3]

For the trierarchy there was a lower but not an upper age limit, which is quite odd, but nonetheless telling, when one considers the formal incorporation of trierarchs into the military establishment. Demosthenes' statement to the effect that he embarked on trierarchic performances as soon as he had come of age (21.154) represents the general rule.[4] That persons past the age limit for military service, sometimes by more than just a few years, could be required to undertake trierarchies is affirmed by prosopographical evidence presented below (p. 97 and n. 29).

Another rule stated that a man was not obliged to perform two different liturgies simultaneously. In 362, Apollodoros was appointed trierarch and shortly thereafter became a member of the proeispherontes who were to fund a naval expedition ([Dem.] 50.4–8). He claims with pride to have agreed to discharge both services without using his trierarchy as a reason for obtaining exemption from the proeisphora, even though he was legally entitled to do so (9).[5] Although no specific instances survive to show this, a man performing some other liturgy was not obliged to undertake a trierarchy (Ps.-Xen. *Ath. Pol.* 3.4).

An especially intricate issue is this: there is no doubt that a trierarch could claim to be exempt from other liturgies in the same year or from a new trierarchy in the next two years, if he performed active service, but did the same apply with those on the list of nominal trierarchs? The record is not clear, though it seems unlikely that this applied after 357/8, when twelve hundred persons were formally needed. Exemption for all twelve hundred means that for the trierarchy alone, thirty-six hundred men would have been required in a period of three years; this is an impossibly high figure.[6]

Demosthenes (14.16) lists five categories of property owners or property that by 354 were excluded from the twelve hundred who were liable for the trierarchy: heiresses (epikleroi), orphans, the property of *klerouchs* (Athenians sent to settle in places under Athenian dominion), the property of corporations (*koinōnika*), and finally *adynatoi* ("those not able" to perform a trierarchy). This list, probably containing the names of male adults (e. g., a deceased father whose property now belonged to an epikleros or a minor boy), prompts us to ask why these properties and property owners were exempt. The traditional view is that, even though they could provide the money needed, the owners were unable to perform personal service.[7] This might be correct for heiresses and orphans, whose property, however, if large enough, was liable for eisphora. Jordan's suggestion (*AN* 67) that the latter were exempt because the state wanted to protect them against financial ruin fails to take into account that eisphorai could be as burdensome as trierarchies: even though a minor, Demosthenes was leader (*hēgemōn*) of an eisphora symmory paying as high a rate as some of the richest Athenians;[8] his two payments of the war tax totaled eighteen hundred drachmas (Dem. 27.37), while his first trierarchy cost him two thousand drachmas (Dem. 21.80). Therefore, and considering that men past military age were not exempt from the trierarchy, it is puzzling that the properties of heiresses and orphans did not carry a similar obligation to finance the fleet. The "military character" explanation will not really do.

Can that explanation apply to *klērouchika* and to *koinonika*? It seems unlikely. Exemption of klerouchika means exclusion of property in *klerouchies* (Athenian settlements in places dominated by Athens), not, as Jordan thinks (*AN* 67 n. 25), of the klerouchs themselves because they were on military duty; if in possession of sufficient property at Athens, klerouchs would still be eligible. The primary evidence for property owned collectively comes from the *hekatostē* inscriptions (*IG* 2².1594–1603) and other documents recording transactions involving the property of demes, phratries, and other cult-corporations (see Behrend *Pachturkunden* 19–42). In the second half of the fourth century, and possibly before that, ownership of such properties conferred liability for the eisphora.[9] And there is one piece of evidence contradicting the view that the personal activity required by trierarchies could not be demanded from corporations: one such body, the Paraloi, carried a permanent obligation to furnish the commander of the sacred ship *Paralos* (*IG* 2².2966). The argument that such properties had the legal status of "undivided" wealth carries no more conviction (cf. pp. 65–66).[10]

A better explanation may be that exemption was a special privilege attached to these properties to make them attractive. At least this seems to be a chief reason for exempting from liturgies investments in leases for mines in the 320s, an arrangement indicating that other leases, particularly of private property, made the lessee liable for liturgies. Such a measure, presented at [Demosthenes] 42.18 as a recent innovation, was probably aimed at encouraging prospective investors. This was perhaps also the case with corporate property (koinonika), especially if the mid-fourth-century involvement (or even intervention) of the state in the leasing of land owned by corporations, cults, and the like can be interpreted as an increasing desire to encourage the exploitation of such properties by offering incentives to the owners and to the lessees.[11]

Agricultural land and buildings (especially those of high value) were the primary object of this concern. In the fifth and fourth centuries, leasing out public and corporate realty was the norm, and this practice occurred on a considerable scale. Joint owners (in addition to their own economic advantage in receiving rent) shared an interest with the state in having their buildings and land looked after and exploited in order that their value be maintained.[12] The ultimate target and real beneficiary of the exemption rule was in all likelihood the lessee of such property. He would have been able to expand his business with the use of a new property that, like the leases of mines in the 320s, did not entail liability, nor did it (or the income derived from it) count in an antidosis-challenge. And it is not surprising that most lessees were indeed men of great substance, who were thus in the liturgical class.

While similar motives can only be assumed with the property of klerouchs, material exists showing the state's concern with estates belonging to orphaned minors. The eponymous archon supervised the leasing of the estates of orphans and heiresses, receiving land as surety (*apotimēma*), and taking to court cases of mismanagement (*Ath. Pol.* 56.6–7). Even though not compulsory (yet seemingly not negligible in scale), leasing out in this case was done to ensure the preservation of a patrimony and the maintenance of the orphans. But since these properties were leased in their entirety and since real security had to be furnished of a value equal to both the estate's worth and the rent, larger estates became accessible only to a limited number of lessees who themselves possessed substantial fortunes.[13] Again, those attracted by the exemption attached to the property of heiresses and orphans were most likely members of the liturgical class.

To the more apparent economic advantages that a lessee expected from such transactions one can add a bonus in store for him. When providing security in land, he put up on his own property a *horos,* marking that it was encumbered. Besides not being liable for trierarchies on account of the orphan estate he had leased, he harvested another benefit in that his own encumbered estate did not count if he was proposed to any liturgy or challenged to an antidosis ([Dem.] 42.5, 9, 28). With the estates of heiresses, orphans, klerouchs, and corporations, then, it seems preferable to focus attention on those actually holding and actively exploiting these estates rather than on their legal owners, and also on the state's interest that the realty involved remained stable.

Exemption from liturgies, finally, was among the honors bestowed on benefactors. It could be enjoyed by the recipient (often a man reputed to be public-spirited, or *philotimos*) for life and, occasionally, by his descendants as well.[14] But not infrequently those honored chose to bear their privilege "nominally and honorarily" (Dem. 20.44), while continuing to perform liturgies. The celebrated Chabrias, to mention one among many examples, conspicuously disregarded the ateleia earned after his victory at Naxos (376).[15] Likewise, men might abstain from using their legal right to regular exemption and eagerly discharge more liturgies than they were obliged to by law (Lys. 21.1–5). This sort of calculated "negligence," well represented in the body of evidence, shows quite convincingly that to the propertied class (in spite of a regularly voiced discontent) the liturgy system had become an indispensable ideological as well as political activity.

In 354, Leptines proposed and carried a law abolishing the grant of ateleia. However, from Demosthenes 20, written when the law was attacked for being passed unconstitutionally, it is clear that the grant of honorary exemption never had included the eisphora and the trierarchy (but on the eisphora, cf. Tod no. 139.35–36). With the exception of the nine archons, no one was to be exempt from the trierarchy. Perhaps, as Rhodes suggests ([1982] n. 13), members of the cavalry may have been formally exempt, but had the option to volunteer for trierarchic service if not currently needed in the cavalry.

It is not certain that this list of the criteria qualifying men for exemption is complete. Still, those attested evince an outspoken concern for the unencumbered functioning of a fiscal rather than of a military institution. An even clearer demonstration of this is furnished by the antidosis.

## The Antidosis

The absence of rules about physical disability or simply old age is accentuated by the presence of an elaborate procedure concerning relative economic debility; personal service came second to monetary contributions. A man could try to be exempt from the trierarchy by pointing out that someone else richer than he did not currently discharge the duty. But before he could go free he was obliged to provide his proposed replacement by making use of the antidosis. If he was successful in transferring his obligation to a financially more able man, he was exempt. If unsuccessful, he had to discharge the service in spite of his allegedly lesser economic potential or insufficient wealth. I have argued elsewhere in detail (Gabrielsen [1987a]) that the entire procedure consisted of two main stages that could (but need not) be coextensive: the antidosis-challenge itself, during which the man originally liable and his potential replacement might try to settle in private the issue of which of the two should discharge the service; and a legal hearing (a diadikasia trial), which ensued only if a private settlement had failed, and at which the jurors, after hearing both parties, decided who should undertake the liturgy. Here I shall deal briefly with antidoseis involving trierarchs, and some features of the procedure and their implications for the trierarchy.

(i) As noted above, antidosis-challenges and diadikasiai occurred on two occasions: when trierarchs were appointed at the beginning of the year, and when men from the pool of nominal trierarchs were called for active service. This is understandable because an individual asked to be active, say, six or eight months after the annual appointment might in the meantime have suffered a considerable financial loss and also discovered that someone else, better off than he, was not discharging a trierarchy currently. Demosthenes complained (4.36) that the Athenians waited until the last minute before the dispatch of a fleet to appoint trierarchs and carry out their antidoseis. It was probably in such circumstances that Thrasylochos successfully challenged Demosthenes to an antidosis about a trierarchy (Dem. 21.78–80; 28.17). Since Thrasylochos had already transferred the trierarchy to a contractor (21.80), and since Demosthenes' service can be dated to between December and the end of 364/3,[16] this challenge concerned the takeover of an active trierarchy. The same may be true of Isokrates' service (15.4–5: he says he "bore that expense" [*dapanē*]) imposed on him through an antidosis.

A decree of 325/4 giving directions for the dispatch of a colonizing force to the Adriatic (*IG* 2².1629.165–271) orders the trierarchs to have their ships ready before 10 Mounichion (ll. 183–90). Then it instructs the thesmothetai to man dikasteria of 201 jurors in order that the strategos of the symmories could introduce the skepseis on 2 and 5 Mounichion. (The terms *skēpseis* and *diadikasiai* are used synonymously for suits arising in connection with claims to exemption: *Ath. Pol.* 56.3; 61.1; Dem. 28.17.) So trierarchs seeking exemption had to produce replacements on 5 Mounichion at the latest.

(ii) The antidosis carried an important functional significance, not least for the trierarchy, which can be gauged by looking more closely at some crucial stages of the procedure. The man challenged was initially offered two options: to undertake the liturgy, or to refuse it, thereby automatically agreeing to exchange properties with the challenger who, now in possession of sufficient wealth, proceeded to discharge the liturgy. Goligher's view that the man challenged had a third option—to refuse both the liturgy and the exchange of properties and enter a diadikasia at the outset—is not supported by the evidence; nor does it seem likely, because it wrongly assumes that a person could circumvent the difficult part of the proceedings at no legal or social cost.[17] Rejection of both options, which were presented at the moment of the challenge (*proklēsis*), also meant refusal to undertake the liturgy.[18] Of course, in principle the man challenged might decline to cooperate just as he or any other man might refuse to comply with an order issued by the authorities. However, with the antidosis he could not do so without risking punishment, and the legal aftermath of his recalcitrance was not, as Goligher and others believe, a diadikasia trial.

Refusal to discharge any liturgy entailed punishment (Dem. 39.8). Trierarchs, in particular, were persecuted if declining to perform their duty (*IG* 2².1629.242–46; [Dem.] 51.4), unless they resorted to supplication or sought asylum in the sanctuary of Artemis in Mounichia (Dem. 18.107). In addition, there was a social cost to be paid by a man challenged who refused both options, for in so doing he demonstrated a total lack of the enthusiasm fitting a public-spirited man (philotimos). Rather than exposing himself to these risks he would therefore prefer, as Demosthenes and Phainippos did,[19] an exchange of properties; but during the negotiations he might try to shun the exchange and so bring the case to trial in the hope of a favorable verdict.

Whether or not the exchange of properties could actually be effective is a problem that has been vigorously debated.[20] But a decree of the deme Ikarion (*IG* i³.254, 440–415?) shows that the possibility of an exchange cannot be in doubt: one of its clauses, regulating the appointment of choregoi, provides for resort to an antidosis as follows (l. 5): *antidosin de enai ton chr[ematon]*. Even though it relates to a single deme, this testimony is rendered valuable by a number of passages in the orators that (directly or indirectly) make the point that an exchange could occur.[21]

However, there is another substantive aspect of the procedure that needs to be recognized as far more crucial than the possible occurrence of the exchange itself: both parties involved in an antidosis could use various means to avoid the completion of a formally initiated exchange. They might reach in private a reconciliatory agreement about who should undertake the liturgy.[22] Or, given that breach of the rules by one party led to an appeal by the other to a law court, and given that legal action canceled the ongoing exchange of property, it was relatively easy for either contestant to transfer the case from the domain of private negotiations to a court of law. For instance, since during the exchange each party was obliged by law (and common oath) to supply the other with an inventory of his holdings drawn up in "a true and just manner" ([Dem.] 42.11), all a man had to do if he wished to bring the matter to trial was to deliver an inventory that manifestly misrepresented his wealth; or neglect to deliver an inventory at all; or accuse his counterpart of having failed on either count. Any of these effectively obstructed the exchange.[23] At the diadikasia the jurors decided which of the two was the wealthier, and that man would have to perform the liturgy.

Hence, although the exchange by law was functionally incorporated into the procedure, the main issue remained throughout that of who should undertake the liturgy. While the exchange was a corollary of the general principle that the largest properties should carry liturgical liability (and surely it only required imagination and cunning for one party to obstruct the exchange), eventually one of the contestants had to discharge the liturgy. Precisely who did so was hardly relevant from the viewpoint of the state. During private negotiations the involvement of the authorities remained minimal. If, on the other hand, the case was brought before a court, the one likely to win was the one who convinced the jurors that his adversary was wealthier than he; sleight-of-hand rhetoric, not sub-stance, was what counted, as each would have it believed that, while he himself had honestly declared his entire wealth, his opponent had con-cealed part of his holdings.[24]

In any event, the state regarded the dispute as a private one in much the same way as it did suits arising from disputes between trierarchs over the return of public equipment or over naval debts; its intervention was always indirect, limited to the availability of legal regulations and the appropriate juridical machinery. What really mattered was that one of these properties should ultimately be employed for liturgical purposes. The responsibility to produce the persons liable for an obligation had been delegated to the propertied class itself, while the questions of who was produced and how remained largely outside the state's field of interest.

In Goligher's judgment, the antidosis was clumsy, absurd, and inane; "the whole liturgical system, in fact, was stupid."[25] On this he might have had the tacit approval of some rich Athenians, and no doubt full sympathy from Isokrates, who overtly branded the liturgies and the anti-dosis as nuisances (8.128). But it is a judgment that can be questioned today. Regarding the trierarchy, the antidosis can be viewed as a device serving two chief purposes. One was to relieve temporarily from expen-diture and toil men claiming financial inability, protecting those individ-uals who were less wealthy against the imposition of a service. However, such a protective function was more apparent than real, in that a chal-lenger was offered no guarantees other than those he himself could pro-vide that the exemption he sought would actually be granted.

Its other chief purpose seems to have been more effectively met: to maintain relative stability in the number of men needed annually to per-form trierarchies by imposing on the same group of individuals the obli-gation to supply replacements. The tactical (and real) significance of this was privatization of the tasks of reporting men who, although liable for the trierarchy, did not currently discharge a service; and of policing po-tential shirkers. These tasks being allocated to the trierarchs themselves, their group functioned as a self-regulating unit responsible for its own replacements. One may ask whether it is possible to separate the antidosis from democracy. Fourth-century Athenians firmly believed that the anti-dosis, like many other democratic institutions, was the work of Solon ([Dem.] 42.1); when airing his dislike of the procedure, Isokrates, one of the critics of the fourth-century political regime, gave a clear sign that there was no room for it at all in his preferred polity. Athenian democracy and the antidosis, it would seem, went together.

One specific point that the antidosis brings out quite forcefully is that trierarchic liability was determined in relative economic terms. Another and more general point is the effective use of coercion (existing side by side with voluntarism). Hence the antidosis can be viewed as a sophisticated mechanism designed by the state in order to exert control over the segment of the citizen body with the economic potential to act as the financial backbone of the navy. Not all those who held up publicly their ostentatious liturgical performances as signs of lamprotes and philotimia had done so voluntarily. Services performed by means of an antidosis were definitely compulsory, even though some people who had been successfully challenged tried to claim the very opposite. The speaker of Lysias 3 boasted of having discharged many liturgies (47), though elsewhere he had to admit his defeat in an antidosis (20). Isokrates stated with pride that he and his son belonged to the twelve hundred who paid eisphorai and performed liturgies (15.145), although in an earlier year he had been forced to undertake a trierarchy through an antidosis (4–5). Demosthenes held up his eagerness to perform voluntary liturgies against Meidias's less honorable performance of a choregy by means of an antidosis (21.156), yet Demosthenes' first trierarchy was discharged after an antidosis (28.17; 21.78–80).

Legally and customarily, a man was expected to channel some of his wealth and time into public service—in this context as naval commander and financier. If he did not do so voluntarily, the antidosis ensured that someone else would see to it that his absence from the trierarchic class would not last long. This was the other side of the state's dependence on wealthy liturgists: what could not be accomplished by incentives was retrieved by way of a subtle coercive contrivance.

## The Hiring Out of Trierarchies

In the fourth century, there existed another, less formal way in which a man might try to free himself from part of the obligation. Although trierarchs were expected to serve in person, a man was permitted to transfer his active period of duty to a substitute. The term used for such transfers was the same as that for the leasing of property: *misthōsis*. There is good reason to believe that this practice was quite widespread.

In 364/3, Demosthenes was forced, through an antidosis, to take over the trierarchy of Thrasylochos, who had already hired it out to a contractor. Accordingly, when Demosthenes "accepted the liturgy" (Dem. 28.17), his obligation consisted merely of handing over to Thrasylochos the sum of two thousand drachmas, which the latter had paid to his contractor (Dem. 21.80). That transfer concerned a syntrierarchy (*APF* 135). Incidentally, this was not the only time Thrasylochos had hired out his obligation; in 361/0, when he "sailed in person on his ship" ([Dem.] 50.52), he was induced by the strategos Timomachos to hire out his trierarchy to Kallippos so that the latter, having assumed full power over the trieres (*autokratōr*), might carry the exiled Kallistratos as he pleased.

The remark that Thrasylochos served in person implies that not all other trierarchs in that squadron had done so. Two indications corroborate this further. First, the same speech says that the syntrierarchs Hagnias and Praxikles (of 362/1) were succeeded by Mnesilochos and Phrasierides (of 361/0). When the latter's turn came to serve his half term, he did not go personally but sent two (or more?) others in his stead, "those who came on behalf of Phrasierides" (41–42), certainly his contractors. Second, the speaker of [Demosthenes] 51 indicates that many of the ships that took part in the engagement at Peparethos against Alexander of Pherae in 361/0 were in the charge of contractors (8).

In 348, Meidias undertook a voluntary trierarchy while serving simultaneously as cavalry commander. In spite of Demosthenes' aspersions (21.163–67), it looks as if Meidias commanded his ship in person when not needed in the cavalry and let the Egyptian Pamphilos take charge of it when he had to perform his duties as hipparchos.[26] In 355, Isokrates complained that whereas in the fifth century the ships were manned with foreigners and slaves, nowadays the Athenians used mercenaries as *hoplitai* but compelled citizens to row the ships (8.48, 79, but cf. 7.54 [circa 357]: Athenians hire foreign oarsmen). Meidias's case, however, brings into focus an even more disquieting trend (if Pamphilos is not a unique example): Athenian triereis were commanded by foreigners.

"On the Trierarchic Crown" ([Dem.] 51) was written for a party in a dispute over the trierarchic crown.[27] The case was heard by the boule, which had to decide whether the award, bestowed on the first trierarch to have his ship prepared for the voyage, should remain in the possession of the speaker, the original recipient according to the boule's earlier decision (4), or should be given to his opponents, a pair of syntrierarchs (*APF* 135–36) who had disputed the award and claimed the crown for themselves. In trying to thwart that claim and discredit his opponents, the speaker says that they had hurried to hire out their service to a contractor, which he found knavish not least because its intent was to evade trierarchic service and expenditure. Demosthenes (21.155) regarded the frequent resort to such a deplorable practice as cheating: some of the Twelve Hundred hired out their obligations by paying to a contractor precisely the sum they had received for performing a trierarchy (one talent), thereby eschewing both personal service and expenditure.

So one can conclude first, that it was possible to hire out a whole trierarchy or a syntrierarchy; second, that a man could do so even when he was already sailing on an expedition (and therefore a misthosis might only cover part of the active term); third, that a syntrierarchy could be transferred to two (or more?) contractors, while, alternatively, a service to be performed by two syntrierarchs jointly could be hired out to one substitute; and finally, that an antidosis–challenge might be made by a trierarch who had already contracted away his service. [Demosthenes] 50.52 used the term *autokratōr;* from this it can be inferred that substitutes assumed full command of the ship.

Occasional boasts by trierarchs to the effect that they risked their lives by joining naval expeditions make it plain that personal service was prized most.[28] Yet instances of misthosis seem far more frequent than the sources document directly. Since hiring out trierarchies rated low in public opinion, it is surely a theme repressed in the speeches (unless it could serve to blacken the picture of an opponent). Moreover, since the original trierarch remained formally accountable for his ship, contractors are virtually untraceable in the official record. Still, the prevalence of the practice can be grasped in a different way: many men performed trierarchies at the age of sixty or more.[29] Only in one case, that of Isokrates, is it indicated that the service simply consisted of an "expense" as opposed to active duty. But one can infer that the remaining examples also represent trierarchies discharged in the same manner. The question this suggests is: what did such transactions mean for the parties involved?

An obvious advantage for the trierarch was that by paying a lump sum he could avoid the hardship and risks of active service. But there is more to it. Describing how he risked his life when serving an additional term, the trierarch Apollodoros also told the jurors of his longing to return to his children, his ill wife, and his dying mother, whom he managed to see only a few days before she breathed her last ([Dem.] 50.59–63). Quite similar were the personal misfortunes of another man while abroad. His opponents in a lawsuit, he explained, intruded into his house, removed his property, harassed his family and attendants, and beat nearly to death an old woman—his former nursemaid and his wife's companion when he was at sea ([Dem.] 47.53–61, 67). Such passionate accounts were meant to evince patriotism, and of course need not be entirely true. Yet they point at the sort of domestic motives that might induce a trierarch to pay another man to take his place on a ship.

Not all the reasons for hiring a substitute were emotional. Economic interests played a fairly large part. "Ships must be launched," says Aristophanes (*Eccl.* 197–98); "the poor men all approve, the wealthy and farmers disapprove." Indeed, farmers were the ones to pay an especially high price, since naval expeditions often coincided with the critical period of peak agricultural activity when the crops needed care or harvesting (barley and wheat became ripe between mid-May and the end of June). Among the personal calamities he suffered while serving overseas, Apollodoros mentions that his land yielded no crops and his orchard no vegetables because of a severe drought that year ([Dem.] 50.61). However, this was less of a problem for owners of large properties, such as Ischomachos in Xenophon's *Oeconomicus* (though one can seriously doubt how typical a farmer he was), whose land was worked and looked after by tenants, hired labor, and slaves. Apollodoros too was not unfamiliar with this practice: whenever he was abroad, his neighbor and trusted friend Nikostratos took over the supervision and management of his estate ([Dem.] 53.4). At any rate, for many men economic considerations certainly added weight to any other reasons they may have had for not going on active service. By hiring replacements, these trierarchs could stay home to attend their personal business while at the same time receiving credit for discharging the duty.

For the sums paid there are only two figures to go by. One is the two thousand drachmas paid by Demosthenes, which compares favorably with the twenty-four hundred drachmas constituting the expenses of Diogeiton's syntrierarchy in a year after 408 (Lys. 32.24, 26–27). Seen in this light, the second known figure, one talent for a single misthosis (Dem. 21.155), is considerably higher and probably pertained to a sole trierarchy. The trierarch's duties to provide a crew and equipment for his ship were inalienable, as were his financial responsibilities in the event of damages or losses.

Demosthenes' equation of *misthōsis triērarchias* with desertion (i.e., *lipotaxia, strateias apodrasis,* 21.164–66) should not be taken *au pied de la lettre.* But even so, the legal position of "lessors" could be insecure. The trierarchs who had contracted their duty in 361/0 were held responsible for the defeat at Peparethos. Aristophon impeached them by an *eisangelia* on the charges of treason and desertion, and proposed capital punishment ([Dem.] 51.8–9). There must have been a substantial enough number of such cases to make the accusations credible, but it is not known whether the accused were actually convicted.[30] On the whole, the hiring out of trierarchies was not, and to the best of my knowledge never became, a right warranted by law; but neither was it directly discouraged, and the incident just mentioned is best understood as a singular reaction to the defeat at Peparethos rather than as a reflection of the systematic prosecution of "lessor" trierarchs.

The contractor, in turn, would have had to meet all current costs from the sum paid by the trierarch. But since the magnitude of expenditure was hardly predictable, he might have had to make additional outlays from his own pocket. The contractors of Phrasierides' syntrierarchy, for instance, had to pay for the part of a prolonged service that fell on Phrasierides ([Dem.] 50.42). The same example suggests that to minimize economic risk, two or more men might undertake jointly half a trierarchy. While at best contractors might manage to balance their expenditure with no substantial loss to themselves, who these people were and what motives they possibly had for taking on the personal and financial risk of others still needs to be explained.

Cawkwell ([1984] 340–41) acutely called them a shadowy lot, and suggested that the best candidates for this job were professional steersmen who, possessing the necessary skill and experience, came in the fourth century to be captains in the real sense. This may well be true. But not all or even most contractors needed to be professionals, and their abilities and ambitions might lie in a different area. The statement in [Demosthenes] 51.7 that two syntrierarchs sought out the one who could undertake the service on the lowest terms possible suggests the existence of an adequate supply of men willing to sail as substitute trierarchs. This is how a scholiast pictures, in his own words, a bargain taking place between two parties just before the dispatch of a fleet: " 'Come on board,' shouted the one party, 'here I supply the money.' 'Hold on a while,' said the other, 'for I still seek out the man who wishes to hire out his trierarchy'" (Schol. Dem. 21.80). Almost certainly contractors accepted trierarchies, occasionally cheaply, because of the prospect of economic gain.

Privateering was not a negligible source of gain, and the official anonymity of contractors afforded them a protective shroud against legal repercussions. As one man put it, "when a person who has taken the trierarchy for hire sets sail, he plunders and pillages everybody [so that] . . . you [sc. the Athenians] alone of all people are unable to travel anywhere without a herald's staff of truce because of the acts of these men in seizing hostages and in provoking reprisals" ([Dem.] 51.13). Behind such a generalization there is a kernel of truth. And this man spoke as if Athenian citizens, not metics, were so inclined. What is said of contractors applies to trierarchs proper.[31] A trieres was involved in a legal action, *phasis* (IG 2².1631.169; 1632.189–90), plausibly because it had been unlawfully used for private purposes.[32] Meidias was accused of having used his ship, when sailing from Styra on Euboia back to Athens, for carrying fences, cattle, and doorposts for his own house as well as pit-props for his silver mines (Dem. 21.167). But this is quite harmless compared to the incident in 355, when the trierarchs Archebios and Lysitheides looted a merchantman from Naukratis; the booty amounted to the considerable sum of nine talents, thirty minas (Dem. 24.11–14). Not very different in nature, though much greater in scale, was the predatory incursion, by the Athenian fleet on its passage to Sicily in 415, on the small coastal town of Hykkara, which, after being captured, had its inhabitants enslaved and used later on as rowing labor in the place of deserting crews (Thuc. 6.62.3; 7.13.3).

Another, not unlawful objective may have been the use, by individuals engaged in trade, of trierarchies in order to establish and maintain a communications network with business connections abroad. Given the almost constant presence of squadrons in areas of notorious importance as sources of grain supply, most notably the Hellespontine area, trierarchs could exploit their presence there. This is not the place to pursue that matter further, but it is notable that in 361, Apollodoros was able to ask for financial support from several of his father's overseas business contacts ([Dem.] 50). Frequent contact with trading centers would allow a man to be well informed about commercial activity, local markets, and people who could supply credit. "Merchants," says Xenophon (*Oec.* 20.27–28), "sail in quest of grain wherever they hear that it is in abundance, crossing the Aegean, the Euxine and the Sicilian seas . . . [and] they carry it to wherever they hear that it is most highly prized and is at a premium." Again, what is said here need not be limited to contractors only.

On balance, therefore, the misthosis trierarchias was generally to the mutual advantage of trierarch and contractor, although the economic gains of the latter cannot be precisely gauged. But what was in it for the state? And more importantly: why was a formal replacement never made of the often complaining trierarch-liturgists (Lys. 29.4) with a group of professionals or semiprofessionals willing to do the job? First, increasing reliance on private wealth in order to meet naval expenditure, in the fourth century, led to increased dependence both on the individuals with the economic potential and on the existing ideological and institutional channels through which their wealth could be made available for such purposes. Rather than circumventing the liturgy system, privatization accentuated its indispensability. Permission to hire out trierarchies made it possible for the state to deploy for the navy the wealth of individuals who, because of old age or other reasons, would have remained virtually outside the trierarchic class. Enlargement of the group of persons potentially liable was, in short, one way of coping with manpower shortages.

Second, given the firm foothold of democratic ideology and government, diversion of the trierarchy away from the liturgical orbit would scarcely have seemed a paying proposition to the economic upper class, inasmuch as this meant loss of an important avenue to distinction for philotimia.[33] And this distinction was worth striving for because of its accepted ideological propriety as a visible manifestation of usefulness to the community, and because of its practical expedience in demonstrating publicly (e.g., in a court of law) that one had incurred "danger and expenditure."[34] An alertness to the elimination of recompensatory elements embodied in liturgical services is evident in a reaction to Leptines' abolition of ateleia from agonistic liturgies: "You deprive the people of those who [sc. through their liturgies] might show philotimia, by giving clear warning that no one who confers a benefit on the people shall gain any advantage at all from it" (Dem. 20.103). In essence, this (like similar utterances in the same speech) is nothing but a stout defense for the preservation of the benefits and honors usually expected to be harvested from

liturgical expenditure. No doubt these were strong reasons for not introducing at Athens a formal substitute for the trierarch, as was done in
the Rhodian navy of the Hellenistic period with an officer called an
*epiplous.*[35]

Certainly, the traditional type of trierarch-liturgist persevered, but it
did so more frequently in spirit than in practice. Permission to all those
who wished to limit their contributions to spending part of their wealth
but not their time represented a further concession made to the trierarchic
class; with this arrangement the state could hope to attract a greater number of naval financiers, while property owners preserved a vital locus in
which to demonstrate their usefulness, even though the twin virtues,
"danger and expenditure," became separated. The misthosis trierarchias
would seem to have offered tangible benefits to all involved.

## PART III

*Financial Responsibilities*

# FIVE

# The Crew

In dealing with a system of naval finance in which one part of the overall cost is paid by the state and another part comes from private outlays acquired through taxation, it is important to try to isolate the spheres of responsibility covered by the two main agents, the state and the trierarchs, and the distribution of burdens among individual trierarchs. I focus here on the financial and legal facets of the duties of trierarchs. The task is not an easy one, nor—with the limited amount of material available—can it be expected to supply rewardingly detailed and satisfactory answers to all queries.

Ideally, this inquiry would move progressively through a description of trierarchic expenditure in connection with the preparation of a ship for sea, during a journey, and after the completion of a term of service. However, what can be gleaned from the sources about the two first stages is disappointingly scanty. In an attempt to overcome some of these inadequacies and offer an account encompassing all three situations, I have chosen to address the question of financial responsibility within a broader context by looking separately at the two main areas of naval infrastructure: the maintenance of crews and of ships.

## The Recruitment of Crews

The use of large triereis fleets forced Greek naval states to deal with the ever-pressing problem of securing manpower. In terms of numbers and expertise, the requirements were so great as to put immense pressure on the resources of states and to occasion strong competition among them about the services of highly skilled professionals. Athens was no exception in this respect; what is exceptional is the survival from there of more full evidence showing how this pressure in part was placed on property owners chosen to command and finance the ships.

The standard trieres complement (*plērōma*) numbered 200 men divided into three main categories: oarsmen (*nautai*), petty officers (hyperesia), and fighting personnel (epibatai and archers).[1] The required number of oarsmen, usually drawn from the thetic class, was 170, with one man pulling one oar. In accordance with the oar system of the vessel in the fourth century, they were distributed into 62 *thranitai* (at the upper level of oars), 54 *zygioi* (at the middle level), and 54 *thalamioi* (at the lower level). It is now firmly established that the term *hypēresia* refers to sixteen specialists: a helmsman (kybernetes), a boatswain (*keleustēs*), a purser (pentekontarchos), a bow officer (*prōratēs*), a shipwright (*naupēgos*), a piper (*aulētēs*), and ten deck hands.[2] The remaining men were soldiers, often, but not invariably, ten hoplites and four archers. A recent suggestion that these were included in the collective term *hypēresia* is not borne out by the evidence.[3] Strictly, the term *epibatai* applies only to the hoplites (*IG* 2².1951), who, furthermore, must be distinguished from the more numerous contingent of soldiers (*IG* 1³.60) aboard troop carriers (*hoplitagōgoi, stratiōtides*).

Nothing is known about the complements of tetrereis and pentereis, the new craft whose numbers increased steadily toward the end of the fourth century. References in the records to components of missile-throwing devices (*IG* 2².1627.322–57) and to a catapult operator (1631.513–14) suggest the employment of ancillary personnel on these vessels, yet the vital question about the number and arrangement of their oars remains unresolved.[4] The available knowledge is limited to the size and functional composition of the trieres complement. And even with this, two hundred men is a conveniently round figure for the normal size of the crew.

The state always provided the fighting personnel, either by regular conscription (Thuc. 8.24.2) or by recruitment of volunteers. A decree of circa 430 (*IG* 1³.60) illustrates how a squadron of thirty ships, sent to collect tribute or to raid the Peloponnesos, was staffed with soldiers: it orders the embarkation on each ship of five volunteer epibatai, forty hoplites, ten archers, and ten *peltasts* (lightly armed soldiers). While the first two groups consisted of Athenian citizens, the latter two were composed of Athenians and of allies in equal numbers. Almost certainly, the five volunteer epibatai made up, or were part of, the standard complement.

With oarsmen and hyperesiai the situation was somewhat different in that the state seems often to have allocated that responsibility to the trierarchs. For most of the fifth and the whole of the fourth century conscription was the exception rather than the rule. For instance, in 428 the Athenians launched 100 ships in order to display their strength along the coast of the Isthmos and make landings on the Peloponnesos. These were staffed by citizens (except the two higher Solonian classes: *hippeis* and *pentakosiomedimnoi*) as well as metics (Thuc. 3.16.1). Since at the same time a force of 150 ships was in commission (100 of them guarding Attica, Euboia, and Salamis, the remaining being at Potidaia and elsewhere, 3.17.1–2), the decision to conscript citizens and metics was no doubt prompted by the need to mobilize all the extra hands available: besides some 25,500 oarsmen on the 150 ships, a further 17,000 would have been needed for the 100 ships cruising off the Peloponnesos.

Xenophon (*Hell.* 1.6.24) mentions a decree ordering the manning of 110 ships in 406 (Arginousai); all those of military age were to embark, slaves as well as freemen. He then notes, as if to underline the exceptional situation, that many of the hippeis class embarked on the ships as well, a clear indication of a manpower shortage among the groups traditionally used for naval service. A total of 18,700 oarsmen were needed for this operation.

Besides being exceptional, conscription may also have been ineffective. A decree of 362 ([Dem.] 50.6) authorized the dispatch of ships to the northern Aegean, and ordered "that the *bouleutai* and the demarchs make lists of the demesmen and return oarsmen." It is not possible to say whether this procedure was a departure from the usual one.[5] What was unusual, Cawkwell points out ([1984] 338), is the resort to conscription itself. At any rate, the state's levy was limited to oarsmen only. Apollodoros dismissed those few who came to his ship from the list of demesmen because of their insufficient number and lack of skill; he then hired others of excellent skill and the best hyperesia, both groups from the open market (7). The strategos Timotheos and his trierarchs were less lucky in 373; having failed to find full crews for their sixty ships at Piraeus, they sailed around the islands to assemble additional manpower, a total of 10,200 oarsmen (Xen. *Hell.* 6.2.11–12).[6]

Frequently, then, the trierarch had to recruit the whole or part of his crew. One case in point is the Sicilian expedition (415), for which the state provided sixty "empty" ships of the rating "fast," forty troop carriers, and the best hyperesiai to man them (Thuc. 6.31.3). The hyperesiai presented no problem: in the fifth century Athens could boast of possessing adequate and able hyperesiai (1.143.1; 8.1.2), while in the fourth century it could supply others with such specialists (*IG* $2^2$.212.59–63; *Hell. Oxy.* 2.1). But the supply of oarsmen did present a problem: in 415 the state provided "empty" ships, *kenas,* which means "without oarsmen," not "without equipment,"[7] because elsewhere in Thucydides (1.27.2; 2.90.6; 4.14.1; 8.19.3) that word is used of ships without crews, and because the state was always obliged to furnish equipment (*IG* $1^3$.127.25–32; 236; [Dem.] 51.5), but not oarsmen. Later, at Aigospotamoi (405), a man hired his own oarsmen and hyperesia (Lys. 21.10), and so did Pasion on five separate occasions before 370 ([Dem.] 45.85). The sixty "empty" ships to Sicily, too, were probably staffed by the trierarchs. All this, in conjunction with reports about "empty" ships after 357 (Dem. 3.5; 4.43), goes counter to Demosthenes' claim (21.154–55) that after that date the state provided crews, whereas previously this was the responsibility of the trierarchs.[8]

Even with fleets of a moderate size, the amount of rowing labor and of specialized deck personnel needed was enormous. The provision of a mere thirty ships with oarsmen and hyperesiai (5,580 men in all) hired by the trierarchs must have represented a labor-purchase transaction the magnitude of which was unmatched by most other sectors of the city-state. While a good part of the funds absorbed by such operations came from the coffers of the state, the share of the trierarchs, consisting in advance payments and bonuses, was by no means negligible.

Finding the cash needed was not so difficult as finding enough fit crews. Recurring recruitment crises had to be solved by scraping together all labor available, not seldom including metics and slaves; contributions of slave-oarsmen by citizens, rare in the body of evidence, need not have been uncommon.[9] Surely, the Athenian demos was renowned for its nautical abilities (Thuc. 1.143.1–2; Ps.-Xen. *Ath. Pol.* 1.2) so that Aristotle could refer to part of it as the "trieres folk" (*triērikon*) or "naval mob" (*nautikos ochlos*: Arist. *Pol.* 1291b24, 1304a22). But this does not mean that they were always eager to go aboard the ships (Isoc. 7.54). Recruitment crises, in addition, render unlikely the assumption that there was a fixed number of citizens among crews;[10] the sacred vessel *Paralos* was definitely exceptional in having an all-citizen complement (Thuc. 8.73.5).

However, was it always the case, as is widely held, that ships were manned with a full complement? Wallinga (1982) challenges this belief, but the evidence he adduces in support of his contention that undermanning must have been habitual is at best circumstantial.[11] I have noted above certain instances in which ships were dispatched without being fully manned. Trierarchs might prove unable to procure in timely fashion a full complement. The speaker of [Demosthenes] 51 seems to have been criticized by his opponents for not having the prescribed number of hyperesia on his ship (6), and also for not having aboard, during the customary trials, oarsmen specifically referred to by the words *nautas oikeious tēs triērous* (17). The latter expression is not entirely clear; but if it means "the oarsmen belonging to that particular trieres," one may suspect (with Kirchhoff [1865] 100 n. 54) that the speaker might have hurried to undergo trials by temporarily filling gaps in his complement with other oarsmen who did not belong to his ship.

Another piece of evidence that ought to be mentioned here is a decree from a year between 440 and 425 (*IG* I³.153). It stipulates that no fewer than [140] men be present when hauling up a ship; no fewer than 120 when launching it; no fewer than ?50/90 when fitting it with *hypozōmata;* and no fewer than 100 when *periormizein* (ll. 6–11). Specification of the minimum number of men needed to carry out the operations of launching and hauling up was made for security reasons; no doubt the same applies to the need for an adequate number of men to fit a vessel with hypozomata (their tension being circa ten tons: Morrison and Coates [1989] 2–3). But why is a minimum number of men specified for periormizein, usually meaning "to bring round a ship to anchor" (LSJ)? It may be noted that the same word, like *kathelkein* (to launch), is used in a more specialized context relating to the standard operation of bringing ships just commissioned to the pier (*chōma*) with the purpose of undergoing trials before departure ([Dem.] 51.4, 7). Also, vessels fitted with hypozomata (*haute hypezōtai, IG* 2².1621.68, to be compared with 1627.50 and *IG* I³.153.9: *hypozonynai*) were those in the list of active ships (*GOS* 295). Therefore, it may be suggested that the fifth-century decree also regulates (though indirectly) the lowest permissible number of members of a ship's crew during trials.

On balance, although ships may at times have set out from the Piraeus with gaps in their complements, it is as good as certain that additional labor was to be obtained by the trierarchs at the first opportunity. Full oar power, used only in battle, emergency voyages, or training, is an altogether different matter. The whole of [Demosthenes] 50 furnishes a good illustration of the trierarch's concern to have a full and competent complement, a concern explicable not least by the need to ensure the ship's performance at sea and by the importance of surrendering it with a full crew to his successor.

## Pay and Provisioning

The meaning of the various terms for pay used in the sources—*misthos, trophē, sitēresion, sitos,* to mention the most important ones—must be determined at the outset. Griffith stated: "Rations, or money for rations, are something without which a soldier cannot begin to fight, and they must consequently be paid *in advance; pay (misthos)* is something which a soldier receives in return for having done some work, and consequently, like any other wages or salary, it is paid at the *end*" ([1935] 265; emphasis in original). Several of the sources cited below render this conclusion invalid, at least as far as crews are concerned. From an exhaustive analysis of the pay vocabulary, Pritchett (*GSW* 1:3–6) concludes that, while in the fifth century these terms were used synonymously, in the fourth century a sharp distinction seems to have been drawn between pay (misthos) and money for rations (e.g., trophe). However, reexamination of the evidence has shown that the sharp distinction postulated is an oversimplification.[12]

It seems best to consider pay and provisioning as complementary, not differentiated, terms. First, as Markle argues ([1985] 295), daily payments of either three obols or one drachma (both labeled trophe) would normally have purchased four or eight days' rations of wheat. If this had to be bought at inflated prices, however, provisioning would demand the entire daily pay. Second, Herodotos's report (8.19) that on retiring from Artemision (480) Themistokles fed his fleet by slaughtering Euboian flocks, and that of Thucydides (3.17.3–4) that each man on the ships blockading Potidaia (431–428) received misthos at one drachma per day, refer to a single fundamental problem: the need to meet a vast logistic burden accruing from the operation of fleets, using human energy for propulsion.

This point is implicitly made in a number of traditions (even though the stories they tell us have little historical value) seeking to demonstrate the ingenuity of commanders when trying to secure the maintenance of their fleets: Themistokles' provisioning of the fleet in 480 by confiscating money hidden in the baggage of those embarking (*FGrH* 323: Kleidemos F 21); or Kimon's hoodwinking of the Ionian allies during the distribution of Persian booty so that he obtained four months' maintenance for the ships (Plut. *Cim.* 9.2–4); or, finally, Perikles' introduction of a training program, "sending out sixty triereis annually, on which large numbers of the citizens sailed about for eight months under pay, practicing at the same time and acquiring the art of seamanship" (Plut. *Per.* 11.4)—a measure widely (but unjustifiably) accepted as historically accurate.[13] Basically, these and other traditions tried to account for the need for a constant flow of resources in order to keep fleets active as well as the relative inability of the state treasury always to fund such operations. The chief sources about naval pay seem to say exactly the same thing.

Such evidence as exists about the rates of pay relates to the period after the beginning of the Peloponnesian War and has been interpreted variously. Some argue that one drachma per man per day was the normal rate during the first years of the war, but after 413 it was reduced to three obols and again to two obols in the fourth century.[14] Others hold that generally three obols was the standard Athenian rate, while one drachma was given only exceptionally.[15] Still others (*GOS* 258–59) point out that, although one drachma was the full pay, crews often received three obols when in service and had the balance of pay given to them on their return home. While none of these views can be rejected, a review of the evidence may show that almost without exception these rates relate to pay given by the state. This need not be, and frequently was not, the total amount received by crews. A clear distinction must be drawn between public and private sectors.

In giving the amount of one drachma per man per day as the pay (misthos) during the siege of Potidaia (431–428), Thucydides (3.17.3) is clearly reporting the expenditure borne by the state (cf. 3.17.4). Also, he thought it appropriate to note that the same rate was given to all ships alike. The Athenian envoys, together with Egestean representatives, returned to Athens from Sicily (in the spring of 415) bringing with them sixty talents of silver for one month's pay (misthos) to sixty Athenian ships (Thuc. 6.8.1); one talent per ship per month works out to one drachma per man per day. Pay at that rate was furnished from Egestean, not Athenian, funds for the duration of one month only; the rate for the remaining period remains unknown.

For the Sicilian expedition (415), which, in Thucydides' words, was "the costliest, most splendid, and best prepared up to that time," the fleet was fitted out "at great expense on the part of both trierarchs and of the state." When Thucydides proceeds to specify pay for the crews, he distinguishes between pay (misthos) at one drachma per day given by the state to each oarsman and bonuses (epiphorai) paid by the trierarchs to a specific group of oarsmen, the thranitai (6.31.1–3). At Thucydides 8.29.1–2, Tissaphernes' pay policy with the Peloponnesian fleet at Miletos (412/11) is mentioned. Tissaphernes gave to all ships a month's maintenance (trophe) as he had promised to do (8.5.5), at the rate of one Attic drachma per man per day. For the future Tissaphernes proposed to furnish three obols and raise this to a full drachma only upon receiving the consent of the king. However, when the Syracusan Hermokrates disapproved of this arrangement, Tissaphernes put forward a new offer. "A sum was agreed upon notwithstanding that was larger by five ships than three obols for each man. For he gave for fifty-five ships thirty talents a month; and to the others, according as there were more ships than this number, pay was given in the same proportion" (8.29.2).

Besides the observation that the Peloponnesian fleet was paid from Persian funds, three further points are worth emphasizing. First, once more Thucydides found it significant to add that one month's maintenance was given to *all* ships. Second, the rate of pay could fluctuate within the duration of the same campaign: one drachma per day was given for the first month; for the future Tissaphernes was to give to fifty-five ships the pay of sixty, which works out to three and a third obols per man per day;[16] then the prospect is mentioned of raising the pay to one drachma. Third, there is a strong impression that a "full drachma" (entelē drachmēn) was the pay normally expected.

On Alkibiades' advice (412/11), Tissaphernes cut down the pay of Spartan crews, "so that instead of an Attic drachma only three obols were given, and that not regularly, and he [sc. Alkibiades] urged Tissaphernes to tell them that the Athenians, who had had experience in naval matters for a longer time, gave only three obols to their own crews" (Thuc. 8.45.2). The final piece of advice given by Alkibiades was that Tissaphernes ought to bribe the trierarchs and strategoi of each city so that they might comply with his pay policy (8.45.3); the implication may be that the latter would be apt to insist on receiving adequate and regular pay, or that they would indulge their crews by extra payments from funds obtained otherwise. As has been rightly pointed out, this source does not say that Athenian crews received only three obols; it rather refers to the practice of withholding part of the sailors' pay until disembarkation in Piraeus in order to avoid desertions.[17]

In 407, Lysander asked Kyros to raise the pay of oarsmen to one Attic drachma a day, explaining that, if this was the rate of pay (misthos), the oarsmen of the Athenians would be enticed by the higher pay offered in the Peloponnesian fleet and desert their ships (Xen. *Hell.* 1.5.4). Kyros responded by referring to the existing agreement "that the King should give thirty minas per month to each ship, whatever number of ships the Lacedaemonians might wish to maintain" (1.5.5). Nevertheless, asked by Kyros later what favor would please him most, Lysander expressed his wish for an additional obol to add to the pay (misthos) of each oarsman. "And from this time onward," Xenophon continues, "the pay [misthos] was four obols, whereas previously it had been three. Kyros also settled the arrears of pay and gave them a month's pay in advance besides, so that the troops were much more zealous" (1.5.6–7).

The speaker of [Demosthenes] 51.11 remarks that, whereas trierarchs who received thirty minas to perform their duty but did not sail in person on their ships were allowed to go unpunished, oarsmen who deserted their ships, even though in possession of only thirty drachmas each, were being imprisoned and punished. One should probably interpret this as meaning that in the mid-fourth century Athenian oarsmen could receive a month's pay in advance at the rate of one drachma per man per day, rather than, as Kirchhoff believed ([1865] 92), three months' rations at two obols a day. In 351 or 349, Demosthenes proposed the establishment of a standing force ready to take action against Philip. Fifty triereis had to be fitted out, plus an unspecified number of horse transports and seaworthy merchantmen (4.16). In addition, ten fast triereis were needed to ensure the safe journey of the fleet (22). When he came to explaining how this force should be maintained, he proceeded from an acknowledgment of the state's limited financial resources (22–24). Expenditure on "the maintenance [trophe]—that is, the bare ration money [siteresion]" of ten fast ships was set at four talents per ship per year, or two obols per man per day.

Although the plan was not realized, two things should be noted. Out of a total force of more than sixty ships, only the crews of ten fast triereis were to receive (regularly or at all) money from the state. And even with these, the amount of two obols a day as ration money (siteresion) was recognized to be insufficient, and therefore resort to other means was advocated for obtaining supplementary funds with which to supply "full pay" (misthon entelē) (29); resort to depredation (23) and the use of booty are foremost among Demosthenes' suggestions.

So what is really known about pay rates primarily concerns the amounts supplied from public funds. These were disbursed either directly from the home treasury of a fleet or indirectly from the treasury of another city-state or a foreign potentate acting as paymaster. Although the concept of "full pay" (entelēs misthos) is often encountered in such contexts, in a number of instances state pay was provided irregularly, at reduced rates or not at all. Moreover, the same rate might or might not have been given to all ships of a fleet or for the duration of a campaign. All these add up to a significant characteristic: as a general rule the aggregate resource demands accruing from the operation of fleets exceeded the amounts actually spent for that purpose by the state.[18] Private funds were therefore needed to supplement the public ones. To illustrate this further I will look at some central aspects of fifth- and fourth-century finance for the fleets.

## Funding the Fleet

Much of the pressure put by naval activity on the state's resources stemmed from expenditures for maintaining the crews. As I have noted, that pressure was transmitted to the trierarchs; but before reaching its destination it was felt by the strategoi commanding fleets. Their responsibility was most eloquently expressed by the Spartan Teleutias who, in 388, addressed his oarsmen as follows: "I have come without money; yet if God be willing and you perform your part zealously, I shall endeavour to supply you with provisions in the greatest abundance . . . I am more desirous of your being supplied than of being supplied myself; indeed, by the gods, I should prefer to go without food myself for two days than to have you go without for one" (Xen. *Hell.* 5.1.14).

Although Teleutias was fully aware of the need to have his crews properly fed, he nevertheless lacked the funds for that purpose. The situation is fairly typical of fourth-century naval finances, those of Athens included. But what about the fifth century? Surely the requirements for funds then were equally great, if not greater, but during most of that century Athenian resources were abundant (though not limitless), and consequently the financial demands on strategoi and trierarchs were of a lesser order.

The expenditure on naval operations before and during the Peloponnesian War gives some idea of the demands on public finances and of the ability of Athens to meet these demands. The record for the campaign against Samos (440: *IG* I³.363; ML no. 55) lists over 1,276 talents paid by the tamiai of Athena to the strategoi leading the nine-month siege with over sixty ships (Thuc. 1.117.2–3);[19] the cost per ship per month would be about 2.3 talents. The record of the expenses for aid to Korkyra (433/2: *IG* I³.364; ML no. 61) lists 26 talents paid in the first prytany to the strategoi of the ten ships dispatched initially (ll. 10–12; Thuc. 1.45), and a further 50 talents (restored) paid later in the same prytany to another squadron of twenty ships (ll. 21–23; Thuc. 1.50–51). These sums are substantial considering that the first squadron perhaps left Athens in mid-July, the second in early August, and both were expected to return before the end of October at the latest (*HCT* 1:196–97). The tamiai of Athena of 418/17 listed a sum in Cyzicene gold staters paid to the trierarchs of Demosthenes' squadron (*IG* I³.370.134–35), and the tamiai of 410/9 (375.34–37) listed several payments (only one, of 3,000 drachmas, is legible) to trierarchs at Samos. In 415/14, 300 talents were sent to Nikias at Sicily, and a further 4 talents, 2,000 drachmas for the expenses of eight ships (Thuc. 6.93.4, 94.4).

These instances, like the total of 2,000 talents spent on the two-and-one-half-year siege of Potidaia (431–428),[20] show how rapidly enormous sums were being swallowed up by naval operations; the element of unpredictability involved is sufficiently great to discredit modern reconstructions of annual naval budgets.[21] But this evidence also tells us another thing: a good deal of the money spent had been borrowed from the treasuries of Athena. While, as Gomme argued (*HCT* 2:31–32), such transactions cannot prove the total absence of a reserve in the state treasury, they definitely reveal the diversity of resources on which Athens could rely; in an eleven-year period (433–422) about 5,599 talents had been borrowed from sacred treasuries, by far the greatest part coming from those of Athena Nike and Athena Polias.[22] The Peloponnesians, in contrast, could only hope for loans from funds stored at Delphi and Olympia to finance their navies (Thuc. 1.121.3, 143.1).

Perikles enumerated the full range of options just before the Peloponnesian War in order to reassure the Athenians of their superior financial ability (Thuc. 2.13.3–5): first, 600 talents came in annually as tribute; second, there were still 6,000 talents in the Acropolis (including the 1,000 talents later set aside as a reserve [2.24.2]) from the previous maximum of 9,700 talents; third, there was uncoined gold and silver worth 500 talents, in addition to the wealth of the temples; fourth, there were the gold plates on the statue of Athena weighing 40 talents of pure gold. When a further 400 talents is added to the tribute, the annual income rises to the 1,000 talents reported by Xenophon (*An.* 7.1.27).

So until the first years of the Peloponnesian War Athens was a very prosperous state, and its trierarchs were not heavily burdened; to them Perikles' stocktaking would have sounded reassuring. But with regard to the more distant future, his optimism about an adequate supply of manpower and funds could scarcely convince those (including himself: Thuc. 1.141.3–5) who foresaw protracted warfare.[23] The drain on the reserves had already started in 433, and it gathered force during the war. "Now the Athenians," Thucydides writes of 428, "finding themselves in need of additional funds for the siege [of Potidaia], having then for the first time resorted to an eisphora to the amount of two hundred talents, also sent to the allies twelve ships . . . to collect tribute" (Thuc. 3.19.1).

The fifth-century imperial tribute made a solid contribution to funding the navy. But deprived of it in the fourth century, Athens saw the need to turn all the more frequently to private means to finance its ventures at sea. The trierarch's share became larger. Another means of raising funds, Thucydides noted, was the levy of eisphora; but often this proved inadequate. Take the levy authorized in 362 to finance naval activity in the northern Aegean. The tax, paid in advance by the proeispherontes ([Dem.] 50.8–9), was to provide money for the crews (10: *stratiō-tika*). Was the amount collected enough to cover the total cost of the enterprise? Probably not.

Demosthenes' complaints that the Athenians were unwilling to pay eisphora may mean that taxpayers neglected to pay in full, or at all.[24] Indeed, from 378/7 to circa 356/5, fourteen talents had accumulated in arrears from eisphorai totaling some three hundred talents (Dem. 22.44), which is not easily reconciled with the application of the proeisphora system. One of the trierarchs in the northern Aegean in 362, Apollodoros, received only periodically pay and ration money (siteresion) from the strategoi during his seventeen-month service. Probably, therefore, part of the unpaid eisphorai stemmed from the levy of 362; this latter had furnished insufficient funds to cover crews' maintenance, while the strategoi had proven unable to raise any additional funds: "The state was neglectful, our allies without resources, and the strategoi faithless," Apollodoros complained ([Dem.] 50.15).

In the fourth century strategoi were frequently sent on expeditions with inadequate state funds, or none at all.[25] This does not mean that the Athenians were being careless or unconcerned with their fleet. Rather, it is indicative of a general tendency to divert a good deal of the naval expenditure from the state coffers. Therefore, commanding officers had to find additional means to pay and provision their crews (see *GSW* 2:59–116). Alternatives did exist. One was plundering.[26] Another was exaction, lawfully or by force, of contributions (*syntaxeis*) from the allies. Yet another was to raise private loans. This is how Demosthenes (8.26) put it before the Athenians in 341: "For where else do you suppose that he [sc. a strategos] looks for maintenance of his troops, if he gets nothing from yóu and has no private fortune to furnish their pay? To the sky? No, indeed; it is from what he can collect or beg or borrow that he keeps things going."

Needing funds for his force of sixty ships in 374/3, Timotheos borrowed 1,351 drachmas from Pasion, and 700 drachmas from each of his sixty trierarchs ([Dem.] 49.6–8, 11–12, 44; Xen. *Hell.* 6.2.11–12)—a total of 42,000 drachmas. He also borrowed 1,000 drachmas from another man in order to pay the Boiotian trierarchs and their crews who had joined his force, "for while our citizens [sc. Athenians] endured their privation and remained at their posts, the Boiotians declared that they would not stay, unless somebody should furnish them with their daily maintenance" ([Dem.] 49.15). Privatizing naval costs, it can be argued, had in the fourth century become the ruling principle.

However, none of these alternative means was secure.[27] In the last resort, therefore, a substantial part of the logistic burden, like any other pressure created by the state's need for resources, was transmitted further down the scale to be borne by the individual trierarch; he alone acted as the formal and ultimate guarantor of the state for the finance of naval operations.

## Logistics and the Cost of Service

Much has been done in the past to demonstrate the significance of an effective commissariat during campaigns.[28] However, the relative share of the trierarch in the overall costs must be isolated. The extent to which the state supplied funds, as well as the ability of the strategoi to obtain supplementary resources, I have argued thus far, determined the amount of trierarchic expenditure. To these pressures from above should be added those from below, stemming from the trierarch's function as the employer of a large complement handling a special craft. Specifically, two further factors determined the magnitude of his outlays: the ship's performance abilities, and his dependence entirely on human muscle and expertise.

Tactically, the raison d'être of the trieres as an offensive weapon lay in its ability to attain high speed under oars. "Why," asks Xenophon (*Oec.* 8.8), "is a trieres, fully manned, such a terror to the enemy and a joy to her friends except by reason of her speed through the water?" Maximum speed averaged seven knots per hour, and to achieve it each oarsman had to produce about one-fourteenth effective horsepower.[29] But this is peak speed used in combat, and could only be kept up for a relatively short period of time, half an hour or slightly more. Oarsmen tired rapidly as their rowing efficiency deteriorated progressively with the increase in the distance they had to cover. For acceleration, vital for ramming tactics, even adequately fit crews had to stretch their efforts to the limit. Turning (*anastrophē*) and backing water (*anakrousis, prymnan krouein*) were just as important tactically and just as demanding.

The oarsmen's limitations (and the effect of those limitations on the ship's tactical capabilities) were well known. In his letter to the Athenians (Thuc. 7.9–15), Nikias gives an account of the deteriorating condition of his troops in Sicily and makes the general remark: "You to whom I write understand that the peak efficiency of a crew lasts for a short period of time and few are the oarsmen who can both set the ship out and maintain their oarstroke" (7.14.1). Occasionally (e.g., Thuc. 3.18.3–4), men were asked both to pull an oar and to fight (*auteretai*); such men faced exorbitant energy demands. The trierarch Apollodoros described the dismay that befell his crew when, tired after a long voyage, they encountered the enemy fleet: having carried out the crossing from Thasos to the southern coast of Thrace, they found the nearby shore too hostile to attempt a landing. "So," Apollodoros continues, "we were forced to ride at anchor all night long in the open sea without food and without sleep, keeping watch lest the ships of the Maronites should attack us in the night" ([Dem.] 50.22).

Apollodoros's report brings into focus another characteristic of triereis fleets. Tactically and logistically, as pointed out by Gomme (1933), oared ships were closely tied to their bases. The relationship between fleets and their bases is a complex one and cannot be treated in full here. Suffice it to note that the radius of action of a trieres was limited by its inability to carry any substantial amount of provisions; a modern suggestion that triereis could carry large supplies so as to operate for long periods of time away from their land bases is definitely wrong.[30] A harbor, a beach, or any friendly stretch of coast always had to be within reach for the crew to bivouac there; one record shows that six ships carried cooking and drinking utensils and tools for hewing wood (*IG* $2^2$.1631.404–9).[31] The water-supply situation was more critical: in 427, Athenian and Rhegian ships were forced to sail against the islands of Aiolos during the winter because of the lack of water there in the summer (Thuc. 3.88.1).[32] For the Sicilian expedition the fighting force was not only accompanied by a train of supplies and logistic personnel but also had to secure access to coastal markets en route to Sicily (Thuc. 6.42, 44). Besides being valuable suppliers of provisions, trading ports could satisfy another important demand: fresh crews.[33] Although one rarely hears about the need for replacements (e.g., Thuc. 8.17), and hardly anything about illness (7.47.2), it may be assumed that neither was rare.

An efficient crew rapidly consumed food and water. One of the first concerns of a trierarch was to satisfy these demands. But what was the consumption rate of food and water per ship? Besides a large amount of grain, the staple food in this period,[34] the diet of crews included fish, meat, oil, and wine. In his vivid picture of victualing in Piraeus, Aristophanes (*Ach.* 544–45) adds garlic, olives, and onions. Elsewhere it is reported that before embarkation the trierarchs provided their oarsmen with barley meal, and a relish of onions and cheese ([Plut.] *Mor.* 349A). The crew of a trieres dispatched for the nonstop voyage to Mytilene in 428 was supplied with wine, barley, and barley cakes made with wine and oil (Thuc. 3.49.3). Foxhall and Forbes ([1982] 48–49, 86–89) set the daily requirements of an "exceptionally active" adult male at 3,822 calories. But particularly for oarsmen (taking here the age group of eighteen to thirty) these requirements may have been higher,[35] probably 4,780 calories, if the men were active for six hours, and 4,070 calories, if they were active for four hours. In the first instance the "basket of goods" would weigh about 1,500 grams, in the second 1,325 grams.[36] The daily food ration for a Macedonian soldier under Alexander the Great has been estimated at 1,362 grams.[37] A complement of 200 (I abstain from discriminating between the diet of the 170 oarsmen and that of the remaining 30 crew members) would then consume, in round figures, 300 or 265 kilograms of food per day. If one sets the absolute minimum requirement for water at two quarts (about 2.27 liters) per man per day,[38] the whole crew would need about a hundred gallons (about 454 liters).

Grain, it is agreed, was the costliest dietary item, while other kinds of foods were so cheap that they are not worth reckoning. From the evidence (primarily from Athens and Delos) relating to the prices of grain in the fifth and fourth centuries, Markle concludes that the price of wheat normally averaged 6 drachmas per *medimnos.*[39] A *choinix* (one forty-eighth of a medimnos, or 839 grams) of harvested (hulled) wheat, which is now reckoned to have been sufficient for an active soldier,[40] cost about three-quarters of an obol. On average, one to one and a half obols would cover most of the provisioning expenses of an oarsman, provided that food could be purchased at normal, uninflated prices. If so, the supply of provision money (siteresion) at two obols per man per day proposed by Demosthenes (4.28) would have been adequate under normal circumstances, as far as basic dietary needs only are concerned. To keep a ship in commission for one month at the cost of one or two obols per man per day on food alone meant expenditure on the order of one thousand or two thousand drachmas. If the trierarch had to bear this cost for, say, two months, which might not have been unusual, his outlays for provisioning only would have amounted to two thousand or four thousand drachmas. The estimate of the total running expenses of a trierarchy at an average of three thousand drachmas may therefore not be far off the mark; if anything, it may be low. Each of the sixty trierarchs sailing under the command of Timotheos in 373 was able to lend the strategos seven hundred drachmas ([Dem.] 49.11), which cannot have been the entire cash reserve they carried on their ships.

A cautionary note is in order here. The estimated daily rate of consumption should be used as an indicator of the requirements of crews, not for postulating that this was the amount of food and water actually consumed every day. But it is fairly certain that failure to supply this amount regularly and for a prolonged period of time was bound to bring the efficiency of oarsmen to an undesirably low level or, even worse, to invite the catastrophic effects of malnutrition and starvation. This was one of the two evils to be avoided by the trierarch; desertion was the other.

Indeed, it would be a serious error to view expenditure on crews as simply a matter of keeping them above the level of starvation. Every trierarch's concern was to get hold of a good complement and to retain it until the strategos authorized its dismissal. Apollodoros's large bonuses and advance payments ([Dem.] 50) have been looked on by his fellow trierarchs and modern scholars as untypically lavish. In some measure this is true. But his outlays made to obtain outstanding oarsmen and hyperesia were motivated by two sound considerations: to secure the performance of his ship, especially to enhance its tactical capabilities in combat; and to ensure that the ship was brought back to Piraeus (or delivered to a successor) in good, seaworthy condition.[41] Hence outlays on crews were really an investment that could save the trierarch from further expenditure arising from compensatory claims.

To have a model crew headed by an outstanding helmsman, even though costly, presented clear advantages. The speaker of Lysias 21 says that after the battle at Aigospotamoi (405) he not only managed to bring home his own ship but also to rescue another (10). All this, he explains, was because of careful preparation; he could afford to hire Phantias, the best helmsman in Greece, as well as oarsmen and a hyperesia to match his professional abilities. Esteemed helmsmen were in high demand,[42] and to induce them to come aboard, trierarchs had to offer pay at much higher rates than those given to other crew members. When a dispute arose between Apollodoros and the aide-de-camp of his strategos over the issue of whether to transport an Athenian exile on Apollodoros's ship, the helmsman Poseidippos chose to obey the orders of his trierarch, reasoning that it was the trierarch from whom he received his pay ([Dem.] 50.48–50). The uniformity in the rates of pay given to a crew, which is frequently assumed for reasons of convenience, is based on a simplified notion not always reflecting reality. Good hyperesiai may have required higher pay than that offered by the state.

Because of the greater technical and physical demands to be met by the upper-level oarsmen, "the *thranites* folk, the saviors of our city" (Ar. *Ach.* 161–62), trierarchs could offer extra pay to them. This was done in the expedition to Sicily in 415 (Thuc. 6.31.3), which need not be an isolated instance. Competition among trierarchs to get hold of skilled oarsmen and hyperesiai would have been common, and the quality of crews determined the amount of extra pay. The expression "fully paid oarsmen" ([Dem.] 50.18: *nautas entelomisthous*) probably refers to professional experts who demanded to be recompensed fully and promptly for their services. The speaker of [Demosthenes] 51 says that he hired the best hyperesia that could be had by giving by far the highest payments (6). Another man (Isoc. 18.60) boasts about the efficiency of his ship by saying: "after persuading my brother to be syntrierarch with me, we gave pay [misthos] to the oarsmen out of our own means and proceeded to harass the enemy."

Thus Apollodoros's bonuses and advance payments were not highly unusual; some, if not all, of his colleagues may have done the same, though on a smaller scale.[43] The unusual thing about him was that he succeeded in making his ship the fastest in the squadron so it would be used on special missions (which earned him the honor of a meal in the *prytaneion,* [Dem.] 50.13) and be chosen by the strategos as his flagship.

Desertion turns out to have been a serious and constant problem in the fifth and fourth centuries. Some causes were lack of pay, inadequate pay, and the offer, by a different employer, of higher rates of pay—a tactic effectively used to paralyze an enemy fleet.[44] As a countermeasure, as noted above, part of the pay supplied by the state was frequently withheld until disembarkation. In such cases the trierarch was compelled to meet his crew's demand for full pay out of his own means. While foreign oarsmen were certainly those most likely to defect, Athenian citizens and metics might stay with their ships as long as they served in some distant field of operations ([Dem.] 49.15). But even these groups could disperse when the ships put into Piraeus; alternatively, they could refuse to re-embark unless they were given more pay ([Dem.] 50.11).

Thucydides (8.57.1) describes the anxiety of Tissaphernes that the Peloponnesian crews would defect if they were not maintained; later (8.78.1) he notes the unrest among the Peloponnesian crews at Miletos, because Tissaphernes was not providing maintenance regularly or in full. Finally, the crews, only half-fed, broke out in open mutiny: "they had never yet received their pay in full [misthon entele], but what was given was short and even that not paid regularly. And they decided that unless they . . . could get subsistence [trophe], the crews would desert the ships" (8.83.1–3).

Nikias gives the reasons why his crews in Sicily deteriorated in numbers (414): the slaves (*therapontes*) deserted; of the foreign oarsmen (*xenoi*),[45] those who had been forced to embark on the ships deserted to their respective home cities, while those who had initially been drawn to service by the attraction of higher pay and thought they were going to make money rather than fight either went over as professed deserters or got away as best they could; and some oarsmen persuaded the trierarchs to take as substitutes for themselves the enslaved inhabitants of Hykkara (Thuc. 7.13.1–2).

A passage from *Hellenica Oxyrhynchia* (15.1) reports an incident (395) when Konon was seeking Persian financial support for his ships at Kaunos (cf. 14.1–2). Some Cypriots among Konon's crews were told that the Persian officers sent by Tithraustes with 220 talents to pay the troops were not going to give the pay that was owing to the Cypriot oarsmen, but only to the hyperesiai and epibatai. The Cypriot oarsmen broke out in mutiny. In 388, the oarsmen of Eteonikos, the Spartan harmost at Aigina, refused to row because he had refused to give them pay (misthos).[46] Oarsmen from Apollodoros's crew defected on three occasions ([Dem.] 50.11–12, 14–16, 23), while in one instance they refused to re-embark unless they were given additional pay (11).

This list of examples is not exhaustive, but it may give a fairly good idea of the size of the problem. It appears, then, that the practical advantages to be gained by the acquisition of a highly paid and outstanding complement were constantly threatened by the possibility that these skilled professionals could defect if they did not receive what was due to them, or if someone else offered them higher rates of pay. As Apollodoros put it, the better the oarsmen, the higher the rate of desertion:

For the more ambitious I had been to man my ship with good rowers, by so much was the desertion from me greater than from the other trierarchs. For the others had this advantage at any rate, that the oarsmen who had come to their ships drawn from the deme-lists, stayed with them in order to make sure of their return home when the strategos should discharge them; whereas mine, trusting in their skill as able rowers, went off wherever they were likely to be re-employed at the highest wages. ([Dem.] 50.15–16)

The trierarch's job as employer of a complement of two hundred was not an easy one.

Much of what has been said above serves to challenge the view (e.g., GSW 2:102), that in the fourth century men accepted military service with the knowledge that no money was in the hands of their officers and that pay must come from booty. A fiscal infrastructure guaranteed by the trierarch effectively prevented the maintenance of crews from being a hand-to-mouth business. Economic support on a large scale and on the spot was absolutely necessary, not only for keeping a sizable complement adequately fed but also for the equally crucial quick employment of manpower reserves.

How much a trierarch would spend on his crew, I have argued, was dictated by the ability or willingness of the state fully to subsidize naval operations, the ability of the strategoi to raise funds, and the need to ensure the tactical capabilities and safety of his ship by obtaining and keeping a skilled complement. If one drachma was the average daily pay expected by and often given to crews, as seems likely, then the sum of thirty minas or one talent per journey received by trierarchs would only cover advance payments for half a month and one month, respectively.[47] Any cost beyond that was shouldered by the trierarch himself.

Although Apollodoros's total expenditure is nowhere stated in [Demosthenes] 50, something can be gained from the list of loans he was compelled to raise totaling well in excess of 5,300 drachmas: (1) hypothecation of his property in order to hire crews in Piraeus; (2) hypothecation of land for the amount of 3,000 drachmas; (3) a loan of 1,500 drachmas with interest; (4) a maritime loan of 800 drachmas; (5) another loan from Pasion's friends at Sestos; (6) an unspecified loan after his crossing from Thasos to Stryme; and (7) a loan from Pasion's friends at Tenedos. Of these, (2) through (7) were raised for the purpose of giving bonuses and advance payments to his newly hired oarsmen and of paying additional sums to the old ones.[48]

It is relevant to mention such other expenditures as are attested in the sources. One Aristophanes spent 8,000 drachmas in three consecutive years, which comes to an annual average of 2,666 drachmas (Lysias 19.29, 42). Diogeiton's syntrierarchy (at the end of the Peloponnesian War) had cost 4,800 drachmas, in other words, 2,400 drachmas per trierarch (Lysias 32.26). Another man says (Lysias 21.2) that he was trierarch for seven years (between 411 and 404) and had spent six talents, an annual average of 5,142 drachmas. (Amounts paid for trierarchies contracted to a substitute are excluded here.) The exact length of actual service in each case is not known. Given that such information strictly relates to what had been paid by the trierarchs themselves, these amounts, in spite of their upward bias, represent substantial outlays.

However, it is more consistent with the evidence to allow for great individual variations in the size of trierarchic expenditure, especially when a constant feature of naval finances was the host of imponderabilia to be encountered each time a fleet was commissioned. And this seems to have necessitated the presence, aboard every ship, of a man who could promptly meet any extra costs that arose. There is basically no difference between the fifth and the fourth centuries in this respect. An important difference, however, was that increasing privatization of naval finances in the fourth century (a consequence of the loss of imperial revenue) entailed a boost in the flow of private cash. True, the burdens borne by the trierarch became in some measure alleviated by the introduction of the syntrierarchy and by subsequent reforms (see chapter 8). By the mid-fourth century, some men could manage to come through their obligation with outlays that were trifling compared to what was expended by others. Yet reckoned by whole trierarchies (or "units"), private expenditure in, say, the 350s must have taken up a larger share of the total cost of campaigns than it had a hundred years earlier. Pay and provisioning constituted one part of that expenditure. The maintenance of the ship constituted the other.

# The Ship

Maintenance of naval matériel entailed huge costs. Generally, the construction of new ships and the proper upkeep of existing ones was to a fairly large degree the responsibility of the state. However, a significant part of that responsibility was in practice allocated to the trierarchs. To what extent and under what circumstances this was done are the main questions I will explore in the sections to follow. In so doing I will use as my vantage point the overall naval strength of Athens in terms of hulls and equipment.

## The Hulls

A rough but useful indication of the amount of resources required for maintenance is provided by figures relating to the size of the fleet. At the height of its strength in the fifth century the Athenian fleet numbered a little over 300 ships. At the start of the Peloponnesian War there were 300 seaworthy triereis (Thuc. 2.13.8; Diod. 12.40.4). The establishment, in 431/0, of an annual reserve of 100 "select" triereis (Thuc. 2.24.2) was probably from the existing 300 seaworthy ships, not in addition to it, which would have made a total of 400.[1] Aristophanes (*Ach.* 545) speaks as if it were possible to launch 300 ships at one time, but such an effort, if ever attempted, would have been exceptional. The largest detachments known to have been in commission simultaneously are 180 (plus 20 manned by the Chalkidians) at Artemision and Salamis; 160 at the end of the Samian revolt (440/39); more than 130 in the summer of 431/0; 250 in the summer of 428; more than 218 in the spring of 413; 110 at Arginousai (406); and more than 140 at Aigospotamoi. All these figures relate to triereis; one hears little of pentekontors and triakontors during this period (IG I³.18.15–16).

For the fourth century, the evidence admits of no certain quantitative statements before the year of the first extant naval record (IG 2².1604). Modern estimates suggest that by mid-387 Athens possessed no more than 50 to 70 triereis.[2] In the context of 388, Xenophon makes the general statement that the Athenians possessed many ships (Hell. 5.1.19). Polybios (2.62.6) speaks of the manning of 100 ships in 378/7—probably the joint force of the Athenians and the Thebans. From 378/7 onward the ground is relatively firmer, as the naval records purport to furnish the total number of ships in individual years with occasional specification of the number of ships at sea and in the dockyards by the end of the year.

The total for the year 378/7 (about 100) is obtained by a count of ship entries that are attested or restored in the record for that year (IG 2².1604). The figures for subsequent years derive from special rubrics known as the sum-total (arithmos) formulas:[3] 283 ships in 357/6; 349 in 353/2; 410 (of which 18 were tetrereis) in 330/29; probably just as many in 326/5 (of which perhaps 50 were tetrereis); 417 (of which 50 were tetrereis and 7 penteteis) in 325/4; and perhaps 365 (certainly 315 triereis and possibly 50 tetrereis) in 323/2.[4] Commentary on the arithmos formulas is essential to an understanding of the nature of the information they provide, since they have hitherto been taken to give, in terms of hulls, the *net* potential of the Athenian navy. This is not always the case.

The formula of 353/2 gives the total of 349 triereis. However, since that total includes 7 ships damaged by storms,[5] 349 is a paper figure; the actual number would be 342 ships. The record of 330/29 reports the total number of triereis in the dockyards and at sea to be 392; then it specifies that of these 52 were at sea, while 3 horse transports had become useless in combat (1627.271–74). It appears then that ships no longer usable were again included in the formula. In addition, while the same document elsewhere lists the receipt and delivery by the dockyard officials of equipment belonging to 9 triakontors (ll. 17–21), these hulls are absent from the arithmos formula; five years later, it will be seen below, some of these triakontors were in commission. Finally, also absent from the formula are some smaller, lighter vessels (*akatoi*, ll. 371–73).

The record of 326/5 (1628) mentions 32 triereis at sea. However, the remaining 328, supposedly in the dockyards, turn out again to be on paper only, for their number includes the following: the 3 useless horse transports also mentioned in the record of 330/29; a number of ships lost in storms, the trierarchs of which had compensated for the losses by cash payments to the *apodektai* (Athenian financial officials) of 328/7;[6] and further ships lost in storms, the trierarchs of which had been ordered by the boule of 326/5 to pay double the cost of losses (1628.484–88, 369ff.). Finally, equipment for 9 triakontors is mentioned (ll. 207–12), but the hulls themselves are absent from the arithmos formula.

Similar problems are observable in the record of 325/4 (1629), giving 32 triereis at sea. The remaining 328 ships include: hulls lost in previous years and compensated for by trierarchs through direct payments to the epimeletai of 325/4 (noted as *eispraxis*), or to the apodektai of the same year, or to officials of a previous year (noted as *apolabē*: 1629.786–88, cf. 475ff.); further ships lost in storms (ll. 788–96); 6 triereis and 1 tetreres lost in storms, the trierarchs of which ships were exonerated from financial responsibility (ll. 796–99; cf. 746ff.); a number of ships given to the Chalkidians as early as 341/0 (ll. 516–43, 799f.; cf. 1623.160ff.); and the 3 horse transports already reported as lost in action (ll. 804–7; cf. 722–29). The last peculiarity to be noted is that no triakontors are recorded in the arithmos formula, even though such ships were in use: the epimeletai of 325/4 noted the receipt of equipment for 9 triakontors and the delivery, at the end of their tenure, of equipment for 5 triakontors (1629.330–35). This is consistent with 4 triakontors (the balance) having been commissioned for the expedition to the Adriatic in that year (ll. 91ff.). Similarly, a triakontor and a penteres, probably active in 323/2 (1631.6–7, 35), are absent from the total for that year (ll. 167–74).

Therefore the totals given by the epimeletai in the arithmos formulas are not net figures of the effective force, but gross totals for bookkeeping purposes, encompassing hulls no longer usable; such vessels are included merely by virtue of having been involved in various legal proceedings. At the same time—and this is an inexplicable peculiarity in the accounting method of the dockyard officials—the formulas seem to be little concerned with certain types of smaller vessels, especially the triakontors, which are not counted among the ships in stock.[7] But having made these qualifications, it is reasonable to infer that the difference between gross and net totals may not have been a substantial one, and that from the early 350s to 323/2 the net number of serviceable hulls was considerably greater than 250 and perhaps not much less than 380.[8] On the whole, and with the exception of the three decades following the defeat of 404, the naval strength of Athens remained remarkably stable.

## The Condition of Hulls

So much for attempting to gain some idea about the resources needed for maintenance by way of determining the number of hulls. What about their seaworthiness? Some suggestions can be made on the basis of the formal descriptions used in the naval records. The epimeletai classified all hulls by rating them in accordance with their age and performance abilities.[9] In this they were assisted by a main register listing ships in a fixed order (part of it is indirectly preserved in *IG* 2².1611.65–134: ships stationed in the harbor of Zea). The manner in which these ratings are described in the records from the 370s and 360s (1604–10) differs from that used in the period after 357/6.[10]

In the pre-357 period, some hulls are classed as "new" (kaine) or "old" (palaia), while others bear neither of these descriptions. Two things should be noted. First, as has been shown (Sinclair [1978] 50–51), "new" (kaine) describes hulls judged to be "as good as new" rather than hulls "built in the past year": for example, *Inscriptiones Graecae* 2².1623.286–89 and 294–99 (of 334/3) list as "new" the triereis *Iousa Archeneo* and *Delphis Epigenous,* which had been constructed in 336/5 and 337/6, respectively. Second, the absence of these terms aims at distinguishing a class of its own.[11] A comparison between 1607.74–96 (of 373/2) and 1611, col. b, from sixteen years later (357/6), reveals that almost all (ten) of the ships mentioned in the first document reappear in the second in nearly the same order, which permits a guarded identification.[12] Since two ships, *Nike* and *Demokratia,* listed as "old" in 373/2 reappear among the rating "second" (deuterai) from Zea in 357/6, it may be deduced that the two ratings are similar. If so, the "new" (kainai), in the early records, would be equivalent to "select" (exairetoi) in the records of the post-357 period, while ships without any description could be an intermediate rating equivalent to the "first" (prōtai) of the post 357-period.

By 357/6, new rating descriptions were introduced. *Inscriptiones Grae-*

*cae* $2^2$.1611 shows that to each harbor were allocated a number of "first" (protai), "second" (deuterai), "third" (*tritai*), and "select" (exairetoi) ships—the latter being especially light, fast-sailing vessels. The date of construction of some "select" ships goes back to 363/2 (1611.106–10). Still, it is not possible to say whether this was also the year in which that rating was officially (re)introduced. In 354, Demosthenes (14.18) mentioned all the ratings except the "select," but his silence is inconclusive.

The ships from Zea in 357/6, for which the record is more fully preserved, numbered 46 "seconds" (or 16 percent of the "national" gross total: 283), more than 37 "select" (or about 14 percent of that total), but only 8 "thirds."[13] Unfortunately, the number of ships rated "first" is not ascertainable. At any rate, these figures are fairly significant, for Zea was the largest and most important naval base. Further information relates to the smallest of the three harbors, Mounichia. Here, in 353/2, there were 12 triereis of the rating "first," 17 "second," and 7 "third" (36 ships in all: 1613.41–43, 60–71). No "select" triereis from Mounichia are attested, but this must be because they were listed separately, in a different part of the record that is now lost.

Although quantitative analysis is hampered by the lack of figures covering all three harbors during a longer span of time, the numerical preponderance of the ships rated "second," in the post-357 records, and of their presumed equivalent, the "old" of the earlier records (about 30 are identifiable in 1604), is quite distinct and hardly fortuitous. It is true that most "old" are also unallotted to a trierarch in a given year: 29 out of the 30 "old" attested in 378/7 (1604). However, this does not mean that hulls of that rating were scrapped as useless (also, ships of the rating "new" are unallotted; for example, 1604.65: *Galateia*). Rather, their overrepresentation should be seen as a result partly of their numerical superiority and partly of the application of the lot during the annual allocation of ships to trierarchs.

In conclusion, it is possible to say that, although "select" and "first" were likely the ships used in special missions because of their outstanding performance in speed and maneuverability, the bulk of the Athenian hulls from the 370s onward consisted of adequately seaworthy "seconds," amply serviceable for most purposes. If one takes the figures for 357/6 as a general guide and makes the reasonable guess that the number of "select" from all three harbors was no less than 60 (Zea alone had more than 37), then slightly over 20 percent of the gross total force (and even a higher percentage of the net total force) was made up of vessels of exceptional ability. The least-able hulls, the "thirds," are also quantitatively insignificant: 8 in Zea (or 3 percent of the 357/6 total) and 7 in Mounichia (or 2 percent of the 353/2 total).

The 340s, 330s, and 320s saw an unprecedented boost in the total number of ships, which, in spite of the difficulty of pinpointing the actual figures, is nonetheless strongly corroborated by the increase in the number of ship-sheds: the total of 372 ship-sheds attested from 330/29 on would be indicative, if not of real strength, then certainly of long-term naval aims. Mounichia, the smallest harbor, with probably no more than 50 ships in 353/2, was now made to accommodate 82 ships, while the largest harbor, Zea, was expanded to take 196 ships.[14] The bleak times of the end of the fifth and beginning of the fourth centuries had long vanished. Already in the early 350s Athenian naval potential had expanded considerably, quickly reaching and surpassing its fifth-century standard. On a practical level, the working of such a labor-intensive machinery on land and at sea sparked a new and greater pressure for human and material resources. On the institutional level, it made highly urgent the broadening and refinement of the fiscal system sustaining that machinery. In the latter area, the year 358/7 was a turning point.

For most of the fourth century (as in the fifth) Athens was not short of seaworthy and properly maintained hulls. "From the place where the fair *triereis* come," responded an Athenian, when asked about his place of origin (Ar. *Av.* 108). Renewing and repairing this force was a matter attended to with great care and efficacy.

## Shipbuilding

The fleet's size was frequently maintained or enlarged by the capture of enemy ships,[15] more rarely by donations from friendly states, and mainly by Athenian shipbuilding projects. New ships were built either by launching extensive programs or by the annually recurring, small-scale shipbuilding at Athens and perhaps also in foreign, or (as Unz [1985] 36 argues for the fifth century) in allied, shipyards. Discussion of each of these topics seems in order here.

The paucity of evidence about Athens's shipbuilding projects after 482–480 is indeed striking. Such sources as do exist shed frustratingly little light on what I would like to know most about: the number of ships, the cost and mode of financing of such enterprises, the supply of materials and labor, the place of construction, and so forth. Moreover, the evidence traditionally adduced in support of certain large programs is now questionable. An extraordinarily large program has been inferred for circa 444/3, because in the Parthenon building accounts of that year (*IG* I².342.40–41) the *trieropoioi* (members of a subcommittee of the boule) are seen to pay back ninety thousand drachmas (restored); this, it is believed (Blackman [1969] 208), was the surplus of a sum allotted to them to finance the enterprise. But in the latest edition of this document (*IG* I³.493.77) the amount is left unrestored, and the name of the board of officials is uncertain.

Again, the accounts of the treasurers of Athena (for 431/0) were previously supplemented (*SEG* 10.226.11–15) to include two payments to the trieropoioi, "one certainly and one probably of 50 talents."[16] Andocides (3.6–7) reports the construction of 100 triereis "during the thirty years of peace after the war because of Aigina" that were to be set aside as a reserve. Also, the *Anonymus Argentinensis* (l. 10) is reconstructed to mention the building of 100 ships in 331/0. Blackman ([1969] 208, 211–12), correcting Andocides' phrase "the war because of Aigina" to refer to the first Peloponnesian War, combined all three sources in order to argue for another large shipbuilding program in 431/0. There are difficulties, however. First, Thucydides (2.24.2) mentions the establishment of a reserve of 100 ships, but not shipbuilding. Second, the accounts of the treasurers have been revised to contain only one, very obscure reference to the trieropoioi (*IG* I³.366.13). Third, the reading and date of *Anonymus Argentinensis* (l. 10) remain controversial.

Finally, Andocides' account has been questioned.[17] Elsewhere (3.3–5), he states that in the period of peace arranged by Miltiades, after the war in Euboia, the Athenians built 100 triereis. Blackman ([1969] 210–12) accepts the facts as being correct but presented in the wrong historical perspective, and infers yet another crash shipbuilding program in 451/0, or 450/49, necessitated by the losses in Egypt of at least 250 ships. While that possibility cannot be ruled out, harder evidence is still needed.[18]

It seems reasonable to assume the occurrence of intensive shipbuilding in the years after the loss of the fleet at Syracuse (Thuc. 7.74–75). However, the only record is of the Athenians' plans to procure ship-timber and money from whatever source they could (8.1.3). The fleet at Samos in 411 numbered 108 ships (including a reinforcement of 26 ships that came from the Hellespont),[19] and as late as 406 only small detachments were sent out. But in the summer of that year 110 triereis were dispatched from Piraeus to aid the main force blockaded in Mytilene only thirty days after the news reached Athens (Xen. *Hell.* 1.6.24). Part of this fleet might have been the result of a building program, provided the latter is reflected in a heavily restored decree of 407 honoring the Macedonian king Archelaos, probably in return for his permission to Athenian shipwrights to build ships with Macedonian timber and in Macedon (*IG* 1³.117; ML no. 91, 279–80).

For the fourth century the evidence hardly improves. A convenient starting point to gauge shipbuilding activity is the surrender of all but twelve ships after the defeat of Athens by Sparta in 404 (Xen. *Hell.* 2.2.20). But Xenophon's general statement (5.4.34) referring to 378/7, "the Athenians furnished Piraeus with gates and set about building ships," is the first and only secure indication of such activity. Attempts made so far to estimate the number of ships built in the years 379/8–377/6 by using the naval record *Inscriptiones Graecae* 2².1604 rely too heavily on hypothetical reasoning to inspire confidence.[20] Dinarchos (1.96; cf. *IG* 2².1627.353–54) speaks of triereis constructed by Euboulos (355–51). But here again, no clues to the nature and extent of the enterprise remain. Finally, Diodoros's report (18.10.2) of a decision in 323/2 to prepare (*paraskeuasai*) forty tetrereis and two hundred triereis cannot, as was suggested by Morrison ([1987] 89–90), mean initiation of an extensive shipbuilding program; why should the Athenians have wanted to add 240 new ships to the 365 they already possessed?

The foregoing review illustrates the dearth of evidence on an important topic. By contrast, more information exists about the organization of regular, annually recurring shipbuilding in the fourth century. Construction was carried out (though perhaps not exclusively) in the Telegoneia shipyards (*IG* 2².1611.132–33) with the professional expertise of naval architects elected by the assembly. A substantial labor force, including shipwrights and other skilled persons (joiners, fitters, makers of rope and sailcloth, and so forth) as well as unskilled personnel, was no doubt permanently employed to perform the practical work for which the trieropoioi had direct financial and administrative responsibility.[21] Finally, the overall supervision of the annual ship construction lay with the boule. A remark (Aesch. 3.30) that the tribes could be required to build triereis is puzzling and perhaps untrustworthy (Kolbe *Re navali* 23).

Occasionally, the assembly decided on technical matters (*IG* i³.153), and regularly determined the condition of hulls, or authorized the delivery of naval matériel.[22] At times, for instance in 347/6, assemblies were held in the Piraeus to deliberate urgent naval matters (Dem. 19.60). But on the whole, the direct involvement of the assembly seldom extended beyond the provision of funds (presumably by a special vote for each consignment of ships in the fifth century, and by an allocation in the annual *merismos* [the distribution of state revenues among the boards of officials] in the fourth century),[23] the types of ships to be constructed, and probably also their number. The last point is controversial, for many scholars endorse the view that there was a fixed annual quota of ships to be built, which quota may well have varied over time. The evidence and arguments that have been put forward in support of this need to be examined more closely.

The *Athenaion Politeia* (46.1) describes one of the boule's tasks as follows: "The Council also inspects the triereis that have been built as well as their rigging and the ship-sheds, and constructs new [*kainas* [*de*]] triereis or tetrereis, whichever [*hopoteras*] the demos votes for." Even though the emendation, by some editors, of the corrupt [*de*] to produce a numeral ("four": Keil [1902] 209–10, or "ten": Wilcken [1907] 399) is now generally rejected, it is still maintained (Blackman [1969] 204 n. 74) that the number of ships to be built annually was fixed beforehand, so that the decision of the assembly concerned only the type of new ships, triereis or tetrereis. However, this passage cannot be made to furnish a figure without violating the text, and the records of the 320s show that both types of craft were built in a year.

Demosthenes 22 (with hyp. 1, 2.8) is an attack on Androtion's proposal to the effect that the boule of which Androtion was a member (359/8 or 356/5) should receive the customary crown, even though at its retirement it had not built the required number of ships. Section 8 reads: "Coming now to the law which explicitly denies to the Council the right to ask a reward, if they have not built the triereis, it is worth while to hear the defence that he will set up . . . The law, he says, prohibits the Council to ask for the reward, if they have not built the triereis." The use of the definite article ("*the* triereis"), it is argued (Blackman [1969] 204), implies that there was a fixed number of ships; but this is an extreme interpretation. No more helpful is the *Anonymus Argentinensis* (ll. 9–11), which is restored to include a decision of the boule, or an order to the boule, to build an annual quota of ten triereis:[24] "[In order that power at sea is maintained] by them, the boule [shall care for] the old triereis [so that they are delivered in good condition.] The boule shall also see to it that, [in addition to the existing ones, ten] new ships are built [every year]"— from the text of Wade-Gery and Meritt ([1957] 164). A serious objection, however, is that the length of line 11 remains unknown, which does not allow safe restorations, and the word interpreted as "ten" is uncertain (Rhodes AB 115–16).

Diodoros (11.43.3) makes Themistokles responsible for the annual building of twenty ships after 480: "And Themistokles persuaded the people each year to construct and add twenty triereis to the fleet they already possessed." From this it is inferred that the annual rate of twenty ships may have remained standard for some years after 477/6, and then been reduced to ten ships.[25] Others (Jordan AN 21–22) contend that the rate of twenty ships continued through the whole of the fifth century. But Rhodes's warning (AB 115) against the reliability of Diodoros's account (perhaps unjustifiably expanding Hdt. 7.144) ought to be taken seriously.

A subsidiary argument rests on estimates of the average length of a trieres' "natural" life; this being ascertained, it is possible to calculate the number of new ships needed annually in order to maintain a fleet force of a certain size.[26] Apart from the objection that this approach leaves no room for such an alternative (and often substantial) source of supply as the capture of enemy ships, it needs to be stressed that no absolutely secure means are at hand with which to trace the careers of ships over the years: the simultaneous existence of homonyms, even of the same rating and harbor (1611.81–82: Nike), is a major obstacle. It is no less difficult to determine whether there was an annual rate of tetrereis, even though the records make it possible to trace their first appearance and increase within a fairly narrow span of time.[27]

So the foundation on which the annual quota view rests turns out to be precarious. Moreover, it is at odds with two observations: eleven "select" ships had been projected to be built in 358/7, of which all but one (the half-finished Boetheia Archeneidou) were delivered completed in the next year (1611.119–33); also, at least nineteen "select" ships had been built in 353/2 (1613.257–67). One can doubt whether only "select" ships were built on these occasions. It seems better to believe that the number of ships to be built in a year was decided by the assembly with due consideration to recent losses or gains and in accordance with current needs and aims and the availability of resources.

## The Replacement of Hulls by Trierarchs

Maintenance of the fleet by the replacement of ships that had been lost and the repair of those that had been damaged led to immense demands for funds and materials. In this area, too, financial responsibility was divided between the state and the trierarchs. Throughout the period, the state was obliged to supply the hulls and equipment, though trierarchs possessing their own equipment might abstain from drawing any from the public. Upon receiving a hull and equipment from the dockyards, a man was listed in a register (diagramma) kept by the epimeletai. A decree of 405/4 granting the Samians permission to use the Athenian triereis at Samos refers to documents where "the trierarchs are publicly registered [as debtors] on account of having received the triereis."[28] No such registers have survived, but the naval records, which drew information from these registers, make it certain that they noted the ship (its name, rating, and naval architect, all for identification purposes), the items of equipment issued, and not least the monetary value of both hull and equipment (the sums to be paid in the event compensation was claimed by the state).

The last item was important, for by being charged with the cost of naval matériel the trierarch became technically (but not yet legally) a public debtor; as noted on p. 83, it is not always possible to distinguish between the expressions "they are in possession of" (echousi) and "they owe" (opheilousi), in literary sources or official documents. A likely reference to the diagramma, in that sense, is made in the division between two cotrierarchs of responsibility to compensate for a hull: one had to pay five-sixths, the other one-sixth "of the amount stated in the diagramma."[29] The handing over of matériel to trierarchs was completed with the delivery to them of a copy from the register, showing the items each had received ([Dem.] 47.36, 43).

From then on, a ship commander had to keep his ship in good condition. Frequent replacement of broken or lost equipment can be assumed without resort to special pleading. Pieces of broken hypozomata lying in the dockyards (1610.26–27) had no doubt been returned by retiring trierarchs; new ones had to be procured from a foreign port, often at high cost. Given the vital importance of oars, it is understandable that thirty spares (*perineō*) should as a rule have been carried on board. But these are the only extra items known to have been regularly issued by the dockyard authorities; any other spare equipment to be used in emergencies would have to be supplied by the trierarch himself.

For current maintenance and repair of the hull he had to buy timber and various other sorts of materials. Flux (*styppeion*), pitch (*pissa*) for caulking, and a special paint (*hypaloiphē*) for coating the vessel's wetted surface were provided in some quantity from the dockyards.[30] But since this was an operation carried out frequently, a considerable amount of such materials, like almost everything else, would be purchased by the trierarch from foreign markets. In the Delian accounts, purchases of pitch amount to about fifteen to twenty-two drachmas per amphora;[31] the amount needed for a single hull would have added up to quite a number of amphoras. In the event of urgent and extensive repair work, the trierarch needed to employ extra hands to assist his own shipwright. One may suppose that these requirements were relatively greater with hulls of the lower ratings, which is true as far as damage caused by age-fatigue is concerned. But ships of all ratings definitely required, and probably received, about the same high standard of maintenance in order to withstand the wear and tear of voyages and combat. (For the forces imposed on tenons when the hull is subjected to bending and shearing actions, see Coates, Platis, and Shaw [1990] 3.) While it is possible only to delineate the trierarch's responsibilities in this area, more is known of his commitments after the termination of his active duty, when he was asked to surrender his hull and equipment.

Regardless of whether he did so to his successor (if still in commission) or to the dockyard officials, he was expected to present his ship in good, seaworthy condition. A provision for accountability seems incorporated in the Naval Law (*IG* I³.236.1–3 and Oliver [1935] no. 1, re-inscribed circa 410–404), and is confirmed by Aeschines (3.19, of 330). For that purpose, the ship was inspected by the epimeletai in collaboration with a "tester" (*dokimastēs:* 1604.56; 1612.220), whose findings—classing hulls and equipment as (*a*)*dokimos,* (*a*)*dokima*—were reported to the boule, plausibly through the trieropoioi (*Ath. Pol.* 46.1). Damages or losses raised the issue of compensation.

In the fourth century (and probably also in the fifth), two different procedures were followed for deciding who should be liable for compensation, both based on official recognition of two distinct causes (though how these latter were defined is unclear). If damage was caused by enemy action, the trierarch was presumably absolved from further financial responsibility. Ultimately, determination of the hull's condition as well as the cause of damage or loss (*kata polemon*) rested with the assembly and was formally ratified by decree. The record of 330/29 lists three horse transports judged as useless through this procedure;[32] all three had been brought back to Piraeus. Since their trierarchs were not asked to pay compensation, they were probably exonerated. However, there is a fair amount of uncertainty about this procedure, for the cases just mentioned (and this is puzzling) are the only ones attested in the records.

More information exists about the second procedure. If damage or loss was caused by storms, the trierarch had his claim treated at a hearing in a law court (diadikasia), where he excused (skepsis) the condition of his hull and equipment with the occurrence of storms (*kata cheimōna*). If he was successful in convincing the jurors that his own negligence had no part in it, he was exonerated: "The following triereis and tetrereis that have been adjudicated for storms were found by a court to have been damaged by/lost in storms" (*IG* $2^2$.1629.746–49, 796–99). Another entry from the record of 325/4 shows that a pair of syntrierarchs who had brought a skepsis were absolved of any responsibility: "Trieres Hegemone, the work of Nausinikos. Trierarch(s): Euthydikos Antiphanous Phegaieus, Diphilos Diopeithous Sounieus. These were succeeded on the ship by Phanostratos Archestratou Gargettios and Ameinias Sokleous Hagnousios who, having brought a skepsis, were acquitted" (1629.771–80).

If, on the other hand, a trierarch was unsuccessful, the jurors made him directly responsible for the replacement or repair of the hull and its equipment. In case he was found liable to replace the ship, he had in addition to demolish the old hull: "Euxenippos Ethelokratous Lamptreus acknowledged his responsibility in court to furnish a new ship to the state and to demolish the old one" (1623.6–13). However, liability for paying compensation did not follow automatically; acceptance of it received legal validation only by the trierarch's personal consent. This was essential in order to avoid legal complications, especially in case the ship thus adjudicated had been in commission under several successive trierarchs.

The juridical fastidiousness of the situation is disclosed by a long and meticulously arranged entry of 1623.14–34. The epimeletai put on record that the trieres *Hippagogos Lysistratou* had been directly transferred three times while at sea. The first to take charge was Aristeides Kephisieus and syntrierarchs; these were succeeded by Lysikles Athmoneus and syntrierarchs who, in turn, surrendered the ship to their successor, Phaiax Acharneus. In spite of preexisting official knowledge that Phaiax was the last one to command the ship, it was nonetheless deemed necessary to involve (and inscribe) all of the trierarchs in the proceedings.

Eventually, Phaiax's acknowledgment in court of his takeover and of his financial responsibility marked the settlement of this case, presumably to the great satisfaction of the remaining individuals; otherwise he would have been entitled, through diadikasiai, to attempt to transfer this liability to any one of his predecessors, to his partners (e.g., 1631.524–30), or even to the whole board of the epimeletai (e.g., 1620.32–55). The effective use of diadikasiai as a means by which to render the trierarchic class a self-controlled unit with its members policing one another has been seen at work with the antidosis, and will receive more attention below.

Finally, each trierarch whose ship had been adjudicated in a skepsis concerning storms, whether convicted or acquitted, was obliged to return the ship's ram to the dockyards, provided, of course, that the ship had been brought back to Piraeus.[33]

## The Cost of a Hull

What did liability to replace a ship mean in economic terms? I shall begin with the hull and return to equipment in the next chapter. Although it is recognized that trierarchs asked to compensate for a hull, in the fourth century, had to pay a lump sum of five thousand drachmas, most scholars maintain that a hull's real cost was higher than that. The current belief still rests on Boeckh's computations that throughout the classical period the hull cost one talent and its equipment a further talent.[34] Thus the attested payments of only five thousand drachmas are explained by assuming that their purpose was either to repair or rebuild the old hull (*Urkunden* 220–23), or to cover part of the cost of a new one.[35] Neither these assumptions nor Boeckh's computations can stand any longer.[36]

First, the notion must be discarded that all ships were built at the same cost at all times. A preeminent factor was access to the sources of supply of vital materials: papyrus, hemp, and flax for cordage; ruddle and resin (i.e., hypaloiphe) for coating the hull; copper and tin for the casting of rams (Murray [1985]); last, but not least, timber. Most of these materials could not be produced from the Attic territory in either the quantity or the quality required (Dem. 17.28).[37] Hanging equipment, sails, and papyrus for ropes came mainly from Egypt (Hermippos fr. 63; *FAC,* apud Athen. 1.27E–F; Theophr. *Hist. Pl.* 4.8.4). In a year before 350, Athens secured the monopoly of ruddle from the Kean cities, Karthaia, Koresos, and Ioulis, perhaps after a short interruption in the late 360s. Of the decrees pertaining to each city (Tod no. 162), that of Koresos prohibits the export of ruddle except on ships authorized by the Athenians, and fixes the transport cost at one obol per talent. Aristophanes (*Ran.* 364) mentions the ban on the export of pitch, leather bags (askomata), and sailcloth, perhaps a permanent measure rather than one merely applying to a short period of crisis.

Of shipbuilding timbers (at least for triereis), the shipwright's first choice was fir (*elatē*) and especially silver fir (*abies alba*) owing to its lightness, strength, longer lengths, and lack of knots, making it particularly suitable for oars and masts; his second choice was pine (*peukē:* Ar. *Eq.* 1300–10), especially mountain pine.[38] Athens's main source of supply throughout most of the fifth and fourth centuries was the forests of Macedon, a well-protected royal monopoly.[39] One clause in the alliance between the Athenians and the Macedonian king Perdicas (circa 417–413) prohibits the export of Macedonian oars to anyone but the Athenians (*IG* 1³.89). Perdicas's successor, Archelaos, was honored in 407/6 probably for his supply of timber and lengths of wood for oars, and for granting permission to the Athenian shipwrights to build ships at Macedon (*IG* 1³.117).

Alongside, or in extension of, interstate agreements, supplies were secured by individuals who acted as intermediaries by exploiting their political connections.[40] In a year between 430 and 405 Antiochides and Phanosthenes were honored for importing Macedonian oars to Athens (*IG* 1³.182). Andocides (2.11) claims to have been a beneficiary when in 411 he supplied oars to the Athenian fleet at Samos for five drachmas apiece by using the friendship of his family with the Macedonian royal house. The strategos Timotheos, through his friendship with the Macedonian king, was able to obtain, in 364/3, a large quantity of Macedonian timber, which was allegedly to be used for his own private building, but the volume of the consignment suggests a different purpose ([Dem.] 49.34–36). Where timber was in adequate supply pitch was also in abundance. In an alliance between the Macedonian king Amyntas and the Chalkidians (circa 393), it is stipulated that "the Chalkidians may export pitch, all building timbers and all ship-timbers except firs, unless the Chalkidian League requires them. The Chalkidian League may export firs, provided that they report it first to Amyntas and pay the prescribed dues" (Tod no. 111).

There is much to suggest, therefore, that the procurement of ship-building materials, above all, depended on the establishment of political alliances, on existing personal contacts, on diplomatic activity, or on the exercise of force, rather than on purely economic determinants. "If some city is rich in ship-timber," says Ps.-Xenophon (*Ath. Pol.* 2.11–12),

where will it distribute it without the consent of the rulers of the sea? Again if some city is rich in iron, copper, or flax, where will it distribute it without the consent of the rulers of the sea? However, it is from these very things that I have my ships: timber from one place, iron from another, copper from another, flax from another, wax from another. In addition, they will forbid export to wherever any of our enemies are, on pain of being unable to use the sea.

The main difficulty with which Athens had to cope seems not to have been lack of funds, public or private, to maintain the fleet, but acute, short-term shortages of supplies. One such situation is described at [Demosthenes] 47.20 as having occurred in 357/6, when materials needed to equip the triereis (sailcloth, flax, and ropes) could not be purchased at Piraeus. Obviously, under normal conditions there was a market able to meet the demand for such commodities.

My argument so far has sought to show that market values were less relevant than political relations between supplier and consumer. Moreover, I wish to stress the fluctuation of costs at different times, not to downplay their significance. Indeed, the specific demands posed partly by the design of the trieres and partly by the particular technique of construction made shipbuilding a costly venture.[41] The costs were not only determined by the purchase price of the timber but also by its transportation, by the size of the labor force needed, and not least by the period of time it took from the moment the trees were felled and shipped until the completed vessel proved its seaworthiness at the inaugural launch. Treatment of these aspects would take me far beyond the scope of the present study. Some cursory remarks, however, may be useful.

First, for hull-planking, masts, and oars, long pieces of timber were required. Transportation of whole heavy trunks by sea was an expensive and cumbersome venture,[42] involving a three-stage process: selection of materials, shipping, and further processing at the shipyards. In order to economize, the timber could be sawn to roughly the required sizes before shipment, but this would seem feasible only with oar and mast timbers: in the 320s lengths of unworked oar-timbers had been purchased for the dockyards, which were dressed into sets of oars in 325/4 (*IG* 2².1629.348–51, 695–99). Most of the planks of the hull that curved would have to be carved into shape by the shipwright himself during construction.

Second, and consequently, a fairly large amount of timber would have been wasted (including timbers scrapped after revealing flaws). Again, to avoid waste, the naval architect and the shipwright (or some other professional expert) would have to travel to the source of supply in order to select timbers of the quality and quantity needed. In short, an extensive and efficient supply network was an indispensable part of the naval infrastructure.

Third, fresh-felled trees contained too much moisture to be suitable for warships (where lightness was important) and first had to be seasoned—a process taking two years or more (Meiggs [1982] 125). References in the sources to *xyla naupēgēsima* may mean "timbers already seasoned for shipbuilding." Suppliers such as Macedon and southern Italy as well as naval powers such as Athens and Corinth would have had a reserve of mature timbers in stock. Quite apart from this, the demolition of severely damaged hulls provided timbers and spare parts for reuse. Finally, it may be right to suppose that silver fir, perhaps used for fast triereis, was more costly than pine.

It is impossible to come up with any particular sum representing the price of a ship in the fifth and fourth centuries, and there may be no such thing as the "standard cost" of a trieres.

## The Significance of Compensatory Payments

If, as seems likely a priori, there were variations in the cost of hulls built in different years and between individual hulls built in the same year, the uniform amounts paid to meet compensatory claims (five thousand drachmas per hull) must carry a special significance. Their purpose can be suggested by an analysis of transactions relating to repairs.

The epimeletai of 356/5 reported that sixty ships were repaired during their term of office (IG 2².1612.232–35). Three different arrangements were used in this connection. One group of hulls (more than eleven) is described as "those lying in the open and that have been surrendered after being brought back from overseas"; it is specified that the epimeletai forced the trierarchs (cf. Thuc. 7.38.2) to deliver these ships to the city in repaired condition (ll. 91–99). It is probable that all expenses were paid directly by the trierarchs. Another group of hulls was repaired by the trierarchs upon receipt of more than 2,560 drachmas from the state (ll. 145–48). It is not known whether the trierarchs were asked to repay that amount, or whether they themselves had to make additional outlays in order to cover the total cost of repair work. A third group consisted of fourteen hulls that had been hauled up in the *neoria* in unrepaired condition. These were repaired at the state's expense (ll. 149–50). The work was contracted to several naval architects; at its completion a "tester" (dokimastes) wrote up the total expenditure (ll. 218–32). Then of this sum (not given in the record), 90 percent was handed over to the naval architects, while the recipient of the remaining 10 percent is unknown (ll. 224–31). The trierarchs were then required to reimburse the state for the cost of repair (ll. 241–46).

In order to make the hulls seaworthy as quickly as possible, the state may have advanced the funds needed for that purpose (as in the second and third groups), and subsequently demanded that trierarchs refund the repair expenses (as in the third group). A similar arrangement, no doubt made in order to circumvent the lengthy money-collecting process and any legal entanglements that might ensue, is attested by the following two cases, which, in addition, show that the sum total of the state's expenditure was divided equally among all trierarchs involved in the transaction.

Contrary to current belief, a voluntary contribution (*epidosis*) did not consist of a gift of a ship to the state, but simply of undertaking a naval obligation that, at that particular time, one was not legally required to fulfill. An illustration of the various, and occasionally peculiar, forms these contributions could take is offered by the transaction discussed here (IG 2².1627.421–35).

In 330/29, three persons were listed as debtors on three ships belonging to the harbor of Kantharos. Their debt accrued because each had volunteered to contribute to the cost of "making the ships ready" for commission (*tōn paraskeuastheisōn*) in the year 338/7. Another reference to the same transaction in the record of 326/5 (1628.562–70) specifies the meaning of "making the ships ready" by stating that these contributions were meant to cover the cost of repair (eis tēn episkeuēn).[43] Since eight years later (330/29) each individual owed precisely 258 drachmas, 3 obols, it is extremely likely that the cost of repair work had initially been advanced by the state, and then was charged to the "contributors" by dividing the total of 775 drachmas, 3 obols, equally among them (see also Kuenzi [1923] 23–24). One would have expected from these volunteers the prompt payment of the money when the job on each ship was done, but clearly this was not the case. While two of them are absent from the last record to mention the transaction (1629.1039–44), the share of the third individual, Philon Meliteus, seems still to have been overdue thirteen years after the event (325/4).

The final case relates to the repair of a considerable number of hulls by or in 323/2. The epimeletai of that year noted the delivery of more than 52,996 drachmas to the treasurer of the dockyards in the presence of the boule, in accordance with Diphilos's law (1631.505–15). Part of that sum consisted of payments made by trierarchs toward meeting the repair cost of their ships (ll. 442–503). But many men still owed part or the whole of their liability by the end of 323/2 (ll. 517–20). It is noteworthy that almost all of the attested sums paid or owed amounted precisely to twelve hundred drachmas (Gabrielsen [1988] 83–85). Since many trierarchs still owed money for ships that had already been repaired, it seems certain that the repair work had been undertaken at the public expense and then the total cost was divided equally among trierarchs; each of these was subsequently faced with a claim to pay twelve hundred drachmas.

The instances presented above strongly suggest that the implementation and finance of repair work, at least whenever the restoration of the ships' seaworthiness seemed urgent, were undertaken by the state. At the ensuing collection of the total spent for that purpose, each trierarch was charged with an equal share in the overall expenditure, regardless of the extent of work done on each hull. The implications of such an arrangement are revealing.

Inasmuch as twelve hundred drachmas charged for the repair of one ship could also cover part of the repair cost of another, some trierarchs would have provided financial assistance to those of their colleagues whose actual liability exceeded twelve hundred drachmas. The system was conducive to a flexibly used, ad hoc pool of funds organized on the principle of self-help on the part of the trierarchs. This was probably also the case with payments of five thousand drachmas demanded for the replacement of a hull. Such an explanation becomes especially likely when seen in light of a marked propensity shown by some trierarchs to let their liabilities remain overdue for quite a long period of time (thirteen years, in the second case above), and of the no less astonishing difficulty the authorities had in recouping from such individuals what was due to the state. Furthermore, time-consuming diadikasiai among trierarchs for settling the issue of responsibility were clearly an impediment to having a fleet ready for immediate deployment.

To circumvent delays, therefore, the state may have undertaken construction of the whole annual quota of replacements needed, and then charged a uniform lump sum to each of the trierarchs liable to provide a hull. Given that these sums were pooled in a central shipbuilding fund, and given the fluctuating costs of construction, the cash collections of five thousand drachmas would normally have provided a solid financial base to cover the trierarchs' share of the overall maintenance. If to this there is added the amount of punitive fines on defaulters, there would have been funds enough perhaps also to cover part of the state's share. The problem, of course, was that not all such sums were duly paid. Finally, besides the five thousand drachmas, a trierarch incurred a further (not negligible) outlay from having the old hull demolished; even though the demolition was probably conducted by dockyard personnel, the records make it clear that the expense of this obligation was borne personally by the trierarch.

The leveling of standard payments for repairs and replacements is a sign of the ongoing process that transformed such liabilities into a tax. At the same time it implies the undertaking, by a group of trierarchs, of collective (as opposed to individual) liability. Indeed, in essence this was one of the principal aims of the institutional arrangements introduced with the symmory system. Here, however, the same principle can perhaps be seen at work across the narrower boundaries of the symmories as it could encompass a random number of trierarchs saddled with a debt. It meant some immediate financial relief for the individual, while it met the state's need for a promptly and adequately maintained fleet.

# SEVEN

# Equipment

## Shortages

My previous assessment of the naval potential of Athens in terms of hulls (guided by the wish to obtain an idea about the magnitude of resources needed for maintenance) led to a clearly optimistic impression. Turning now to a similar assessment of equipment for the ships, the picture that emerges is a forthrightly pessimistic one. During most of the period covered by the naval records (and one may suppose also in the fifth century) Athens suffered from a shortage of equipment. How serious was that shortage, and how is it to be accounted for?

Previous assessments are based almost exclusively on the stocktaking rubrics of the naval records.[1] The picture that can be derived from these rubrics is surely that there was less equipment in stock than there were hulls. Nevertheless, the deficiencies documented by these rubrics seem not to sustain an altogether pessimistic view. On the whole (and bearing in mind the incomplete state of the records), even though there were shortages, especially of the more easily perishable hanging equipment, the situation does not seem terribly gloomy. To take one of the most vital items, oars, the record of 357/6 shows that 233 hulls (82 percent of the gross total force) could be fitted out with a complete set (1611.19–21). The corresponding figures for a year toward the end of the period are 297 hulls (82.5 percent of the gross total) at the beginning of 325/4, and 289 hulls (80 percent) at the end of that year (1629). Likewise with rudders: 225 ships (79.5 percent) could be equipped in 357/6; 254 ships (70.5 percent) could be equipped at the beginning of 325/4. However, all this is deceptive.

For it turns out (again) that these rubrics do not give net figures of the equipment in stock, but what ideally should have been the gross potential of the dockyards. One illustration of the difference between the ideal and the actual situation comes from the record of 357/6 (definitely not a typical year; cf. [Dem.] 47.20). According to the overall stocktaking rubrics of the epimeletai who drew up 1611, there should have been complete sets of poles (*kontoi*) enough to fit out 225 ships (79.5 percent of the gross total force, ll. 33–37). But a different part of the record reveals that in fact there were poles in the dockyards for only about 49 ships from Zea (the largest harbor, which had 46 "second," 8 "third," more than 37 "select," and an unknown number, well over 16, of "first" ships). Similarly, there were just enough poles in the dockyards to equip 8 ships from Kantharos, and hypozomata in the storehouse (*skeuothēkē*) for only 16 ships from the same harbor (1611.196, 268–70). Of the 283 ships possessed in 357/6, only about 89 could be fully equipped by the end of that year. All this confirms the depressing remark made by the speaker of [Demosthenes] 47 that there was not (enough) equipment in the dockyards when a fleet had to be commissioned in 357/6 (20).

This situation was not unique. Detailed information survives from 353/2 to show the state of affairs in Mounichia, which is represented in the record with 36 hulls (of all ratings except the "select"). Of these, 7 lacked complete sets of oars (*tarroi*), 19 lacked rudders, 19 lacked mainmasts, and 29 lacked boat-sails (1613.41ff.). These figures should be compared to the total dockyard potential as stated by the epimeletai of that year: tarroi for 291 ships (83 percent of the total; i.e., 58 ships lacked tarroi); rudders for between 280 and 290 ships (83 percent of the total; i.e., 59 ships lacked rudders [1613.303–5]); mainmasts for 311 ships (89 percent of the total; i.e., 38 ships lacked mainmasts [1614.140]).

Thus, even though a glance at the stocktaking rubrics creates a positive impression, closer examination furnishes good reasons to believe that Athens suffered from a serious and chronic shortage of equipment that was occasionally aggravated by short-term crises. So the picture one gets really depends on which part of the records one looks at, and, unfortunately, the part listing the real deficiencies (entries showing how many ships could in fact be fully equipped with individual items of wooden and hanging equipment) has not always survived.

One source of discomfort are the figures of the stocktaking rubrics relating to hanging equipment, which are alarmingly low in the pre-330/29 period. The gross number of sails in 356/5 was just enough to fit out 97 ships (1612.62–63), while in 353/2 there were ropes for 111 ships (32 percent of the gross total force), and anchors for 136 ships (39 percent of the total force [1614.161, 163]). Considering that these figures include what was owed by naval officials and trierarchs, the most economical explanation for the missing items is that they could not be accounted for—that is, they had vanished from the dockyards and the dockyard officials were unable to record who should be made responsible for their return.[2] By contrast, the records from 330/29 onward show a remarkable and substantive improvement in the situation, not least because of a decision, in the same period, to store a reserve of hanging equipment for 100 ships on the Acropolis.

Wooden equipment was kept together with the hulls in the ship-sheds (neōsoikoi) of the three naval bases.[3] A circuit wall (remains of which have been found at Zea) isolated possibly the entire harbor area from the rest of the city (Garland [1987] 96, 156), offering protection to naval installations and matériel.[4] For hanging equipment, separate storehouses (skeuo-thēkai) were used. The earliest mention of them is reportedly made in one of Aischylos's lost plays (Psychagogoi fr. 274 [TrGF]; cf. Poll. 10.10). A boundary stone from the early fifth century is supplemented to read: "boundary of the ropes of the ships" (SEG 10.384). Permanent facilities had probably been established by Themistokles and were later developed at the initiative of Perikles.[5]

The fourth-century naval facilities are epigraphically attested. Various storehouses were in use simultaneously, but toward the end of the period a strong emphasis developed on the centralized upkeep of hanging equipment. Such items appear from the 370s to 353/2 stored in a building simply referred to as the "house" (oikēma: 1610.6–7; 1613.270), but in 330/29 this seems to have been used only for miscellaneous matériel (1627.359, 416–17). Another storehouse, consistently mentioned in the singular (skeuotheke), was also used for storing hanging equipment as late as 348/7,[6] but in 330/29 the same building is referred to as the "old skeuotheke" in an entry listing only "rotten leather bags" (askomata: 1627.352). In 330/29 "wooden skeuothekai for the hanging equipment of

278 triereis" are recorded (1627.320–21, 396); almost certainly, they were in use previously,[7] though seemingly not for long after 330/29. Yet another building, "the large house [oikema] by the Gates," appears from 330/20 onward to have been employed for the storage of miscellaneous matériel.[8]

Most hanging equipment was subsequently gathered under one roof in Philon's skeuotheke (four hundred Attic feet long, fifty feet broad, thirty feet high), which, according to the surviving written specifications of 347/6 (*IG* 2².1668), was to be built at Zea: "beginning from the Propylaion that leads from the Agora, as you come from behind the shipsheds, which are roofed together."[9] Work started in 347/6 (*IG* 2².505 and add. 661, giving the mode of finance), and after an interruption in 339/8, because of the war against Philip, it was resumed and completed by Lykourgos so as to be put into use perhaps in 330/29.[10] It is likely that the supervision of the new skeuotheke was entrusted to a separate "treasurer of hanging equipment" (*tamias kremastōn*), who may have collaborated with two or more from the annual board of the epimeletai ton neorion.[11] In addition, complete sets of hanging equipment for 100 triereis were by 330/29 (and probably already by 334/3, or even earlier) stored on the Acropolis, in the Chalkotheke at the Opisthodomos.[12] This measure may be comparable to the creation of a reserve of 100 ships in 431/0.

With regard to the shortages of equipment: how are the deficiencies to be accounted for? The answer is straightforward: equipment was owed by naval officials and trierarchs. Explicit statements of this are made in the arithmos formulas—for example, "Wooden and hanging equipment . . . owed by the officials and trierarchs" (1611.10–18). At first sight there seems nothing sinister in these debts; they are just what one would have expected as the natural outcome of the frequent give-and-take between naval officials and trierarchs. However, on closer scrutiny not all such debts are so innocent as they appear to be. There is much to suggest that one or the other group (trierarchs or officials) was constantly and seriously draining the dockyards of public equipment.

## Misappropriation of Equipment by Officials

It was not at all unusual for naval officials to withhold either equipment or its equivalent in cash. The fragment *Inscriptiones Graecae* 2².1617, columns b and c (probably from 357/6), lists various boards of epimeletai from three consecutive years (369/8, 368/7, 367/6) and one treasurer of the "triereis construction fund" (*tamias triēropoiikōn*) as debtors of equipment from several ships. But since only a small part of the record is preserved and this concerns wooden equipment only, the original list of debtor-officials (and the volume of debts) may well have been considerably larger.

Much richer and hence more illustrative are the data relating to transactions, in the period 345/4–342/1, conducted during a large-scale collection of debts from naval officials of previous years (1622.379–579). The collection was carried out by "those who had held office in the neoria" in the years 345/4–342/1, a board of officials that may or may not be identical with that of the epimeletai.[13] Be that as it may, it is important to note that the earliest of these debts date from 378/7. During the collection of the 340s most debtors (of the twenty-eight attested) paid relatively small amounts, from about 55 to 300 drachmas. However, this tells us nothing about the original size of these liabilities. For instance, the sum of over 316 drachmas paid by the three heirs of Mantias Thorikios, *epimeletes* in 377/6 (ll. 435–43), may be just one of several installments made in the intervening years. By contrast, Philagros Phalereus, epimeletes in 348/7 (only two years before the debt collection), paid a much higher sum, 1,637 drachmas (ll. 549–52). Another epimeletes, Apemon Phlyeus (of 360/59), initially paid 50 drachmas, and subsequently 2,709 drachmas in the *bouleuterion,* where the council met, because he was convicted in a diadikasia he himself had entered against Theophrastos Kopreios, presumably one of his colleagues to whom he attempted to transfer part of his liability (ll. 520–30).

Much of what these and other naval officials seem to have indulged in was the retention, use, and perhaps misuse of public equipment. Euthynos Lamptreus, tamias trieropoiikon in 346/5, was one such misappropriator. He had been in possession of a number of oars, which he eventually returned (*tōn paradotheisōn*) to the officials carrying out the debt collection in 345/4–342/1. However, as many as eighteen hundred oars were brought by Euthynos into the dockyards (*eisēnegken*) in useless condition, and therefore he was made to pay 3,600 drachmas (2 drachmas per oar) in compensation (ll. 387–97).[14] Although it cannot be proved, it is at least plausible that these oars had become useless by way of a private (unofficial) transfer from Euthynos to some trierarch(s); the latter would only be too happy to bypass any formal dealings with the naval administration (cf. [Dem.] 47.23), perhaps in return for a gratuity to the supplier. If it is right to suggest that such dealings were not exceptional, two implications follow. First, a great many important transactions concerning the fleet took place outside the official channels. Second, as the following examples may demonstrate, men holding key positions within the naval administration were making a good profit.

Of even greater magnitude are the debts of Mnesikles Kollyteus, an official of 346/5 described as "the one elected by the boule," and of Euthymachos E[——], treasurer of the neoria in 347/6. The former withheld a formidable amount of equipment: almost complete sets of hanging equipment belonging to as many as eighteen ships (ll. 420–31)—which is equivalent to one-half of the force stationed at Mounichia in 353/2. The latter had at the expiration of his tenure formally surrendered to the incoming board of officials equipment that he had received from the trierarchs. But while he had observed the first part of his duty, to record the delivery on the stele (*grapsas en tēi stelēi*), he failed to perform the second and most important part, to replace the matériel itself in the dockyards (*ouk eisēnegke*). Eventually, Euthymachos was made to return an enormous amount of equipment: hypozomata for 16 ships, mainsails for 35, *hypoblēmata* for 36, *topeia* for 18, *katablēmata* for 25, *pararrhymata leuka* for more than 31, *pararrhymata trichina* for more than 22, ropes for 30, and anchors for 34 ships (that is, 68 anchors!) plus three complete sets of oars (a total of 510 oars! ll. 446–77). It is also noteworthy that simultaneously with the return of these items Euthymachos paid an unknown sum in compensation for additional items that he presumably had kept for himself.

What Mnesikles and Euthymachos had misappropriated was not a trifling matter, nor are these just isolated instances. The whole board of the epimeletai of 325/4 and their secretary did much the same thing as Euthymachos: they recorded the surrender of equipment on the stele, but neglected to replace it in the neoria. In addition, they failed to deliver thirty-three drachmas, two obols that had been in the possession of their predecessors in office since 331/0; their debt, consisting of a not negligible amount of equipment, is recorded in the document of 323/2 (1631.410–29; cf. 1627.234–37).

Several tamiai trieropoiikon were also listed for the tardy return of equipment. Demokrates Eiteaios (of 332/1) withheld equipment from several tetrereis until 330/29 (1627.374–75). Antiphon Erchieus (of 335/4) withheld equipment for two tetrereis until 330/29, and poles for two tetrereis until 325/4 (ll. 33–34; cf. 1629.343–45). Eupolemos Myrrhinousios (of 334/3) surrendered topeia for five tetrereis in 330/29 (1627.73–75). Leotrephides Kropides (of 333/4) surrendered in 330/29 topeia for twelve tetrereis and hanging equipment belonging to two trDe ereis (ll. 155–71). These belated deliveries have been previously explained (Schmitt [1974]) by the assumption that the treasurers (and the whole board of trieropoioi) had been unable to keep to the annual schedule of ship construction. But one of their colleagues of 328/7, Polykrates Aphidnaios, who by 323/2 had *not* yet returned rudders from four ships, is expressly recorded as a debtor (*opheilōn:* 1632.14–16); moreover, the tamias trieropoiikon of either 359/8 or 356/5 absconded with fifteen thousand drachmas from the shipbuilding fund (Dem. 22.17). When seen in conjunction with the cases presented above, and considering that the equipment concerned consisted of miscellaneous items, not of complete sets (as one might have expected in cases of belated construction), these instances render more likely the explanation that retention of public equipment by the tamiai trieropoiikon is in question. One last instance (which will be fully treated below) is this: Kephisodoros Kydathenaieus, tamias of the dockyards before 325/4, withheld equipment for no fewer than ten triereis (1631.350–403).

The economic implications of this can be understood by looking at the monetary worth of equipment—its official value (*timē*) as currently set by the authorities, not its market value.[15] For the most part sums listed in the records are a poor guide to the value of equipment, since it cannot be decided whether they represent full payments or merely installments. To identify full payments it is necessary to isolate instances where both the amounts and the equipment to which they relate show a satisfactory degree of uniformity. These requirements are met by several entries revealing the value of trieres and tetreres equipment in different years.

The monetary value of a complete set of trieres equipment (attested from about 345/4) was 2,299 or 2,169 drachmas;[16] the difference, 130 drachmas, arises because the first sum relates to a set with a more costly "light" sail, the second to a set with an ordinary, "heavy" sail.[17] By 323/2 the value of a set with a light sail had been almost doubled. A series of debts listed in *Inscriptiones Graecae* 2².1631.517ff., although it shows no absolute uniformity (mainly because some of the amounts are not fully preserved), set it at circa 4,100 drachmas.[18] Unfortunately, the extant figures relating to tetreres equipment do not reveal the total monetary value. However, they certainly point at the order of magnitude, as every one of them amounts to more than 6,000 drachmas.[19]

The difference is striking. It is telling that for a complete set a man had to pay almost as much as when asked to compensate for a hull if his liability related to trieres equipment, or even more if it related to tetreres equipment. Two complementary explanations can be put forward to account for the marked increase attested in the second half of the fourth century. First, it may be due to the effects of external factors such as the need for Athens, in that period, to turn to distant sources of supply. Second, and perhaps more important, the near doubling of values may have been the result of a deliberate policy aimed at deterring trierarchs and naval officials from misappropriating public equipment either by lengthy retention or by taking possession of the items they withheld through compensatory cash payments. What remains in question is why the value of tetrereis equipment was so much higher than that of triereis equipment.

The hanging equipment for eighteen ships that Mnesikles Kollyteus withheld (1622.420–31) represented a substantial fortune. This phenomenon can hardly be accounted for as the petty misappropriation of matériel normally occurring in any bureaucracy. Given the fragmentary state of the evidence, the frequency with which retention of equipment by officials is attested is remarkable; in more than a few cases the amount of equipment involved is so large that the withholder must have needed a private storehouse to accommodate it. The number of items needed for a single trieres was considerable; the oars (each about four meters long) alone numbered two hundred. It is fairly clear that such conduct was on the threshold of, or well beyond, what was permissible by law.[20] But it is much less clear what the legal consequences, if any, were in each case.

## Misappropriation of Equipment by Trierarchs

With regard to trierarchs it is easier to suspect misappropriation on a large scale than it is to prove it. It is known that a number of individuals owned private equipment. In 362, Apollodoros fitted out his ship entirely with his own equipment, receiving nothing from the public, and so did his colleague Hagnias ([Dem.] 50.7, 42). The speaker of [Demosthenes] 51.5 boasted that he equipped his ship at his private expense, using none of the equipment furnished by the state. The speaker of [Demosthenes] 47 stated that in the many trierarchies he had performed before 357/6 he had never received equipment from the dockyards, but provided his own (23).

Because of a serious shortage of equipment in the dockyards in 357/6 and of the failure on the part of those withholding it to clear their debts, a decree proposed by Chairedemos ordered, inter alia, those owning equipment to sell it to the state, and made disobedience punishable with confiscation of the offender's property ([Dem.] 47.20, 44). The introduction of such a measure must have been based on preexisting knowledge that the number of owners was substantial. Further evidence points in the same direction.

A number of entries in the naval records listing equipment under the formula "someone introduced" (eisēnegken) have been correctly interpreted as concerning privately owned equipment introduced into the dockyards.[21] In Inscriptiones Graecae 2².1609, the formula is used in order to mark off such items on a ship that had been introduced by an individual (not necessarily the current trierarch), which for practical purposes had to be distinguished from other items such as, for instance, those transferred from another, temporarily inactive ship (e.g., ll. 68–69). The formula recurs in another document with the purpose of specifying the provenance of three complete sets of oars, those having been introduced in the dockyards by Phormion Peiraieus, Eudraon Thorikios, and Archedemos Pitheus. Two of them are securely (and one tentatively) attested as trierarchs (1622.472–77).[22]

The earlier view that equipment listed under the heading eisēnegken represented payments of an eisphora levy in kind is refuted because a number of oars that had been introduced into the neoria by Sopolis (and were recorded as such under the same heading) were confiscated with the rest of his property after he had failed to discharge a naval liability on behalf of his brother. This and the remaining instances reflect, therefore, a practice occasionally resorted to by trierarchs, of lending their private equipment to the dockyards.[23]

All in all, ownership of a partial or a complete set of equipment by trierarchs or individuals who can be assumed to have belonged to the trierarchic class is well documented. The next question is how these persons came into possession of equipment. Almost certainly, some would have purchased it in the same manner—and from the same sources of supply—as the state. Makartatos, Isaeus 11.48 says, was able to buy a whole trieres. The procurement of oars by Andocides and of timbers by Timotheos (in both cases from Macedon) has already been mentioned. The stock purchased by Timotheos was too large to be reconciled with the allegation ([Dem.] 49.29, 36) that it was to be used to build his private house; in fact, he may have invested in ship-timber (Meiggs [1982] 364). If Meidias was able to transport on his trieres various commodities from Euboia for his private use (cattle, doorposts, and timber: Dem. 21.167), there is no reason to doubt that some trierarchs should have obtained naval matériel whenever they came in contact with the sources of supply. Alternatively, they may have used the market in Piraeus supplying the naval administration: for example, Euboulos purchased lengths of rope (*neia*: 1627.353–54); by 328/7 or 327/6 Demades had bought fifteen (or more) sets of undressed oars for the dockyards, though the capacity in which he acted is not known (1629.348–51, 695–99).

Individuals expecting to perform trierarchies would have procured their own equipment either because they wished to have as few dealings as possible with the dockyard administration, as the speaker of [Demosthenes] 47.23 says he did, or because they found it worthwhile to invest in spares, which would prove valuable in case of breakage during a journey.

So far everything looks orderly, legitimate, and guileless. But there are other indications (too numerous to be passed over unmentioned) of public equipment coming into private hands in a less straightforward or honorable manner. Time and again individuals are mentioned who, although liable to return equipment they had retained, either refused blatantly to surrender it (cf. [Dem.] 47.25, 28) or ultimately chose to reimburse the state for its monetary value rather than return the equipment itself. Since it would be pointless to cite all the evidence, I will mention only a few examples.

In 328/7 or 327/6 Lysanias Sounieus received hanging equipment and a mast on the newly built tetreres *Salpinx Demotelous*, and he retained this until 325/4, in which year he paid 5,603 drachmas toward its cost (1628.10–12). Moreover, the epimeletai of 325/4 found that Lysanias had also received a set of undressed oars but had neglected to enter that fact in the record (1629.689–90). For this he was made liable to pay a further 415 drachmas. There can be little doubt that by means of these payments the items concerned subsequently became Lysanias's lawful possessions, and that, had his negligence gone unnoticed, he would have been successful in misappropriating a whole set of oars.

In 357/6, Demophanes Alopekethen owed several items of equipment from three different ships on which he had served in previous years (1611.434–41). These he kept (and presumably used) during his lifetime, for in one of the years between 345/4 and 342/1, Themistokles Phrearrhios, perhaps a relative of his, compensated the state for the matériel on Demophanes' behalf (1622.331–50; APF 219).

In 357/6, Archestratos Alopekethen withheld equipment from four different ships (1611.440–48). His earliest service on one of these may well date from 369/8 or earlier, if one (quite hesitantly) assumes that he had observed the two-year exemption rule. At any rate, Archestratos never returned that equipment, but paid 460 drachmas in compensation during the period 345/4–342/1 (1622.249–63). Curiously, in a document of a year before 361/0 (possibly as early as 371/0: 1609.84) the same man is listed as having introduced into the dockyards (and hence was the owner of) a complete set of wooden equipment. Also, Praxiteles Batethen, who by the end of the 340s paid 690 drachmas toward defraying an old debt for equipment for a ship (1622.769–83), is listed in 1609.64 as having introduced certain items. Less certainly, Stephanos Euonymeus, who owed equipment in a year shortly after 357/6 (1618.83–91), may be identical with an individual recorded in 1609.85 as having introduced equipment.

There is a paradox to be accounted for here in that men introducing their equipment later appear also as debtors for such matériel. Is it the case that they had engaged in a questionable kind of generosity by lending to the dockyards equipment that they already had misappropriated? Or is one to infer that they chose to employ in acts of munificence what they themselves owned, and to draw public equipment for performing their trierarchies?

These examples can be easily multiplied. Although one may suppose that the very nature of the records does much to overrepresent such cases, in this area the documents convey a widespread trend also detectable in the literary sources. Possibly in 356, Satyros, in his capacity as epimeletes ton neorion, collected 34 talents (204,000 drachmas!) from those owing public equipment (Dem. 22.63).[24] The magnitude of the amount is as good an indication as possible (it is doubtful that all debts concerned complete sets) that the number of items owed as well as the number of debtors involved in this transaction alone were immense. The great shortage (in the pre-330/29 period) of hanging equipment that could not be accounted for by the naval officials (see p. 148) admits of no other explanation than that the matériel in question had by obscure routes ended up in private hands. A number of the cases discussed so far seem to contradict Davies' argument ([1969] 315) that retention of equipment could derive not from any wish to embezzle public property or to divert it to one's own personal use, but from motives of efficiency and philotimia. Indeed, the extensive misappropriation of equipment by naval officials bespeaks the less noble motives of both officials and trierarchs.

In the long run, the flow of public equipment away from the dockyards through lengthy retention or misappropriation had its own impact on naval administration and organization. Recognition of the need for better supervision and protection as well as more efficient methods of recovering matériel called for innovation and reforms. First, from 357/6 onward bookkeeping became increasingly elaborate and refined. Second, concentration of equipment into a few, large storehouses admitted of better control: after construction of Philon's skeuotheke, probably in 330/29, most hanging equipment was brought under one roof and also under the supervision of officials with special responsibility for its upkeep; likewise, from the 330s onward, complete sets of hanging equipment for 100 triereis were safely placed under the guardianship of the goddess Athena on the Acropolis. Last, but not least, with the introduction of the symmories a new legal and institutional environment was created, where responsibility for the retention of equipment by one individual was, in some measure, delegated to the group to which he belonged. These and other facets of the development after 357/6 are given more thorough treatment below.

## The Recovery of Naval Debts

The first legislative measures dealing with naval defaulters were introduced at about the same time as the inception of trierarchic symmories and the formal definition of the number of those annually needed to perform trierarchies as twelve hundred property owners; the crucial years are 358/7 and 357/6. What prompted at least some of these measures was an embarrassing crisis in which a fleet could not be commissioned because equipment that should have been in the dockyards was in the hands of individuals who refused to return it ([Dem.] 47.20). Yet little of this was new.

First, a large number of debts owed by trierarchs and naval officials in the 350s and 340s had been outstanding since 378/7. Incidentally, it would be rash to assume (as Davies does, [1969] 313–14) that such liabilities went no further back, because no publicly inscribed records were kept before that year; the circumstance that eisphora arrears had also been overdue since 378/7 (Dem. 22.44–45) precludes any explanation based on the peculiarities of (or disruptions in) dockyard bookkeeping. A more likely explanation may be that previous debts had been cleared during an earlier large-scale debt collection conducted by 378/7.[25]

Second, the records from the 370s and 360s show that ships about to be commissioned lacked equipment, and had to be fitted out by borrowing supplementary items from other ships or from individuals who possessed their own equipment. It seems certain that shortages were a real and pressing issue calling for a solution at that time as well. No doubt, the legislative measures of the early 350s constituted the first in a series of active steps to address a situation that had been left uncontrolled for many years, and that could no longer be tolerated. Still, this does not explain the timing of a decision to abandon the attitude of laxity toward defaulters: why was a more severe line not adopted before 358/7? The answer, it can be argued, is to be sought in the insufficient number of men assembled annually to perform trierarchies in the years before Periandros's law, and in the increase of their number to twelve hundred by that law.

Tolerance toward defaulters should not be confused with negligence and indifference, nor, as has been claimed, with the inability on the part of naval officials to pressure offending trierarchs because of fear of retaliation by powerful political figures.[26] On the contrary, it was the outcome of a deliberate choice to deal with the worse of two evils: a shortage of equipment because of failure on the part of withholders to return it, and an inability to recruit enough trierarchs to serve in a year. Enforcement of coercion with a view to improving the stock in the dockyards was likely to produce the undesirable effect of lessening the enthusiasm of naval financiers to undertake voluntary trierarchies. Given, therefore, that the solutions to these two problems were mutually exclusive, avoidance of further deterioration of the recruitment situation obviously received priority in the period before 358/7.

Two decrees and one law, all providing guidelines for the collection of debts after 358/7, are palpable indications of the seriousness with which the situation was addressed. Most of the available information comes from [Demosthenes] 47; but since the speaker confines his account to the legal particulars relevant to his own case, the informativeness of this source leaves much to be desired. Nevertheless, the speaker's description of the legal and administrative proceedings brings out fairly clearly the following elements.

Chairedemos's decree, possibly of the boule (19), may have been particularly concerned with the recovery of equipment for the ships about to sail in 357/6 (20). To implement this the dockyard superintendents of 357/6 (referred to as "the recipient officials": *hē paralabousa archē* [22]) were instructed to allot defaulters—listed on the stele surrendered by the previous officials (of 358/7)—to the trierarchs about to sail and to the epimeletai of the symmories (21). Perhaps the same decree ordered owners of equipment to sell it to the state, and further stipulated that refusal to do so, like the failure of withholders to return public equipment, was punishable by confiscation of the offender's property (44).

A provision of Periandros's law generally rendered it compulsory to receive the lists of debtors (21). Who was to receive the lists is not specified in the text. But since the speaker has just mentioned the trierarchs about to sail and the epimeletai of the symmories, and since he found it worthwhile to stress that it was this law that had created the symmories (something most of his listeners would have known), it is almost certain that from 358/7 on the ultimate recipients of lists of debtors were the epimeletai of the symmories and symmory members in charge of the ships about to put to sea. Further confirmation of this comes from the next decision.

A decree of the assembly, presumably expanding and reinforcing the procedure laid down by the boule, obliged the dockyard officials to surrender the list of debtors to the trierarchs about to sail and to the epimeletai of the symmories in order that the latter might themselves carry out the collection of debts from each of the defaulters allotted to them (21).

It is regrettable that the speaker says so little about Periandros's law, but it may well be supposed that its provisions constituted the main legal matrix on which the subsequent decrees were modeled. Yet whatever the exact relation of these three measures, enough of their content has survived to disclose their sharing of a preeminent concern: to define more rigorously than before the obligation incumbent on trierarchs (and now also on the newly created epimeletai of the symmories) to act as debt collectors on behalf of the state. A chief principle they thus helped promote was privatization of the irksome task of exacting naval debts. Compared to the previous (but poorly preserved) Naval Law from the fifth century (IG $1^3$ 236.3–9 and Oliver [1935] no. 1), the legislative measures of 358/7 and 357/6 are innovative in at least two areas.[27]

First, while the old law seems to have ordered the surrender of equipment by a trierarch to his successor, and to have given the latter the right to enter legal action in case the withholder refused to cooperate, the new legislation rendered it peremptory for the successor/recipient to recover equipment from the debtor. At first glance the difference between the two procedures might seem slight, but on closer scrutiny it turns out to be an important one. Before 358/7 a man could decide at will whether to use the legal means afforded by law in order to exact equipment from his recalcitrant predecessor. Alternative methods by which to achieve a private settlement of the matter were arguably not infrequently used, and almost certainly some would have been less keen to be involved in a diadikasia if they were able to fit out their ships with equipment they possessed in private. Therefore, a certain freedom afforded previously to the collector-trierarch to opt for a settlement without use of the legal machinery could be exploited by the withholder with a view to prolonging his retention of public property. The effects of this have been described above. The post-358/7 legislation, however, sought to obstruct or considerably eliminate such instances by requiring a recipient trierarch to recover public equipment under any circumstances.[28] Successor trierarchs were forced into the role of debt collectors.

Second, but equally important, after 358/7 the obligation to recover equipment was extended to apply both to the successor trierarch and to the epimeletes of the symmory to which he belonged, and possibly also, formally, to the entire symmory. A new principle, that of extended liability, was beginning to gain in significance in this and other areas. Judged in terms of the purposes they were designed to serve, the new regulations seem substantially more concerned with expanding while at the same time tightening the responsibilities of debt collectors than with placing legal constraints on debtors. The discussion of Theophemos's case below will illustrate this point more clearly.

How effective were the new measures? Not so effective as it was hoped they would be. A dossier of documents can be adduced to show that once put into effect, they led to the prompt clearance of some but far from all debts. A good impression of the list of defaulters surrendered by the epimeletai of 358/7 to their successors of 357/6 is given by the record of the latter year (1611.374ff.): it reveals not only the volume of some debts but also the approximate length of time they had been overdue (inferred from the number of ships involved in each entry). The record of the following year (1612.262ff.) lists some of those who used the opportunity to clear their debts, but there were many others who did not do so.

Still other records bear witness that the legislation of 358/7 and 357/6 was followed by the systematic and thorough registration of debtors in accordance with the principle of extended responsibility described at [Demosthenes] 47.21–22. Especially important are the "symmory documents." Four fragments (1615, 1617, 1618, and 1619), dating from about 357/6, but assumed, without good reason, to be of a single naval inscription from after 357/6,[29] have their rubrics arranged in the same manner as two other fragments of different years (1616, 1625). Each rubric gives the name of the epimeletes of the symmory to which a ship belonged, specifies which items of equipment from that ship were present in the dockyards, and finally lists those owing equipment—for example, 1615.88–104:

Europe, in need of repair, belonging to the symmory of Pythodoros Thriasios. On this ship are present: useless rudders, useless big sailyards, ladders, one of them useless. The following owe [sc. equipment]: Demophilos's heir, Sostratos Euxitheou Acharneus: a complete set of oars; Strombichos Euonymeus and Dorotheos Anagyrasios: mast-partners; Stephanos Myrrhinousios and Demonikos Lakiades: a mainmast.

This is part of a balance sheet of the stock in the dockyards. The men listed as debtors are sole trierarchs or syntrierarchs (for example, Strombichos Euonymeus and Dorotheos Anagyrasios)[30] who had been in charge of the same ship in different years. Here they are grouped together because they owed items of equipment from that ship. The symmory to which *Europe* belonged was in that year supervised by the epimeletes

Pythodoros Thriasios; in a different year it was headed by another man, Phano[——], who took over the entire group of debtors (1616.117–30). What these entries probably reflect is the allocation of defaulters in accordance with the proceedings recounted in [Demosthenes] 47.21–22.

By 345/4 the bulk of the naval debts seems still to have remained uncleared, necessitating the decision to undertake yet another large-scale collection. Parallel attempts to recover other public debts are also attested in the same period.[31] The pertinent naval transactions cover the period 345/4–342/1. Records exist of at least two individuals, Archestratos and Demophanes, who should have discharged their liabilities by 357/6, but had not: the first owed equipment from four, the second from three ships.[32] Moreover, in about 356/5 the superintendent of the dockyards, Satyros, exacted naval debts from Kallikrates Aphidnaios and Leptines ek Koiles (Dem. 22.60, 63). Yet both individuals made further payments in 345/4–342/1 (1622.165–84, 361–64). It looks, then, as if the latter pair as well ought to have cleared their debts, but actually did not do so, in 356/5 or before.

In sum, neither of the two known major debt collections, during the early 350s and the late 340s, had the effects that the new legislative measures (first and foremost, Periandros's law) were intended to produce; in 342/1, Menestheus Rhamnousios's debts from two ships were still noted with the remark "he paid nothing" (1622.721–36). A chief reason was the particular attitude of the authorities toward naval defaulters.


## The Treatment of Defaulters

The collection of the cash paid to meet naval debts was conducted by the dockyard officials, who forwarded the amounts exacted to the apodektai (IG 2².1627.200–233). Alternatively, payments might be made directly to the apodektai (1629.585–99, 674–83). In most cases recalcitrant debtors were brought to a law court, which levied a punitive fine of double the amount of their original debt (diplōsis).[33] Legal action was initiated by the epimeletai.[34] This much can be confidently regarded as standard practice. But a look at the stand taken toward those still refusing to discharge their liabilities reveals a variety of procedures, some recurring, others ad hoc. A characteristic common to all, however, is that they generally placed naval debtors in a distinctly more favorable position than other public debtors and, more importantly, may even have afforded milder treatment to one naval debtor than to another.

Whereas other public debtors were exposed to imprisonment and loss of civic rights, defaulting trierarchs, treated more like private debtors, astonishingly were not.[35] Another punishment that could be inflicted on debtors was confiscation of their property. Indeed, there were individuals whose property was confiscated because of failure to defray a naval debt that had been doubled. But three such cases are the only ones I know of (of which one concerns a naval official), and these probably come under the category of *apographai,* in which the person making the denunciation acts in collusion with the defaulter in order to help him clear his liability.[36]

In 334/3, Demonikos Myrrhinousios had his debt on *Hygieia Archenikou* doubled by a court to 2,028 drachmas, 2 obols (1623.218–24). This sum remained unpaid until his property was denounced by Theodoros Myrrhinousios (in 327/6), after which annual installments of 210 drachmas were paid in the period 327/6–323/2 (1631.288–325). Probably, the debt was to be discharged within ten years (210 × 10 = 2,100 drachmas), if it is assumed that the confiscated property consisted of land (*Ath. Pol.* 48.3), and that either a fine (71 drachmas, 4 obols) had been added to the original 2,028 drachmas, 2 obols, or less was paid in the tenth year.

The naval record *Inscriptiones Graecae* 2².1631.350–403 contains a decree of the boule proposed by Polyeuktos Hestiaios in 324/3 concerning the debt of Sopolis. The case arose from the failure of Sopolis's brother, Kephisodoros, to return equipment for ten triereis after his tenure as treasurer of the neoria. Because Kephisodoros was dead, or else had absconded by 325/4, Sopolis was held responsible for the equipment but refused to return it. In consequence, the epimeletai of 324/3 brought him before a court, which sentenced him to pay more than double the amount of the original debt (ll. 359–60; cf. *Urkunden* 212).

Sopolis's subsequent defiance of the court's order led to the extension of the legal proceedings by his imprisonment, his loss of civic rights, and the involvement of the boule that passed the pertinent decree. The proposer, Polyeuktos, confiscated the whole of Sopolis's property, which included a number of oars described as "the oars of Sopolis that have been introduced in the dockyards" (ll. 360–65). However, it appears that Polyeuktos's interest was to ensure the proper clearance of Sopolis's debt. In one provision he let his lawful reward for bringing the *apographē* be reckoned against Sopolis's debt so that the latter could resume his civic rights (*eis tēn epitimian:* ll. 365–68). Further provisions order the epimeletai of 324/3 to record that the state had taken possession of Sopolis's oars by reckoning three drachmas per oar against Sopolis's debt, while their treasurer, upon receiving the oars, was to count them and add up the total of their monetary equivalent. Finally, the decree instructs the secretary of the Eleven and all naval officials about how Sopolis's debt should properly be written off, prescribes the fine to be paid by them in case of malfeasance, and gives Sopolis and his relatives the right to bring an eisangelia, if they were subjected to unjust treatment.

Stesileides Siphnios owed 12,117 drachmas, 2 obols, a debt of which part went back to 336/5 (1623.202–17). The entire amount remained overdue after Stesileides' death by 330/29 (1627.194–99), and was ultimately discharged by Leodikos Siphnios, the guardian of his still minor heirs, through an apographe brought by Hermodoros Acharneus (in 324/3: 1631.429–41).

It seems certain that in all three cases the sum raised by the apographe corresponds to the amount of the debt, while the individual making the denunciation (most clearly in Sopolis's case) is assisting rather than attacking the debtor. The arrangement followed with Demonikos compares favorably with that of Aristogeiton, whose public debt (doubled to 10 talents, 2,000 drachmas) was cleared by having a plot belonging to him confiscated (by another man?) and bought by his brother Eunomos for precisely the amount of the debt. Eunomos initially paid two installments totaling 2 talents, 400 drachmas, and was obliged to defray the residue (8 talents, 1,600 drachmas) within ten years (Dem. 25. hyp. 2–3).

Consider the case of an impudent defaulter, Theophemos. The well-known story of his liability, as reported in [Demosthenes] 47, brings out most clearly three important characteristics: the conversion of a public responsibility to a private one; a fair degree of tolerance on the part of the public authorities toward defaulters; and exploitation of both of the foregoing by a defaulter with the intent to prolong settlement of his liability as much as possible, or, ultimately, until his defiance was viewed as an offense against the state itself.

In his capacity as epimeletes of a symmory and one of the trierarchs about to sail (357/6), the speaker of [Demosthenes] 47 was made liable to recover equipment lacking from his ship; it was withheld by the syntrierarchs Demochares and Theophemos (21–23; all subsequent references are to this speech). As the syntrierarchs refused to surrender the items in their possession, the speaker, formally acting as a debt collector, summoned them before the apostoleis and the epimeletai ton neorion who at that time collaborated in introducing such cases to a law court. At the diadikasia trial, Demochares and Theophemos were held liable for the retention of public equipment and were ordered to return it; Demochares discharged his part of the liability, but Theophemos did not (26–29, 33).

After several unsuccessful attempts to make Theophemos comply with the court's order, the collector referred the matter to the apostoleis and the boule; the latter reacted by passing a decree authorizing him (and other collector-trierarchs in the same plight) to exact the debts in any way possible (33). Empowered with the right of compulsory execution, the collector proceeded to seize some of Theophemos's holdings as security, but all he accomplished was to be assaulted by the defaulter (38–39)—the culmination of Theophemos's audacity. Having reported to the boule that Theophemos had resisted the execution, the boule took the view that the offense now was no longer against a private person but against itself, the demos, and the pertinent statute (41), and instructed the collector to bring an eisangelia on a charge of breach of the law and of impeding the dispatch of the fleet. At the ensuing eisangelia Theophemos was convicted. But when the boule was about to deliberate whether to levy the maximum fine in its power (five hundred drachmas) or to refer the case to a court for a heavier punishment, the collector conceded that an additional fine of twenty-five drachmas would suffice (41–44).

Although Theophemos eventually discharged his debt, some crucial details about the manner in which this was done and the precise financial consequences of his offense remain unclear. Obviously, he surrendered the equipment in his possession,[37] and he must have paid an additional fine of 25 drachmas (43). But additional to what? A diplosis is nowhere mentioned, even though, based on similar cases, one would expect this to have been prescribed either at the diadikasia or later by the boule.[38] Nor is this all. The collector acted on the legal basis of three statutes (one of which ordered the confiscation of the defaulter's property) in addition to a court's decision and an authorization by the boule to take as a pledge part of the debtor's holdings. Yet, curiously enough, Theophemos would suffer none of these. The unexpected generosity displayed by the collector in the course of the eisangelia may encourage one to suspect that a private settlement was finally reached, even though the offense at that stage was already viewed as one against the public. Although the power to decide the dispute had been placed in the hands of public authorities, the matter apparently never lost its private character.

The conclusion one is led to draw from this case is that the general attitude of leniency toward naval debtors, which I have traced for the 370s and 360s, was not entirely abandoned after 358/7. In consequence, the real effect of Periandros's law (and of the additional legislative measures) turned out to be quite limited. Notwithstanding the existence of punitive sanctions, a debtor was still able to maneuver past most legal obstacles. He could do so partly because settlement of naval liabilities was largely regarded as a private affair in which the responsibility to recoup public property was assigned to individuals from the trierarchic class itself; and partly because in the end what seems to have mattered most to the authorities was the recovery of equipment rather than the punishment of a defaulter. The same overriding concern is discernible from a variety of attested ad hoc arrangements by which defaulters were offered favorable terms to clear their debts.

(i) The boule of 326/5 sentenced to diplosis trierarchs who had failed to discharge their obligation to replace hulls and who now owed 10,000 drachmas per hull. Some of these liabilities had been outstanding for quite a long time—since 334/3.[39] In conjunction with the boule's decision, a decree of the assembly, proposed by Demades Paianieus, gave permission to the debtors themselves as well as to other individuals to reckon their voluntary contributions (epidoseis) to the corn fund against the amount owed in each case (1628.339–49).[40] This was doubtless a handsome gesture, and some trierarchs made use of the opportunity to clear their debts. One example will suffice to illustrate how this was done. Konon Anaphlystios paid 5,000 drachmas to meet his original debt, and had his contribution of 1,000 drachmas to the corn fund reckoned against his liability. To defray the remaining 4,000 drachmas he enlisted the help of two individuals, Panther Lakiades and Meidon the Samian, whose epidoseis to the corn fund amounted to 3,000 and 1,000 drachmas, respectively (1628.353–68).

Clearly, the arrangement was brilliantly designed to the advantage of the state: it facilitated the exaction of debts that might have gone unpaid for several more years; it enabled the state to mobilize extra resources to meet the urgent need for corn; and the doubling of these liabilities by the boule may indeed have been a tactical step toward raising additional

funds. However, the deal was no less advantageous to defaulting trierarchs who, besides being able to fulfill two obligations by paying for
one, actually were offered a discount through permission to transfer a
substantial part of their liability to a larger group of individuals: Konon
Anaphlystios paid 6,000 drachmas, whereas he should have paid 10,000
drachmas. Besides, a total of seven persons are attested to have rendered
financial support to Konon in order to enable him defray a series of similar liabilities that he had incurred either alone or jointly with his trierarch
partners.[41] The principle of extended liability was here expanded to operate beyond the boundaries of the symmories and, as many of those rendering financial assistance were not trierarchs, also outside the trierarchic
institution itself. More examples survive to show the principle of extended liability at work.

(ii) Of special interest is the transaction concerning the debt of Pausanias Agrylethen, the essentials of which are furnished by the record of
334/3 (1623.144–59). In a previous year, Pausanias was made liable to
replace the trieres *Epideixis Lysistratou*. Because he had failed to discharge
his debt, the epimeletai of 334/3 brought him before a court, which sentenced him to diplosis, his debt now totaling 10,000 drachmas. On the
same occasion, or shortly thereafter, the strategoi and the Twenty (probably to be identified with the epimeletai of the twenty trierarchic symmories) appointed Onetor Meliteus as Pausanias's syntrierarch, certainly not
with a view to performing active service (since Pausanias's term of duty
had expired in a previous year), but to assist the original debtor in defraying his liability on a joint basis. Pausanias was to pay five-sixths and
Onetor one-sixth of the amount stated in the register: that is, 8,333
drachmas, 2 obols, and 1,666 drachmas, 4 obols respectively.[42]

By or in 325/4, Onetor paid 783 drachmas, 2 obols (probably only an
installment) toward meeting his part of the debt. The involvement of
the epimeletai of the symmories in Onetor's appointment as syntrierarch
accords well with their prominent role in the recovery of trierarchic
debts,[43] and may render likely the inference that Onetor's responsibility
to provide financial support resulted from his membership in the symmory to which the ship *Epideixis* belonged. Perhaps the epimeletai of the
symmories, in collaboration with the strategoi, sought out a symmory
member who would undertake to help a fellow trierarch clear his debt.
Be that as it may, the arrangement just described was by no means
unique.[44]

(iii) The record of 323/2 (1631.442–654) lists trierarchic debts that were either paid or still owed by the end of that year. Mention has already been made of one part of these debts, relating to the cost to repair each ship. The other part consisted of the liability of the same trierarchs to compensate for equipment. In most cases a complete set was in question. While each trierarch undertook responsibility to pay for the repair of his ship on his own, some men shared their liability for equipment with one (or, rarely, two) *synteleis*. Not all transactions were fully preserved, but from those that are legible or can be fairly securely restored it can be seen that a liability is divided as in the following two examples: the trierarch of *Stilbousa Smikrionos*, Kineas Lamptreus, was charged to pay 3,460 drachmas (five-sixths), his synteles Ly[——] 630 drachmas (one-sixth); the trierarch of *Hellas Archeneo*, Thoudippos Araphenios, was charged to pay 2,776 drachmas, 4 obols (five-sixths), his synteles 941 drachmas, 4 obols (one-sixth).[45]

Most cases in 1631 reveal a fairly consistent adherence to the principle of allocating approximately five-sixths of the debt to the original trierarch and one-sixth to a synteles, if two men were involved, while a roughly similar apportionment was undertaken if three men were involved. Those listed as synteleis were not syntrierarchs in the sense in which the latter term is usually understood (i.e., a group of persons sharing an active trierarchy): first, the latter are clearly distinguished by the epimeletai of 323/2 (1631.635–59)—a distinction bespeaking the co-existence of two nominal groups within the body of trierarchs with separate functions; second, syntrierarchs, as a rule, shared a liability equally between them. The term *synteleis* designates those assisting the original trierarch in defraying a liability incurred after the expiration of his service.

The striking resemblance between the transactions of 323/2 and the division of liability between Pausanias and Onetor (cf. p. 167) convincingly precludes the idea of mere coincidence, and instead suggests a recurring method of recovering naval debts by distributing financial responsibility progressively among debtors proper and one or two joint contributors. The notion that synteleis were saddled with a smaller fraction of the total debt can only be sustained if one considers what they paid toward a single liability. But since a man could appear as synteles in as many as three different debts, his total outlays in 323/2 might amount to nearly as much as the outlays of each of the original debtor-trierarchs:

Nikeratos Kydantides, synteles on three different ships, undertook to pay over 2,051 drachmas.[46] Organization and implementation of debt exactions were, no doubt, tasks entrusted to the symmories and their epimeletai.

By such arrangements, then (and those attested are only a small sample), naval defaulters were treated differently in relation to one another, and as a group in relation to other public debtors, even though often the nature and size of their debts were identical. Obviously, in introducing one or the other deal, the state was trying to solve a practical and often serious problem: the recovery of naval matériel (or its monetary equivalent) that had remained, and otherwise might still remain, in private hands for a considerable length of time, either because of cumbersome legal proceedings, or because of the debtor's recalcitrance, or both. Inherent in each deal was the double objective of securing the interest of the state on the one hand and of exerting as little pressure as possible on defaulting trierarchs on the other.

In this area, too, maintenance of balance in the relationship between state and trierarchs was a prime concern. Most prominent among these arrangements were those permitting financial assistance to be rendered by another party (i.e., extended liability), and one might take the view that the apographai discussed above had a similar effect. The practice of spreading trierarchic costs to a larger group of persons was completely consonant with the raison d'être of, and in effect institutionally embedded in, the symmory system.

## PART IV

*Institutional Transformation*

# EIGHT

# The Reforms

## The Syntrierarchy

As Thucydides makes plain, wealthy Athenians were foremost among the champions of the oligarchic movement that in 411 spread from the army at Samos to Athens. The heavy burdens they had to bear because of the ongoing war became a breeding ground for financial grievances, and this factor gave additional impetus to their chief political intention, soon to materialize in the replacement of the democratic constitution. In proceeding to implement their scheme to overthrow the democracy, the conspirators at Samos, counting among their numbers trierarchs of the fleet stationed there, passed a resolution that would have been pleasing to the ears of an ardent oligarch whose criticism of democratic institutions had been publicized some two decades earlier (Ps.-Xen. *Ath. Pol.* 1.13): they resolved "zealously to contribute from their own private resources either money or whatever else should be necessary, feeling that from now on the burdens they would bear would be for no others than themselves" (Thuc. 8.63.4; cf. 48.1). Against this background, one may concede, it was almost inevitable that with the restoration of democratic rule after the brief and unsuccessful oligarchic venture, amendments had to be made in the area of trierarchic obligations.

The introduction of the syntrierarchy (cotrierarchy) was the first known major concession made to the propertied class. It reflected the realization that the financial and personal requirements accruing from trierarchic service had become exorbitant for many men. By way of this institutional innovation, the previous firm adherence to the principle "one man to a ship" was loosened, and permission was given to two or more individuals who wished to cooperate toward discharging a single service. At the same time, this meant the introduction of a new principle, extended liability, which was applied to the allocation of financial burdens and personal labor; as mentioned above, this principle was further developed and hence gained in significance in the period after 358/7. A similar concession made in the field of choregic performance toward the end of the fifth century highlights a prevailing concern to distribute the liturgical burdens among a larger group of men—a policy probably adopted with the intent to encourage volunteers.

While the year of its introduction cannot be firmly established, it seems certain that the new system was operative during the final years of the fifth century.[1] The syntrierarchy of Diogeiton with Alexis Aristodikou (Lys. 32.24, 26) dates from a year between 408 and 406. Another man says that after he persuaded his brother to be his syntrierarch they engaged in some naval activity that took place between Aigospotamoi (405) and the defeat of Athens by Sparta (404) (Isoc. 18.59–60). Co-trierarchies are also attested in a list of crews believed to have fought either at Arginousai (406) or at Aigospotamoi (IG 2².1951).

A scholiast (to Ar. Ran. 404, citing Aristotle as his source) notes that in 406/5 the principle of two men sharing a choregy was introduced for the comic and tragic performances at the Dionysia. However, even though synchoregies by two or three men appear to have been common at the Rural Dionysia (e.g., IG 2².3095), inscriptional evidence strongly indicates the absence of the practice at the City Dionysia in the period 398–329. Therefore, the occurrence of synchoregies at the City Dionysia had most likely been confined to a single year, or to a few years.[2] Insofar as the grant of permission (in one area only temporary, in another permanent) for joint liturgical performances constituted a "package deal" seeking to mitigate the burdens carried by property owners during the distressing final years of the Peloponnesian War (and the increase of the length of respite from one to two years after a trierarchy could belong to a similar context), one may locate the beginning of syntrierarchies in the immediate vicinity of 408/7.

It is confirmed, not least epigraphically, that syntrierarchies, like sole trierarchies, remained a stable feature throughout the following period (until 323/2), remarkably surviving a series of subsequent reforms. Co-operation between two individuals was the norm, especially during the first half of the fourth century.[3] However, joint performances by three or more persons, although rarely attested, were permissible (four: 1609.76–77). From the 350s onward, instances of collaboration among three, and some times up to seven and even ten, syntrierarchs become distinctly more numerous.[4]

Almost nothing is known about the method of arranging groups of syntrierarchs. But it seems certain that whether to serve as sole trierarch or as syntrierarch was a choice that lay with the individual. Isaeus 5.36 implies that Dikaiogenes had the option of undertaking a single trier-archy or a syntrierarchy (cf. Wyse 459). In more than one sense it must have been an advantage to have a dependable partner, and the obvious preference would be for relatives and friends. As noted, a man persuaded his brother to be his cotrierarch shortly after 406 (Isoc. 18.60). Stratokles Diomeieus was joined by his son Eudemos on the trieres *Hene* (before 357/6) and again on *Naukratis Xenokleous* (1612.132–38, 271–73). Pytho-doros Acharneus and a relative of his, Menon, were syntrierarchs on *Eukleia* (356/5: 1612.247–49; *APF* 282–83). Surely, a voluntary syntrier-archy of Demosthenes with Philinos Lakiades on *Heos* stemmed from their decision to cooperate (Dem. 21.161; *IG* 2².1612.301–10). A collabora-tion might arise from an existing business partnership. Davies surmised that the seven syntrierarchies of Aristolochos Erchieus and Antidoros Phalereus could be due to the circumstance that the two men perhaps were partners in a banking business.[5] But other motives are equally pos-sible: the joint service of Nikostratos Halaieus and Polymnestos Ana-phlystios on *Hikane* (1622.265–67) may well have come from a desire to repeat a successful collaboration on *Trieteris* in the 370s (1605.38–39). Such instances, then, cannot be explained except on the supposition that men were generally free to choose both their colleagues and the manner in which to discharge their service. Alternatively, the strategoi might act as intermediaries, grouping together individuals who wished to serve as syntrierarchs.

Firmer inferences can be drawn about the division of responsibility among syntrierarchs. As a rule, if two men took charge of a ship, they shared their active term of duty equally ([Dem.] 50.39–40). But since partners could conclude a private agreement (*synthēkē*) laying down the length of time for which each was obliged to serve ([Dem.] 50.68), I suspect that they were also allowed to deviate from the general rule and fix the length of their respective terms at their convenience. Again, an ever-present possibility that one's partner might not show up enhanced the need to share the service with a dependable colleague, all the more so when, as seems likely, the state did not intervene to furnish a replacement. Isaeus 6.1 may represent a rare instance of two syntrierarchs in charge of their ship simultaneously. The speaker explains: "When Chairestratos set sail as trierarch to Sicily, although, having sailed there myself before, I knew well all the dangers I should encounter, yet, at the request of these friends of mine, I sailed with him and shared his misfortune, and we were both made prisoners of war." Clearly, if a syntrierarchy was really in question, this form of cooperation was exceptional, arising from a special request to an experienced trierarch to help his inexperienced colleague during a long and difficult voyage (cf. also Dem. 24.11–13).[6]

Usually, syntrierarchs shared equally all expenses arising from their term of active duty.[7] The principle of equal distribution of any subsequent financial liabilities (for example, replacement or repair of hulls and equipment) is also consistently encountered in the naval records.[8]

## Effects and Defects

Even though the new system was definitely conducive to lessening in some measure the burdens on certain individuals and to attracting volunteers, in the long run it contributed to the creation of a new problem: difficulties in recruiting enough trierarchs to serve in a year. To discover the main reasons for this one must look first at the number of persons needed to perform trierarchies both before and after the introduction of the syntrierarchy.

For the fifth century the only fairly secure piece of information available is Pseudo-Xenophon's statement (*Ath. Pol.* 3.4) that 400 trierarchs were appointed each year. Kalinka ([1913] 80–81) rightly noted that this should not be taken as evidence for the existence of four hundred instead of three hundred serviceable ships. Therefore, the selection of 400 persons for the trierarchy needs explanation. Davies has made a good case that the number of appointments to festival liturgies was more than 97 in an ordinary year, rising to more than 118 in a Panathenaic year, and that from the 400 men annually selected to perform trierarchies about 100 were or could be temporarily exempt from that obligation because of their engagement in festival liturgies.[9] Indeed, this squares well with the circumstance that the number of trierarchs who might be needed to serve simultaneously (at a time when the principle of "one man to a ship" was still in force) cannot have been higher than the total number of ships Athens is known to have possessed in that period, three hundred. However, while Davies' conclusion that the same class of men performed festival liturgies and trierarchies is unquestionable, his estimate of that class at 300 to 400 property owners throughout the fifth and most of the fourth centuries appears to be too low.[10]

Three points need to be made. First, there was not a distinguishable body of men always performing trierarchies only; rather, rich men discharged trierarchies and festival liturgies. This is firmly established by the vast material from which the liturgical record of wealthy Athenians is reconstructed in *Athenian Propertied Families*.[11] Second, the exemption rules had a direct and significant impact on the number of both those performing trierarchies and those performing festival liturgies. Third, since such an impact worked reciprocally between festival liturgies and the trierarchy, and moreover extended to cover three or more consecutive years, its real force remains undisclosed if one confines consideration to the number of men needed in only one year. For the period during which the rule of one year's respite after any liturgy might have been applicable, one can reckon the numbers needed by taking a three-year interval.

Festival liturgies required monetary outlays and personal involvement for a limited period of time during a year. They had certain essential features in common with the trierarchy (e.g., the exemption rules at large, and particularly the antidosis). But there were fundamental differences as well. A most obvious one was the role of the trierarchy as the nerve-center of naval defense. Again, whereas trierarchs used (and were held financially accountable for) costly material belonging to the public, festival liturgists did not.

Festival liturgies are distinguished by their relative institutional stability. No major reforms comparable to those undergone by the trierarchy occurred in this area: the synchoregy from 405 to about 398, the abolition of honorific exemption in 354 (though the law was attacked for being unconstitutional; Dem. 20), and minor adjustments in the procedure concerning the appointment of choregoi before 348/7[12] are the only changes mentioned by the sources. Emphatically, festival liturgists did not dis-

charge their service with one or more partners, they never became organized into symmories or "joint contributors" groups (*synteleiai*), and they
were not allowed to hire substitutes to perform their duty. One good
indication of the trierarchy's preeminence, militarily, financially, and politically, is the interest it aroused in reformers; another is of course the
higher prestige attached to it compared to other liturgies (Lycurg. *Leoc.*
139–40). Such a privileged place in the liturgical organization may justify
the inference that in decisions pertaining to the recruitment and designation of liturgists at large, trierarchic matters received priority.

The accepted view is that about 100 men were needed annually to
perform the festival liturgies. Furthermore, one may assume that 250
(not 300, as in a less conservative estimate) men were required for the
fleet. While the total of 350 persons would undertake all these obligations
in the first and third years, just as many men would be needed in the
second year. Simply for the system to work effectively in a three-year
period, the number of property owners had to be nearer 700. With regard
to the period during which the syntrierarchy and the two years' respite
after a trierarchy applied (both of which are likely to have been operative
from the final years of the fifth century), a model covering a four-year
interval must be employed.

I proceed from the assumption, based on a guarded reckoning, that
most (four-fifths) of 250 trierarchies—understood as "units"—were to be
performed by single trierarchs, and a smaller number (one-fifth) by pairs
of syntrierarchs; hence in one year there would be needed 200 sole trierarchs and 100 syntrierarchs, 300 in all. Because of the uncertainties
surrounding the continuing existence of the synchoregy, 100 is retained as
the number of men required for festival liturgies. While the 300 trierarchs
of the first year could be deployed again in the fourth year, two new
groups each of an equal size would be necessary in the second and third
years. Festival liturgists, allowed only one year's exemption, would still
total 200 in a three-year period. In sum, within four consecutive years the
class of liturgists should number 1,100 (900 trierarchs plus 200 festival
liturgists); in a less conservative calculation it would approximate 1,200.

A different estimate ought to be made for the first decades of the
fourth century (from the 390s to perhaps the 370s) in that the number of
men needed for the fleet had by then fallen considerably. By how much
one cannot say, nor are any reliable figures forthcoming before the first
extant naval record (1604), which indicates that in 378/7 the number of

trierarchies—again, "units"—was 100 or slightly more. Applying the rates of three-fourths and one-fourth for the distribution, from this year onward, between sole trierarchies and syntrierarchies respectively, there would now be needed 75 single trierarchs and 50 syntrierarchs (125 in all) in one year, and 375 in a four-year period; these together with 200 festival liturgists bring the size of the class to 575.

But any decrease in the field of trierarchies was, in some measure, offset by the introduction (378/7 or shortly after) of the proeisphora. It too was a liturgy normally requiring 300 persons a year. Unlike all other liturgical obligations, it involved no personal labor or (ideally) expenditure other than the supply of a relatively short-term loan; whenever an eisphora tax was levied, the proeispherontes collectively advanced the entire amount, which they then tried to recover individually from a group of taxpayers. In practice, however, the proeispherontes could suffer financial loss as they might prove unable to recoup all or part of the sum they had paid ([Dem.] 50.9). Since they were entitled to exemption, the number of men required in a three-year period would be 600 if eisphora was actually levied in three consecutive years or, alternatively, if the Athenians took such a possibility into account when introducing the system. Hence the total number of liturgists needed in the 370s would have been slightly higher than at the end of the fifth century, that is, 1,175; the approximation to 1,200 then needs no special pleading.

However, each of the latter two models is artificially rigid and bound to break down (1) in the certain presence of individuals exempt because of service in the cavalry (probably 1,000 men after 431),[13] or (2) in the event that syntrierarchies might gain in popularity after circa 408, or, finally, (3) if old members who dropped out of the class at any period could not be promptly replaced by just as many new ones, the replacement rate probably being about 40 men in a year.[14] Admittedly, there were some who discarded the exemption rules and embarked on performance of successive liturgies for a series of years (e.g., Lys. 21.1–6). On the other hand, there were also those insisting on their right to exemption (Isoc. 18.60). Due allowance should also be made for performance of festival liturgies by metics. However, their number seems to have been insignificant; challenging Leptines, Demosthenes (20.20) says "if he can point to five such men, I will eat my words."

The upshot of this is twofold. First, legislative innovations intended to lessen the trierarchic burden on each individual had, if not as a chief objective, then definitely as a major effect, the nominal broadening of the liturgical class with almost twice as many men as were needed for most of the fifth century. Second, and consequently, the estimates of the size of that class at 1,200 property owners by Jones ([1957] 85–86) and Rhodes ([1982] 3–5, 11) come closer to what the actual requirements may have been by the end of the fifth century. My own opinion is that no fewer than 1,200 to 1,500 persons would have been needed if the system were to function properly in a four-year period. The demographic implications of this will not be pursued here. What should be noted, however, is that by setting the number of men annually required to perform trierarchies at 1,200, Periandros's law of 358/7 seems to have formalized a previously unofficial though practically used definition of the size of the propertied class.

But what I have been dealing with so far is simply the numbers *required,* not those actually obtained in any one period; and there are distinct signs that periodically the system did not function smoothly or properly at all. Manpower shortages possibly occurred in the area of festival liturgies[15] (and Leptines' proposal of a law in 356/5 ordering the abolition of exemption from festival liturgies can be seen as an attempt to remedy this situation), and certainly in that of trierarchies.

In the naval record of 378/7 (1604), forty-seven ships are seen (or can be inferred) to bear the description "unallotted," which suggests that about half of the fleet that could be mobilized had to remain passive because of unavailability of single trierarchs or syntrierarchs to take charge of them. In the incompletely preserved record of 373/2 (1607 and 1608), twenty "unallotted" ships are attested; that is, slightly less than one-fourth of the effective force needed commanders. Similar manpower shortages were probably experienced in other years as well. Although the evidence is not crystal-clear on this matter, some measures may have been adopted to counterbalance the disproportion between the number of men (and properties) needed to run the fleet and the number of those actually obtained in a year.

It is possible that syntrierarchies were temporarily suspended so as to achieve a higher ratio of trierarchs to ships. Or trierarchs about to retire might have been induced or forced to remain at their post for an extra term. Either of these could have been applied on a particular occasion. In Mounichion 374/3, the strategos Timotheos departed for his journey around the Peloponnesos with sixty ships in the charge of sixty trierarchs.[16] In reporting Iphikrates' takeover of Timotheos's fleet in the Aegean islands during the next year (373/2), Xenophon (*Hell.* 4.2.14) states that Iphikrates, in order to carry out the planned periplous, effectively obtained crews for the sixty ships that Timotheos had taken under-manned from Athens "and exercised force on the trierarchs" (*kai tous triērarchous ēnagkaze*). Xenophon's laconic and puzzling statement invites the question of what kind of force Iphikrates exercised. The sixty trierarchs had been serving since Mounichion 374/3 (or shortly thereafter), and would have needed to be replaced by fresh trierarchs appointed at the beginning of 373/2. Because of such shortages as reflected in the naval record of 373/2 (1607 and 1608), there may not have been enough men available at Athens to be sent to relieve Iphikrates' trierarchs. So it can be argued that in 373/2 Iphikrates forced the old trierarchs to serve a prolonged or extra term because insufficient replacements, if any, were forthcoming from Athens.[17] In addition, when the sizable fleet of sixty ships was to be manned in 374/3, the right to perform syntrierarchies might have been suspended. However, no evidence can be adduced to buttress the latter contention.

Yet another measure, for which clear evidence exists, was the unofficial acceptance that a gradually growing number of men preferred to perform their service as absentee trierarchs by having their duties transferred to a substitute. Also, old age was no longer a deterrent. More properties able to furnish cash for the fleet was what really mattered; more men to take charge of the ships personally was a secondary issue. If there had been an official pretense that the trierarchy was primarily a military duty requiring valor as well as expenditure, with the departure from the "one man to a ship" principle and with the increasing occurrence of hired trierarchies, that pretense practically vanished, only being rejuvenated (for altogether different purposes) in the law courts.

In conclusion, the concession made to the trierarchic class with the introduction of the syntrierarchy and the rule of two years' respite seems to have aimed at solving (and may in effect have solved) one problem, but in the long run it created another: an occasionally great gap between the formal requirement in any four-year period for many more men to function within a broader network of fiscal obligations, on the one hand, and a substantive inability always to obtain just as many men as were needed, on the other hand. How is this to be explained? Obviously, simple lack of economic potential may still have set a limit on the ability of some to meet their obligations with the frequency and eagerness expected of them. But the picture cannot be complete—however unglamorous it may now look—without taking into account the circumstance that yet others who did possess the economic potential remained averse to employing their wealth in trierarchic expenditure, even in the presence of the option to share the burden with someone else. Favorable treatment of those actually coming forth to serve in a year and leniency toward defaulters seemed therefore a necessary and prudent stand to take.

## Periandros's Reform

The heavy dependence of the state on a well-organized and efficient fiscal system with which to finance the fleet made the serious defects shown by that system in the mid-fourth century a source of growing concern. As argued above, a chief vexation lay partly in the difficulty of securing enough men to expend their time and wealth for the purpose of running the navy, and partly in the lack of effective means to prevent (or at least curtail) shortages of naval matériel. A no less serious problem was to find a way to improve the situation in either area without affecting negatively the cooperation of property owners. Maintenance of an appropriate balance between the elements of option and compulsion as well as stability in the relationship between state and naval financiers seemed imperative, perhaps even more so now than before.

Recognition, by the early 350s, of the urgent need for reform led to the enactment of Periandros's law, probably in 358/7 (*Urkunden* 178). That law remained in force until 340, in which year it was superseded, but not entirely supplanted, by Demosthenes' law; some of the principal components it had introduced persisted as intrinsic features of the trierarchy until 323/2. It is useful to note that a good deal of what is known about Periandros's reform comes from criticisms of its efficiency, which are incorporated in proposals for further changes.

Two chief innovations occurred in 358/7. One is that the group of property owners annually liable to perform trierarchies was officially defined as twelve hundred persons who in formal or informal parlance could also go under the name "joint contributors," synteleis.[18] Another is that this group was organized into twenty divisions of sixty members each, the symmories.[19] Certainly, both of these had a significant impact on the transformation of the institutional setting, yet each was indisputably a corollary of further and equally significant (though less transparent) changes in the way in which the machinery was meant to function in the future. My immediate concern is therefore twofold: to establish the particulars of the new organization, and to reconstruct the main intentions underlying this reform with regard to the obligations and functions of trierarchs.

## One or Two Symmory Systems?

For almost two centuries, the question of how the trierarchy was organized by Periandros's law has been a field rife with conflicting views far too numerous to be addressed in full here. One crucial problem that calls for special treatment, however, not least because of a revival of the debate in recent years, is whether the symmories into which the trierarchy was organized in 358/7 were the same as those established in 378/7 for the eisphora (*FGrH* 328: Philochoros F 41).

In a context exclusively concerned with the trierarchy, the speaker of [Demosthenes] 47.21 explains that it was in accordance with Periandros's law that the symmories were constituted (*synetachthēsan*). Traditionally, "constituted" is taken to mean "created for the first time" and to refer to symmories for the trierarchy as distinct from those used for the eisphora.[20] This view, however, has recently been impugned by Ruschenbusch and Mossé, who argue that the reform of 358/7 did not create new symmories for the trierarchy but reorganized the existing ones so as to accommodate those liable for both the eisphora and the trierarchy.[21]

Particularly, Ruschenbusch maintained (in 1978 and in a series of subsequent articles) that after 358/7, all twelve hundred members of a single symmory system were identical with those who paid the eisphora, and that only three hundred of them were liable for the trierarchy and all other liturgies.[22] MacDowell subscribes to the "one symmory" view, but proposes a distinction between those among the twelve hundred members who performed trierarchies in person, on the one hand, and those who merely contributed to naval costs and paid eisphora, on the other; he argues that, even though in practice trierarchs were always men who were also in the list of the Twelve Hundred, appointment to, and performance of, trierarchies were matters different from membership in a symmory, since the latter also included persons unable to perform personal service; after 340, however, the symmories were used exclusively for the trierarchy, since "there is in fact no evidence at all for the use of symmories for the collection of *eisphora* after 340."[23]

Rhodes defends the traditional view. He follows the contention of Jones and others that the class of men liable for the eisphora was wider than the class of men liable for the trierarchy. He holds that after 357, those liable for the trierarchy were defined as the twelve hundred richest citizens, less those who could claim exemption, and that these men were grouped into symmories especially created for the trierarchy.[24] As is often the case, such diametrically opposed views mainly spring from different interpretations of the scanty body of evidence now available. Admittedly, none of the sources inherently possesses the strength needed to deliver the *coup de grâce* to one or the other theory, so the disagreement will in all likelihood persist. Still, the evidence seems to justify the older view in the form in which it has most recently been put forward by Rhodes. This entails a commitment to reconsider the main sources and arguments that have been employed in the debate.

The argument from silence seems to me to be the least valid of all. Scholars accepting the "one symmory" view list a number of passages that mention the symmories but that, in their opinion, fail to draw a distinction between eisphora and trierarchic symmories, and explain this by saying that such a distinction did not exist.[25] How much truth is there in this? One relevant passage is Demosthenes 14.16–18. Here, MacDowell argues ([1986] 439), Demosthenes "talks about 'the 1200' and symmories for several sentences before mentioning triremes; it is not likely that he would have left his listeners in the dark so long before making clear which system of symmories he was talking about, if there were in fact two systems." One answer to this (which MacDowell himself offers) is that Demosthenes' mention (as early as 14.16) of the Twelve Hundred would have made it plain to his listeners which of the two symmory systems he meant (at 21.155 he explicitly links the Twelve Hundred with the trierarchy), especially when much of what is said in the pertinent speech is about naval preparation.

Incidentally, MacDowell seems elsewhere not to be in doubt that Demosthenes 14.16–18 mentions the symmories in a specifically trierarchic or naval context.[26] Moreover, the identification of the Twelve Hundred as payers of eisphora rests on the connection made at Demosthenes 14.19–20 between the valuation (timema) of Attica (six thousand talents), on the one hand, and the twelve hundred *triērarchountes* and their symmories, on the other. But in fact, Demosthenes does not say that eisphora should be paid, or that the overall timema was possessed, by only twelve hundred persons. What he proposes is simply to graft upon the Twelve Hundred, by way of allotment, the total amount of wealth declared for eisphora purposes. How to raise funds, first and foremost by means of eisphorai, is a theme he addresses in subsequent sections (14.24–29).

Another passage is Demosthenes 18.103, in which Demosthenes speaks of the navy and suddenly mentions the leaders (*hēgemones*) of the symmories. Assuming (against Rhodes) that the title hegemon was used both for the leaders of the eisphora and for those of the trierarchic symmories, MacDowell infers ([1986] 439) that Demosthenes referred to (and his listeners understood) only one symmory system. The context to which this passage belongs is Demosthenes' reform of 340, which is addressed in detail below. Here it is sufficient to note that, while hegemones is the title consistently used for the leaders of eisphora symmories, there is not a single piece of evidence to show that the same title was borne by the leaders of trierarchic symmories. The gloss of Harpocration (s.v. "hegemon symmorias"), cited by MacDowell to buttress his contention that it was, proves unhelpful in this regard: the lexicographer merely says (with reference to Dem. 18 and a lost speech of Hypereides, fr. 159 [Kenyon]) that a hegemon was the richest member of a symmory—which kind of symmory one cannot say from this gloss alone. So Demosthenes (18.103; cf. 312), could very well say that his law of 340 transferred the trierarchic burdens to the three hundred richest Athenians without necessarily meaning that these persons held the same position within the trierarchic symmories as they did within the eisphora symmories. There may be less ambiguity in this passage than MacDowell thinks.[27]

Indeed, there is little ambiguity in another passage in which the hegemones of the symmories and the Three Hundred are mentioned in connection with the eisphora (Dem. 2.29 and 13.20): "Before, Athenians, you used to pay eisphorai by symmories, now you conduct your politics by symmories. A rhetor is hegemon of each symmory, with a strategos under him and three hundred to do the shouting. The rest of you are assigned some to the one, some to the other [sc. hegemon and strategos]." The body politic is here likened to the organization responsible for the eisphora: the symmories are headed by hegemones who are immediately followed by the three hundred richest Athenians, and then by the remaining taxpayers. An important clue to the size of the eisphora-paying class may be furnished by the parallel drawn between a large number of Athenians and ordinary taxpayers. To sum up, the argument from silence carries no force.

Beyond this, three sources are commonly adduced in support of the theory that one and the same symmory system incorporated all eisphora-payers and trierarchs.

(i) One (and the most important) of these contains Demosthenes' proposals presented in 354 with a view to altering certain aspects of the Periandric system that until then had purportedly functioned unsatisfactorily. Foremost among these shortcomings was an inability to achieve the goal of recruiting all of the twelve hundred persons formally required in a year. To remedy this, Demosthenes (14.16–17) proposes the following:

> I say that you must enlarge the 1200 and make 2000, by adding 800 to them; if you designate that number, I believe that, when heiresses, orphans, property of cleruchs and corporations, and any disabled men [adynatos] have been deducted, that will give you 1200 persons. Out of these I think you should form 20 symmories, as there are at present, each containing 60 persons. Each of these symmories you are to divide into 5 parts of 12 men, matching the richest with the poorest in every case. (Tr. MacDowell [1986] 441)

Since the twelve hundred symmory members, it was argued by Lipsius ([1878] 296), included certain categories of property owners who for various reasons could not be asked to go on active service as trierarchs, and since the number of those exempt (eight hundred) is too high for that group to have come into existence in the few years between Periandros's law and 354, it follows that the Twelve Hundred must have been constituted for a different purpose, that is, the eisphora, and that those of the Twelve Hundred not eligible for the trierarchy were only liable to pay eisphora. A case in point is a man described as "adynatos," a word interpreted variously: some think it refers to physical disability, and suggest that such a man would have the economic potential to pay eisphora but not the ability to perform an active trierarchy in person;[28] others think it refers to financial inability, and suppose that the same man would have possessed property enough to be liable for the eisphora but not enough to discharge trierarchies.[29]

(ii) Ruschenbusch finds the latter view confirmed by the second source to be discussed here. In his attack (355/4) on Leptines' law, which ordered the abolition of exemption from festival liturgies, Demosthenes (20.28) makes the remark: "So those who have too little property to justify a trierarchy will make contributions to the war in payments of *eisphora,* while those who attain the level for service as trierarchs will be of use to you in both ways, trierarchy and *eisphora*" (tr. MacDowell [1986] 440).

Such a distinction, in economic terms, between those liable for the trierarchy and those liable for the eisphora is believed to be consonant with the idea that men among the Twelve Hundred who possessed less than the minimum amount of property entailing eligibility for the trierarchy (in Ruschenbusch's opinion, four talents, two thousand drachmas) would have had to pay the tax only.[30]

(iii) Finally, the existence of a single symmory system is thought to be implied by Isokrates' boastful enumeration (in circa 354/3) of his own and his adoptive son's public outlays. Speaking of himself, he says (15.145): "You have enrolled not only yourself but your son among the Twelve Hundred who pay the eisphorai and perform the other liturgies, and both of you have discharged three trierarchies, and have performed all other liturgies with greater expense and splendor than the laws require." Isokrates' words, contend the supporters of this theory, are most obviously interpreted as meaning that the twelve hundred persons were identical with those paying eisphora and performing liturgies.[31]

However, neither of the interpretations under review is tenable.[32] First, consider Demosthenes 14.16–18. Lipsius did not take into account the possibility that the Twelve Hundred might have been selected by means of a procedure identical (or similar) to that used for the appointment of trierarchs in the fifth century (Ps.-Xen. *Ath. Pol.* 3.4): the preliminary determination, every year, of a gross body of persons potentially liable, and then the selection of a net body of persons who were de facto liable after deducting those entitled to exemption. Four hundred trierarchs were appointed annually during a period (the early 420s) in which Athens had about three hundred ships, each to be headed by a single trierarch, and when a hundred men from this group could be exempted from the trierarchy on various counts. It is possible, then, that the Twelve Hundred were also a preliminarily assembled body of property owners required to discharge liturgies in a year, among whom there were persons not legally obliged to discharge a service. In this view, it is not necessary to suppose that the Twelve Hundred existed before 358/7, or that a good many of them were only liable to pay eisphora.

Second, a serious error is the inference from Demosthenes 14.16–17 that the categories of property owners exempt from trierarchic service (heiresses, orphans, klerouchs, corporations, and adynatoi) nevertheless retained their membership in symmories. This seems to be both self-contradictory and the opposite of what Demosthenes says. Obviously, his legislative scheme did not intend to alter the provision of the Periandric law that twelve hundred persons should perform trierarchies, but to propose a means by which so many men could actually be obtained. This, Demosthenes suggested, should be done by initially selecting a group that was larger than twelve hundred by as many property owners as were usually exempt (in his opinion, eight hundred persons). When those entitled to exemption had been deducted from the initial group of two thousand, then the Athenians would get a net body of twelve hundred persons to fill the twenty symmories, precisely as prescribed by Periandros's law. Ultimately, therefore, the eight hundred persons exempted did *not* become members of the symmories and the formal body of trierarchs either in Demosthenes' scheme or under the Periandric system currently in force. One must simply distinguish between the body of property owners initially assembled (which included persons and properties entitled to exemption), on the one hand, and the net body of twelve hundred required by law to perform trierarchies after exemptions were granted, on the other.

Third, the presence of adynatoi among the categories exempted remains disturbing, and is unexplained by the current interpretations. Physical inability is rendered less likely by the presence, in the trierarchic class, of persons incapable of performing active service in person (Isoc. 15.5). One Epigenes was forced to be trierarch in spite of his poor health and loss of possessions during the Dekeleian War (Lys. fr. 35 [Thalheim]). Nikeratos, son of Nikias, characterized as "physically an utter weakling" (Dem. 21.165), had an impressive trierarchic record.[33] In addition, there was the option offered to all to transfer their service to a contractor (cf. pp. 95–102). Financial inability seems not to constitute a more viable alternative because exemption on this ground was obtained through the antidosis; since a petitioner had to furnish a replacement, no reduction in the numbers of those liable, such as the one claimed at Demosthenes 14.16, would have ensued.

Another and perhaps better interpretation of the term *adynatoi* ("those not able" to perform a trierarchy) may be the following. Even if a man was both physically and financially capable of undertaking a service, he might nevertheless have been unable to do so for legal reasons—that is, because he was discharging another liturgy at the time. Apollodoros boasts of his willingness to advance the proeisphora in 362 by saying: "Of these [sc. persons selected in that year to pay the proeisphorai] I was the first to pay the proeisphorai, nor did I seek to get myself excused on the ground that I was serving as trierarch and could not [*ouk an dynaimēn*] perform two liturgies at the same time, or that the laws did not allow such a thing" ([Dem.] 50.9). If a person, in 362, could consider himself adynatos (not able) to perform two liturgies simultaneously because the law did not permit such a thing, nothing prevents the supposition that in 354 Demosthenes could well call "adynatoi" persons claiming exemption for much the same reason. This interpretation has the additional advantage of including in the Demosthenic list of persons entitled to exemption (14.16) the considerable group of men currently performing some liturgy other than the trierarchy.

Finally, it is often taken for granted that the Twelve Hundred consisted of a standing and clearly defined body of property owners registered for fiscal purposes (the eisphora or the trierarchy), which body included heiresses, orphans, and the like. But this view is unsupported. As I argued in chapter 3, no such official and currently kept trierarchic registers can be traced in the entire body of evidence.

Once the interpretation of Demosthenes 14.16–18 as indicating the inclusion in the Twelve Hundred of all those who paid the eisphora is disposed of, Demosthenes' remark at 20.28 (see p. 187) can simply mean that there was a group of persons rich enough to perform trierarchies and pay eisphora, and another group financially able to contribute to the tax only. "So this person," Demosthenes (20.26) says, "who owns much, contributes much to these objects [sc. trierarchies and eisphorai]; there is no getting out of it." Consider also the following. In 403 no more than about five thousand citizens would have lost their civic rights as a result of Phormisios's proposal to limit citizenship to those who owned land in Attica (Dion. Hal. 32, *Lys.* 526 = Lys. 34 hyp.). Diodoros (18.18.5) reports that nine thousand persons retained their citizenship when the limitation of the franchise to those owning property worth 2,000 drachmas or more was carried out after Antipatros's abolition of democracy in 322/1.[34] According to Polybios (2.62.6–7), the taxable capital of Athens in 378/7 amounted to 5,750 talents; for 354 Demosthenes (14.19) gives it as 6,000 talents. On this evidence Boeckh (Staatsh. 1³.615–16) correctly remarked that the figure twelve hundred for all those liable to pay eisphora is too low.

Alternatively, assume for the sake of argument that the taxpaying group numbered no more than twelve hundred. In that case, attestation of a certain individual as liable to pay eisphora by virtue of being the lessee of property worth a mere 700 drachmas would unavoidably lead to the conclusion that the same man was a member of an organization comprising the twelve hundred richest Athenians.[35] This is impossible. For that reason alone Isokrates' words (15.145; cf. p. 187) must be taken to mean that the Twelve Hundred performed all the liturgies and paid eisphora because they were the richest citizens, unlike other, less wealthy citizens who did not perform liturgies but paid eisphora.[36] Perhaps one should take seriously the implication at Demosthenes 2.29 that the number of eisphora-payers was much larger than twelve hundred.

A few more sources adduced in support of the "one symmory" theory will be treated below. But none of the passages just reviewed can sustain the skepticism of some scholars about the institution, by Periandros's law, of symmories exclusively used for the trierarchy and distinct from those used for the eisphora.

## The Number and Composition of Symmories

Whatever the number of eisphora symmories (it is widely believed they totaled one hundred: Jones [1957] 28), those for the trierarchy were apparently always twenty intended to be composed of sixty members each. In 354, Demosthenes (14.17) could say, no doubt with reference to the current Periandric regime, that there were presently twenty symmories that should, but did not always, comprise sixty persons each.[37] However, there is disagreement about the number of symmories after 354.

Scholars holding the "one symmory" view argue that at least one of the proposals put forward by Demosthenes in that year was carried into effect: a subdivision of the existing twenty symmories into one hundred parts.[38] Demosthenes calls the latter simply "parts" (mere); but since mention is made of the "twenty large symmories" (14.19, 21), by implication, these parts could also be called (small) symmories. The same scholars find this affirmed by a fragment of Kleidemos (*FGrH* 323: Kleidemos F 8), which they date to circa 350, and which, inter alia, reports that there are one hundred symmories. Ruschenbusch ([1978] 282–83) seeks to confirm that hypothesis by citing four fragments, believed to be from a single naval inscription, listing ships under the names of more than twenty individuals acting as heads of symmories (*IG* 2².1615, 1617, 1618, 1619). On these grounds, and because the Three Hundred, who were affected by Demosthenes' subsequent reform of 340, are commonly identified with the hegemones (leaders), *deuteroi* (seconds) and *tritoi* (thirds) of the hundred eisphora symmories,[39] it is then concluded that from 354 onward the number of symmories (used for both the eisphora and the trierarchy) was one hundred. However, each component upholding this theory turns out to be precarious.

First, as noted by Schaefer (*Demosthenes* 1:468–69), Demosthenes' proposals of 354 were never carried out. Their economic practicability, Davies points out (*Wealth* 35), was all too easily assumed, and "one receives the unfortunate impression that in 354 Demosthenes was thinking more in terms of arithmetical neatness and administrative convenience than of individual circumstances and personal burdens." An even more disturbing observation is that in 330 Demosthenes (18.102–8) praised highly his law of 340, while at the same time delivering a devastating attack on the trierarchic law previously in force; unless one assumes the introduction of another law between 354 and 340 (for which there is no evidence), it is most unlikely that he would so fiercely attack his own legislation of 354.[40]

Second, the fragment of Kleidemos cannot be securely or approximately dated to any specific period in the fourth century. To use Demosthenes 14.16–17 in order to do so would involve a circular argument; neither is it possible to say whether it speaks of trierarchic or eisphora symmories, though this is not a problem for those who maintain that there was only one symmory system. Third, the number of individuals listed as leaders of symmories in the fragments assumed to belong to one naval inscription can only indicate the number of symmories if it were proven (and it is not) that all men listed there acted in such a capacity in the same year; it is distinctly possible that they may have served in separate years, and no evidence has been adduced for the claim that all of the relevant fragments really belonged to the same inscription (Laing [1968] 245 n. 4). Fourth, there is no evidence to support the assumption that the Three Hundred formally functioned as hegemones, deuteroi, and tritoi within the trierarchic system before or after 340;[41] indeed, they all were liable to perform, and most of them performed, trierarchies because they were the richest citizens (Dem. 18.171). The crucial question, however, is whether they had a more formal affiliation to the trierarchy than just that.

Almost all of the sources that make explicit mention of that group (or some of its members; cf. note 39) unanimously associate it with the eisphora, proeisphora, and symmories. One might argue that, since the strategoi supervised the affairs of the Three Hundred, as well as of tri-erarchs,[42] the symmories to which the hegemones, deuteroi, and tritoi belonged had responsibility for the eisphora (and proeisphora) and the trierarchy. But this argument is rendered invalid by evidence showing that, whereas in the early 320s antidoseis for the Three Hundred were still carried out by the strategoi ([Dem.] 42.5), in the same period these and other tasks pertaining to the trierarchy had been transferred to one strategos with special responsibility for the trierarchic symmories (*Ath. Pol.* 61.1; *IG* 2².1629.208–10).

Given the likelihood of a significant degree of continuity of member-ship among the Three Hundred (Wallace [1989] 479), it would have been perfectly possible, in any case, to view them (and speak of them) as a clearly defined body, both functionally and corporately. For these rea-sons, it can be argued, one could say that they were greatly affected by Demosthenes' trierarchic law of 340 (Dem. 18.103–4, 312; Aesch. 3.222; Din. 1.42; Hyp. fr. 134), without necessarily implying that this body formally functioned as hegemones, deuteroi, and tritoi also within a tri-erarchic framework. In conclusion, no good evidence can be cited to show a further reorganization of the system in 354 aimed at increasing the number of trierarchic symmories to one hundred.

To return to other changes documented (or inferred) to have occurred after 358/7: Periandros's law assigned the supervision of each of the twenty symmories to one of their members who acted as superintendent (epimeletes) of his own group. The Twenty (*hoi eikosi*), referred to in a naval inscription from 334/3, are very probably the epimeletai of the symmories (1623.155). Presumably, their tenure lasted one year, though a man could volunteer to hold the position more than once. Part of their job must have been to supervise the affairs of their respective groups, to act as formal representatives of the symmories vis-à-vis the naval administration, and to assist, individually or as a unified body, the strategoi in the management of naval matters.[43]

Symmories were formed at (or soon after) the annual appointment of trierarchs by way of a more or less even distribution of the persons available in a year into twenty groups. It is probably true that often (perhaps every year) and for various reasons the prescribed number of twelve hundred persons could not be obtained in full; in 354, Demosthenes (14.16) claimed that about eight hundred were lacking in a year. Possibly the composition of symmories was arranged by the strategoi (in the late fourth century by the strategos of the symmories) so as to obtain a fair representation of the wealthiest men in each group.[44] An ingenious attempt has been made to determine the various levels of wealth possessed by members of synteleiai groups (joint contributors), and to reconstruct the distribution, within each group, of the burdens carried by each individual in proportion to his wealth. The findings of such an investigation would have laudably added much to our knowledge, but unfortunately in this case the calculations are based on questionable grounds.[45]

Finally, after 358/7 all Athenian ships were distributed among the twenty trierarchic symmories (instead of among individual trierarchs, as previously) so that members of a symmory in a given year served only on ships belonging to that symmory. As noted above (p. 82), the description of hulls as "unallotted" is completely absent from the records of this period; the fragments *Inscriptiones Graecae* 2².1615 through 1619 and 1625 list ships according to their symmory; and [Demosthenes] 47.29 indicates that trierarchs served on the ships of their common symmory.[46] Again, no absolutely equal distribution seems always to have been possible. Inasmuch as the total number of ships could not be divided into exactly twenty parts (for instance, the 283 triereis in 357/6), some symmories must have had fewer ships than others. For the same reasons one should expect an unequal representation of "select" ships (or any of the other ratings), and of tetrereis.

So much for the new institutional setting. But what about the way it was meant to function?

## Trierarchs and Synteleis

With sixty members in each symmory to take care of fewer than twenty ships, it was hoped in 358/7 that the stark disparity, experienced in previous years, between the number of available trierarchs and the total number of ships should be effectively eliminated in the future. With regard to the performance of active service, however, Periandros's legislation left the pre-358/7 system basically unchanged: the naval records of the period from 357/6 to circa 342/1 make it plain that trierarchies continued to be discharged by sole trierarchs or by groups of syntrierarchs, not by groups of joint contributors (synteleis). Since the total number of ships probably never exceeded 350 in the same period, it is virtually certain that only some of the twelve hundred men to be selected annually were expected to be active at any time. But if so, what were the functions of the remaining segment?

One of the most welcome outcomes of the symmory debate is an incipient recognition of the existence of two functionally differentiated groups within the body of the Twelve Hundred: men performing active trierarchies (trierarchs in the proper sense), and groups of joint contributors (synteleis) providing financial assistance to members of their symmories who were currently serving or had just served on a ship. However, there is nothing to recommend the idea of either obligation being carried by two distinct groups of men.[47] Rather, the distinction was simply a nominal one determined by the function performed at a given time, since a man acting as a joint contributor in one year might have been a trierarch proper on a different occasion or might be asked to sail as an active trierarch later in the same year.[48] It turns out that all twelve hundred could be called trierarchs as well as synteleis (Dem. 14.20; 18.104).

Regrettably, the evidence is too poor to enable us to unravel the modus operandi of the *synteleia* system in detail. Demosthenes (21.154–55) stresses the differences between performing trierarchies before and after 358/7: whereas previously, he claims, men bore all costs from their own means, now a man like Meidias could undertake a trierarchy with little or no cost to himself. The degree to which evasive action was made possible by exploiting the current system, one may suspect, is exaggerated here. Yet this point aside, there is no reason to question the central claim in Demosthenes 18.104 that a sole trierarch could now be helped financially by the synteleis.

At Isaeus 7.38 the point is again made that it was far more demanding (and hence more virtuous) to perform trierarchies under the previous system, when trierarchic symmories were not in existence. For Thrasyllos Leukonoieus, states the speaker in 354, "not only performed all the other liturgies, but also served as trierarch continuously, not [making the ship] while acting as a member of a symmory, as people do now, but from his own means, not jointly with another man but alone, not taking two years off but continuously, not doing it perfunctorily but furnishing (or preparing) everything as well as he could."

The expression in brackets could provide an important clue to the function of the symmories. But most modern editors doubt its authenticity because, they think, it makes no sense: trierarchs (or the symmories) could not be possibly asked "to make [build] a ship." Some suggest that it ought to be emended to other expressions, such as "to furnish the ship," "to prepare the ship," or "to man the ship."[49] Rejecting all these alternatives, Wyse (580–81) preferred to omit the expression altogether, reasoning that the antithesis of "from a symmory" and "from his own means" is false: "Both before and after the creation of the symmoriai the trierarch 'paid out of his own pocket.'" But this is not entirely true: like Demosthenes 21.154–55, this source insists (and almost all agree at least on this) that trierarchs were helped financially by their colleagues—that is, members of their symmories or synteleis. Commentators, in short, have sought to alter or dispose completely of the expression, but this they do on the basis of some unsatisfactory assumptions. To say "to make a ship" in such a context may pose a problem only if it is taken literally. However, one cannot be certain that it should be understood that way.

Since the naval records make it clear that sole trierarchs or syntrierarchs remained wholly responsible for their ships and equipment, it is possible to rule out two things: (1) that the *total* trierarchic expenditure was shared by a wider group of synteleis, and (2) that active trierarchies were discharged by synteleis. Even though Demosthenes (21.155) calls all of the Twelve Hundred synteleis, his own voluntary service with Philinos Lakiades in 358/7 or 357/6 is described as a (syn)trierarchy (21.161; 18.99), and the same is true of Meidias's service in 348 (21.160–61, 167). It looks as if there was a tendency to use, inappropriately, the terms *trierarch* and *synteles* as synonymous (Dem. 18.104). In addition, I have noted that syntrierarchs shared their expenses equally, but not so with any synteleis they might have. Consequently, the financial obligations of synteleis were limited to certain areas.

One area in which a group of synteleis would have collaborated was that of making one or more ships from their symmory ready for a journey. The expression "to make a ship" in Isaeus 7.38 may refer specifically to that duty. Indeed, a ship was looked after within a particular symmory. This is likely the context of Demosthenes' statement that sixteen synteleis were responsible for one ship (18.104). Again, that figure is thought to be improbably high, because it is unconfirmed by the naval records; hence it is emended to yield groups of seven and eleven.[50] But this is unnecessary. Although Demosthenes' figure (sixteen synteleis to one ship) might be an exaggeration, or else represent an extreme case, the need for emendation is strictly unwarranted, not least because such a group of sixteen, if its function really was to contribute to the cost of preparing the ship only, would hardly be expected to appear in the naval records, unless its members somehow had incurred a debt payable to the naval administration. Another source, which says that before 340 trierarchies were performed by groups of six and seven (Hyp. fr. 134), is fully compatible with the view that a number of men cooperated to prepare one or more ships.

There are no specific reasons why one should assume with MacDowell ([1986] 442–44) that only the richest among the Twelve Hundred were to discharge active trierarchies. On the contrary, one specific complaint exists to the effect that the richest members might spend less than their less wealthy colleagues, and another states that all men in a synteleia contributed the same share regardless of economic position (Dem. 21.155; 18.102–8). Considering the option of introducing the principle of synteleia into choregic performances (as had already been done with the trierarchy), Demosthenes (20.23) stated in 354, "in that case each man will make a small contribution from his own means, and none would be hardly treated, even if his property were quite small." Rather than alluding to a proportional allocation of economic burdens, this passage may simply mean that the contributions of synteleis generally were so small that even men with relatively small properties could afford the cost. But there may be some rhetorical distortion in this. It is easy to envisage a situation in which less wealthy individuals at times had to bear the burdens of an active trierarchy, while a number of their wealthier fellows only contributed relatively small amounts toward the cost of putting the ship to sea. If this is more or less what Demosthenes wanted to alter in 340 (18.104), as seems likely, there can be no doubt that for some the system worked unjustly.[51]

Timely preparation and dispatch of a fleet were preeminent objectives pursued by various other means as well. A significant one was the regular provision, by the state, of an amount to each trierarch just before a voyage, probably for the purpose of covering part of his expenditure on crews. Two sources can be adduced in support of this. The first ([Dem.] 51.11) is fairly forthright and says that each trierarch received three thousand drachmas per voyage. The second needs to be discussed at some length. Traditionally, a passage reporting how Meidias performed his first trierarchy (Dem. 21.155) has been translated as follows:

He has only put his hand to the task since you made twelve hundred citizens joint contributors [synteleis], from whom such men as Meidias exact a talent and then contract for the equipment of the trireme at the same price. After this the state provides the crews and furnishes the tackle; so that some of them succeed in really spending nothing at all and by pretending to have performed one public service enjoy exemption from the rest.

Virtually all commentators take the key sentences of this passage to mean that rich men like Meidias collected a talent from the twelve hundred synteleis, with which they then paid for the expenses of their trierarchy.[52] But this, it can be argued, is not quite what Demosthenes says, and the accepted translation contains a disturbing improbability, namely that a trierarch received contributions from all twelve hundred synteleis. An alternative rendering, which is closer to the Greek text, and which eliminates that improbability, is the following: "you [sc. the Athenians] have made [*pepoiēkate*] twelve hundred synteleis, you yourselves [*hymeis*], from whom [*par' hōn*] they [sc. men like Meidias] collect a talent."[53]

According to this translation, a trierarch collects a talent not from the twelve hundred synteleis but from the state. Hence, except for the difference in the amounts paid (one talent may have been given to a sole trierarch, three thousand drachmas to each syntrierarch), Demosthenes 21.155 and [Demosthenes] 51.11 seem basically to refer to the same thing: trierarchs about to assume active service cashed in an amount from the treasury. By being provided with ready cash, the trierarchs (some of whom may have had to spend some extra time in raising loans with which to fund their obligation) could thus proceed to hire their complements more quickly than before.

Another means employed to avoid delays was the intervention (financial or otherwise) of the state in order to speed up the process of repairing ships. The evidence relating to the particular procedures followed was set forth in chapter 6. But it is useful to recall that in trying to recoup its expenditure from the trierarchs charged with the cost of repair, the state introduced arrangements recognizably modeled on the philosophy of self-help and joint contributions (synteleia). So this is probably another area in which groups of synteleis within a symmory assisted the trierarch. Explicit evidence for the performance of that task by synteleis comes from a year after 340 (IG 2².1631) and is best treated under the system of that period. Here I will merely note that adherence to this principle served the double objective of spreading the financial perils among more men and of having the fleet promptly repaired and constantly maintained.

No clear picture exists of what precisely the synteleia system entailed in terms of monetary contributions toward the performance of trierarchies. Yet a probable explanation that fits all the evidence is that groups of men provided financial support to those among their fellow symmory members who were currently assigned to an active trierarchy. Arrangements of this sort were solidly founded on a principle offering tangible advantages to both trierarchs and the state: that of extended liability. Appreciably clearer is the operation of that principle in the field of outstanding naval liabilities, addressed in detail in chapter 7. By Periandros's law the responsibility to recover public equipment from defaulters was delegated to the new administrative and fiscal units, the symmories. Their epimeletai as well as those of their members about to assume active service were obliged to act as debt collectors, and hence became formally accountable for the whole volume of debts owed within their own group. The process of transforming the trierarchic obligation into a tax proper was well under way.

Although many details remain unknown, it is possible to offer a general evaluation of the main intentions of Periandros's reform and to say something about its merits and shortcomings. Probably the most remarkable feature of the Periandric system is that it ambitiously sought to address both sources of previous concern (shortages of manpower and equipment) in a single rectification scheme. Essentially, in order to increase the efficacy of the system, the principle of extended liability was more rigorously defined and expanded, while at the same time a further concession was made to the trierarchic class. First, the official designation of twelve hundred as the number of individuals needed to undertake trierarchies in a year was intended not only to ensure an adequate supply of commanders who would share among them the overall burdens but also to make a wider circle of men answerable for deficiencies in naval matériel. Second, the allocation of all responsibilities (and of the ships) to twenty symmories was aimed at delineating far more clearly the fiscal duties incumbent on each symmory (and ultimately on each individual), on the one hand, while it allowed the state to exercise a greater degree of control over its naval financiers, on the other.

However, even though some of its elements proved quite successful (first and foremost the symmories), an insoluble conflict within its main objectives—to increase the fiscal efficiency of the system without causing discontent in the trierarchic class—rendered the scheme as a whole an impossible circle to square. One of its most fierce critics could point to two shortcomings: that the burdens were distributed unequally among individuals, and that not all of the twelve hundred men required annually were always obtained (Dem. 14.16; 18.102–8). Inevitably, therefore, further changes were to follow (see pp. 207–13).

## Voluntary Naval Contributions

A significant development beginning in the early 350s was that wealthy citizens were frequently requested to come forth voluntarily and undertake responsibility for part of the naval burden. In principle there was nothing new in this; volunteer trierarchs (*ethelontai*) did exist also in the preceding period (e.g., Isoc. 18.59–60). What constituted a novelty by the mid-fourth century (and distinguished these particular contributions from individual acts of largess) was the introduction into the naval sphere of a practice already resorted to in other areas whenever the regular channels of obtaining revenue either had failed or, for some reason, could not be used: a formal appeal for public subscriptions, epidoseis.

Little can be said today about the general characteristics of such subscriptions without repeating (here summarily) the views of A. Kuenzi and L. Migeotte. In short, epidoseis were exceptional arrangements, formally introduced and organized by the state, that in addition to setting forth the occasion, the purpose, and even the size of contributions, also specified the honors to be bestowed on contributors. Their implementation involved a three-stage process. First, a resolution was passed by the political authorities (generally the assembly). Second, promises were made by donors to contribute; by so doing they legally validated their obligation to provide what was required of them, thus placing themselves in a position analogous to that of public debtors (at any rate until they had fulfilled their promise). Third, payment of contributions was usually followed by publication of official lists, both of those who had and, less praiseworthily, of those who had not kept their promises.[54]

The latter two stages are referred to in the earliest account securely attesting the implementation of a subscription, Isaeus 5.37–38 (of circa 389):

> Though so many eisphorai for the cost of the war and the safety of the city have been made by all citizens, Dikaiogenes has never contributed anything, except that after the capture of Lechaion (392), at the request of another citizen, he promised in the assembly a subscription of three hundred drachmas . . . This sum he promised but did not pay, and his name was posted on a list of defaulters in front of the statues of the eponymous heroes, which was headed: "These are they who voluntarily promised the people to contribute money for the salvation of the city and failed to pay the amount promised."[55]

While men failing to keep their promises ran a considerable risk of being faced with public disdain, it is not clear whether any (and if so, which) juridical sanctions were applied to them.[56] On the other hand, it is beyond doubt that, being subject to the controls of statute and to a fair degree of social pressure, epidoseis were in reality appreciably less voluntary than they might appear to be at first sight. Their true significance came closer to a tax (Migeotte [1982] 51). Exactly when they were used for the first time at Athens is a problem still debated, but it seems certain that they had been established by the final years of the fifth century.[57]

Within this general framework, then, naval epidoseis came to occupy a distinct position. They differed from all other state-organized subscriptions by virtue of their sometimes idiosyncratic forms and special field of application; also, unlike individual cases of optionally undertaken trierarchic expenditure, they were contributions collectively solicited, organized, and monitored by the state.

But what did naval epidoseis mean precisely? Historians have traditionally answered this by saying that they consisted of two often (but not always) coextensive acts: to make a gift of a ship to the state, to perform a voluntary trierarchy, or both. Some wealthy individuals, it is maintained, put their privately owned warships in the service of, or presented them to, the state; they may or may not have commanded them as trierarchs. Other individuals responded to epidoseis simply by presenting themselves voluntarily for trierarchic service or offering to take on the cost of running a ship.[58] However, some crucial elements of this view can be challenged. First an important question must be reconsidered: did certain citizens, in the late fifth century and throughout the fourth century, own warships that could occasionally be deployed in the Athenian fleet?

In the Introduction I mentioned Kleinias's participation in the naval engagement of 481/0 with his own trieres and crew, and made the point that this example, typical of previous practices, is also the last to appear on record as far as Athens is concerned. The only other known example encountered in the following period that can securely attest the private possession of a warship is that of Makartatos son of Apolexis, who "sold his land-plot and bought a trieres, which he manned and sailed away in it to Crete," where he perished in battle (Isae. 11.48). But although this instance, probably to be dated between 386 and 380 (*APF* 85), bespeaks the relative ease with which an individual could purchase his own trieres (provided that he possessed the financial means), it alludes to a situation fundamentally different from that of Kleinias: Makartatos employed his ship not as a member, or in the service, of the military establishment but in order to embark on the pursuit of his own interests as a privateer, perhaps assisting some Cretan city or cities at war with the Spartans.

That an Athenian citizen in command of a regular warship acted beyond the control of the political authorities almost caused a serious diplomatic incident (as it was feared that his action would imperil the peace between Athens and Sparta) and gave rise to enough anxiety at Athens for it to become the subject of a debate in the assembly. Quite different (but equally disturbing) was the episode concerning Demainetos's unauthorized use of a trieres in order to join Konon's Persian fleet (396). Because he deployed a public vessel for an entirely private purpose, he was subject to punishment (*Hell. Oxy.* 1.1–3; 3.1–2). True, there is nothing to suggest that private possession of warships was prohibited by law. Still, it certainly looks as if the only man known to have had one,

Makartatos, operated outside the institutional boundaries of the "national fleet."

Several individuals are believed to have possessed and employed their own warships in national service, but the evidence for this is weak and ambiguous.[59] In describing Alkibiades' diplomatic activity in the summer of 415, Thucydides (6.50.1) says: "After this Alkibiades sailed in his own ship (*tēi hautou nēi*) over to Messene and made proposals to the Messenians for an alliance."[60] Dover stated with certainty that "his own ship" means "literally his own (cf. Thuc. 61.6), not simply the ship in which he sailed as general."[61] But this conclusion is not warranted by the language of Thucydides, since it was perfectly possible for somebody to speak of a ship as being "his own" in the sense that he merely was in charge of it. This is brought out by two different instances concerning trierarchs manifestly in charge of public vessels.[62]

In addition, Xenophon (*Hell.* 1.5.11) reports under the year 407 that "Alkibiades, hearing that Thrasyboulos had come out from the Hellespont and was investing Phokaia, sailed across to see him, leaving in command of the fleet his helmsman Antiochos, with orders not to attack Lysander's ships. Antiochos, however, with his own ship [*tēi te hautou nēi*] and one other sailed to Notion into the harbor of Ephesos and coasted along past the very prows of Lysander's ships" (1.5.12). Clearly, "his own ship" does not mean that Antiochos was the actual owner, but only that he was temporarily in charge of Alkibiades' flagship.[63] Probably, then, this is the sense in which the expression "his own ship" is used by Thucydides (6.50.1), namely, that Alkibiades sailed on his flagship, and the same may also be true of Plutarch's statement (*Per.* 35.1) that "Perikles had gone aboard his own trieres [*epi tēn heautou triērē*]."

With a single exception, then, the examples considered so far do not furnish proof that individuals possessed their own warships, while the one that does (Isae. 11.48) concerns a privateer engaged in a conflict between foreign states. Besides, the latter case highlights the awkward political entanglements likely to result insofar as the state was not in a position to restrain the ventures of men who, by virtue of owning a warship, could act in the double capacity of privateers and Athenian commanders. In the light of a major emphasis on naval strength after 483/2, implementation of the policies projected by the political bodies in war as well as in peace could only be ensured through seizure by the state of absolute control over an entirely "national fleet." (Ships supplied by the allies became subject to that control.) In the post-Themistoklean naval organization, the duplicate functions performed by Kleinias and others before him (i.e., owners of private ships and commanders in the fleet) were effectively severed so as to guarantee the state's monopoly of armed violence at sea. In 355, Xenophon (*Vect.* 3.14) could contrast "the state ownership of public triereis" with the private ownership of merchant vessels. It is not unlikely that he alluded to the current concept of a "national fleet" in which privately owned warships had no place.

I now return to naval epidoseis. The first, Demosthenes states (21.161), were made for the campaign to Euboia in the summer of 357—an expedition that resulted in the conclusion of an alliance with the Euboian cities.[64] Among the public-spirited citizens to respond promptly to this request were Demosthenes and Philinos Lakiades, who cooperated as syntrierarchs on a ship. Like a number of other men, they presented themselves for service as volunteer trierarchs (Dem. 21.161). Since both men were held accountable for a considerable amount of equipment (*IG* $2^2$.1612.301–10), their naval contributions in 357 (like those of others) consisted in performing ordinary trierarchies on ships supplied and equipped by the state.

By describing the epidoseis of 357 as the first to occur, Demosthenes no doubt wanted to say that these were the first subscriptions formally solicited and organized by the state, as opposed to similar, albeit informal and isolated, contributions spontaneously made by individuals in the past.[65] The wealthy banker Pasion, for instance, had at some date before 370 made voluntarily epidoseis of five triereis: "and he voluntarily contributed five triereis [*pente triēreis ethelontēs epidous*], and manning them at his own expense he discharged [five] trierarchies [*kai par' heautou plērōsas etriērarchēse triērarchias*]" ([Dem.] 45.85). This does not mean that he donated five ships (which would have represented an extraordinary feat, whether one supposes that he himself possessed so many triereis or that he had paid for their construction). It means, rather, that he optionally performed five separate trierarchies on ships for which he had supplied crews at his own expense. An analogous instance may be that mentioned by Xenophon (*Hell.* 2.3.40): during the Peloponnesian War, Antiphon had supplied (*pareicheto*) two fast-sailing triereis. Again, such a benefaction probably did not consist of a donation to the state of two triereis that Antiphon himself owned, as Jordan believed (*AN* 91–92), but of his offer to pay for the staffing and operation of two ships (*APF* 327).

Demosthenes (21.161–62) reports two subsequent appeals for epidoseis. One of these was made for the dispatch of a force to Olynthos in 349/8, and is commonly associated with the first of three expeditions recorded by Philochoros: the Athenians sent thirty triereis under Chares, and "completed the manning of a further eight ships" (*FGrH* 328: Philochoros F 49). While Demosthenes and Philochoros may well refer to the same event, there are no compelling reasons to suppose, with Migeotte ([1983] 141) and others, that subscriptions were limited to the eight additional ships. The other appeal is mentioned by Demosthenes as a recent event, possibly related to a new Athenian intervention in Euboia in the following spring (348).[66] As in 357, both of these subsequent appeals were for volunteer trierarchs, not, as is widely maintained, for subscriptions consisting of a double generosity: to perform trierarchies and to offer ships.[67] The next known call for epidoseis, in the spring of 340, seems to have been of much the same kind. Its double objective was pursued by introducing two parallel arrangements.

One was designed with a view to obtaining naval commanders *and* financiers. Hypereides Kollyteus (the orator) is recorded as having sailed off in 340/39 on "the trieres he had contributed voluntarily" (*epidosimos triērēs*) under the strategoi leading the force sent to besiege Byzantion, Phokion and Kephisophon (1628.436–52; 1629.957–75; [Plut.] *Mor.* 848E). As has been suggested, this trieres may well have been part of the force sent in the spring of 340 to assist the Chalkidian Kallias, which numbered forty triereis "assembled by way of epidoseis on the initiative of Hypereides, who was the first to make an epidosis of two triereis on his own behalf and on behalf of his son."[68] Again, it is supposed that some, if not all, of these contributions (and certainly those of Hypereides) represented gifts of triereis.[69]

However, such a supposition corresponds poorly with Hypereides later being made liable to replace the trieres in his charge by paying five thousand drachmas, which sum, because of his failure to advance it, was in 325/4 doubled to ten thousand drachmas (1628.436–52; 1629.957–75). It is improbable that Hypereides would have been presented with such a claim if he really had donated that ship. More unlikely, furthermore, is that prior to the dispatch of a squadron to help the Chalkidians each contributor would have accomplished the formidable task of either building or procuring a ship. (Hypereides would have had to supply two!)

Finally, can it be the case that subscriptions were prompted by a shortage of ships? Definitely not. Especially after 358/7, Athens was well supplied with seaworthy hulls (cf. chapter 6). The number of ships for 340 is unknown, but it would almost certainly lie somewhere between 349 (the total for 353/2) and 392 (that for 330/29).[70] The appeal of 340, then, could hardly have been for hulls. On the contrary, what seems to have been urgently needed was men willing to take charge of the ships and provide the funds required for their operation. It may be concluded that trierarchic epidoseis, on this and all other occasions, did not consist of a gift of a warship to the state, but generally of undertaking voluntarily a naval obligation that, at that particular time and in those circumstances, one had no legal obligation to undertake.[71]

The other arrangement in the spring of 340 had as its prime objective the conversion from public to private of further naval costs accruing from the military aid to the Chalkidians. A number of Athenian ships lent to the Chalkidians were placed under the collective financial responsibility of a group of Athenian citizens. Mention of the relevant transaction is made in the naval record of 334/3, which introduces a list of twenty-three persons—most of them prominent men of their day—under the heading: "[The following are] guarantors of [triereis]," and ends by stating: "These owe an additional 845 drachmas for the value of equipment."[72]

Sixteen years after the subscription (in 325/4), fifteen of these twenty-three individuals made a payment, personally or through an heir, toward meeting their debts, while the remaining eight had either already defrayed their liabilities or simply had paid nothing, which meant they were not mentioned in the record of that year (1629.516ff.). It looks as if the enthusiasm of some was not matched by their eagerness to make a cash contribution. At any rate, since the individual payments in 325/4 are of a quite uniform size (some of 256, others of 285 drachmas), the 845 drachmas listed as overdue in 334/3 cannot be the sum total owed by all twenty-three persons (1623.197–99). Rather, it must represent a uniform sum to be paid by each of them. There is nothing to indicate that the ships lent to Chalkis by way of epidoseis had been gifts.[73]

It looks then as if twenty-three guarantors had undertaken collectively financial responsibility for the equipment of the ships for Chalkis. Because of the failure on the part of the Chalkidians to return (or make good the loss of) this equipment, each guarantor was charged with an equal share in the total amount to be paid in compensation. The size of their original debt is not known. But since by 334/3 each of them still owed a uniform sum, it is likely that they had made previous installments of a likewise uniform amount. Finally, in 325/4, following a decree of Demades ordering that these debts be cleared, some guarantors paid further (perhaps the last) installments.

Certain similarities between these proceedings and other known transactions in which the overall naval costs are distributed equally within a wider group of men strongly encourage the belief that in this instance, too, expenditure was shouldered by individuals as a kind of tax. Typically, the formal (and first attested) description of a group of naval financiers as "guarantors" not only reflects but is also fully consonant with the current tendency to privatize any excessive financial risks accruing from naval enterprises, and to introduce a functional distinction between trierarchs, in the old sense, and contributors to naval costs. Indeed, both elements are recognizably at work in another instance of epidoseis discussed above (see pp. 143–44): three individuals owed exactly 258 drachmas, 3 obols each, because in 338/7 they had promised to contribute to an epidosis toward the repair expenses of three ships.

What all these men were really required to do by occasional appeals for epidoseis was to take on their shoulders an economic burden that the state had no interest in lifting in the long run, and that could not currently be sustained from within the regular network of trierarchic obligations. Prompt cash payments did not always matter greatly. From 358/7 on, men and funds required in addition to those that could be obtained through the established institutional channels were assembled by means of exceptional resort to formal subscriptions.

While coercion—in the guise of social and political pressure in the boule or assembly—played a distinct role in these measures, the epidoseis were brilliantly enriched with a face-saving element manifest in the opportunity offered to an individual to be the recipient of honorary rewards in return for contributions officially stamped as "voluntary." However, incorporation of naval subscriptions into a formal legal structure should not be seen as a sign that the established trierarchic system had not stood the test of time, but perhaps as symptomatic of the state's attempts to privatize an ever-increasing part of its naval expenditure without adding to the fiscal burdens already borne by that system.

## Demosthenes' Reform of 340

Certain elements of the Periandric regime were soon found to function unsatisfactorily. In consequence, a new reform aiming to rectify that system was introduced in 340. Evidence relating to two squadrons commissioned in separate years will help illustrate the adjustments carried out by means of this reform.

One squadron was to escort a corn transport in 326/5. The record of that year makes reference to the decree authorizing the dockyard officials to issue a number of tetrereis (six or so) under the command of the strategos Thrasyboulos Erchieus (1628.37–42). One ship, *Hegemonia*, was entirely in the charge of the treasurer of the sacred ship *Paralos* (1628.79–88); the remaining four tetrereis for which information exists were delivered to groups of three or four syntrierarchs. While each of these four ships was in the charge of a principal trierarch,[74] a different group of men functioned simultaneously as syntrierarchs on two or three of these ships. For example, Kephisodotos Sybrides was syntrierarch on *Kratousa Smikrionos* with three colleagues, on *Paralia Demotelous* with two others, and on [——]nos Chairestratou again with two others.[75] This confirms my point that active service continued to be performed by sole trierarchs or syntrierarchs, not by synteleis.

It seems, then, that the syntrierarchic obligations of certain men in this squadron were extended to cover more than one ship. Given that syntrierarchs shared equally all costs of service, the financial responsibility of Kephisodotos Sybrides really amounted to one-quarter of the costs from *Kratousa,* one-third of the costs from *Paralia,* and one-third of the costs from [——]nos Chairestratou. But since all these add up to almost an entire trierarchy on a single ship, what was the point, one may ask, of not assigning Kephisodotos to a sole trierarchy? Three complementary explanations can be offered, each of which evinces the advantages of this arrangement both to individual trierarchs and to the state.

First, a man's current economic potential may have been insufficient to sustain expenditure on a whole trierarchy; it might be precisely for this reason that Alkibiades Thymaitades' liability was limited to one-quarter of the costs of one ship (*IG* 2².1628.51–62). Second, whereas Kephisodotos Sybrides would have carried virtually all costs on his own if he were assigned to a single trierarchy, by acting as an equal partner with seven others on three ships, he could count on receiving financial support from his colleagues on each of these ships. Third, any economic risks related to a claim for compensation on account of damages or losses were conveniently spread (to take the same case) among eight men and three different ships.

Another squadron was commissioned for the colonizing expedition to the Adriatic in 325/4; it consisted of triereis, tetrereis, and triakontors. The naval record of that year preserves the rubrics for only ten ships (1629.1–164, 272–78). An interesting and revealing feature is the distribution of men to ships as well as the composition of groups of syntrierarchs.

To begin with, in conformity with standard practices, some persons were simply principal trierarchs or syntrierarchs on just one ship. For instance, Aristogenes Philaides served as sole trierarch on the tetreres *Eueteria Archeneo* (ll. 272–78), while Kritodemos Lamptreus served as principal trierarch with two syntrierarchs on the trieres *Kouphotate Tolmaiou* (ll. 1–21). But there is another group of men who acted simultaneously as principal trierarchs or syntrierarchs on as many as three different ships. One of them, Derkippos Kopreios, was a syntrierarch on the triereis *Kouphotate Tolmaiou* with two colleagues, on *Euphemia Epigenous* with one colleague, and on *Stephanephoria Hagnodemou* with two colleagues; that is, he shared responsibility for three ships with five other men (ll. 1–63). Equally energetic was Phrynaios Athmoneus, who served as principal trierarch on the triakontor *[——]ia Antandrou* with one colleague, as sole trierarch on another triakontor, *[——]a/e Chairestratou,* and as syntrierarch on a third triakontor, *[——]era Chairionos* with one colleague—three ships were now in the hands of three men (ll. 91–144). More or less the same pattern is shown in the services of others.[76]

So here one can detect a trend unmistakably similar to that revealed by the squadron of 326/5: the actual liability of Derkippos Kopreios, reckoned in terms of his share in each ship, consisted of one-third of the costs from *Kouphotate Tolmaiou,* half of the costs from *Euphemia Epigenous,* and one-third of the costs from *Stephanephoria Hagnodemou.* Together these amount to more than the cost of a sole trierarchy. By the same reckoning, the burdens of *Phrynaios Athmoneus* are tantamount to two sole trierarchies. What the record makes fairly plain is that of the ten persons attested, five shared responsibility for nine ships belonging to one and the same squadron. On average, this yields a ratio of ships to trierarchs of almost two to one; this is not (even though it might appear to be) a return to and expansion of the fifth-century system. Last, but not least, there is a distinct (albeit not steep) graduation in the individual trierarchic burdens borne by the men in this group. I will now turn to the motivations for, and effects of, Demosthenes' trierarchic law of 340, as recounted by the author of the reform himself (18.102–8).

First, a word on the date of its introduction and the length of time it remained in force. Although explicit evidence is lacking, the law probably belongs to 340.[77] However, it is widely believed that on Aeschines' initiative the law was either amended or completely superseded by the enactment of another law shortly after 338.[78] This view must be rejected as invalid on two counts. Aeschines' attack (3.222) cannot be dated precisely; while, as Schaefer plausibly suggests (*Demosthenes* 2:527 n. 2), it may not have been launched in the same year in which Demosthenes proposed his law, nothing indicates that it took place several years after 340. Also, Aeschines' charge seems to have been specifically directed against alleged misdemeanors (or simply the mismanagement of naval affairs) perpetrated by Demosthenes during his tenure as superintendent of the navy, *epistatēs tou nautikou* (3.222), which he held *after* his law was carried out and not before, as Schaefer and others believed.[79] I therefore conclude that the system introduced by Demosthenes probably remained in force at least until 323/2.[80]

What were the innovations introduced by this reform? One of Demosthenes' cardinal claims (Dem. 18.102–8) is that the navy was in a state of dissolution because the overall burdens were unfairly distributed between those members of the trierarchic class who owned much and those who owned less. Accordingly, seeking to remedy the shortcomings intrinsic in the Periandric system, his legislation introduced an equitable method of allocation by forcing "the [very] wealthy to do what was just" (namely, to contribute in accordance with their economic standing), while preventing the wrongful oppression of the less wealthy. In short, the solution was to transfer the trierarchies (which, as Dem. 18.107–8 makes plain, does not mean the obligation to perform trierarchies as such but part of the trierarchic expenditure) from men with lesser means to men of great affluence.[81] On a practical level, this goal was accomplished by fixing the contributions of each man in proportion to his property, so that an individual who was formerly one of sixteen contributors to a single trieres might now appear to be trierarch on two ships (104).

Just how the principles of the new law were put to work and what sort of rearrangements they occasioned in the distribution of services and costs among trierarchs are patently demonstrated by the evidence relating to the squadrons dispatched in 326/5 and 325/4. Numerous other examples can be cited from the naval records of the post-340 period to show that Demosthenes' reform was implemented successfully and—as far as one can tell—remained a sound piece of business. In essence, then, this law obliged a very wealthy person to act as principal trierarch on one or two ships, or to discharge simultaneously a number of syntrierarchies whose cumulative expenses could quite often be equal to, and sometimes in excess of, those for two sole trierarchies. At the same time, it gave less wealthy men the opportunity to spend on a term of service shares proportionate to their economic ability.

Regarding the extent to which the previous system was altered, it appears that Demosthenes' reform cut fairly deeply in a single but profoundly sensitive area, that of distribution. Not unexpectedly, the new regulations provoked reactions from those most likely to be directly affected: the three hundred richest Athenians, or the hegemones, seconds, and thirds of the symmories. Much of what is known of their endeavors to quash the enactment of the law both before and under the legislative proceedings cannot be taken at face value, as it is embedded in the passionate accounts either of Demosthenes himself or of his political opponents. The list includes attempts to bribe Demosthenes to withdraw his scheme as well as an unsuccessful indictment of the proposal by a *graphē paranomōn* while it was preliminarily treated in the assembly; moreover, Dinarchos (1.42) raised the accusation that Demosthenes did actually accept bribes to alter and redraft his proposal in every meeting of the assembly.

Whatever the credibility of these allegations, at least this much seems certain: the Three Hundred (or a number from that group) were opposed to the new scheme because it transferred to them a greater economic burden than they had to carry hitherto. But is it true, as many scholars maintain, that Demosthenes' law reduced the number of men liable to perform trierarchies from twelve hundred to only three hundred?[82] Davies, who believes the normal size of the trierarchic class to have been on the order of three hundred persons, claims that "far from creating a new, and unprecedentedly restricted class of men liable to the trierarchy, Demosthenes' law merely rectified a serious anomaly by restoring and systematizing the status quo . . . The one attempt to alter its [sc. the trierarchic class's] size, that of Periandros, was a disastrous failure."[83] However, if there was an area in which Periandros's law was *not* a failure, this is it, and there are substantial reasons now to endorse the alternative (and older) view that officially those liable to perform trierarchies in a year continued to number twelve hundred.[84]

First, although the three hundred richest citizens were indisputably among the Periandric group of twelve hundred, no proof exists to the effect that their specific functions as leaders, seconds, and thirds of symmories formally applied to the trierarchy.[85] Second, most sources seem to say that the reform of 340 caused grievances among the Three Hundred, not that it limited liability for the trierarchy to that group only,[86] and one passage (Dem. 18.107) says (or at least implies) that relatively poorer members of the trierarchic class continued to discharge trierarchies under Demosthenes' law, though now they were greatly relieved by its equitable distribution of burdens. A fragment from a speech of Hypereides (159 [Jensen/Kenyon]), preserved by a lexicographer (Harp., s.v. "symmoria"), says that "there are fifteen men in each symmory." On the assumption that this refers to a year after 340 and to the twenty trierarchic symmories, Rhodes infers ([1982] 6, 10) that the total number of men liable must have been three hundred. Yet the speech "Peri Polyeuktou peri tou Diagrammatos," to which this fragment belongs, cannot be dated with certainty, and, more importantly, all of the extant references in this speech to the symmories or the hegemones exclusively concern the eisphora (cf. Harp., s.v. "diagramma," "diagrapheus," "hegemon symmorias," "symmoria"), not the trierarchy.

Third, epigraphic evidence can now be adduced to suggest that twelve hundred trierarchs were formally required in a year after Demosthenes' reform. I have attempted elsewhere to reconstruct the list of members (and ships) of a particular symmory in the year 324/3.[87] The persons attested in that symmory add up to at least thirty-six and could possibly have been as many as forty. These are shown to have served simultaneously in syntrierarchic groups of various sizes (i.e., in pairs or groups of four or even ten) on seventeen different ships. While in the light of evidence referring or alluding to manpower shortages it is doubtful whether the formal objective of obtaining twelve hundred persons was achieved every year (Dem. 14.16), it is quite likely that the total number of men in the symmory of 324/3 came fairly close to sixty. Moreover, given that approximately four hundred ships were allocated into twenty symmories in 324/3, the attested seventeen ships belonging to the symmory in question would be near the maximum number.

Demosthenes' reform did not affect the Periandric innovation holding that officially twelve hundred men should undertake trierarchies, but effectively imposed on the three hundred richest persons from that group the obligation to carry heavier financial burdens. Hence, rather than reflecting a decline in the capital resources of Athens (Davies *Wealth* 23), this measure signifies a prodigiously gallant and bold resolution to offer relief to many among the Twelve Hundred by means of diverting into the naval-fiscal channels a greater share of the wealth possessed by a few of their notoriously affluent fellows.

Yet the new legislation was not entirely concerned with riding roughshod over the Three Hundred: an appreciable concession was made to this group as well by allowing them to spread their enlarged financial responsibilities and risks over more ships and to share their services with a group of colleagues. Preservation of the goodwill of naval financiers was still of prime importance; the naval records corroborate the view that the Demosthenic legislation may have proved successful in eliminating a growing discontent imminently threatening, under the Periandric system, the relationship between the state and a majority of property owners.

Nor did Demosthenes' reform change the number of trierarchic symmories, which continued to be twenty.[88] Many details of the arrangements made within each symmory and the possible cooperation between various symmories still remain dismally obscure. But the general lines of development are now easy to see; because of the new principle of proportional distribution, the symmories had undergone the sort of adjustments likely to produce the patterns of sole trierarchies and syntrierarchies shown by the discussion of the squadrons of 326/5 and 325/4.

The synteleia principle and that of extended liability were, however, still applied (even though Dem. 18.104 might create the impression that the term *syntelēs* became obsolete). As noted in chapter 7, Onetor Meliteus was in 334/3 officially appointed a syntrierarch of Pausanias Agrylethen with the sole purpose of helping the latter defray his outstanding liability to replace a ship. Likewise, in 323/2, a substantial number of men formally called synteleis did much the same by financially helping out trierarchs owing equipment (*IG* $2^2$.1631.442ff., 517ff.). By the 330s, the meaning of the term *(syn)trierarch* had become broad enough to unite appropriately the functions of commander of a warship, naval financier, and taxpayer into a single and (in spite of its institutional complexity) unobtrusively simple concept.

## *The Sociopolitical Profile*

One last question is this: what was the political and social profile of the individuals performing trierarchies? Their supreme economic position is beyond doubt, while the sources of their wealth are now known to a satisfactorily detailed degree (*APF; Davies Wealth* 38–72). Several of the topics I have discussed relating to the magnitude of their affluence may have demonstrated clearly that they definitely did *not* come from "all walks of life," nor, as one scholar claimed, did they belong to the middle class—whatever may be the criteria used to define that class.[89] "We are the men who perform liturgies, we are those who pay the proeisphora, we are the rich," Demosthenes (21.153) makes Meidias brag with self-complacency and, in this context, a good measure of audacity (cf. also the general statement in Arist. *Pol.* 1291a33–34). The fundamental and incontestable truth of this utterance is that men of the trierarchic class, in particular, constituted—and so when dealing with them one stands face-to-face with—the top segment of the Athenian aristocracy of wealth. But it would be satisfying to know more about them. Concretely, besides the bare ascertainment of their economic circumstances, what other features of their position and activities within Athenian society could possibly justify such pride as shown in Meidias's statement?

To begin with the political arena, the narrower issue of allegiance to democratic or oligarchic ideology and government, although important in other respects, is not of concern here. Much more essential to my present purposes is the question whether (and if so, to what degree) members of the trierarchic class might try to exert an influence on decision making in the democracy. As far as simple attendance at the assembly and law courts is concerned, wealthy Athenians generally did not lack interest or enthusiasm for engaging in political activity, even though it is still a point of scholarly disagreement whether the numerically dominant group during sessions was actually the "rich," the "poor," or a largely hypothetical "middle class."[90] More significantly, systematic and diligent collection of prosopographical data from the whole of the classical period fully confirms the active participation of the wealthy in Athenian public life, both as holders of military, financial, and other magistracies and as members of the council.[91]

Yet three principal elements embodied in the democratic constitution or custom opened these positions also to a far larger group of citizens, and effectively prevented the system from being contaminated by co-optation. First, with the exception of certain major magistracies subject to direct election (e.g., the generalship), most offices were filled through application of the lot. Second, property qualifications were generally disregarded, even though they were explicitly ordained by law. Third, the majority of officeholders were remunerated from public funds.[92]

A different and clearer picture emerges when one moves beyond the issue of simple participation in the assembly, law courts, and magistracies to examine the representation of the wealthy in positions requiring a substantially more active involvement in, as well as offering the option of greater influence on, political decisions. Hansen has argued persuasively that these were the positions held by rhetores (those addressing assemblies or the council, or proposing laws, decrees, and the like) and the board of ten annually elected military commanders, strategoi. The combined group of rhetores and strategoi was "the nearest equivalent of what we with a much vaguer and less formal term call 'politicians' or 'political leaders.'"[93]

To his study of this core of politically active citizens, Hansen appends a list of the names of 373 attested rhetores and strategoi, which list, he notes, cannot claim to be complete.[94] The remarkably high representation of the wealthy in this group is revealed in that 114 (or about 30 percent) are present in Davies' register of liturgists in *Athenian Propertied Families*. But I should enter the important caveat that this percentage may be somewhat inflated, since Davies' register also includes the relatives of those known to have performed liturgies. Therefore, a more secure method, albeit one confirming rather than altering the basic pattern already exposed, is to examine how many among the attested rhetores and strategoi are known to have performed trierarchies. Among the 373 persons listed by Hansen, I can single out 58 trierarchountes (or 15.5 percent). This is quite significant, not least because if a complete list of rhetores and strategoi existed, the proportion of the trierarchic class would be expected to have been even higher. In an equal representation of the various social components of the citizen body, the number of trierarchs should not have exceeded about 4 percent, that is, their proportion (twelve hundred) in a total citizen population of thirty thousand.

So the conclusion one is compelled to draw is that the higher economic stratum, and specifically the trierarchic class, had more than its share of possibilities to exert influence on political decisions. True, education, possession of skills (especially in rhetoric), leisure, and perhaps a greater motivation for active participation by those in disagreement with current political trends go a good way toward explaining this phenomenon. A most potent factor, ably and fully treated by Ober (1989), was the preservation, under democracy, of a balanced relationship between the majority of citizens and the economic elite, in which the latter were granted prestigious leading positions in the state in return for their contributions—be they in the form of military leadership, good counsel, or financial outlay. But one must make allowance for the presence, within the same class, of political quietists, or those who minded their own business (*apragmones*). Although their number remains unquantifiable, there is good evidence to show that these men cherished a different ideology, deeming it morally commendable to stay away from the forefront of public life, or even to abstain from participating in the assembly, the law courts, and the nomination of candidates to offices and the council.[95]

Thus Meidias's self-complacent boast "we are the men who perform liturgies, we are those who pay the proeisphora, we are the rich" (Dem. 21.153) was comfortably sustained by—and indeed contained a hidden reference to—the strong political profile of his class. But its justification derived also from another hard fact: that mainly through their liturgical outlays people of Meidias's standing made an enormous contribution to the national revenue. This needs demonstration.

Bearing in mind that "averages" are artificial constructs obscuring important variations (and fluctuations over time), one can attempt to estimate what may have been spent annually on the fleet. It seems likely that the running costs of a trierarchy amounted to about 3,000 drachmas (expenditures on trierarchies transferred to a contractor will not be taken into account here). One individual is known to have spent 8,000 drachmas on three trierarchies, or on average 2,666 drachmas per service (Lys. 19.42; cf. 19.29). Another was trierarch for seven years and claims to have spent 36,000 drachmas, an annual average of 5,142 drachmas (Lys. 21.2). I do not know how these services were discharged; theoretically, some or all might have been syntrierarchies, in which case the cash actually spent would have been well in excess of the attested amounts. In another instance, each of two syntrierarchs paid 2,400 drachmas, a total of 4,800 drachmas (Lys. 32.26).

This last piece of information stems from the accounts of current expenditure kept by one syntrierarch; therefore, it certainly does (and the other sums might) relate only to running costs. Compensatory payments, usually amounting to a further 5,000 drachmas (but frequently enlarged by fines), raised expenditures to a higher level. To be on the safe side, one can set the average cost of an entire trierarchy at 6,000 to 7,000 drachmas. The real magnitude of these contributions can be judged by setting them against the daily earnings of contemporary laborers. In the last decade of the fifth century, a skilled worker was paid 1 drachma, or more rarely 1.5 drachmas, per day (cf. the Erechtheion accounts, 409/8–407/6: IG 1².373–74 = IG 1³.474–79). Toward the end of the period, an unskilled worker was paid 1.5 drachmas, and a skilled worker 2 to 2.5 drachmas, per day (the Eleusinian accounts, 329/8 and 327/6: IG 2².1672–73). Granted, this is a rough guide, because one cannot always be sure that such earnings made up the whole of a man's daily income. But since it is doubtful that any supplementary amounts would have made more than a trivial contribution, these figures are still valid for my point that, even if he worked every single day in a year, it would take some five to eight years for an ordinary Athenian to earn what a trierarch spent in one year.

Assuming now an annual number of sixty trierarchies, the total private cash spent on the fleet is on the order of 360,000 to 420,000 drachmas (60 to 70 talents) a year. When the expenditure on one hundred festival liturgies (each averaging at least 1,000 drachmas) is added,[96] the total contributions of the whole liturgical class rise to 460,000 to 520,000 drachmas (roughly 77 to 87 talents) a year. According to Hansen's calculations ([1991] 315–16), the cost of Athenian democracy in the 330s was about 100 talents a year. It is instructive to note that at one point in the mid-fourth century, when the revenue annually coming into the treasury totaled no more than 130 talents, the annual liturgical contributions equaled about 59 to 67 percent of that amount! At a slightly later date, at the end of the 340s, when the incoming annual revenue had risen to 400 talents, the liturgical contributions still equaled a respectable 19 to 21 percent.[97]

Certainly, payments of eisphora and proeisphora would have taken either percentage considerably higher, but it is best to exclude these contributions here because they were irregular, and because in principle the amounts forwarded with the second obligation were expected to be recovered. Yet even without these services, it is easy to see that in economic and social terms, too, the trierarchic class had powerful reasons to develop a self-awareness—and insist on wide recognition—of its being not only the backbone of the navy but also one of the pillars of Athenian society at large.

# Epilogue

The huge requirements for funds to operate the awesome but costly engines of war, it has been argued, rendered the presence of an efficient fiscal infrastructure indispensable right after the creation at Athens of a large, state-owned fleet in the years 483/2–481/0. In particular, the unprecedentedly heavy logistic burden (posed partly by the structural and tactical characteristics of the new man-of-war, the trieres, and partly by its sizable complement), coupled with the immense expenditure accruing from maintenance, necessitated the presence aboard each ship of a financier capable of aiding the state treasury by supplying funds quickly and on the spot, and by undertaking financial responsibility for damages or losses.

Despite the unavailability of direct evidence for the character of the trierarchy in early fifth century, it now seems hard to accept the previous postulate about a pristine initial stage in which the trierarchic institution was solely or even predominantly a military one. The Themistokles decree cannot affirm that contention. This is not to say that militarily the trierarchy was an empty shell; the point I wish to emphasize is rather that its fiscal significance was pronounced from the outset.

Such a conspicuous military expansion and reorganization as that witnessed in the final years of the 480s—motivated by the objective of achieving naval supremacy, and purportedly championed by Themistokles—proved politically and socially disruptive in two important respects. For one, creation of a corps of warship commanders, the trierarchs, who were to take charge of ships exclusively belonging to a "national" fleet, transferred an important occupation from its previous locus of private ship ownership, based on the archetypal values of aristocratic military prowess and status-determined munificence, to the financial repository of the liturgy system. For another, the diversion of the naval command into the liturgical orbit placed munificence in this area under the regulatory mechanisms of democratic statutes that generally but unequivocally spelled out the obligation incumbent on wealthy citizens to serve the state (or the people) with their "body and property" (*tōi sōmati kai tois chrēmasi tēi polei lēitourgein*).

Both processes, it has been suggested above, led to—and reflect—the emergence of a single institutional framework formally encompassing a section of the citizen body distinguished for its possession of wealth: that is, the liturgy of the trierarchy. No direct evidence survives to show the trierarchy as a liturgy during these early stages, but enough is now known about its vital role in naval finances during the subsequent and better-documented period for the onus of proof to be shifted to those who claim that it was not. An observation of a positive character should also be added: the operation of the liturgy system by 481/0 in the area of choregic performances renders the expansion of that system with the incorporation of the trierarchy perfectly possible and likely.

In some measure, this new institutional structure seems to have been erected partly on the foundations of an earlier one, though in terms of evidence it would be unwise to identify this latter specifically with the naukrariai; it is a prevalent ethic rather than a narrowly delineated institutional entity to which one should properly turn to discover a possible precursor. "Ever for the sake of *aretai*," uttered Pindar in his praise of the avenues to aristocratic excellence (*Ol.* 5.15), "do toil and expense strive to achieve a deed whose outcome is shrouded in danger and uncertainty; but when men are successful they seem wise even to the citizens" (tr. Adkins [1960] 160).[1]

The originally aristocratic idea (accepted at the heart of democracy and successfully cultivated throughout the fifth and fourth centuries) that toil and expenditure not only mark the excellence of a whole class, but also are honored by equals and unequals alike with the rewards of social and political esteem, made the terms of the liturgy system acceptable to most, if not all, wealthy Athenians. Due observance of his trierarchic duties in general, like his display of zeal to have his ship promptly fitted out and commissioned, earned the trierarch the honor of a crown and the much coveted title of philotimos.[2] By the mid-fourth century the honorific attribute philotimos ideally embodied the twin virtues of munificence *and* military valor; this is succinctly brought out by Demosthenes' ruthless attack on Meidias (21.159–67), and by other sources as well.[3]

Yet, paradoxically, although the notion of military valor persevered as an ideal worthy of emulation, in real life its significance had noticeably begun to fade away. The process can largely be described as the domestication, under Athenian democracy, of the aristocratic warrior. One must enter the reasonable qualification that perhaps the ideal could be upheld as long as trierarchies were discharged in accordance with the principle that one man should be wholly responsible for, and serve in person on, a single ship. But with the departure from that principle in the last decade of the fifth century, that notion was progressively eroded as successive reforms transformed and redefined the network of obligations in a way that ill fits the image of the warrior, but fits quite well that of the taxpayer.

The extension of responsibility for one ship to a larger group of men (syntrierarchs and synteleis), the increase in the number of absentee trierarchs who hired out their services to substitutes, the emergence of a functional distinction between commanders proper and naval financiers, the organization of trierarchs into symmories, and not least the use of coercion to prevent attempts to evade the obligation, all were distinct signs that the traditional striving for the reward of arete through "toil and expenditure" survived in the liturgical context by perpetuating a myth about aristocratic military valor. It met the needs of the community for resources and personnel to ensure its defense, and, in the long run, it offered a convenient arena of activity within which the members of the propertied elite could amass the credit and prestige required to pursue their personal ambitions. My findings on the criteria determining eligibility for the trierarchy lend further weight to this.

Indeed, as far as the evidence admits of firm conclusions, eligibility for the trierarchy was based not on the ability to command, or on technical skills in navigation (though possession of either could prove advantageous), but exclusively on the criterion of possession of wealth; this was always reckoned in relative, not absolute, terms. The absence of any specific lower limit (however narrowly or broadly defined) for properties incurring liability to the duty was plausibly born from the wish to ensure the constant presence of a sufficiently large number of men to serve as trierarchs, notwithstanding possible fluctuations in the level of wealth owned by that group overall.

No definite lists of those liable have been attested. The assumption that the diadikasia documents were such lists can be questioned. Generally, men entered the trierarchic class—either voluntarily or compulsorily—by being notoriously wealthy, or by having inherited properties that had previously supported trierarchies, or possibly by being the testators of a deceased trierarch. A petitioner could leave that class by claiming that another man wealthier than he ought to take his place; even then he would have to put his claim to the test through the often unrewarding legal mechanism of the antidosis. To ensure stability in the size of the trierarchic class it was incumbent upon the man seeking exclusion (of a temporary nature, never permanent) to supply a replacement financially capable of carrying the obligation.

All these, then, are features of a population segment that functioned much more as a fiscal entity than as a recruiting ground for candidates to positions within the established military hierarchy.

It comes as no surprise, therefore, that a good many sources voice discontent with, and grievances over, the financial burdens accruing from trierarchic performances. The relevant passages are well known. Isokrates did not hold back his annoyance that those who possessed property found life burdensome because of the multitude of duties imposed on them—the liturgies and all the nuisances connected with the symmories and with the antidoseis (8.128). "I observe that already the state is exacting heavy contributions from you," Xenophon makes Sokrates say to wealthy Kritoboulos (*Oec.* 2.6), "and if war breaks out, I know they will require you to discharge so many trierarchies and pay so many eisphorai that it will nearly crush you." But how much substance is there in these claims?

Undeniably, the financial demands that could be made were far from negligible, occasionally rising to levels that might even challenge the ability of notoriously affluent households to provide ready cash. During the second half of the fourth century, a requirement to make compensation for a trieres hull entailed payment of 5,000 drachmas; for a complete set of equipment the requirement was 2,169 or 2,299 drachmas, depending on whether a heavy or a light sail was included. Added together, these claims represented the substantial sums of 7,169 or 7,299 drachmas. I do not know what the corresponding figures may have been in the preceding period, but I find no cause to believe that they were of a much smaller order. Be that as it may, it is certain that by the final years of the 320s compensatory payments for equipment had almost doubled, so that the sum required for a whole ship now amounted to about 9,100 drachmas. If a tetreres was in question (on the assumption that a lump sum of 5,000 drachmas was demanded for these hulls as well), then the amount would rise to approximately 11,100 drachmas. To this must be added possible punitive fines of double the amount owed resulting from failure to clear such liabilities promptly. Still, to grasp the real scale of the economic demands, it is much more appropriate to consider trierarchic expenditure in the light of cumulative liabilities over a series of years. The attested liabilities of Konon Anaphlystios son of Timotheos can serve as an example.

These accrued from eight distinct trierarchies that he had performed either alone or jointly with one or more colleagues in the period from about 342/1 to 325/4, and consisted of his obligation to replace several ships as well as a considerable amount of equipment. Reckoned together, they amounted to the respectable sum of 34,923 drachmas.[4] Besides, Konon had served on three further ships for which no liabilities are documented, while another debt of his relating to equipment from some smaller vessels is not specified in the records.[5] But this only covers the expenditures incurred after the term of a service had expired. If one includes what Konon would have spent during each of these eleven known trierarchies by taking 3,000 drachmas to be a fairly reasonable average of the current expenses per service,[6] the attested financial claims with which he was faced within a period of seventeen years totaled 67,923 drachmas. Against this background, the complaints about the oppressive character of trierarchic obligations would seem justified.

However, this is only part—and perhaps not a very large part—of the whole picture. While it can be doubted whether Konon's case was unique, his abnormally high expenditure certainly lay too close to the extreme end of the scale to be taken as typical. Most individuals did not undertake trierarchies with the frequency he did, nor were they burdened by such immense compensatory claims. In addition, the inferred average of 3,000 drachmas relating to current expenditure does not take into account that some men served only a short spell of duty and hence spent much smaller amounts, while others, like Apollodoros in 362–360, may have had to be active for a very long period and thus spend even more than that. The existence of considerable diversity is a necessary and trenchant qualification. To be designated a trierarch at the beginning of the year often meant to be initially appointed as nominal trierarch and then to be called later on to assume active service for a certain period of time that year. Lastly, men could opt for a syntrierarchy with two, three, or occasionally more partners, while in the years from 357 to 340 some may have gotten away with quite small outlays made within a synteleia group (Dem. 18.104; 21.155). Thus, at the opposite end of the scale there were almost certainly men who in a ten-year period could manage to limit their expenditure by undertaking fewer trierarchies than were strictly required by law or custom; these men, like all others, were allowed, if they so wished, to have their services transferred to contractors by paying a lump sum of about 2,000 drachmas.

Because of the tendency of the state to privatize a gradually growing part of naval expenditure, whole trierarchies, reckoned as "units," might well have been costlier by the middle of the fourth century than they had been a hundred years previously. But, if so, this need not mean a corresponding and unconditional rise in the outlays of each and every man. The balance sheet must therefore cover the great individual variations in trierarchic expenditure that existed between the two extremes just outlined. Seen in this light, the grievances in the sources over the distressingly heavy fiscal demands, one may suspect, reflect perhaps another notion quite dear to the hearts of the trierarchic class but not wholly vested with substance.

More than a few features of the way the institution worked, and of the development it underwent from the end of the fifth century onward, bear witness that the relationship between the state and the naval financiers was one of reciprocity and interdependence. An important prerequisite for membership in the trierarchic class, I have noted, was possession of visible wealth. Demosthenes credits his relative Demochares with the performance of trierarchies and other liturgies all undertaken by virtue of his gallant decision to own his possessions unconcealed (28.3); such praise is particularly significant for its implication that it was within the power of Demochares, had he so wished, to do otherwise. Conversion of wealth into invisible property, imaginatively practiced by some proprietors with the prime objective of evading their obligation (and potentially open to

others as a tactical means of obtaining the same end), constantly threatened the state's ability to mobilize for naval finance purposes as many
property owners as were currently required. Therefore, the need to preserve the financial potential of a vital source of tax revenue and the
need to ensure the cooperation of naval financiers arguably became dominant influences on the ensuing reforms that vigorously transformed the
trierarchy.

Most important, the introduction of the syntrierarchy in circa 408/7
represented the first major concession to the trierarchic class, above all
because it signaled the emergence of a new principle that was later to
permeate many areas of the institution: that of extended liability. It has
been argued that already in its first form, joint trierarchies, that principle
aimed at lessening the burdens falling on an individual by spreading the
personal and financial risks equally among members of a wider group.
But the syntrierarchy—combined with the rule of two years' respite after
a trierarchy and one year's respite after performance of any other liturgy—triggered a need for more men to serve in a period of four consecutive years.

A serious problem with which the naval administration had to cope,
especially in the first half of the fourth century, was manpower shortages;
the situation is credibly reflected in the fairly large number of ships that
remained unallotted to trierarchs in a given year. An attitude of startling
leniency toward naval defaulters and misappropriators of naval matériel,
documented in the same period, can best be explained as conditioned by
the wish to avoid a further widening of the disparity between the number
of men needed and that of men actually obtained to serve in a year. By
358/7, the inevitable effects of this had become manifest in two juxta-
posed vexations greatly undermining naval efficacy: recruitment difficulties and a worrying shortage of equipment in the dockyards.

A solution to both problems was attempted with Periandros's reform
of 358/7. The number of men liable to perform trierarchies in a year
was thereby formally set at twelve hundred. These were organized into
twenty fiscal-administrative entities, the symmories—to be distinguished
from the symmories used for eisphora purposes—each of which had sixty
members. At the same time, all the ships were distributed among the
symmories. More men should thus have shared the overall burdens. Two
further innovations may be noted. First, while active service continued to
be performed by sole trierarchs and syntrierarchs, the principle of ex-

tended liability (enforced within each symmory) probably enabled those discharging an active trierarchy to enlist the help of their fellows in the symmory (groups of synteleis) to make their ships ready. Second, under the new system the responsibility for recovering naval debts was delegated to the symmories. A functional differentiation ensued between trierarchs in the proper sense and naval financiers.

All that the next reform, carried out by Demosthenes in 340, altered in that system was that the distribution of financial burdens was now made in accordance with each man's economic standing. Consequently, and in contrast to previous practices, the wealthiest citizens among the Twelve Hundred—those commonly referred to as the Three Hundred—were made to pay more than their less wealthy colleagues. The earlier view that Demosthenes' reform limited liability for the trierarchy to only three hundred persons can now be questioned on the basis of epigraphic evidence. Information relating to the dispatch of two squadrons, one in 326/5 and the other in 325/4, shows the reformed mode of distribution at work, while at the same time it highlights the continuing adherence to the principle of extended liability.

Although the recruitment situation and that of shortages in naval matériel seem to have improved considerably, neither reform was entirely successful in effectively eliminating the causes of irregularities. By 354, and perhaps as late as 323/2, it was still not always possible to obtain all of the twelve hundred men needed in a year. Extra manpower and funds had to be mobilized on several occasions through appeals for voluntary naval contributions (epidoseis). Naval debtors continued to be treated with relative leniency, and in order to recover debts long overdue the state had to introduce ad hoc deals offering tangible advantages to defaulters who wished to clear their liabilities. All in all, preservation of the goodwill of the trierarchic class remained a preeminent concern.

This does not imply the absence of coercive mechanisms specifically designed to exercise control over and regulate the contributions of naval financiers. Disobedience entailed punishment. Men refusing to perform their obligations could be imprisoned. The antidosis procedure was another highly effective means by which to make the trierarchic class a self-controlled entity. In some measure it was responsible for the recruitment of its own members; at the same time it performed the useful task of policing individuals apt to shirk their duty. Coercion was in this case administered personally by the very group of men whom it was likely to afflict. Similarly, armed with the right to enter diadikasiai against any of his colleagues, a trierarch was compelled to act as a debt-collector on behalf of the state, and hence could, as the speaker of [Demosthenes] 47 did, find himself embroiled in cumbersome legal or personal quarrels. Yet, whether by force or by consent, many men discharged their obligations without further ado.

Besides offering the prospect of honorific attributes, political leadership (particularly as rhetores and strategoi), and the reward of charis, trierarchic performances served also to maintain and justify a man's economic position—above all because they could be put forth as hard proof of his having prudently channeled his wealth into the conduits of public utility. At a certain time in the fourth century, liturgical contributions in a year equaled more than half (about 59 to 67 percent) of the amount of the total national revenue, which was derived from other sources. And even when the public finances improved shortly thereafter, the annual expenditure of liturgists was still equivalent to one fifth (about 19 to 21 percent) of the revenue coming into the state coffers.

The point is often made in a legal context and in stereotypical terms, but it is now clear that it cannot have been meaningless:[7] "My father died while serving as trierarch," says the speaker of Lysias 19, pleading with the jurors to be allowed to retain his property, "and I will try to do what I saw him doing, and raise, by degrees, some little sums for the public services. Thus in practice it continues to be the property [of the state: Dobree]" (62). "You would be justified in considering our case with benevolence," sounds another such plea by the speaker of Isaeus 7, "especially since our adversaries have made away with and sold an estate of five talents that used to discharge trierarchies and reduced it to desolation, whereas we have already performed liturgies and will continue to do so in the future, if you ratify the intentions of Apollodoros by restoring to us the estate" (42).

What arguments of this kind were meant to demonstrate was that private wealth had been zealously placed (or was intended to be placed) in the service of democratic ideology. Yet surely such utterances, unequivocally familiar to the fourth-century economic elite, would have had a disconcertingly alien ring to the class represented by Kleinias son of Alkibiades.

# Appendix

## Standard Equipment

In the naval records, the standard set of triereis equipment is classified by "wooden" and "hanging," and consists of the following items. (Full discussions and explanations of each item are offered in *GOS* 289–307, and Casson *SSAW* 82–92, 224–67, and the glossary, 389–402.)

I. "Wooden"

1. *Tarros* (170 working oars)
2. *Perineō* (30 spare oars)
3. *Pēdalia* (2 rudders)
4. *Klimakides* (2 ladders)
5. *Kontoi* (poles, probably 3)
6. *Parastatai* (2 mast-partners holding the boat-mast in place; cf. Casson *SSAW* 237 n. 59; Morrison and Coates [1986] 160 n. 1)
7. *Histos megas* (mainmast)
8. *Histos akateios* (smaller boat-mast)
9. *Keraiai megalai* (big sailyard, composed of two spars)
10. *Keraiai akateioi* (boat sailyard, composed of two spars)

II. "Hanging"

1. *Hypozōmata* (ropes undergirding the hull horizontally from stem to stern; normally four were carried on board)

2. *Histion* (sail: consistently in the singular in the records, but Xen. *Hell.* 2.1.29: *megala histia* and *histia akateia*)
3. *Topeia* (rope tackle used in connection with the sails, and consisting of 1 *ankoina*, 2 *himantes*, 3 *podes*, 3 *hyperai*, 1 *halinos*, and 8 *kalōs*)
4. *Hypoblēma* (canvas screen or awning)
5. *Katablēma* (canvas screen or awning)
6. *Pararrhymata leuka* (white canvas screens, always in plural)
7. *Pararrhymata trichina* (screens "of hair," i.e., made of hide, always in plural)
8. *Schoinia* (ropes of varying thickness and length)
9. *Agkyrai* (2 anchors)
10. *Askōmata* (leather bags covering the lowest oarports)

A change occurred after the mid-fourth century. From the naval record *Inscriptiones Graecae* 2².1624 on (of a year after 336/5; cf. ll. 42–49 with 1628.369–95; 1629.889–914, contra H. Fränkel, "Attische Inschriften," *AM* 48 [1923]: 11–13, who proposed a year between 336/5 and 331/0), the wooden equipment of triereis is reduced to only six items: *tarros, pēdalia, klimakides, kontoi, histos,* and *keraiai.* This seems to coincide with the introduction of the tetrereis. At that time the only difference between the equipment of triereis and tetrereis was that the latter did not carry a *hypoblēma.* (Fränkel, ibid., 11, held that this item is absent from the triereis of *IG* 2².1631.257–65, because it was no longer issued by the dockyard officials, but its absence is probably due to an omission by the stone-cutter; the *topeia* of tetrereis are missing from 1629.1068–84, but present in 1631.276.) Since the obsolete items (*parastatai, histos akateios,* and *keraiai akateioi*) were never used on tetrereis, the implication may be that the wooden equipment of triereis was brought into concord with that of tetrereis. The way in which such changes may have influenced the design of triereis is an issue awaiting examination.

# Notes

## Introduction

1. Hdt. 8.17; cf. Plut. *Alc.* 1.

2. *APF* 15.

3. *GOS* 254. *Trireme*, stemming from the Latin *triremis*, is the name commonly used in English for a particular type of warship. Here I have preferred to retain the Greek form *triērēs* (plural: *triēreis*). By the same token, *tetrērēs/eis* and *pentērēs/eis* are used instead of "fours" and "fives" for the types of craft that made their appearance in the fourth century B.C. However, *triakontors* (thirty-oared ships) and *pentēkontors* (fifty-oared ships) seem preferable to their Greek forms, *triakontoroi* and *pentēkontoroi*.

4. Hdt. 5.47. Plutarch (*Alex.* 34.2) reports that the celebrated athlete Phayllos of Kroton fitted out a ship at his own cost and fought on it in the battle of Salamis. Phayllos was a victor in the Pythian games (Hdt. 8.47).

5. The evidence for this is presented in n. 4 to the Epilogue.

6. Andreades (1933) 323; Jordan *AN* 134.

7. Mainly, Ruschenbusch (1978); Mossé (1979); Rhodes (1982); MacDowell (1986); Gabrielsen (1989b) and (1990).

8. Din. 1.71: *rhetores* and generals had to own land in Attica and to have legitimate children in order to be worthy of the trust of the people; cf. *Ath. Pol.* 4.2. That the law was not enforced: Rhodes *Commentary* 511; M. H. Hansen, "The Athenian 'Politicians,' 403–322 B.C.," in Hansen (1989) 1–23, esp. 6–7.

9. Rodgers (1937) xiv, 117–20, 127–29.

10. The "sea-power" orthodoxy is the idea that naval power and superiority

played a decisive role in the history of the modern world; Mahan (1890). Further-more, Rodgers's view was solidly based on the "modernistic" orthodoxy that commercial interest determined the policy of the ancient state, a thesis refuted by Hasebroek (1928), (1931).

11. For a reappraisal of the significance of naval warfare and sea power, stress-ing their restricted role in ancient history, see Lazenby (1987b), but cf. Starr (1989) and the review of that work by P. De Souza in *CR* n.s. 40 (1990): 506–7. Tarn (1930) 142 wrote: "What is called the command of the sea at this time [sc. the Hellenistic period] only meant that the Power who claimed it had a good prospect, if challenged, of getting a fleet to sea, which might defeat the challenger." The traditional view is held by Brockmeyer (1971). Little can be gained from Charles (1946). A most useful analysis of attitudes to naval power in general is offered by Momigliano (1944); the attitude of the Attic orators in particular is treated by Ober (1978).

12. The warships of other states were commanded by trierarchs: e.g., Hdt. 6.14 (Samian), 7.181, 8.93 (Aiginetan), 8.46 (Naxian), 8.90 (Phoenician), 8.85 (Greek); Thuc. 8.45.3 (Peloponnesian); Arist. *Pol.* 1304b29 (Rhodian). But next to nothing is known about the character of the trierarchy outside Athens, and Gomme's inference (*HCT* 3:448), from Thuc. 4.11.4–12.1, that Spartan trierarchs were similar to the Athenian ones is unwarranted.

13. See generally Adkins (1972); M. I. Finley, *The World of Odysseus*, 2d ed. (London, 1977). On *leitourgia,* see N. Lewis (1960) and (1965); the only penetrat-ing inquiry into the term remains that of H. Strathmann, in *Theologisches Wörter-buch zum Neuen Testament,* ed. G. Kittel (Stuttgart, 1938) 4.4:221–38.

14. Davies (1967). On deme liturgies, see D. Whitehead (1986) 150–52.

15. Abolition of the liturgies by Demetrios of Phaleron (317/6–307/6): *FGrH* 76: Douris F 10; cf. W. S. Ferguson, *Hellenistic Athens: An Historical Essay* (Lon-don, 1911), 55–58; H.-J. Gehrke, "Das Verhältnis von Politik und Philosophie in den Werken des Demetrios von Phaleron," *Chiron* 8 (1978): 149–93, esp. 171.

16. *IG* 2².3073–88: a publicly appointed *agōnothetēs* performed liturgies on behalf of the people. Cf. H.-J. Gehrke, "Das Verhältnis von Politik und Philoso-phie in den Werken des Demetrios von Phaleron," *Chiron* 8 (1978): 171; de Ste. Croix (1981) 305–6.

17. Lauffer (1974), (1980). M. I. Finley's remarks (*The Ancient Economy,* 2d ed. [London, 1985], 152) meet nicely the arguments of those denying any links be-tween the liturgy system and democracy: Veyne (1976) 186–200; Roberts (1986).

18. *Staatsh.* 1³.670.

19. Andreades (1933) 132, 293, 323, 358–63. His "confiscatory tendency" view (277 n. 3) was taken from Vilfredo Pareto, *Les systèmes socialistes* (Paris, 1902), 1:155, 157.

20. Davies *Wealth* 128–30; cf. 92–95; Ober (1989) 226–33.

21. Lycurg. *Leoc.* 139–40: "To earn your *charis* he must, instead, have been distinguished as a trierarch, or built walls to protect his city, or subscribed generously from his own property for the public safety. These are services to the state: they affect the welfare of you all and prove the loyalty of the donors, while the others [sc. liturgies] are evidence of nothing but the wealth of those who have spent the money." Cf. Thuc. 6.16.1–4; Lys. 18.23; 20.31; 21.25; 25.12–13.

22. E.g., [Dem.] 50; liturgies: Ant. 2.2.12; Isae. 5.41; 6.60–61; Lys. 7.31; [Dem.] 42.23; Isoc. 18.63; cf. 58–60.

23. Parading liturgies in court: e.g., Dem. 8.70–71; Isae. 5.41–42; 6.60; Lys. 25.12–13. I am not entirely convinced by Garner's argument that parading trierarchies in court was indirectly connected with religion (i.e., the "salvation of the city" aspect), so that "reverence was fully due those who financed the fleet"; Garner (1987) 49.

24. Litigants promising that they would continue or increase their public outlays, if they were acquitted or allowed to retain their wealth: Isae. 6.61; Lys. 19.62; 21.12–15 (quoted in the text); Dem. 28.19–20, 24.

25. Carter (1986) 51, who goes so far as to view the liturgies as an insurance policy (104).

26. Thuc. 6.39.1: defending Syracusan democracy, Athenagoras is made to say that the wealthy are the best guardians of property, and the many (*polloi*) the best judges; Dem. 14.25–28: wealth is best kept in the hands of its owners until the state needs it for paying for the war.

27. M. I. Finley, *Economy and Society in Ancient Greece*, ed. B. D. Shaw and R. P. Saller (London, 1981), 90–91; and more extensively, H.-J. Gehrke, *Stasis: Untersuchungen zu den inneren Kriegen in den griechischen Staaten des 5. und 4. Jahrhunderts v. Chr.*, Vestigia, no. 35 (Munich, 1985), 326–27; cf. 213, 231, 344.

28. An excellent description of the relationship between "mass" and "elite" was offered by Ober (1989), who argues that the sociopolitical equilibrium was, above all, achieved by means of rhetoric: its symbolic language helped bridge, on the ideological plane, the gap between the social reality of inequality and the political ideal of equality. However, while this may be true in a general context, I argue that reciprocity and interdependence were to a much greater extent centered on more tangible, economic benefits.

29. A. Wilhelm, "ΕΠΙΓΡΑΦΗ ΠΕΙΡΑΙΩΣ," *AE* (1901): 81–84 (= *IG* 2².1604\*; *IG* 1³.498); *Collections Froehner*, vol. 1, *Inscriptions grecques*, ed. L. Robert (Paris, 1936), 1ff., no. 2 (= *IG* 2², part 2, p. 811, 1604\*a; *IG* 1³.499); Robinson (1937) (= *IG* 1³.500).

30. For Ross's letter to Boeckh, see *Urkunden* viii–xii. K. S. Pittakis offered extensive commentary on the texts and, from his own observations, proposed corrections to Boeckh's (and Ross's) transcripts: *AE* (1853): 835–40; (1857): 1504–43, 1552–73, 1574–79, 1580–85, 1604–36; (1858): 1652–76, 1680–83, 1716–33.

31. Kirchner added only two fragments unknown to Köhler (*IG* 2².1609, 1624). Five fragments found in Athens in 1934–36 were taken by E. Schweigert to be from a copy of *IG* 2².1611; Schweigert (1939) no. 5. But the similarity of entries between the two is no proof that a copy is in question. Sundwall (1910) 51–52 (cf. D. M. Lewis, "Notes on Attic Inscriptions," *BSA* 49 [1954]: 44) identified 1611 as the record from the beginning of 357/6 and 1612 from the end of that year. However, the separate stocktaking of equipment in the dockyards in both 1611.42–64 and 1612.47–84 is a good indication that they are records from different years. Also, Boeckh (*Urkunden* 25–26) took 1611 to be an exceptional record from the beginning of 357/6, because instead of announcing the usual *paralabē* (receipt) and *paradosis* (delivery), the preamble states: "The dockyard [superintendents recorded, *anegrapsan*] the following." But the formulaic expression does not warrant such a dating; see, e.g., *IG* 2².120. Ruschenbusch (1987a) dated 1611 to the middle or second half of 357/6, yet he bases this on the unproven—and in my opinion untenable—view that the *epimeletai* of that year were untimely replaced by a fresh board of officials who drew up 1611. [Dem.] 47.20–48 mentions the epimeletai of 357/6 several times, but not their supposed dismissal.

32. (a) Epimeletai: *Urkunden* 48–64; G. Glotz, in Daremberg-Saglio 2:669–73; Rhodes *AB* 117–18. Jordan argues that the epimeletai of *IG* 1³.236.5, 6, are the same as those of the fourth century (Jordan *AN* 30–46, pace Rhodes *Commentary* 545), and so also are *[hoi epime]lomenoi to neorio* of *IG* 1².73.19 (= 1³.153) and the neoroi of 1².74.11 (= 1³.154) and 2².1.30 (= 1³.127). Ps.-Xen. *Ath. Pol.* 3.2 speaks of the "supervision of the dockyards" by using the words *epimelēthēnai tōn neōriōn*. (b) Publication of their records: Jordan (following Sundwall [1910] 53) mistakenly thinks that before the 330s the epimeletai published their annual accounts (*diagrammata*) only in the fourth year of each Olympiad (Jordan *AN* 31; cf. *Urkunden* 1–12). (c) Replacement of the epimeletai by other officials in the years 348/7–334/3: suggested by Rhodes *AB* 119, 239–40, with reference to an unpublished essay by D. M. Lewis, apud Cawkwell (1963) 57 n. 62. If so, their *archē* (office) might have been transferred to *hoi epi to theōrikon* (the board of the theoric fund, Aesch. 3.25), but Cawkwell (ibid.) has objections. Davies (1969) 316 n. 35 is in error in stating that the board of epimeletai is attested for the last time in *IG* 2².1623.3–5 (334/3).

33. Gabrielsen (1988) 74–75.

O N E : *The Origin of the Trierarchy*

1. *Staatsh.* 1³.636–37; Kolbe *Re navali* 22, 26; Martin "Naukraria"; Brillant "Trierarchia" 42–43; Hommel "Naukraria"; Strasburger "Trierarchie" 107; Labarbe *Loi navale* 43–49; Wüst (1957); Thomsen (1964) 120–38 and (1977); Amit *AS* 103–7; Jordan *AN* 9–16; Cozzoli (1977); Haas (1985); Lambert (1986); Figueira

(1986) 257–79. For further references see Cozzoli (1977) 552 nn. 2–3, and Gabrielsen (1985) 21 n. 1.

2. Hignett (1952) 71; Haas (1985) 41 n. 61; Starr (1989) 28; Wallinga (1993) 17–18. Wallinga's thorough study (which rightly stresses the use of privately owned ships in the preclassical period, though within the institutional context of the naukrariai) appeared when it was too late for me to note in detail my agreement or disagreement with his main views.

3. Keil (1902) 224 n. 1; Gabrielsen (1985). A. French, "Solon and the Megarian Question," *JHS* 77 (1957): 238–46, esp. 238, accepted the connection between naukrariai and the fleet but denied the existence of any system of taxation for financing naval operations.

4. The archaeological evidence: Torr (1894); *GOS* 18–28; Gray (1974) 22–26, 57–61. Connection with the naukrariai: Helbig (1898). On whether the ship-scenes depict real events: Ahlberg (1971) 58, 69—positive; F. Chamoux, "L'école de la grande amphore du Dipylon: Étude sur la céramique géométrique à l'époque de l'Iliade," *RA* 23 (1945): 55–97—negative. Identification of the Lenormant relief: Beschi (1969–70).

5. Hdt. 5.71.2. Cf. also Thuc. 1.126.3–12; Plut. *Sol.* 12.1–11; Schol. Ar. *Eq.* 445.

6. Jordan (1970) proposed the reading *enemon⟨to⟩*, and translated "who at that time collected the revenues of Athens," but cf. Rhodes *Commentary* 152. Political/fiscal duties: Wright (1892) 30–33; Glotz (1900); Kahrstedt *Staatsgebiet* 247–48; Hignett (1952) 71; Thomsen (1964) 133; Figueira (1986) 270–74. Wüst (1957) 176–78 identified the naukraroi with the Areopagos and their prytanies with the archons. Lambert (1986) argues that the prytanies of the naukraroi were the constitutional ancestors of the bouleutic prytanies.

7. See the discussion of their provenance in Beloch *GG* I².2.237; Hignett (1952) 20–22, 69; Thomsen (1964) 133–34; Rhodes *Commentary* 151–53.

8. *FGrH* 324: Androtion F 36, Schol. Ar. *Av.* 1541. A scholiast (to Ar. *Nub.* 37) states that the naukraroi had been in charge of the Panathenaic procession. Combining these testimonies, Jordan (1970) 160, 172–73 argues that Athens built and operated its earliest ships for religious purposes; the vessels were constructed and controlled by the prytanies of the naukraroi (cf. Jordan *AN* 10–11). But even if the naukraric fund had financed a single sacred embassy, it does not follow that the naukraroi had religious or naval functions.

9. "And in the laws it is stated: '*an tis naukrarias amphisbētēi*' and '*tous naukrarous tous kata tēn naukrarian,*'" *FGrH* 323: Kleidemos F 8, Photios *Lex.*, s.v. "naukraria." I have left the pertinent clauses untranslated because their exact meaning is still debated; cf. Thomsen (1964) 131–33. The first clause, especially, has been associated with the antidosis; Kahrstedt *Staatsgebiet* 282 n. 2. This is refuted in Gabrielsen (1985) 38–41.

10. It is so used by Thomsen (1964) 120–21, and Jordan *AN* 10–11.

11. Hommel "Naukraria" 1948; Thomsen (1964) 121–22.

12. Most of the attempts to date Kleidemos's book to circa 354–350 rest on Paus. 10.15.5 and on the assumption that the symmories referred to in F 8 are to be associated with the one hundred subdivisions of the twenty symmories proposed by Demosthenes in 354 (14.17); cf. *FGrH* 3b (suppl.) 1:58. J. K. Beloch, "Das Volksvermögen von Attika," *Hermes* 20 (1885): 255, dated it to after 378/7, Thomsen (1964) 85–89 before that year.

13. That membership of a naukraria was determined by the same wealth criteria as the Solonian census classes is pure conjecture: W. Schwahn, "Tele," *RE* 5.A1 (1934): 247ff.; Busolt-Swoboda *GS* 2:820ff.; Thomsen (1964) 139; Vélissaropoulos (1980) 20.

14. Ammonios, s.v. "naukleroi and naukraroi": "naukleroi are the owners of ships, naukraroi those collecting the public property, and naukraria the localities in which the properties lay." See also *Suda*, s.v. "demarchos," "demarchoi"; Schol. Ar. *Nub.* 37; Photios, s.v. "naukraria."

15. Solmsen (1898), relying heavily on Poll. 8.108; Hommel "Naukraria" 1938; P. Chantraine, *Dictionnaire étymologique de la langue grecque* (Heidelberg and Paris, 1974), 736–37.

16. It is also attested in the dialect form *nēos* (Ionic), *nāwos* (Laconian), and *nauos* (Lesbian).

17. See Gabrielsen (1985) 48, and Lambert (1986) 111 n. 26.

18. Rihl (1987); Cecchini (1982–83) 554–55, 560–61, referring to Hesychios, s.v. "nausteres." Cf. also N. Wecklein, "Der Areopag, die Epheten und die Naukraren," *SBAW* 3 (1873): 1–48.

19. Kahrstedt *Staatsgebiet* 246–48; cf. Labarbe *Loi navale* 43; Wallinga (1993) 17–32. The inception of the navy is dated variously; eighth century B.C.: Ahlberg (1971) 58, using the archaeological evidence; early sixth century B.C.: Amit *AS* 60–61; Jordan *AN* 6–7, using mainly Herodotos's report of an Athenian expedition (between 600 and 575) to seize Sigeion and a war with Mytilene on Lesbos (5.94–95), and also of the conflict (end of the seventh century, or beginning of the sixth) between Athens and Aigina (5.84–89).

20. Humphreys (1978) 166–68 n. 13, and generally M. I. Finley, *Early Greece: The Bronze and Archaic Ages,* new rev. ed. (London, 1981).

21. Haas (1985) 33–35, 39–40. In a law believed to contain Archaic elements (Just. *Digest* 47.22.4, quoting the Roman jurist Gaius), "those away for booty or for trade" are listed among the bodies and associations permitted to pass sovereign enactments, provided they do not contravene public law. See W. S. Ferguson, "The Attic Orgeones," *HThR* 37 (1944): 62–66, and D. Whitehead (1986) 13–14. Representations of vessels of the Geometric and Archaic periods appear in *GOS* 18–37, 73–117. Use of pentekontors by the Phoenicians for long-distance

trade, and of a larger vessel, the *samaina,* by the Samians in the sixth century B.C.: Hdt. 1.163.2 and Plut. *Per.* 26.3–4, respectively; see Snodgrass (1983), but cf. C. Reed, "Maritime Traders in the Archaic Greek World: A Typology of Those Engaged in the Long-Distance Transfer of Goods by Sea," *AncW* 10 (1984): 31–44. Piracy: Ormerod (1924); Ziebarth (1929); Garlan (1989) 173–201.

22. Garlan (1989) 173–201, esp. 201; Bravo (1977).

23. Miltiades the Younger was sent by the sons of Peisistratos on a trieres to take control of the Chersonese in circa 516 (Hdt. 6.39). Again in the early 490s, he is reported to have sailed home to Athens with five triereis (Hdt. 6.41). It may be right to suppose (cf. Haas [1985] 43–44) that these ships were privately owned in the service of aristocratic foreign enterprises. Diod. 8.19.1: private possession of a pentekontor.

24. Accepted by *Staatsh.* 1³.636; B. A. van Groningen, *Aristote: Le second livre de l'Économique* (Leiden, 1933), 73; but cf. Amit *AS* 103.

25. Earliest mention of trieres: Hipponax (*floruit* circa 540) fr. 45 (Diehl³). The origin of triereis is debated: (*a*) at Samos circa 540–523 B.C., Davison (1947); (*b*) at Corinth in mid-seventh century B.C., *GOS* 129–30; Lloyd (1972), (1975), and (1980); (*c*) Phoenician invention, Basch (1969), (1977), and (1980).

26. Hdt. 7.144.1–2; Thuc. 1.14.1–2; *Ath. Pol.* 22.7; Plut. *Them.* 4.1–3; Polyaenus 1.30.5; Nep. *Them.* 2.2; Aristid. 46.187; Just. *Epit.* 2.12.12; Liban. *Decl.* 9.38; [Nicol.], *Progymn.* 8.7. See also *FGrH* 107: Stesimbrotos F 2, apud Plut. *Them.* 4.3, for Miltiades' opposition to Themistokles' plan. K. Meister, "Stesimbrotos' Schrift über die athenische Stadtsmänner," *Historia* 27 (1978): 274–94, esp. 283, argues that Aristides and not Miltiades opposed the scheme.

27. Hdt. 3.57.2: distribution of mining revenue among the Siphnians in the sixth century. See Latte (1968).

28. Followed by Plut. *Them.* 4.3; Nep. *Them.* 2.2–3; Liban. *Decl.* 9.38; [Nicol.] *Progymn.* 8.7. Insofar as they diverge from their primary source, these later traditions show no sign of having independent authority; cf. Podlecki (1975) 201.

29. In the way Labarbe posed the problem—"100 ou 200 navires? 100 ou 200 talents?"—he made the number of ships interdependent with the question about the total mining revenue (*Loi navale* 21ff., 42, 123); but see T. J. Cadoux, review of Labarbe, *Loi navale, JHS* 79 (1959): 184–85; S. A. Accame, review of Labarbe, *Loi navale, Gnomon* 31 (1959): 507–10; S. Lauffer, review of Labarbe, *Loi navale, Historia* 8 (1959): 382–84; Podlecki (1975) 201–2; Lenardon (1978) 54.

30. See Hammond (1982) 80 n. 26. Hdt. 7.144.2 mentions the plans for future shipbuilding. Diod. 11.43.3 reports a decision to build an annual quota of 20 ships. Kolbe (*Re navali* 7–8) combined *Ath. Pol.* 22.7 and Diod. 11.43.3 to postulate the construction of a consignment of 100 ships in 483/2, and three annual consignments each of 20 ships in the years 483/2–481/0.

31. Rhodes *Commentary* 278, noting that Athens had a fleet of 70 ships in 489 (Hdt. 6.132)—this force might have included the 20 ships from Corinth (Hdt. 6.89). Amit *AS* 18 sets the size of the fleet in 489 at 70 ships, but maintains that the Athenians did not have more than 50 ships during the war with Aigina.

32. Maridakis (1963) 14–17, 24–25, 29–32, 42–45, and Papastavrou (1970) 40–43.

33. Holladay (1987); Hegyi (1969).

34. Hdt. 5.94–95; 6.36–41, 138–40; Strab. 13.1.38 (C 599); cf. *IG* I².948, a dedication from Lemnos.

35. The entangled chronology in Herodotos is discussed by A. Andrewes, "Athens and Aegina: 500–480 B.C.," *BSA* 37 (1936–37): 1–7; N. G. L. Hammond, "Studies in Greek Chronology of the Sixth and Fifth Centuries B.C.," *Historia* 4 (1955): 371–411, esp. 406–11; L. H. Jeffery, "The Campaign between Athens and Aegina in the Years before Salamis," *AJPh* 83 (1962): 44–54; A. J. Podlecki, "Athens and Aegina," *Historia* 25 (1976): 396–413; T. J. Figueira, "Herodotus on Early Hostilities between Aegina and Athens," *AJPh* 106 (1985): 49–74; Figueira, "The Chronology of the Conflict between Athens and Aegina in Herodotus Bk. 6," *QUCC,* no. 57 (1988): 49–89.

36. Burn (1984) 293; Garland (1987) 15n, 178. On Miltiades' Parian expedition, see P. Bicknell, "The Date of Miltiades' Parian Expedition," *AC* 41 (1972): 225–27, and R. Develin, "Miltiades and the Parian Expedition," *AC* 46 (1977): 571–77.

37. Frost (1968) 113. Themistokles' archonship: denied by C. W. Fornara, "Themistocles' Archonship," *Historia* 20 (1971): 534–40, accepted by R. J. Lenardon, "The Archonship of Themistokles, 493/2," *Historia* 5 (1956): 401–19; D. M. Lewis, "Themistocles' Archonship," *Historia* 22 (1973): 757–58; W. W. Dickie, "Thucydides 1.93.3," *Historia* 22 (1973): 758–59. A. A. Mosshammer doubts both the archonship and the initiation of a naval program: "Themistokles' Archonship in the Chronographic Tradition," *Hermes* 103 (1975): 222–34.

38. A. Kleingünther, *Protos Euretes: Untersuchungen zur Geschichte einer Fragestellung, Philologus* suppl. 26 (1933); cf. M. H. Hansen, "Solonian Democracy in Fourth-Century Athens," in W. R. Connor et al., *Aspects of Athenian Democracy, C&M* Dissertationes, no. 11 (Copenhagen, 1990), 82.

39. Diod. 11.41.2: completion of the program in 477/6; cf. Plut. *Them.* 19.2. J. H. Schreiner, "Thucydides 1.93 and Themistocles during the 490s," *SO* 44 (1969): 23–41, adopts a different reading of Thuc. 1.93.3–4, and argues that the development of the Piraeus and the expansion of the fleet were parts of Themistokles' (first) naval program during his archonship. See also M. Chambers, "Themistocles and the Piraeus," in *Studies Presented to Sterling Dow on His Eightieth Birthday, GRBS* suppl. 10, ed. K. J. Rigsby (Durham, N.C., 1984), 43–50.

40. Morrison and Coates (1989) 20.

41. The lot: *Ath. Pol.* 22.5; cf. Hdt. 3.80; M. H. Hansen, "When Was Selection

by Lot for Magistrates Introduced in Athens?" *C&M* 41 (1990): 55–61. Kleisthenes' reforms: *Ath. Pol.* 20.1–22.1; Hdt. 5.68–69. Cf. M. Ostwald, *Nomos and the Beginnings of the Athenian Democracy* (Oxford, 1969), 137–60; J. S. Trail, *The Political Organization of Attica, Hesperia* suppl. 14 (Princeton, N.J., 1975).

42. *IG* 2².2318 and E. Capps, "A New Fragment of the List of Victors of the City Dionysia," *Hesperia* 12 (1943): 1ff., no. 1.

43. Date: Capps (1904) 25–29, and "A New Fragment of the List of Victors of the City Dionysia," *Hesperia* 12 (1943): 10–11, pace Pickard-Cambridge (1968) 72, 102–3, who proposed 509/8. Less forcible is M. Treu's argument that a quasi-choregy existed under Peisistratos: "Eine Art von Choregie in Peisistratischer Zeit," *Historia* 7 (1958): 385–91. See generally Deubner (1966) and Davies (1967).

44. Competition between the traditional aristocracy and the "new rich": Adkins (1972) 39–41, esp. 40–41; cf. Garner (1987) 11–13.

45. Jameson (1960), (1962); revised text in ML no. 23.

46. Andreades (1933) 323; Brillant "Trierarchia" 448; Strasburger "Trierarchie" 113; Alexandres (1950) 196. A recent claim by Roberts ([1986] 362), that the trierarchy carried with it the heaviest of political involvements, is misguided: neither the events that ended with the conviction of the strategoi after Arginousai (406: Xen. *Hell.* 1.7.4–35) nor Apollodoros's refusal to obey the strategos ([Dem.] 50.48–50) can be made to show that trierarchs held "the highest military office in the state . . . what was simply the second highest office in the government."

47. Jameson (1963) 396; Jordan *AN* 134. Vartsos (1978) 241 believes that the trierarchy may have attained its liturgical character during the Peloponnesian War. On the requirement for legitimate issue, see the critical remarks of Habicht (1961) 4.

48. Earlier bibliography is given by S. Dow, "Bibliography of the Purported Themistokles Inscription from Troizen," *CW* 55 (1962): 105–8, and Chambers (1967) 166–69; current bibliography is found in *SEG* and in *REG*'s *Bulletin épigraphique*. The provisions about trierarchs are used by those on both sides of the authenticity debate, but each side assumes the very point it sets out to prove. Jordan *AN* 31–32 forces the argument to its limit when says that the author was familiar with the syntrierarchy because he specifies that there should be one trierarch to a ship.

49. N. Robertson (1982). Date: Dow (1962); Étienne and Piérart (1975), esp. 62 n. 37.

50. Hammond (1982) 81–87 eliminates that difficulty by dating the mobilization provisions to September 481 and associating the event with Hdt. 7.44.3 (81). A hundred ships were to resist the Persian advance at Artemision, and another hundred were to deter or to act against attacks from the second enemy, the Aiginetan fleet. Thus the Thermopylai-Artemision defense by the Greek forces is seen as a different and later enterprise to be dated to August 480, while the evac-

uation of Attica was decided in September 480, not by decree but by proclamation (Hdt. 8.41). However, the decree speaks throughout of the defense against the barbarians (esp. ll. 5–6, 45), not against the Aiginetans, as might reasonably be expected had a sizable force of one hundred ships actually been employed with that intent. Moreover, Hammond's reconstruction of the events (85–86) presupposes the replacement of [kai Aiginētōn], line 17, with [Chalkideōn]. Finally, and worryingly, Hdt. 7.144.1–2 says quite explicitly that the new ships were never used for the purpose for which they had been built (the war with Aigina); the simultaneous use of the fleet against both the Aiginetans and the Persians is only claimed in the dubious report of Polyaenus 1.30.5. See also Lehmann (1968) 282–83.

51. Schachermeyr (1963); D. M. Lewis (1961).

52. On the sailing seasons: Hes. Op. 663–65; cf. G. L. Snider, "Hesiod's Sailing Season (W&D 633–665)," AJAH 3 (1978): 129–33. See generally Semple (1932); Naval Intelligence Division, Book of Reference 516–516A: Greece, Geographical Handbook Series 1–2 (Cambridge, 1944); Casson SSAW 272, 282ff., 286ff., 297.

53. The particulars of these tactics are still debated; cf. Lazenby (1987a) and I. Whitehead (1987), pace Morrison (1974).

54. Thucydides stresses the importance of helmsmen in several naval engagements during the Peloponnesian War: 2.87; 7.70.3, 6; cf. 4.75.1 (Samian); 7.39.2 (Corinthian). Among the few instances in which he does mention trierarchs, one is the report that they are forced to repair damaged ships (7.38.2), another that they are urged by the strategoi not to back water and retreat from the ongoing engagement (7.70.8). Highly exceptional skills must have been possessed by Alkibiades' helmsman, Antiochos, who in the Notion campaign was temporarily entrusted with the command of the whole fleet (Xen. Hell. 1.5.11). Pausanias (10.9.8–9) reports that Lysander's helmsman was honored with a statue at Delphi and citizenship at Megara. Cf. also Lys. 21.10; Pl. Resp. 488C–D; [Dem.] 50.46–48.

T W O : Qualifications by Wealth

1. The fullest analysis of these terms is still Hemelrijk (1925); his view that plousioi and penetes do not describe socially opposed and polarized groups (English summary, 140–42) is endorsed by Davies Wealth 10. But see the discussions of Vernant (1965); Gauthier (1976) 38–39; Gabrielsen (1981) 123–25; de Ste. Croix (1981) 69–80; Finley (1983) 1–23; and Ober (1989) 194–98.

2. Jones (1957) 75–96; Casson (1976) 29–59; Davies Wealth 28–37, with graph facing p. 36; Andreev (1983).

3. Two talents, Staatsh. 1³.145, 537, 561, and Fränkel's note in 2³.111* n. 756;

three talents, G. F. Schoemann and J. H. Lipsius, *Griechische Altertümer* I⁴ (Berlin, 1897), 502; more than three talents, Busolt-Swoboda *GS* 2:893 n. 1. But Jones (1957) 86 spoke of "average trierarchic fortunes" worth two talents or less. Kahrstedt (*Staatsgebiet* 218 nn. 2–3) insisted that no minimum of wealth was required, and that liturgists were selected from a fixed number of Athenians.

4. Casson (1976) 30, 32: "a fortune of 3 or 4 talents made a man a liturgist"; cf. Ober (1989) 128. Brun (1983) 15–18, distinguishing between liturgical properties and trierarchic properties, sets the latter at about ten talents. But this is not confirmed by the evidence he cites.

5. Ruschenbusch (1985c); cf. (1978) 279 n. 17; in (1990) it was raised to four talents, two thousand drachmas. But (*a*) the view that the same assessment method was used for both eisphora and liturgies is a conjecture; (*b*) the rates of five, four, three, two, and one mina to be paid for each twenty-five minas are surmised from a single instance showing the rate of five only for eisphora, the remaining rates being a guess; and (*c*) the need to raise the amount to four talents, one thousand drachmas, to make it divisible by twenty-five minas, makes the whole construct questionable.

6. Wyse 365–67, followed by *APF* xxiii–xxiv, and Brun (1983) 16–17.

7. [Plut.] *Mor.* 349B, commenting on the dangers of excessive display that has led choregoi to near-bankruptcy.

8. *IG* 2².417 (of a year after 330); cf. Davies (1967) 39.

9. *APF* xxiii; cf. Brun (1983) 6.

10. Davies *Wealth* 28–29. But see Casson (1976) 49–51; R. K. Sinclair, "Lysias' Speeches and the Debate about Participation in Athenian Public Life," *Antichthon* 22 (1988): 54–66, esp. 56–57.

11. Finley (1952) 91; Millett (1991) 64–71.

12. He actually says that forty-five hundred drachmas was his patrimony. But since this is spoken of separately from his investments in the silver mines, lost recently (3), it must have constituted the residue of his estate when the speech was made.

13. Finley (1952) 207–10 nn. 19–20, against the previous belief in land registers, J. K. Beloch, "Das attische Timema," *Hermes* 22 (1887): 371; H. Francotte, *Les finances des cités grecques* (Paris, 1909), 37ff. M. B. Walbank, "The Confiscation and Sale by the Poletai in 402/1 B.C. of the Property of the Thirty Tyrants," *Hesperia* 51 (1982): 74–98, 86 n. 28, assumes that land registers existed in each deme.

14. Dem. 21.156–57; 27.7, 37; 28.4, 7, 8; 29.59–60; generally, Polyb. 2.62.7; Dem. 14.19, 27; *FGrH* 328: Philochoros F 46. Cf. Wallace (1989) 488–89. Earlier views are found in Thomsen (1964) 24–37 and 45–71.

15. References to previous opinions appear in Gabrielsen (1986) 101 n. 7.

16. Visible and invisible refer to cash: Lys. 12.83; Isae. fr. 15 [Thalheim]; Isoc. 17.7; Aesch. 1.101; [Dem.] 45.66; 48.12, 35, Ep. 3.41; Din. 1.70; or to debts: Andoc. 1.118; Dem. 38.7. In Lys. fr. 79 [Thalheim], visible refers to land, invisible to cash; cf. Ar. Eccl. 601–2. Realty only: Lys. 20.33; [Dem.] 50.8; Xen. Hell. 5.2.10; but in Isae. 8.35, visible includes land, slaves, money, and furniture; cf. Isae. 6.30; Dem. 38.7.

17. Isoc. 17.2–11. At [Dem.] 48.12 (cf. 48.33, 35), it is thought important to stress that a sum deposited with a bank remained visible.

18. Isae. 5.43; 7.39; 11.47; Dem. 28.2, 7, 24; [Dem.] 42.23; Isoc. 7.35; 18.48, 60; Aesch. 1.101; Din. 1.70.

19. Cf. Dem. 28.7 (property disclosed through payment of eisphora); Din. 1.70 (while some possess their property as visible and pay eisphora, Demosthenes keeps his own as invisible); Lys. 22.13 (some refuse to pay the tax, making poverty their pretext). IG 2².1581 indicates that a man risked confiscation of his property if he failed to declare his timema; cf. Lipsius AR 299ff.; de Ste. Croix (1953) 34 n. 16.

20. E.g., Demosthenes' inheritance: APF 126–35; the estate of Aristophanes, son of Nikophemos, APF 202; that of Hagnias, Stratokles, and Theopompos, APF 87–88.

21. De Ste. Croix (1953) 60 and n. 121 assumed that usually the councilors acted on behalf of the symmories. D. Whitehead (1986) 133 n. 73, accepting Meier's supplement ⟨tous dēmarchous kai⟩, argues that the reports were made by the demarchs and the councilors; Thomsen (1964) 210 endorses Thumser's view (De civium 57–58) that the procedure of 362 aimed at, or else contained, the establishment of the three hundred proeispherontes. Cf. also Davies Wealth 143–46; Rhodes (1982) 14. Wallace (1989) 474–78, reviewing thoroughly the opinions about this passage, holds that the procedure it describes was used continuously from the inception of the Three Hundred until 323/2.

22. The date of origin of the proeisphora is unknown. De Ste. Croix (1953) 59, Jones (1957) 27, and Davies Wealth 17–19 argue for 378/7. Others place it after 378/7: Thomsen (1964) 211–12, 220–26; P. Brunt, review of Thomsen (1964), in JHS 86 (1966): 245–47. Wallace (1989) 485 rightly insists that the principal and only evidence is Isae. 6.60, which supports an origin sometime in the 370s.

23. See the objections of Rhodes (1982) 14, and Wallace (1989) 477.

24. Davies Wealth 143–50, followed by Rhodes (1982) 13 and D. Whitehead (1986) 132–33.

25. At [Dem.] 45.78, Apollodoros contrasts the liturgical activity of citizens by birth to that of naturalized citizens. His father Pasion was distinguished by his largess ([Dem.] 45.85; IG 2².1424A, p. 800, ll. 128–29, 139–40; 1609.85–87), a course also followed by Phormion (IG 2².1622.472; 1623.245; 1629.645–56; Dem. 21.157). Trierarchies of metics? (a) Kallaischros Siphnios (IG 2².1609.27) and his

son Stesileides (1623.204–5, 251–52, 268–75; 1631.435); however, they are exceptional since Kallaischros was a lessee of the silver mines, an owner of land in the mining district, and one who enjoyed isoteleia; cf. R. J. Hopper, "The Attic Silver Mines in the Fourth Century B.C.," *BSA* 48 (1953): 200–254, esp. 246. (*b*) Herakleides Erythraios's services (*IG* 2².1491.26; 1492.106) are of a late date (306/5 or 305/4). (*c*) Antimachos of Chios (*IG* 2².40.10; 1604.79) was not a trierarch, pace Jordan *AN* 90 and M. J. Osborne, "Entertainment in the Prytaneion at Athens," *ZPE* 41 (1981): 153–70, esp. 155. Henceforth the full name of an individual will be given as a transliteration of the original formula: personal name followed by (patronymic and) demotic.

26. The key words are [*eschēkotas*] ("they had in their possession") and [*opheilein*] ("they owe"), lines 61, 63.

27. I take the sentence "my father died while serving as trierarch" to bear a causal relation to the preceding sentence "at this moment, too, I discharge a trierarchy."

28. "Serving as trierarch" need not imply personal command of the ship. The service of the father is dated to 389 or 388, that of the son to 388 or 387 (Lys. 19.55); cf. *APF* 200.

29. E.g., the debt of Charidemos Acharneus on *Aura* (before 330/29) was paid in that year by his three sons, Eurymedon, Phylakos, and Troilos (*IG* 2².1627.207–22); that incurred by Hieronymos Lamptreus on *Strategis* was defrayed by his heir Philokrates Lamptreus (1622.587–88); Diodotos Philinou Hamaxanteus, the heir of Diomedes Hamaxanteus, accepted responsibility to replace *Eukarpia* on behalf of his testator (1623.97–123).

30. Cf. *APF* 199. Lys. 19.29, 42, showing a son serving as choregos on his own account and on account of his father, renders the inference plausible, but not certain.

31. I accept Kirchner's restorations [*triērarchos*] and [*syntriērarchos*] as likely.

32. This is inferred because "Nikias's household" is mentioned separately; Lys. 19.47; cf. 18.6. Also, Nikias's property was transferred to his son Nikeratos; then the property (allegedly worth only fourteen talents) passed to his grandson Nikeratos (Lys. 19.47). For this reason, it is kept out of consideration in Lys. 18.21.

33. This is implied by the statement "we possess enormous wealth" (Isoc. 15.154; cf. 158).

34. On co-ownership and partition of inheritance, see Beauchet *Droit privé* 638ff.; Lipsius *AR* 575–77; Biscardi (1955); Kränzlein (1963) 130–37; Asheri (1963); Harrison *LA* 1:239–43. D. M. MacDowell, "The *Oikos* in Athenian Law," *CQ* n.s. 39 (1989): 10–21, esp. 11–15, claims that an oikos belonged only to one man. However, this claim, which remains unproven, is based on too sharp a distinction between the terms *ousia* and *oikos* (when the latter means "property")

and on two unsupported assumptions: that joint ownership of an oikos (especially by two brothers) was exceptional, and that the simultaneous presence of father and son in the liturgical class must mean that each owned his own property.

35. Harp., s.v. "koinonikon," completely misunderstood *koinōnikōn* in Dem. 14.16, as he took it to refer to brothers who, while possessing a trierarchic inheritance jointly, were ineligible because their individual shares were insufficient to qualify for trierarchic duty.

THREE : *Appointment*

1. That these katalogoi were lists of citizens with various degrees of wealth, with statements of their assessments for the trierarchy, was the view of W. W. Goodwin, *Demosthenes on the Crown* (Cambridge, 1904), note ad loc. Boeckh (*Urkunden* 181, *Staatsh.* 1³.662) inferred from the spurious document in Dem. 18.106 that each trierarch was rated for a trieres according to his valuation—one trieres from ten talents.

2. Mossé (1979) 39–40 associates a list of men eligible for the trierarchy with the *diagramma* in Harp., s.v. "diagramma" (citing Hyp. frs. 102, 152 [Jensen/Kenyon]), *Lex. Seg.* 236.13, and *Suda*, s.v. "diagramma." However, that document, presumably kept by a *diagrapheus,* bears no relation to the trierarchic diagrammata (on which see Gabrielsen [1988] 73–77), but rather to the eisphora; Thomsen (1964) 188–90, 246; Brun (1983) 10, 32; Rhodes (1982) 18 n. 49; Wallace (1989) 488–89.

3. A. Andrewes, "The Hoplite Katalogos," in *Classical Contributions: Studies in Honour of Malcolm Francis McGregor,* ed. G. S. Shrimpton and D. J. McGargar (Locust Valley, N.Y., 1981), 1–3.

4. Cf. Gabrielsen (1990). True, as Rhodes (1982) 8 notes, "an estate which belongs to an *epiklēros* today will one day belong to an adult male citizen again." However, any such list including *epiklēroi,* orphans, and the like can hardly be called "a list of those liable." Moreover, there is a certain contradiction between two of Rhodes's statements: "it is not impossible that in reforming the trierarchy the Athenians should have taken a longer view and have started with a gross list of potentially trierarchic estates" (ibid.), and "from 357 onwards there was a definite list of men liable for the trierarchy" (3).

5. *IG* 2².1928–32; E. Schweigert, "Inscriptions from the North Slope of the Acropolis," *Hesperia* 7 (1938): 277, no. 12, and 306, no. 29; K. Pritchett, "Greek Inscriptions," *Hesperia* 15 (1946): 160, no. 17; cf. D. M. Lewis, "Notes on Attic Inscriptions," *BSA* 49 (1954): 37. *IG* 2².1928.2–3 contains the heading [*hoi*]*de diedikasant*[*o*———] *kata to to dēmo* [*psēphisma*]; cf. 1930.2; 1931.3.

6. Davies *Wealth* 133–50. The Thousand are attested in Lys. fr. 54 [Thalh.], and Isae. fr. 33 [Thalh.], apud Harp., s.v. "chilioi diakosioi." Older view: U.

Köhler, "Aus den attischen Inschriften," *AM* 7 (1882): 96–111, originally challenged by Goligher (1907) 504.

7. For details, see Gabrielsen (1987b).

8. A. Stschoukareff, "Ein unedirter attischer *'Catalogus iudicialis,'*" *AM* 12 (1887): 131–35.

9. *Ath. Pol.* 56.3; Dem. 20.28, 130; 21.13; 39.7.

10. *IG* 1².897–901, with Dem. 14.22–23; cf. Siewert (1982) 10–13, 142. Tribal selection of trierarchs: Armstrong (1949); Jordan (*AN* 63–65) endorses Kolbe's view (*Re navali* 29) that the method was abandoned in the fourth century, though he finds it resumed in *IG* 2².1622. However, neither the listing, in this record, of trierarchs in the tribal order, nor Nikias's addressing of trierarchs by patronymic and phyletic at Syracuse (Thuc. 7.69.2), tells us anything about the method of selection.

11. For a general discussion of political obligations and optional decisions, see J. Dunn, *Political Obligation in Its Historical Context: Essays in Political Theory* (Cambridge, 1980), 243–99.

12. Dem. 21.171–74; *Ath. Pol.* 61.7; *IG* 2².213.6–8; 1254; Dain (1931); the tamiai were simultaneously trierarchs (*IG* 2².2966; Isae. 5.6; Plut. *Them.* 7.5), often on other ships as well (*IG* 2².1623.225–29; 1628.8–16 and 1629.689–99; 1628.79–88).

13. In exceptional cases, the verb also refers to transfers from one ship to another; *IG* 2².1632.25–35, 233–39.

14. Jordan *AN* 65–67; cf. *Urkunden* 167–68, *Staatsh.* 1³.629; Kolbe *Re navali* 27.

15. Lists of soldiers were handled in similar fashion. The speaker of Lys. 9, having recently returned from abroad, found himself enrolled (*katalegēn stratiōtēs*) and complained to the strategos that he had already done service (4). This he did *after* he had learned of his enrollment; had he been selected personally by the strategos, he would have objected instantly. See also S. Hornblower's comment on the view about Kimon and "his 4000 hoplites" in 462: "we have no right to assume that he chose them personally; four thousand are a lot of people to know by name" (*The Greek World, 479–323 B.C.* [London and New York, 1983], 36).

16. Kahrstedt *Staatsgebiet* 222 n. 1; de Ste. Croix (1953) 58 n. 109; Thomsen (1964) 210–11 n. 83. MacDowell (1986) 439–40 n. 14 considers the passage as one in which the context does not make clear which kind of symmory is meant. But see Rhodes (1982) 11 n. 30, and p. 184 above.

17. [Dem.] 47.21–23; Lys. 32.26; *IG* 2².1629.567; 1612.136, with [Dem.] 50.

18. Cf. Lys. 19.57: "my father . . . was trierarch seven times"; Isae. 6.60: "Phanostratos has already been trierarch seven times." One begins to feel uncomfortable with the recurring claim of seven trierarchies. However, no definite clues are forthcoming about whether, and if so why, the number seven had become rhetorically attractive, perhaps other than the impression that a record of seven

trierarchies would give of a man who, for a good part of his adult life, had been spending his wealth on trierarchies: i.e., at least twenty-one years, if the two years' respite had been consistently used.

19. Jordan *AN* 66; Cawkwell (1984) 337. Boeckh's (*Staatsh.* 1³.630) inference, from [Dem.] 50.11: *katalysis triērous* ("breaking up a trieres crew"), that a trierarch's term expired when the ship put into the Piraeus, was shown by D. S. Robertson (1927) to be mistaken. Exemptions: Lys. 21.2; Isae. 7.38; *Ath. Pol.* 56.3.

20. Cawkwell (1984) 339–40; cf. [Dem.] 50.41–42, with 51.8.

21. Apollodoros feared imprisonment when he defied the orders of the strategos to sail the exiled Kallistratos to Thasos, 46–51. See generally *Ath. Pol.* 61.2; Dem. 18.107.

22. *IG* 2².1623.26–28: "He acknowledged [*hōmologēsen*] in a law court that he had received this ship"; cf. ll. 234–36, 257–58, 301–5. The legal issues likely to arise with the takeover of equipment are hinted at in [Dem.] 47.29–32.

23. The rules for proper military conduct seem to have been specified in the laws *peri tōn strateuomenōn*, Dem. 3.11. *Graphē lipotaxiou* (desertion): Andoc. 1.74; Lys. 14.5–9; 15.11; Isoc. 8.143; Dem. 15.32; 21.103, 110; Aesch. 2.148; 3.175–76. A *graphē anaumachiou* (not participating in a naval battle) is attested in Andoc. 1.74; cf. also *Suda*, s.v. "anaumachiou," but the only evidence for a *graphē liponautiou* (deserting a ship) is Poll. 8.40, 43. On all three *graphai*, see Lipsius *AR* 452–54; Harrison *LA* 2:32; Hansen (1976) 72.

24. Pace Davies (1969) 318.

25. The Themistokles decree (ML no. 23.22–23) has the appointment of two hundred trierarchs followed by an epiklerosis to just as many ships. If this is the work of an editor, he took little account of the possibility that at least some of the two hundred ships had been assigned to trierarchs already before the decision for full mobilization was made. To carry out a new allotment of all available ships hardly seems sensible in an emergency situation.

26. Other entries listing nominal trierarchs: *IG* 2².1606.7–10, 45–47; 1607.26–27, 101–14, 136–38; 1608.52–54.

27. Cawkwell (1962) 36–37, but cf. Schweigert (1939) 15. The expedition set off in the summer of 357; Schaefer *Demosthenes* 1:162, 164.

28. [Dem.] 47.20: "but those from whom it was due [*hoi opheilontes*], who had in their possession [*echontes*] such equipment, had failed to return it." Cf. 44 for the use of *echōn*.

29. Ruschenbusch (1987a) dates *IG* 2².1953 to 360/59, because, he thinks, Aristokles Eleusinios and Periandros Cholargeus (syntrierarchs in 1611.290–92) in the dedication appear as trierarchs each on his own ship; hence the two documents attest different trierarchies. However, 1953 lists only the dedicators, without specification of who served as sole trierarch or syntrierarch and on which ship.

FOUR : *Exemption*

1. Accepted by Rhodes *Commentary* 625. The only other evidence implying it is a decree of the deme Ikarion (*IG* 1³.254, circa 440–415?), which orders (ll. 3–4) the appointment of choregoi from members and residents of the deme who had not discharged that liturgy before. But cf. D. Whitehead's (1986) warning to exercise extreme caution in applying the evidence for procedures and institutions from one deme to another deme or to the whole polis.

2. Rhodes (1982) 2–3, meeting Davies' argument (*Wealth* 17 n. 16) that the rule did not apply in the fifth century.

3. That it may have been abolished in 358/7: *Staatsh.* 1³.539, 544, 630; Rhodes *Commentary* 625, 682, and Rhodes (1982) n. 68. Wallace (1989) 486 n. 38 (cf. Cawkwell [1984] 343 n. 28) states that Isae. 7.38 may imply an interval of two years for the trierarchic liturgy, but in 357 the exemption rule may have changed (from two years to one) in light of the reduced cost. However, the evidence suggests not a general reduction of costs, but that in the period from 358/7 to 340 some were burdened more heavily than others, and that after 340 the system was reformed so as to work more equitably (cf. Dem. 18.102–7, and pp. 207–13 above).

4. The speaker of Lys. 21.1 says that he discharged a choregy in the year of his *dokimasia*. The rule mentioned at Lys. 32.24 (referring to a year before 400), that orphans are exempt from all liturgies for a year after their dokimasia, probably applied to the sons of those who fell in the Peloponnesian War; cf. Rhodes *Commentary* 509. *Ath. Pol.* 42.5 says that the *epheboi* "are exempt from all duties," but these duties are not specified. If they included the liturgies, I would prefer the view (pace MacDowell [1990] 371) that exemption of the epheboi may have been introduced after the organization of the *ephebeia* (circa 335) into a two-year compulsory national service for all young men; Rhodes *Commentary* 494–95, 509. An attempt to impose a liturgy on a minor (Menestheus) represents an extreme case (Arist. *Rh.* 1399a35ff.; cf. *IG* 2².1622.199–200).

5. Thomsen (1964) 212 doubts that this passage can be used to show that the exemption rule applied to the proeisphora, but his suspicion that Apollodoros is lying is unfounded; cf. Gabrielsen (1987a) 8 n. 4, and Wallace (1989) 486.

6. MacDowell infers from Dem. 21.155 that whereas a trierarch was a liturgist with a right to exemption from other liturgies, a contributor to naval costs (in his opinion, one of the Twelve Hundred) was not a liturgist and thus not entitled to exemption: MacDowell (1986) 443, (1990) 373. But this rests on the questionable supposition that not all of the Twelve Hundred were regarded as trierarchs; see p. 194 and n. 47 above.

7. Jordan *AN* 67; Davies *Wealth* 137–38; Rhodes (1982) 8, 10; Ruschenbusch (1978) 282.

8. Dem. 21.157; 27.7; 28.4; 29.59–60.

9. *IG* 2².1241.14–17; 2492.24–27; 2496.25–28; 2497; 2498.7–9; 2499.37–39.

10. *Staatsh.* 1³.631, 633, citing Poll. 8.134; Finley (1952) 89, 275 n. 5.

11. D. M. Lewis (1973) 196–97; M. B. Walbank, "Leases of Sacred Properties in Attica," *Hesperia* 52 (1983): 100–135, 177–231, esp. 228–30.

12. Osborne (1988) 285–92.

13. Ibid. 308–10, 313–19; cf. Finley (1952) 38–44.

14. The Bosporian ruler Leukon enjoyed ateleia from the liturgies at Athens; Dem. 20.31ff. Cf. *IG* 2².212 (347/6). Cf. also *IG* 2².1140.12–15 (decree of Pandionis); 1147.1–2, 9–11 (decree of Erechtheis).

15. Dem. 20.75, 84–85, 146, with 21.64 (a choregy between 359 and 356).

16. Dem. 30.15–17 (cf. 21.155), with Schaefer *Demosthenes* 1:290 n. 2.

17. Goligher (1907) 506–7. My objections are laid out in Gabrielsen (1987a) 23–24.

18. It is possible that in other cases of proklesis, refusal of both options (e.g., Isae. 6.16) did not have serious legal consequences. But the Athenians had good reasons for taking a much more stern view toward the liturgies and especially the one related to the navy.

19. Dem. 21.78–80; 28.17; [Dem.] 42; cf. Gabrielsen (1987a) 31–36.

20. For the view that it was a real possibility, see *Staatsh.* (1851, 2d ed. without H. Fränkel's annotations) 1:749–52; T. Thalheim, "Die Antidosis," *JKP* 115 (1877): 613–18; T. Thalheim, "Die Antidosis," *Hermes* 19 (1884): 80–91; Lipsius *AR* 588–99. For the view that it was impracticable, see Dittenberger (1872); H. Fränkel, "Die Antidosis," *Hermes* 18 (1883): 442–65; Beauchet *Droit privé* 722–37; L. Gernet, *Démosthène, plaidoyers civils* (Paris, 1957), 2:71–77. H. Francotte, *L'antidosis en droit athénien* (Paris, 1895), combined both views.

21. Lys. 24.9; Dem. 20.40; 21.78; 28.17; [Dem.] 42.19, 27; cf. Gabrielsen (1987a) 15–16, 36.

22. This kind of agreement would be concluded at a meeting referred to as *synodos peri tōn dialyseōn,* [Dem.] 42.12; cf. 11, 14. Lys. 4.1–2 describes a reconciliation, but textual problems render the terms of the agreement less clear; possibly the man challenged agreed to discharge the liturgy (3).

23. There is an allusion to these and similar means in Dem. 28.17: "I accepted the exchange [*antedōka men*], but I obstructed [the proceedings] [*apekleisa de*] because I aimed at a diadikasia trial [*hōs diadikasias teuxomenos*]." MacDowell (1990) 297–98 interprets *apekleisa* narrowly as meaning refusal by one party to let the other enter and inspect his property. The speaker of [Dem.] 42 entered a diadikasia because of Phainippos's failure to deliver his inventory (1, 2, 12, 14, 30);

Phainippos, in turn, charged his counterpart with having delivered a faulty inventory (17); cf. Gabrielsen (1987a) 34–36.

24. See the remark of de Ste. Croix ([1966] 113) about the estate of Phainippos as described by the speaker of [Dem.] 42: "The speaker may or may not have taken in the dicasts: he has certainly taken in scholars wholesale."

25. Goligher (1907) 512. Garner, even though he does not subscribe entirely to Goligher's view, concludes that "certainly a cumbersome dependence on quantity alone caused many oddities in Athenian law": Garner (1987) 73.

26. Cf. J. M. Carter, "Athens, Euboea, and Olynthus," *Historia* 20 (1971): 418–29, esp. 422–24.

27. A full analysis of the speech appears in Kirchhoff (1865), who dated it (86–87) to a year after 357. But *APF* 135–36 (following F. Blass, *Die attische Beredsamkeit*[2] [Leipzig, 1887–98], 3.1:243) argues that it concerned Demosthenes' trierarchy of 360/59 (Aesch. 3.51–52 with schol.).

28. Lys. 6.46–47; 19.20; 21.3; Dem. 21.165; [Dem.] 50.59 (*synepipleōn*).

29. Agapaios Eleusinios: trierarch in the 360s (*IG* $2^2$.1609.112) and in the late 320s (1632.186), when 60+ years old; Aischylos Paionides: born by 370 (D. M. Lewis, "Dedications of Phialai at Athens," *Hesperia* 37 [1968]: 374, no. 51.8–9) and trierarch in the late 320s (*IG* $2^2$.1631.497), when 60+; Aristeides Kephisieus: probably born by 420 (his father Euphilitos was *tamias* of Athena in 420/19 [$1^3$.236.16]) and trierarch in the 330s ($2^2$.1624.83), 70+; Antisthenes Kytherios: choregos in 380 or 370 (1138.27ff.; D. M. Lewis, "Notes on Attic Inscriptions," *BSA* 50 [1955]: 21) and trierarch in the 330s (*IG* $2^2$.1623.233–34), 70+; Demades Paianieus: probably born by 380 (Lewis, "Notes," 34) and trierarch in the late 320s (*IG* $2^2$.1631.499–501 and passim), 60+; Euetion Sphettios: *diaitetes* in 329/8 (1925.16–17) and trierarch in the late 320s (1632.11–14), 60+; Isokrates Erchieus: 82 in 354/3 and trierarch in circa 356 (Isoc. 15.5, 9), 80 or more; Kallias Thorikios: diaitetes in 329/8 (*IG* $2^2$.1925.18–20) and trierarch in the late 320s (1632.151–52), 60+; Ktesippos Aixoneus: probably over 70 in 378/7 (Lewis, "Notes," 24) and trierarch in circa 378/7 (*IG* $2^2$.1604.87), 70+; Lykinos Palleneus: *archōn* on a ship in 361/0 ([Dem.] 50.53) and trierarch in the late 320s (*IG* $2^2$.1631.466), 70+; Meidias Anagyrasios: slightly younger than 50 in 347/6 (Dem. 21.154, 162) and trierarch in the 330s or 320s (*IG* $2^2$.1629.770), 60+; Menexenos Cholargeus: born before 420 (Isae. 5.33; Wyse 404) and trierarch in the early 350s (*IG* $2^2$.1612.114), 60+; Telesias Probalisios: diaitetes in 330/29 (2409.38–39) and trierarch in the late 320s (1631.524–25), 60+; Phaidros Sphettios: probably born by 390 (strategos in 347/6, 213.18) and trierarch in the late 320s (1632.329, 342), 60+; Philomelos Paianieus: trierarch in 378/7 (1604.90) and in 336/5 (1628.373–74; 1629.893), 60+; Charidemos Paianieus: diaitetes in 330/29 (1924.16) and trierarch in the late 320s (1632.70, 311), 60+; the father of the speaker of Lysias 19: trierarch at the age of 70 (58, 60, 62).

30. Cawkwell (1984) 340. For details, see Kirchhoff (1865) 103; Lipsius *AR* 190–91; Rhodes *AB* 154 n. 1, 180 n. 2; Hansen (1975) 118–19.

31. Allegations that trierarchies could be discharged with a view to personal gain: Lys. 28 (esp. 2, 4) and 29 (esp. 4).

32. On phasis: Isoc. 17.42; cf. *Urkunden* 230, 521; E. Ruschenbusch, *Untersuchungen zur Geschichte des athenischen Strafrechts,* Gräzistische Abhandlungen, no. 4 (Cologne and Graz, 1968), 70–73.

33. Philotimia was equated with expenditure on the state: *IG* 2².1629.200–204; Dem. 8.70; 18.257; 28.22; [Dem.] 42.25; 50.15; 51.22; Lys. 19.56; 26.3; Aesch. 3.19; Isae. 7.35–36; Isoc. 18.60–61.

34. Usefulness: Dem. 4.7; 19.281–82; 28.24; 36.58; [Dem.] 42.25 (useful and philotimos with his property and person); Isae. 4.27; 7.41–42; 11.50; cf. Aesch. 1.105 (an unprofitable citizen). Danger and expenditure: Dem. 20.10; 21.162–66.

35. Segre (1936) 228, line 3, and 232–33; cf. A. Maiuri, *Silloge epigrafica di Rodi e Cos* (Florence, 1925), no. 5.

FIVE : *The Crew*

1. *IG* 2².1951; O. Broneer, "Excavations on the North Slope of the Acropolis in Athens, 1931–1932," *Hesperia* 2 (1933): 393, no. 12; O. Broneer, "Excavations on the North Slope of the Acropolis in Athens, 1933–1934," *Hesperia* 4 (1935): 164, no. 24, listing the crews of eight triereis. Cf. Laing (1965), esp. 107–8.

2. Jameson (1963) 389–92; *GOS* 257. Jordan's view (*AN* 243–59) that the term *hypēresia* refers to those of the oarsmen who were state-owned slaves can no longer be accepted; cf. Welwei (1974) 67–70; E. Ruschenbusch, "Zur Besatzung athenischer Trieren," *Historia* 28 (1979): 106–10; Morrison (1984).

3. Morrison (1984) 50–53, 56. But Thuc. 6.31.3, 8.1.2, and [Dem.] 51.5–6 do not support that view, while [Dem.] 50.10, 25, 29, 32, 35, 36, and 44 do distinguish among nautai, hyperesia, and epibatai, as does *Hell. Oxy.* 15.1 between hyperesia and epibatai. Jameson (1963) 389 argues that in the Themistokles decree *hypēresia* refers to the fighting men, but in the fourth century to a group separate from nautai and epibatai. The usual number of epibatai: *GOS* 263–66; Casson *SSAW* 304. Jordan *AN* 187 argues that Athenian triereis carried large numbers of marines. However, Thuc. 1.49.1 says quite the opposite: at the battle of Sybota (433) the Corinthians and the Korkyraeans had many epibatai on their decks, because, unlike the Athenians, they lacked experience.

4. Reconstructions in Tarn (1930) 122–41; *GOS* 291; Casson (1969) and *SSAW* 99–103.

5. Davies *Wealth* 144.

6. Other references to conscription: (*a*) Xen. *Hell.* 5.4.61 (376); (*b*) Isoc. 8.48,

79 (of 355); (*c*) Dem. 3.4 (352); (*d*) Dem. 4.36 (of circa 351); (*e*) *FGrH* 328: Philochoros F 49 (349/8); (*f*) Aesch. 2.133 (347/6); (*g*) Diod. 18.10.2 (323/2).

7. So *Urkunden* 201; Morrison (1984) 50. Jordan (*AN* 256) proposed the reading *kainas* (new). There is no support for the view (*HCT,* vol. 4, commentary on 6.43) that the forty troop transports to Sicily were rowed by hoplites and carried a skeleton crew of sailors.

8. Accepted by *Staatsh.* 1³.641 and D. Whitehead (1986) 134; questioned by Cawkwell (1984) 342–43.

9. *IG* 2².1951 (cf. Ar. *Ran.* 190–92, 693–94; *FGrH* 323a: Hellanikos F 25 [171]). *IG* 2².505 attests to the contribution by an individual of twelve oarsmen, probably his slaves, for the Lamian War. See Welwei (1974) 65–104, correcting both *Staatsh.* 1³.329–30 (extensive use of slaves) and R. L. Sargent, "The Use of Slaves by the Athenians in Warfare, II: In Warfare by Sea," *CPh* 22 (1927): 264–79 (denial of their employment).

10. Amit *AS* 29–48; Meiggs (1972) 439–41: citizens formed a considerable proportion. Strauss (1986) 71–78 estimates the number of thetes during the Peloponnesian War by using Ruschenbusch's formula ("Zur Besatzung athenischer Trieren," *Historia* 28 [1979]: 106–10): eighty citizens + sixty metics + sixty foreigners per ship, thus taking it for granted that the equation thranitai = citizens had been the rule; cf. Williams (1983); Hansen (1985) 21–25.

11. Cf. Wallinga (1993) 169–85. (*a*) What was unusual about Kleinias (Hdt. 8.17) was that he provided his own crew, not that the latter numbered two hundred; (*b*) the meaning of *a*[*n*]*a hekaton arithmon,* in ML no. 23.32, is still debated (N. Robertson [1982] 37); (*c*) that horse transports had sixty oars does not mean that troop transports had fewer than 170 oarsmen; (*d*) the difference between sixty "fast" triereis and forty stratiotides (at Thuc. 6.43) cannot be one between fully manned and undermanned ships (cf. *HCT* 4:309–10); (*e*) Thuc. 1.49.1–3 (Sybota, 433) refers to the difference between old and new tactics, not that triereis may be undermanned when using boarding tactics; (*f*) Thuc. 8.74.2 (cf. 86.9) says that the crew of *Paralos* was transferred to a troop carrier, not that the latter was a trireme with a skeleton crew.

12. Gabrielsen (1981) 67–81, 151–55; A. Dreizehnter, "Zur Entstehung der Lohnarbeit und deren Terminologie," in *Soziale Typenbegriffe im alten Griechenland und ihr Fortleben in den Sprachen der Welt,* ed. E. C. Welskopf (Berlin, 1981), 3:269–81.

13. Eddy (1968) doubts only the number of ships involved, which he emends to sixteen; cf. Jordan *AN* 104–5, 112; Meiggs (1972) 427. Not that training was unimportant (Thuc. 1.142.9), but, as contemporary sources insist, experience was gained through frequent service on expeditions (Ps.-Xen. *Ath. Pol.* 1.19–20; Thuc. 3.115.7–8; Xen. *Hell.* 6.2.27–30).

14. Jones (1957) 32 and 142 n. 54; Dover, *HCT* 4:293; Andrewes, *HCT* 5:97–99; Jordan *AN* 111–16.

15. *Staatsh.* 1³.342–45; Gomme, *HCT* 2:275–76; *GSW* 1:17; Amit *AS* 51–52: three obols before and after the Peloponnesian War, but one drachma for most of the war.

16. Cf. *GSW* 1:16; Andrewes, *HCT* 5:70–72, discussing the textual and arithmetic problems.

17. *GOS* 259, but Andrewes (*HCT* 5:98) has objections. Thuc. 8.45.2: Athenian crews received only three obols per day not so much because of a lack of money as to prevent illness or desertion. Ar. *Eq.* 1366–67: "First of all, to all who row long ships I will give their full pay [*misthon entelē*] when they come into port" (Sommerstein [1981] ad loc.); *Hell. Oxy.* 15.1. Polyaenus 3.9.51: Iphikrates always kept on hand a quarter of his army's monthly pay as security against desertion. Cf. *GSW* 1:24–29.

18. Attempts to calculate the "operational expenditure" of the fleet in the fourth century (Robbins [1918]; Wilson [1970], esp. 305–16; Burke [1985] 256–58), in my view, tend to underestimate the total costs of expeditions.

19. See *AFD* 48–56 and *ATL*, vol. 2, doc. D18. The higher sum of over fourteen hundred talents in the record (l. 19) is explained as including payments for the campaign against Byzantion (ML 51), but cf. Meiggs (1972) 188–95, esp. 192; R. P. Legon, "Samos in the Delian League," *Historia* 21 (1972): 145–58; C. W. Fornara, "On the Chronology of the Samian War," *JHS* 99 (1979): 7–19.

20. Thuc. 2.70.2; Isoc. 15.133 gives 2,400 talents.

21. Peacetime cost of the navy (448–431): Eddy (1968) 155–56; naval costs to 431/30: Unz (1985) 24–28. Cf. A. French, "The Tribute of the Allies," *Historia* 21 (1972): 1–20.

22. *IG* 1³.369; cf. ML 214–17; *ATL* 3:341–44; Gomme, *HCT* 2:432–36.

23. The funds available could finance the first four or five years (G. Busolt, *Griechische Geschichte bis zur Schlacht bei Chaeroneia* [Gotha, 1904], 3.2:876–78, 893 n. 3), or three years of the war (D. Kagan, *The Archidamian War* [Ithaca, N.Y., 1974], 37–40).

24. Dem. 8.21–23 (342/1); cf. 1.6, 20 (349/8); 2.24, 27, 31 (349/8); 3.20 (349/8); 4.7 (351); *Ex.* 41.2; and Lys. 28.3–4, 29.4, 9. Cf. B. D. Meritt, "Indirect Tradition in Thucydides," *Hesperia* 23 (1953): 185–231, esp. 223–24; Thomsen (1964) 165–66, 173–74; H. B. Mattingly, "Athenian Finance in the Peloponnesian War," *BCH* 92 (1968): 450–85, esp. 451, 455.

25. *GSW* 2:84–85, 101. Dem. 4.23–24 (of 351): a force must resort to raids, for no misthos or trophe can be supplied from the treasury; 10.37 (shortly after 355 or 342/1?): the revenues of the city did not exceed 130 talents; 23.209 (of 352): the treasury had not one day's *ephodia* (provisions); 3.30 (of 349/8): complaint about lack of pay; 2.28; 8.24–26; 23.171: strategoi do not receive sufficient funds. In

358/7, a force was sent to Euboia without maintenance (siteresion) and had to provision itself there; Arist. *Rh.* 1411a9–10.

26. In 389/8, Thrasyboulos was sent to Rhodes with forty triereis, but he first carried out raids in the Hellespont and on the Thracian coast in order to obtain funds to pay his squadron: Xen. *Hell.* 4.8.25–31; Lys. 28; Diod. 14.94.2, 99.4. In 373/2, Iphikrates maintained his crews at Korkyra from booty captured from Syracusan ships and sold for sixty talents: Xen. *Hell.* 6.2.35–38; Diod. 15.47.7, 16.57.2–3; Polyaenus 3.9.55.

27. In 343/2, Diopeithes was not given funds from Athens, nor was he allowed to use the syntaxeis to maintain his crews in the Hellespont: Dem. 8. hyp. and 21; 9.15; *FGrH* 328: Philochoros F 158; he therefore had to resort to raids and to exacting money from merchantmen (Dem. 8.8–9, 19, 21–28, 46–47).

28. *GSW* 1:30–52; cf. Tänzer (1912).

29. Speed: Casson *SSAW* 128, 280 nn. 42–44; Morrison and Coates (1986) 103–6. Effective power: Coates and McGrail (1985) 60–62, fig. 17; Morrison and Coates (1989) 84–97; Coates, Platis, and Shaw (1990) 20–31, 84–86.

30. Jordan *AN* 108–9. *GSW* 1:32–33 furnishes evidence to show that they could have taken provisions for one to three days. Cf. Gomme (1933) 8; Morrison and Coates (1986) 95, 99, 102.

31. Nikias reported that his oarsmen at Sicily were being wasted because they were forced to go a distance for wood and forage, thus falling prey to the enemy's cavalry (Thuc. 7.13.2).

32. Water supplies: C. Müller, ed., *Geographi Graeci Minores* (Paris, 1855), 1:427–514; [Plut.] *Mor.* 303C; Ath. 5.208A. Cf. Gomme (1933) 18 n. 9.

33. Lampsakos, Xenophon says (*Hell.* 2.1.19), was full of wine, grain, and all kinds of provisions when the city was captured by Lysander in 405. [Arist.] *Oec.* 2.2.7 mentions Lampsakos in his example of wartime inflation in the price of barley, oil, wine, and other commodities occurring when a large fleet was about to put to harbor. When the trierarch Apollodoros suffered desertions, he sent his pentekontarchos to Lampsakos to employ new oarsmen, while he himself secured others from Sestos ([Dem.] 50.18).

34. Foxhall and Forbes (1982) 44 n. 10, 56, 71, 74; P. Garnsey, "Food Consumption in Antiquity: Towards a Quantitative Account," in Garnsey (1989) 36–49 with tables (68–88).

35. Cf. Garnsey (1989) 39.

36. In these calculations the Basal Metabolic Rate (= 318 kj/hour) is multiplied by a factor for very hard work (6.6), for sedentary activity (1.5), and for sleep (1); cf. *Energy and Protein Requirements: Report of a Joint FAO/WHO/VNU Expert Consultation,* Technical Report Series, no. 724 (Geneva, 1985), 71 (table 5), 178 (annex 1), 203–4, and annex 5, esp. 189. Energy requirements (based on a distribution of 10 percent protein, 35 percent lipid, and 55 percent carbohydrate):

20 mj (for 6 hours' work), requiring 1,500 g of food (= 700 g wheat, 150 g fish/ mutton, 150 g oil, 500 g wine), and 17 mj (for 4 hours' work), requiring 1,325 g of food (= 600 g wheat, 100 g fish/mutton, 125 g oil, 500 g wine).

37. Engels (1978) 18, 123–26.

38. Guilmartin (1974) 63.

39. Markle (1985) 279–81, 293–97. Barley meal was cheaper by half (279; cf. Foxhall and Forbes [1982] 53–54 n. 39). The nutritional value of wheat and barley by weight is closely equivalent: Markle (1985) 277; cf. F. B. Morrison, *Food and Feeding* (Ithaca, N.Y., 1954), 1114, 1128; Foxhall and Forbes (1982) 46, 53.

40. See Foxhall and Forbes (1982) 55 n. 46—arguing mainly against A. Jardé, *Les céréales dans l'antiquité grecque* (Paris, 1925), 129—and 51–62 for a discussion of the Greek sources.

41. Dem. 18.107: some trierarchs abandon their ships abroad; one reason might be inability to pay the crews; cf. 108.

42. Thuc. 7.39.2, 62.1; Ar. *Eq.* 541–44; Pl. *Resp.* 341C–D; Xen. *Hell.* 1.5.11; Paus. 10.9.8.

43. [Dem.] 50.15 indicates that the other trierarchs in Apollodoros's squadron had also suffered desertions, though to a lesser degree. Since the deserting oars-men are contrasted to those supplied from the deme lists (16), it follows that the other trierarchs had hired extra labor.

44. Thuc. 1.31.1, 143.1; 7.13.2; Xen. *Hell.* 1.5.4; [Dem.] 50.14.

45. Jordan *AN* 213, 251–52 n. 27 argues, against Kolbe *Re navali* 44, that therapontes and xenoi must be distinguished from nautai. But cf. Morrison and Coates (1986) 117–18; A. J. Graham, "Thucydides 7.13.2 and the Crews of Athenian Triremes," *TAPhA* 122 (1990): 257–70.

46. Xen. *Hell.* 5.1.13; Dem. 4.24: a strategos is unable to command if he does not provide pay.

47. [Dem.] 51.11; Dem. 21.155. In 375, a trierarch received one talent, one thousand drachmas for having transported the *theoroi* and choruses to Delos for the Greater Delia: *IG* 2².1635.34–35. Payment of one talent, seven hundred drach-mas by the Delians to the trierarch Mantias Thorikios may have had the same purpose; cf. the inscription reported by O. Alexandri, *AD* 25, part B.2 (1970): 60 and pl. 56a, with D. M. Lewis, apud Clark (1990) 54.

48. [Dem.] 50.7, 17–19, 23, 56.

SIX : *The Ship*

1. The latter opinion is held by several scholars: *GOS* 228; D. Kagan, *The Archidamian War* (Ithaca, N.Y., 1974), 26 n. 38; E. Lévy, *Athènes devant la défaite de 404: Histoire d'une crise idéologique,* BEFAR, no. 22 (Paris, 1976), 274; Burke (1985) 257 n. 34. But this is not what Thuc. 2.24.2 seems to be saying; cf. Kalinka (1913)

280. Andocides (3.9) claims that during the peace of Nikias there were four hundred ships (a figure defended by D. M. MacDowell, "An Expansion of the Athenian Navy," *CR* n.s. 15 [1965]: 260), but in view of the other evidence one should prefer Aeschines (2.175), who, referring to the same years, says that there were three hundred seaworthy ships; cf. Blackman (1969) 213. Xen. *An.* 7.1.27 mentions the number of ships at the start of the Peloponnesian War, but the manuscripts vary between three hundred and four hundred.

2. Robbins (1918) 366; Amit *AS* 25, citing the evidence for the size of squadrons operating in the 390s and 380s; Wilson (1970) 310–11; Sinclair (1978) 49–51. *IG* 2².31.20 (restored) is interpreted to suggest naval activity in 386/5 in the northern Aegean and Propontis; but A. Höck, "Das Odrysenreich in Thrakien im 5. und 4. Jahrhundert v. Chr.," *Hermes* 26 (1891): 453–62, and Tod no. 117 attempt no restoration.

3. Their development is discussed by Ashton (1977).

4. 357/6: *IG* 2².1611.3–9; 353/2: 1613.284–92; 330/29: 1627.266–78; 326/5: 1628.481–500; 325/4: 1629.783–812 (on the number of pentereis [7 or 2], see Ashton [1979]); 323/2: 1631.167–74; cf. Ashton (1977) 4–5, Morrison (1987) 90–92, contra the less probable reconstruction of Schmitt (1974) 80 n. 1.

5. *Diadedikasmenai* ("adjudicated"), *IG* 2².1613.224–26; cf. 205–6, 291–92, and U. Köhler, "Aus den attischen Seeurkunden," *AM* 6 (1881): 21–39, esp. 24.

6. 1628.483–84 and 1630, which are now joined to continue and complete col. b (after l. 338) of 1628; cf. E. Schweigert, "The Naval Record of 326/5 B.C.," *Hesperia* 9 (1940): 343–45, no. 43; Laing (1968) 246–47.

7. See the Introduction (p. 15). On Greek accounting in general: G. E. M. de Ste. Croix, "Greek and Roman Accounting," in *Studies in the History of Accounting,* ed. A. C. Littleton and B. S. Yamey (London, 1956), 14–74; R. Macve, "Some Glosses on Ste. Croix's 'Greek and Roman Accounting,'" in Cartledge and Harvey (1985) 233–64.

8. The largest fleets known to have been simultaneously in commission in the fourth century are 120 ships at Embata in 356 (Diod. 16.21.1), and 170 ships in 323/2 (Diod. 18.15.8).

9. However, only the ratings of triereis are known; the only exception to this known to me might be *IG* 2².1628.81–84: "[Tetreres Heg]emonia, the work of [———], new, [tested,] built in the archonship of Niketes" (332/1). But the word "new" was no longer used as a rating description in this period.

10. An attempt to alter the traditional date of 1604 (377/6) to 379/8 (Clark [1990]) is not convincing; a more plausible alternative is the year 378/7. Cf. Gabrielsen (1992); 1606 is of 373/4, 1607 and 1608 of 373/2. No precise date can be established for 1605 (which is probably part of the same stele as 1604) and for 1610, but the context of the 370s is indisputable; for 1609 several dates have been pro-

posed, all within the same chronological environment, but no criteria are readily at hand to favor a definite year; cf. Gabrielsen (1989a) 99 n. 20.

11. Sinclair's assumption ([1978] 50 n. 83) that ships without a description must be taken as "old" is unsupported.

12. *Nike, Eleutheria, Demokratia, Kleo, Arete, Europe, Synoris, Euphemia, Neotate, Aphrodisia.*

13. *IG* 2².1611: "seconds" (ll. 73–96); "select" (ll. 107–33, 135–40, 157–70, 185–89); "thirds" (ll. 97–103).

14. *IG* 2².1627.398–405; 1628.552–59; 1629.1030–36.

15. E.g., Thuc. 2.103.1; 3.50.1; 4.16.1–3; 8.19.3; cf. 7.24.2: capture by the Syracusans of forty masts belonging to Athenian ships; *IG* 2².1606; 1607, col. b; 1610.23–24; 1629.145.

16. Blackman (1969) 208; cf. *AFD* 83–86, noting (85) that the restoration is hypothetical.

17. See the works cited in Blackman (1969) 209 n. 86.

18. The losses in Egypt (454: Thuc. 1.104, 109–10 with *HCT*, vol. 1, ad loc.) were perhaps not so great (Meiggs [1972] 101–8, 439–41, 473–77), but cf. A. J. Holladay, "The Hellenic Disaster in Egypt," *JHS* 109 (1989): 176–82.

19. Thuc. 8.30.2; 79.1–6, with Andrewes, *HCT* 5:30–31, 273–74.

20. Sinclair (1978) 51 does not see a significant reconstruction of the navy, and argues from the occurrence of ships described as "new" (in 1604) that twenty-nine ships were built in the two-year period; however, that description admits of no secure dating criteria. Wilson (1970) 310–11 postulates an upsurge of shipbuilding at Athens and believes that forty-one ships were built in the same period. For equally optimistic estimates, see Robbins (1918) and Amit *AS* 25.

21. *Ath. Pol.* 46.1; *IG* 1³.153.4; 117.8–9; 182; 366.13.

22. Condition of hulls: *IG* 2².1627.241–48; 1628.460–65; 1629.722–45; 1631.100–105. Deliveries: 1623.309–13; 1628.37–42; 1629.11–15, 32–36, 153–57; 1631.214–16 (decree of the boule and the demos); cf. 1604.64–65 (decree of the demos or the boule?).

23. Rhodes *AB* 99–100, 103, 117 n. 6. *IG* 1³.117 (407/6) possibly ordered the strategoi to borrow money from the apodektai and then to hand it over to the shipwrights for building ships. This arrangement perhaps reflects an emergency situation where the trieropoioi had temporarily exhausted their shipbuilding grant and a decree was necessary before the apodektai could advance the money against later repayment (ML 280). The normal procedure would have been for the Hellenotamiai to disburse funds from the combined state and imperial treasuries to the trieropoioi, and for the latter to forward the money to the shipwrights; cf. Meritt (1936); *ATL* 3:361.

24. Keil (1902) 10–17, 41–43, 74–75, 135–40 connected the *Anon. Arg.* with Andoc. 3.5, and argued for the building of one hundred triereis, though he also considered the option of an annual building of ten ships. Kolbe (1901) 409, 411–13

held that the program was a fleet expansion: *kainas epinaupēgein hekato[n]*, not a replacement as Andocides suggests. Wilcken (1907) 387–403 dated the event to 431/0, and argued that it was a recurring program of ten triereis beginning in that year. Wade-Gery and Meritt (1957) proposed that lines 3–11 are one section, commenting on Dem. 22.13, and referring to a Periklean decree of 450/49 ordering the reduction of the rate from twenty to ten triereis. Detailed commentary on the various restorations is found in Blackman (1969) 204–7 and Jordan *AN* 26–29.

25. Wade-Gery and Meritt (1957) 187; Blackman (1969) 203–4, 21; but cf. Eddy (1968) 146; *GOS* 225.

26. Keil (1902) 201–11, citing examples of "lives" of twenty-five, thirty-three, and thirty-seven years; cf. Kolbe (1901) 386–407; Amit *AS* 27; Blackman (1969) 203, 215; Casson *SSAW* 90.

27. Schmitt's (1974) calculations, yielding an annual average of seven tetrereis, are vitiated by the unreliability of his principal dating criterion: the return, by various tamiai *trieropoiikon,* of tetrereis equipment to the dockyards; see pp. 151–52 above.

28. ML no. 94; cf. A. L. Boegehold, "The Establishment of a Central Archive at Athens," *AJA* 76 (1972): 23–30, esp. 23–25; *IG* I³.127.

29. *IG* 2².1623.152–58; cf. Gabrielsen (1988).

30. Styppeion: [Dem.] 47.20; *IG* 2².1629.1151–52, 1631.336. Hypaloiphe: 1627.313–17; 1622.715, 740.

31. Meiggs (1982) 453, table 3.

32. *IG* 2².1627.241–48; cf. 1628.460–65; 1629.722–45; 1631.100–105.

33. Those acquitted: *IG* 2².1629.841–58; 1631.148–67, 199–211. Those convicted: 1623.6–13; 1628.609–18; 1629.826–40, 1085–92; 1631.176–84, 184–99, 279–83.

34. *Urkunden* 196–210 (*Staatsh.* I³.139–41). Labarbe *Loi navale* 44 n. 2: one talent included the cost of equipment. S. K. Eddy, "Four Hundred Sixty Talents Once More," *CPh* 63 (1968): 184–95, esp. 189–92 (followed by Blackman [1969] 184), sets the cost of a triereis in the 480s at one talent, because, he argues, the ship-contributing allies in the early fifth century were assessed with the conversion formula of one trieres = one talent of tribute. But (*a*) a comparison between ship contributions in the 480s and the later tribute assessments is arbitrary; (*b*) the instances of correlation he cites (e.g., Aigina: thirty ships at Salamis, thirty talents in tribute) can be pure coincidence; (*c*) even if this were correct, one talent might be a nominal valuation, not the cost of building a ship; and (*d*) if a ship cost one talent at Athens, it does not follow that it cost the same elsewhere. Gomme, *HCT* 2:33 n. 1, refers to M. Holroyd's suggestion that the equation was one trieres = three talents of tribute, because many of the tributes from larger cities were three talents or a multiple or a fraction of three. But cf. N. D. Robertson, "The True Nature of the Delian League, 478–461 B.C.," *AJAH* 5 (1980): 64–96, esp. 65.

35. Köhler (1879) 81–82; Köhler unjustifiably assumed that the old hull became the property of the trierarch and then was returned to the state together with payment of five thousand drachmas.

36. (a) Payments for repairs were specified as such: *episkeuē triērous/tetrērous*, *IG* 2².1612.91–99, 145–50; 1628.562–69; 1631.442–48, 517–20. Payments of five thousand drachmas, in contrast, had a different purpose: 1623.6–13, 26–34, 113–23. (b) Not all hulls for which payment of five thousand drachmas was made could be rebuilt (Boeckh) or returned to the dockyards (Köhler), simply because some never returned to Piraeus; 1623.124–32: "Delias, the work of Timokles . . . [The trierarchs] acknowledged in court their responsibility to provide a new one to the state," where the absence of instructions to demolish the old hull and to return the ram indicate that the ship was lost. Cf. Gabrielsen (1988) 68–69.

37. Unlike, for instance, Cyprus, where ships could be built and equipped completely from local materials; Amm. Marc. 14.8.14. On the imports of materials by naval states: Johnson (1927); Semple (1932) 275–82; Meiggs (1982) 116–53, 188–217.

38. Johnson (1927) 201; Meiggs (1982) 119; Morrison and Coates (1986) 180–82, 189.

39. Another source was Thrace, probably exploited since 476/5 with the establishment of an Athenian settlement at Eion at the mouth of Strymon. Also, Amphipolis (occupied from 437/6 to 424/3) "was useful to Athens for the timber it sent and for the silver revenue" (Thuc. 1.98.1; 4.108.1). Another but distant source of supply was the forests of southern Italy, to which Athens presumably had to turn after the breakdown of its relations with Macedon in the second half of the fourth century; cf. Demosthenes' statement (17.28, shortly after 336) that it was difficult to get timber for the fleet and it had to come from a long distance. Southern Italy, it is argued, had probably supplied timber for the ships built in the 480s (Meiggs [1982] 124–25).

40. The circulation of natural products along the networks of ritualized friendship is discussed by G. Herman, *Ritualised Friendship and the Greek City* (Cambridge, 1987), 82–88.

41. Casson *SSAW* 201–13, and (1985); Morrison and Coates (1986) 192–222.

42. Burford (1969) 185–86, and Burford, "Heavy Transport in Classical Antiquity," *EHR*, 2d ser. 13 (1960): 1–18; Casson (1956); Snodgrass (1983).

43. For *paraskeuazein* meaning *episkeuazein*, see Thuc. 7.38.2–3.

SEVEN : *Equipment*

1. *IG* 2².1611.3–64; 1613.284–310; 1614.140–65. Cf. Davies (1969) 315–18; *GOS* 289–307; Cawkwell (1984) 341. The items of equipment mentioned in this chapter are explained in the Appendix.

2. E.g., in giving the overall total of sets of oars, 233, which were (*a*) in the dockyards, (*b*) in commission, and (*c*) owed by officials and trierarchs, the record of 357/6 separately mentions that of these sets 881 single oars were missing, i.e., they were impossible to account for (1611.21–22, with 10–18).

3. The best-preserved remains of ship-sheds are those of Zea: B. Graser, "Athens Kriegshäfen," *Philologus* 31 (1872): 1–65; I. C. Dragatzes, "ΕΚΘΕΣΙΣ ΠΕΡΙ ΤΩΝ ΕΝ ΠΕΙΡΑΙΕΙ ΑΝΑΣΚΑΦΩΝ," *Praktika* (1885): 63–71; D. Blackman in *GOS* 181–92.

4. *Ath. Pol.* 24.3: five hundred guards of the dockyards; Ar. *Ach.* 916ff.; Dem. 18.132: fear of being destroyed by fire.

5. Pl. *Grg.* 455D–E; cf. *GOS* 225.

6. *IG* II².1621.7, 28, 101; cf. 1609.21; 1611.13, 269; 1613.241–42, 282.

7. *Urkunden* 310, 324; cf. Kirchner's note to *IG* 2².1611, for the view that column e of the inscription listed equipment from these skeuothekai.

8. *IG* 2².1627.280–81; 1628.501–3; 1629.976–78; 1631.212–14.

9. Marstrand (1922), citing the earlier literature; Jeppesen (1961) 221–23; Lorenzen (1964); A. Linfert et al., eds., *Die Skeuotheke des Philon im Piräus* (Cologne, 1981).

10. Interruption: *FGrH* 328: Philochoros F 56a; resumption: [Plut.] *Mor.* 841D; cf. Xen. *Vect.* 6.1; Din. 1.96; Aesch. 3.25. Mentioned in 330/29: 1627.288, 292, 296, 301–2, 407, 420; although none of these entries directly proves that the skeuotheke was already put into use, the specification of the earlier building as "the old skeuotheke" (1627.352) indicates that strongly. The levy of annual eisphorai in the period 347/6–323/2 to finance the building of ship-sheds and the skeuotheke need not mean that the work itself was completed in 323/2, as Jeppesen (1961) 69–70 n. 2 believes. Probably, the hanging equipment listed in 1628.228ff. (326/5) and 1629.356ff. (325/4) as being stored in the neoria was actually placed in the new skeuotheke.

11. Laing (1968) 246, (326/5) ll. 341–44; *IG* 2².1629 (325/4) ll. 464–66: "The following we received from the treasurer of hanging equipment, Antisthenes Phalereus, and from the dockyard superintendents serving in the archonship of Antikles" (325/4), stated by the epimeletai of 325/4. Boeckh (*Urkunden* 58, 478), rightly noted that the epimeletai referred to were "einzelnen Aufsehern der Werfte des Amtsjahres."

12. *IG* 2².1627; 1628; 1629; cf. 1471 B, col. 2, 61ff.; 1479 B, 41ff., 64ff.; 1481 B; 1641 C; 1648; 1649.

13. Rhodes *AB* 119, 239–40; cf. an unpublished essay by D. M. Lewis (apud Cawkwell [1963] 57 n. 2), which I have not been able to consult. See also note 32 to the Introduction.

14. Cf. *Urkunden* 54; Gabrielsen (1989a) 95.

15. *Timē skeuōn:* [Dem.] 47.32; 50.26; *IG* 2².1620.65–73; diagramma (register) stating the time skeuon: Dem. 14.21; [Dem.] 47.36, 43; *IG* 2².1623.144–59, 207–9, 215–17; 1629.622–27, 647–54, 656–64; 1631.417–18, 641–52.

16. For 2,299 drachmas: *IG* 2².1623.35–49 and 1629.486–93 (Menestheus Rhamnousios's service on *Amphitrite Lysikleidou,* probably in 345/4; cf. 1443.106–8); 1623.268–75 and 1627.194–99 (Stesileides Siphnios on *Iaso Lysikratous*). For 2,169 drachmas: 1624.63–70 (Diokles Eleousios on *Nike Aristokratous*); 1624.42–49, 1628.369–95, and 1629.889–914 (Philomelos Paianieus and syntrierarch on *Charis Archeneo*).

17. *IG* 2².1623.368–75; 1629.667–73. The epimeletai of 325/4 delivered two heavy sails (*histia pachea*) when they should have delivered two light sails (*histia lepta*). For that reason they were compelled to pay an additional 300 drachmas "according to the register [diagramma]" (1631.415–17). A light sail was at that time valued over 150 drachmas, but that transaction took place in 323/2, when the value of equipment had risen drastically.

18. E.g., ll. 44–48 (Philokles Eroiades on *Boetheia Smikrionos*).

19. E.g., 6,105 drachmas, 3 obols: *IG* 2².1629.639–46 (Philokomos Paianieus on *Aktis Epigenous*); 6,000 drachmas: 647–56 (Archippos Paianieus and syntrierarchs on *Homonoia Archineo*).

20. On misappropriation of public funds, see Lys. 19, 27, 28, 29. Cf. D. Cohen, *Theft in Athenian Law,* Münchener Beiträge zur Papyrusforschung und Antiken Rechtsgeschichte, no. 74 (Munich, 1983), esp. 49–51.

21. H. Fränkel, "Attische Inschriften," *AM* 48 (1923): 3–23, esp. 20; R. Sealey, "*IG* II² 1609 and the Transformation of the Second Athenian League," *Phoenix* 11 (1957): 95–111, esp. 97; Davies (1969) 318–19; Brun (1985).

22. Phormion Peiraieus: 1623.245–59; 1629.647–56; Eudraon Thorikios: 1623.143–49, 246–52; Archedemos [Pitheus]: 1609.57.

23. Sopolis's case: 1631.350–403; cf. Gabrielsen (1989a) 97–98.

24. Satyros might have acted on authorization of the legislative measures of 358/7 and 357/6; cf. Cawkwell (1962) 44; Davies (1969) 316; Develin *AO* 276.

25. Gabrielsen (1987b) 47–51.

26. Cf. Köhler (1879) 84; Davies (1969) 316. Andreades (1933) 325 n. 1 saw the ineffectiveness of the navy as being due to the "criminal leniency of the courts."

27. Rhodes (*AB* 157) observes two differences: (*a*) the old law does not mention the *apostoleis,* who in 357/6, together with the epimeletai, brought disputed cases to trial; (*b*) jurisdiction, in the old law, remained with a *dikasterion* instead of passing to the boule if the original court order was ignored.

28. Cf. [Dem.] 47.23: "It was therefore a matter of necessity [*ex anagkēs*] for us to receive them. I must tell you that hitherto, although I had often served as trierarch for you, I had never taken equipment from the dockyards, but had supplied it at my own private expense whenever need arose, in order that I might

have as little trouble as possible with the state. On this occasion, however, I was compelled to take over [*ēnagkazomēn paralabein*] the names [sc. of defaulters] in accordance with the decrees and the law."

29. Laing (1968) 244–54; but cf. Gabrielsen (1990) 99.

30. Cf. *IG* 2².1616.122–23; 1618.106–7, for their cooperation on *Aianteia Lysikleous*.

31. A decree of 354 provided for *zētētai* (boards of officials appointed to help the state recover public debts), before which information might be laid against anyone holding public money, sacred or secular (Dem. 24.11 and hyp. 2.1–3).

32. Archestratos: *IG* 2².1622.249–63, cf. 1611.440–48. Demophanes: 1622.331–50; cf. 1611.434–41.

33. Diplosis by a dikasterion: *IG* 2².1623.57–58, 68–71, 87–96, 109–12, 136–43, 147–51, 218–24; 1628.634–36; 1631.255–60 (liability of a naval official). On diplosis: Rhodes *AB* 148–58; Hansen (1991) 262.

34. [Dem.] 47.24–26; *IG* 1³.236.6; 2².1631.353–55.

35. Public debtors: their debts might be doubled, normally in the ninth prytany (*Ath. Pol.* 48.1; Andoc. 1.73–74; but cf. Dem. 24.39–40 and passim [law proposed by Timokrates in 353]); they could suffer loss of civic rights (Dem. 59.6), and be imprisoned by the boule until they had discharged their debts (Andoc. 1.92–93; *Ath. Pol.* 63.3). Cf. Rhodes *AB* 148–51, 179 n. 3, and D. M. MacDowell, *The Law in Classical Athens* (Ithaca, N.Y., 1978). On trierarchs: Hansen (1976) 59 n. 22. Boeckh's claim (*Staatsh.* 1³.631) that the apostoleis could imprison those in arrears is not borne out by the source he cites (Dem. 18.107). Philokrates' prosecution before a dikasterion for having misappropriated funds (first as a treasurer of, then as a trierarch under, the strategos Ergokles; Lys. 29) bears a different significance.

36. Osborne (1985a) 1–6 and (1985b) 44.

37. The register (diagramma) held by Theophemos, which listed the items owed, was submitted at the eisangelia (43). The speaker did finally sail on his ship; *IG* 2².1612.313–16 probably records the return of equipment by Demochares and Theophemos in 356/5.

38. Rhodes (*AB* 156) assumes that a diplosis was included in the deliberation of the boule during the eisangelia.

39. That of Konon Anaphlystios, Onetor Meliteus, and Euboios Anagyrasios on *Delias Timokleous: IG* 2².1623.124–35; 1628.396–418; 1629.915–39; that of Phaiax Acharneus on *Hippagogos Lysistratou:* 1623.14–34; 1628.420–35; 1629.940–56.

40. For the disruption of food supply after Chaironia (cf. Demosthenes' appointment as grain commissioner after the war) with three subsequent food shortages (in 336/5, 330/29, 328/7), see Garnsey (1988) 154–55.

41. *IG* 2².1628.350–68, 369–95, 396–418.

42. For details see Gabrielsen (1988), arguing against the interpretations of Boeckh (*Urkunden* 108–10, Urk. XIV.c.26–32), Köhler (1879) 8off., and Kirchner (note to *IG* 2².1623). On the Twenty, see Köhler (1879) 87.

43. [Dem.] 47.20–23; *IG* 2².1615, 1616, 1617, 1618, 1619, 1625.

44. To the examples in which debtors receive financial assistance may be added the following: (*a*) Philomelos Cholargeus took over (*anadexamenos*) the liability of Eupolis Aixoneus (1623.60–71); (*b*) the original trio liable to compensate for *Delias Timokleous* in 334/3 (Konon Anaphlystios, Onetor Meliteus, and Euboios Anagyrasios) was later (326/5) joined by Phaiax Acharneus (1623.124–43; 1628.396–418; 1629.915–39; 1631.10–15 [restored]); (*c*) the case of Nausikles Oeithen and his heir Klearchos Aigilieus, discussed on p. 63.

45. *Stilbousa*: 1631.448–52, 585–88, 652–54; the exact division is 5.1/6 and 0.9/6. *Hellas*: 1631.470–73, 592–601, 678–79; the precise division of the attested sums is 4.5/6 and 1.5/6. In transactions where the cost of repair and of equipment are given as one sum, the amount relating to equipment only can be obtained by deducting 1,200 drachmas from the total.

46. On *Aura Lysikleidou* as synteles of Euthynos Hagnousios, whose share in the debt was 2,372 drachmas, 3 obols (1631.582–85; cf. 457–62, 496–99); on *Phosphoros Archenikou* as synteles of Lykinos Palleneus, whose share was 3,216 drachmas, 4 obols (1631.588–91; cf. 466–70); on *Phaule Chairestratou* as synteles of K[——]on, whose share was 3,400 drachmas (1631.551–56).

EIGHT : *The Reforms*

1. *Urkunden* 177; *Staatsh.* 1³.637–38. However, Boeckh's assumption (672) that Xen. *Oec.* 2.6 refers to one of the earliest attested syntrierarchies can be questioned.

2. Cf. E. Capps's reconstruction of *IG* 2².2318 in "A New Fragment of the List of Victors of the City Dionysia," *Hesperia* 12 (1943): 5–8; Pickard-Cambridge (1968) 48, 87, 102. K. J. Maidment, "The Later Comic Chorus," *CQ* 29 (1935): 1–24, esp. 2–4, dated the disappearance of the *synchoregy* in circa 394/3.

3. Dem. 21.154: "Moreover, as soon as I came of age (364), I performed trierarchies, at the time when we discharged the duty in pairs of trierarchs." If Demosthenes wants to imply that no syntrierarchies by pairs of trierarchs were performed after 358/7 (cf. 155), his claim cannot be true. It should be noted, however, that the first record from the 370s and 360s to list any significant number of syntrierarchies is *IG* 2².1609.

4. Three syntrierarchs: Schweigert (1939) no. 5, fr. E, ll. 1–4; *IG* 2².1613.210–14; 1622.351–55; 1623.20–25, 125–29, 133–36; 1628.43–46, 66–69, 71–75; 1629.3–7, 45–50; 1631.635 (and 1632.26–30); 1631.641–45. Four or more: 1623.246–53 (four);

1628.54–59 (four), 136–42 (four); 1632.56–59 (five), 85–89 (five), 67–71 (seven); 1628.20–27 (nine); 1632.307–12 (ten).

5. *APF* 35–36; *IG* 2².1609.70; 1612.352–59; 1622.131–36.

6. Boeckh (*Urkunden* 175) inferred from [Dem.] 50.37 that two syntrierarchs could serve together on their ship, but the source does not warrant that inference.

7. Lys. 32.24, 26; [Dem.] 50.30–31, 33, 38–40, 42. The view (*Urkunden* 208–10) that syntrierarchs drew up a diagramma stating the relative share (not always equal) to be paid by each man toward the running expenses of their service is unsupported. The entry on which it rested (1629.544–68, cf. *Urkunden* 482–84) shows only that the principal trierarch, Demostratos Kytherrios, paid several installments on his own behalf and on behalf of his two partners in order to compensate for *Proplous Demotelous.*

8. Such payments are frequently specified as follows: (*a*) "This man paid one-half [*to hēmisy* or *ta hēmisea*]," *IG* 2².1622.45, 74, 130, 136, 144–45, 183, 196–98, 244–47, 269–70, 328–29; 1629.572; (*b*) "This man paid one-third [*to triton meros*]," concerning a debt paid by one of three syntrierarchs, 1622.115, 294–95, 359–61, 373–75; (*c*) "This man/each of these men paid his own share [*to kath' hauton* or *to kath' hautous meros*]," 1624.95; 1627.213, 219.

9. Davies (1967), *APF* xxviii–xxxix, and *Wealth* 16. In the latter two works Davies muddles the issue a bit by making the erroneous statement that diadikasiai (in general and not only those concerning antidoseis) would not reduce the total number of men assembled to discharge trierarchies.

10. Davies *Wealth* 15–24, 26–27, and *APF* xx–xxi, followed by Ober (1989) 117, 128. But see the critique of Rhodes (1982) 4–5. Ruschenbusch (1978) and (1985c), too, believes that trierarchies and other liturgies were performed by only three hundred men.

11. Demosthenes' statement (355/4) to the effect that "since the richest citizens perform trierarchies, they are already exempt from the choregies [here in the sense 'festival liturgies']" (20.19) is an oversimplification; cf. Isae. 6.60. A man who had previously undertaken a trierarchy was free to perform a choregy or any other festival liturgy as soon as the term of his exemption was over and, on this ground, obtain exemption from a new trierarchy.

12. Dem. 20.28, 130; 21.13; 39.7, to be compared with *Ath. Pol.* 56.3.

13. G. R. Bugh, *The Horsemen of Athens* (Princeton, N.J., 1988), 39–78. Rhodes (1982) 5 believes that whereas members of the cavalry ought to have been exempt from the trierarchy, there is no reason why they should not have performed festival liturgies.

14. T. H. Nielsen et al., "Athenian Grave Monuments and Social Class," *GRBS* 30 (1989): 411–20, esp. 417 and n. 22. The authors set the number of adult male citizens at 30,000 (cf. Hansen [1985] 65–69 and passim), and assume that

during the period circa 420–320 the members of the liturgical class must have totaled about four thousand. With a reconstructed life expectancy at birth of about twenty-five years and an annual growth rate of about .5 percent, the annual replacement of *lēitourgountes* is calculated to about 3.3 percent of 1,200 × 100 (years) = 3,960, rounded off to 4,000.

15. Dem. 21.13 with Platonios's comments on the failure of men to present themselves for service as choregoi at the Dionysia in 390/89; cf. A. Meineke, *Fragmenta Comicorum Graecorum* (Berlin, 1839), 1:532. The reported unwillingness of some to serve as choregoi cannot be pure conjecture (so Pickard-Cambridge [1968] 87 n. 4; K. J. Maidment, "The Later Comic Chorus," *CQ* 29 [1935]: 9–10), and is compatible with Dem. 21.13. Cf. Davies *Wealth* 25.

16. [Dem.] 49.11; cf. 49.6; Xen. *Hell.* 6.2.11.

17. A different explanation is given by Davies (1969) 324–25.

18. The Twelve Hundred: Dem. 21.155 (347/6); 14.16–17 (354); Isoc. 15.145 (354/3 or slightly earlier); Isae. fr. 18 [Thalheim] = 74 [Sauppe], apud Harp., s.v. "chilioi diakosioi"; cf. *FGrH* 328: Philochoros F 45; Poll. 8.100, s.v. "chilioi kai diakosioi"; Schol. Dem. 21.154, 155. Synteleis: Dem. 18.104 with Schol. to 105, 106; 20.23; 21.155; Lib. *Dec.* 23.1.37; Schol. Dem. 21.80; *Suda,* s.v. "synteleis"; *Harp.*, s.v. "synteleis."

19. IG 2².1615, 1616, 1617, 1618, 1619, 1625, 1629.209–10; Isae. 7.38; Dem. 14.16–17; 39.8; [Dem.] 47.21–22, 29; *Ath. Pol.* 61.1; *P. Oxy.* 1804, fr. 4, 7–13; possibly, Isoc. 8.128. Hyp. fr. 159 [Jensen/Kenyon] = 173 [Sauppe] is uncertain.

20. F. A. Wolf, *Demosthenis Oratio adversus Leptinem* (Halle, 1789), ci–cvi, rev. ed., ed. J. H. Bremi (Zurich, 1831), 58–59; *Staatsh.* 1st ed. (1817), 2:59–62, and 1³.609, 615, 618, 647; *Urkunden* 178; Thumser *De civium* 63; Kolbe *Re navali* 28–29, 40; Kahrstedt *Forschungen* 224, cf. 209; Strasburger "Trierarchie" 108–9; Brillant "Trierarchia" 446; Jones (1957) 28; de Ste. Croix (1953) 45; Thomsen (1964) 88–89; Jordan *AN* 74.

21. Ruschenbusch (1978) with no explicit reference to [Dem.] 47; Mossé (1979) 31–42, on the meaning of the word *synetachthēsan,* 37 n. 12, and MacDowell (1986) 440. Mossé's opinion differs slightly from that of Ruschenbusch, in that she believes that the eisphora-paying class was the same as the liturgical class. The view about one symmory system for the eisphora and the trierarchy was also held by G. G. Schoemann, *Antiquitates iuris publici Graecorum* (London, 1838), 327–28 n. 8; *Staatsh.* 2³.123*, Fränkel's n. 834; *FGrH* 3 b, suppl. 1, p. 58.

22. Ruschenbusch (1978) 282; (1985b) 240, 245, 247; (1985c) 237–38; (1985d) 251–52; and (1987e) 80—endorsing MacDowell's view that 300 persons performed trierarchies, while the remaining 900 symmory members contributed to naval costs. Ruschenbusch (1990) argues that from the Twelve Hundred only 300 persons were liable for the proeisphora, agonistic liturgies, and the trierarchy; but

since 120 among the 300 were usually exempt, the number of those really performing trierarchies was 120. However, see Gabrielsen (1990).

23. MacDowell (1986), quotation from 446 n. 34, and (1990) 373: "We should therefore conclude that the 1200 were not trierarchs."

24. Rhodes (1982) 5–11; cf. Gabrielsen (1989b) 151–52; Jones (1957) 28; *Staatsh.* 1³.616–18, with Kahrstedt *Forschungen* 222; de Ste. Croix (1953) 32; Thomsen (1964) 202, 205; Strauss (1986) 42–43; Ober (1989) 128–29, 199–200.

25. Mainly, Dem. 14.16–18; 18.103; 39.8 (which is treated at p. 77 above). MacDowell (1986), who thinks the argument from silence is one of the strongest, offers detailed discussion of these passages (439–40); cf. Ruschenbusch (1978) 277; Mossé (1979) 37.

26. MacDowell (1986) 441: "From this passage [Dem. 14.16–17] it is clear that in 354 the 20 naval symmories did not consist entirely of active men." Cf. Ruschenbusch (1978) 280: "In der Symmorienrede (14,16) des Demosthenes (354) heisst es im Zusammenhang mit der Trierarchie" (quotation follows).

27. Demosthenes (21.157) says: "I was hegemon of a symmory for ten years," which comes shortly after his criticism of Meidias's insufficient trierarchic contributions (155); "any juror knowing that there were two kinds of symmory," MacDowell argues ([1986] 440), "would surely have taken it as a reference to a naval rather than an *eisphora* symmory. But in fact the symmory of which Demosthenes was leader for ten years was a symmory for payment of *eisphora*." This reasoning, however, is not cogent: at 21.152–53, Demosthenes introduces his attack on Meidias's poor performances of trierarchies and agonistic liturgies; at 154–55, he deals in detail with trierarchies, and at 156 with festival liturgies, after which (157) he mentions his own eisphora contributions as hegemon of a symmory. There is a clear thematic division, and the context in which Demosthenes says that he acted as hegemon is well separated from that in which Meidias is accused of dodging trierarchies.

28. Rhodes (1982) 10; MacDowell (1986) 441 with nn. 17–18.

29. Ruschenbusch (1978) 282. But Ruschenbusch (1990) interprets adynatoi as "körperlich oder geistig Behinderte," and defines the eisphora payers as those owning property worth over three talents, two thousand drachmas.

30. Ruschenbusch (1990); cf. (1978) 282, and (1985c).

31. Ruschenbusch (1978) 277; Mossé (1979) 37; MacDowell (1986) 442.

32. My objections are laid out in more detail in Gabrielsen (1990).

33. *IG* 2².1618.6; 1627.200–203; 1629.494–99, 544–68, 826–36; 1631.189–90, 551–56, 582–85, 588–91; Dem. 21.165.

34. In this Diodoros is following a good source, Hieronymos of Cardia: J. Hornblower, *Hieronymus of Cardia* (Oxford, 1981), 110. Cf. also Plut. *Phoc.* 28.7.

35. *IG* 2².2496 (cf. Behrend *Pachturkunden* no. 35): concerning a workshop

with an adjoining house and a smaller house. The fifty-four drachmas to be paid as annual rent is 7.7 percent of the valuation (timema = seven hundred drachmas) of the property, which accords well with the return usually expected from landed property, about 8 percent (Isae. 11.42).

36. Cf. *Staatsh.* 1³.615; Thomsen (1964) 200–201; Rhodes (1982) 7–8. Mac-Dowell's reasoning (1986) 442 that "the words *tous eispherontas* immediately follow the figure 1200 and must be associated with it" carries little weight.

37. A lexicographer (*P. Oxy.* 1804, fr. 4, ll. 7–13) claims, without giving a date or source, that there were twenty-six trierarchic symmories of sixty members each. But besides a number of manifest improbabilities (e.g., symmories were headed by hegemones who defrayed the expenses from their own means and then recovered the amounts from members of their symmories), the figure twenty-six is probably an error for twenty; cf. B. P. Grenfell and A. S. Hunt, eds., *The Oxyrhynchus Papyri,* pt. 15 (London, 1922), 17.

38. Ruschenbusch (1978) 282; MacDowell (1986) 445. Cf. p. 22 above.

39. Dem. 18.103, 312; Aesch. 3.222; Din. 1.42; Hyp. fr. 134 [Jensen/Kenyon] = 160 [Sauppe]. The three hundred richest Athenians are mentioned in Dem. 18.171. Isae. 6.60 says that the Three Hundred paid the eisphora, while [Dem.] 42.25 (cf. 3–5, 21) says that they were liable for the proeisphora; the proeisphora and proeispherontes are mentioned in [Dem.] 50.8–9; Dem. 21.153.

40. I am indebted to M. H. Hansen for drawing my attention to this observation.

41. C. Mossé's reference ([1979] 38–39) to "the first," "second," and "third" in *IG* 2².1611 and 1612 cannot be to the Three Hundred, since, as Rhodes pointed out ([1982] n. 31), the inscriptions list ships' ratings. Jordan (*AN* 77) puts forward the improbable view that "the Three Hundred were not included in the 1,200 symmoritai, but formed a special college which furnished the financial leadership of the symmories. The 1,200 on the other hand were not especially wealthy citizens, but belonged to what we may call the middle class." Thomsen believes that the three hundred proeisphora-payers were not included in the trierarchic symmories of Periandros ([1964] 234).

42. The Three Hundred: Dem. 2.29 (and 13.20); [Dem.] 42.5; trierarchs: Dem. 35.48; 39.8; *IG* 2².1623.153–59.

43. [Dem.] 47.21ff.; *IG* 2².1615, 1616, 1617, 1618, 1619, 1625; 1623.144–59.

44. Speaking of the malfunction of the system before 340, Demosthenes (18.102, 104, 107, 108) points specifically to the unfair distribution of burdens among the wealthy and the less wealthy men within a symmory; again, in 354 he proposed (14.17) to match the richest with the poorest in each symmory.

45. Ruschenbusch (1985b), (1985c), using *IG* 2².1622.580–783. But (*a*) many of the sums listed there are installments, not full payments (cf. ll. 631–38); (*b*) since certain men in a group had their debts doubled (ll. 643–55, 741–57), their

liabilities date from an earlier year than those of the other men in their group; (c) none of these groups is called synteleis; a group of seven might have been in charge of a ship simultaneously (ll. 608–10), but elsewhere (1632.67–71) seven men on one ship are called syntrierarchs.

46. Gabrielsen (1989b) 149–50. I have not been able to see on which evidence MacDowell (1986) 447 n. 38 thinks that a trierarch did not have to be a member of the symmory that paid money for the maintenance of his ship; this he bases merely on the unsupported supposition that in a particular year a particular symmory might find that its richest citizens were all ineligible, because they were heiresses, orphans, and the like.

47. MacDowell (1986) 442–43 and (1990) 372–73. But (a) the speaker of [Dem.] 47.21ff. cannot be made to say that some members of his symmory were not trierarchs; (b) Hyp. fr. 134 [Jensen/Kenyon] calls the members of groups of six and seven "trierarchs" (*syn pente kai hex triērarchountes*); (c) Dem. 21.155 calls *all* of the Twelve Hundred synteleis without specifying that some of them were trierarchs; (d) Dem. 18.104 disproves MacDowell's theory: it says that groups of sixteen synteleis performed a liturgy, and that some men called themselves synteleis instead of trierarchs.

48. E.g., Nikeratos Nikiou Kydantides: (a) epimeletes of a symmory around 357/6 (*IG* 2².1616.8); (b) trierarch on *Eleutheria Archeneo* before 330/29 (1627.200–203); (c) trierarch on *Symmachia Hagnodemou* before 325/4 (1629.494–99, 834–36; 1631.189–90); (d) syntrierarch on *Proplous Demotelous* before 325/4 (1629.544–68); (e) synteles with Euthydemos Hagnousios on *Aura Lysikleidou* by 323/2 (1631.582–85, 457–62, 469–99); (f) probably, synteles with Lykinos Palleneus on *Phosphoros Archenikou* (1631.588–91, 466–70); (g) possibly also synteles with another man on *Phaule Chairestratou* (1631.551–56).

49. *Tēn naun porisamenos; tēn naun paraskeuazomenos; tēn naun plērosamenos.* Cf. Wyse 581. *Urkunden* 194: "ein neues Schiff bauen lassen."

50. W. Christ, "Zu Demosthenes de cor. §104," *Philologus* 45 (1886): 383–85; H. Wankel, *Demosthenes Rede für Ktesiphon über den Kranz* (Heidelberg, 1976), vols. 1–2, ad loc.

51. Cf. Davies *Wealth* 22.

52. *Staatsh.* 1³.652–53; Jordan *AN* 83; MacDowell (1986) 441–44 and (1990) ad loc.

53. Since the relative sentence *par' hōn eisprattomenoi talanton . . .* immediately follows *hymeis* (itself related to *pepoiēkate*), it must be connected with it, not with the *diakosious kai chilious synteleis*. The unorthodox position of *hymeis* may have been chosen for additional emphasis.

54. Kuenzi (1923) 1–6 (definition); Migeotte (1982), (1983), and (1984) 238–46, no. 69, using the anecdotes in Plut. *Alc.* 10.1; *Phoc.* 9.1–2; Theophr. *Char.* 22.2–3, and correctly giving the verb *epididonai* the rendering "offrir" ([1983] 134). That

contributions were forwarded in the assembly is also attested by Ath. 4.168F; Diog. Laert. 7.12.

55. Cf. P. Roussel, *Isée, Discours,* Budé ed. (Paris, 1960), 87. Wyse 460–64, de Ste. Croix (1953) 32 n. 6, and Migeotte (1983) 135 note the ambiguous use of the term *eisphora.*

56. See Dem. 20.100, 135; [Dem.] 49.67; *Ath. Pol.* 43.5: the law dealing with the offense of failing to keep a promise to the demos; on this charge *probolai* might be made that could lead to an eisangelia; cf. Hansen (1975) 13–14, 38–39. But there is no clear evidence for the application of this procedure in connection with epidoseis; cf. Migeotte (1983) 138–39.

57. Kuenzi (1923) 57: introduced about the end of the fifth or beginning of the fourth century; Migeotte (1982) 50, (1983) 131: probably as early as in the initial years of the Peloponnesian War.

58. *Urkunden* 190–91, 196; *Staatsh.* 1³.657, 685–86; Köhler (1879) 89; Kolbe (1901) 389; Brillant "Trierarchia" 454; Kuenzi (1923) 24, 37–41; Strasburger "Trierarchie" 111, 113, 114; Amit *AS* 107; Jordan *AN* 91–92; Migeotte (1983), (1984) 238–42, esp. n. 379a.

59. Amit *AS* 107; Jordan *AN* 91–92.

60. Cf. 6.61.6: "So he [sc. Alkibiades], in his own ship [*echōn tēn heautou naun*], and those who were accused with him, sailed off in company with the Salaminia from Sicily, as if for Athens." See also Plut. *Cim.* 8.6: Kimon "on his own ship."

61. *HCT* 4:316, 338. Cf. Jordan *AN* 91; Cawkwell (1973) 759; Migeotte (1983) 139.

62. Lys. 21.6: "At first Alkibiades . . . was aboard my ship"; [Dem.] 50.52: "[Timomachos] himself came on board my ship, and sailed around here and there until he reached the Hellespont."

63. The same meaning is carried by Xenophon's report later on (*Hell.* 1.6.23): "Kallikratidas, however, sailed down upon him [sc. Diomedon] suddenly and captured ten of his ships, Diomedon escaping with his own ship [*tēi te hautou*] and one other."

64. There is disagreement about whether it took place in 358/7: Schweigert (1939) 15; O. Picard, *Chalcis et la confédération eubéen* (Paris, 1979), 237–40; Ruschenbusch (1987a), (1987c), or in 357/6: Beloch *GG* 3.2:258. But cf. Cawkwell (1962) 35–37; H. Wankel, "Demosthenes erste Trierarchie und die Euböaunternehmens vom Jahre 357," *ZPE* 71 (1988): 199–200.

65. So also Kuenzi (1923) 36, 51; but Migeotte ([1983] 141) has reservations.

66. These subscriptions were organized by (and were originally made before) the boule, not the assembly: Kuenzi (1923) 37; Migeotte (1983) 141–42, but cf. Schaefer *Demosthenes* 2:82. Meidias's promise to contribute (allegedly a decision made on second thought) was announced in the assembly; cf. Demosthenes' re-

mark (21.162) that he hurried to make his offer already before the *proedroi* had taken their seats.

67. *Staatsh.* $1^3$.657; Schaefer *Demosthenes* 2:82; Kuenzi (1923) 37–38; Jordan *AN* 92. Migeotte (1983) 142 points to several statements in Dem. 21.160–67 to the effect that Meidias had made an epidosis of a trieres (160: *triērē epedōken,* with 163 and 165), and infers that the subscriptions in the spring of 340 consisted also of offers of ships. However, this remains undocumented, and I do not believe that expressions such as *triērē epedōken* and *epidosimos triērēs* are to be taken literally.

68. [Plut.] *Mor.* 849F. On the date see F. Ladek, "Über die Echtheit zweier auf Demosthenes und Demochares bezüglichen Urkunden in Pseudoplutarchs Βίοι τῶν δέκα ῥητόρων," *WS* 13 (1891): 81; Schaefer *Demosthenes* 2:495 n. 1; Kuenzi (1923) 39; Migeotte (1983) 143.

69. *Urkunden* 190–91, 196; Kuenzi (1923) 39–40; Migeotte (1983) 143–44, 147 n. 96.

70. *IG* $2^2$.1613.284–92; 1627.266–78. In 354, Demosthenes (14.18) claimed that the triereis totaled three hundred—perhaps an error, or more probably a rounded-off figure to ensure the arithmetical neatness of his scheme (16–21).

71. The epidoseis recorded in *IG* $2^2$.1623.309–33 (334/3) carry the same significance: "Of the trierarchs who have made epidoseis of triereis, the following are in possession of equipment in accordance with the decree proposed by Nausikles" (ll. 309–13). Obviously, the three trierarchs listed had in an unknown year received, and by 334/3 or later still owed, public equipment. They all had served on public hulls (pace Köhler [1879] 89; Kolbe [1901] 389–90) as volunteer trierarchs. Migeotte's claim (1983) 142–44 that these were spontaneous offers of ships is unconfirmed.

72. *IG* $2^2$.1623.160–99; F. W. Mitchel, "Derkylos of Hagnous and the Date of I.G. II$^2$, 1187," *Hesperia* 33 (1964): 337–51, esp. 338–39; 1629.516ff., 799–800; cf. Dem. 18.87; Aesch. 3.89–105. Probably, the Chalkidians' request for ships from Athens included a request for funds to run that force; compare the request for war matériel and funds made by the Cypriot envoys in Lys. 19.21–22.

73. So Migeotte (1983) 143–44. Migeotte, however, realizes (144) the difficulty raised by his view: i.e., if so many Athenians had supplied their privately owned ships, what sort of guarantee was to be obtained by the state through this arrangement? But cf. Migeotte (1984) 241–42.

74. Demokles Teithrasios on *Hiera Demotelous;* Charias Kydathenaieus on *Kratousa Smikrionos;* Diphilos Pitheus on *Paralia Demotelous;* Klearchos Aigilieus on *[——]nos Chairestratou.*

75. *IG* $2^2$.1628.51–62 (1629.700–706); 63–70; 71–78. Similarly, Konon Anaphlystios was syntrierarch on two ships (ll. 43–50; 51–62 [1629.700–706]); Pythokles Acharneus on two ships (ll. 43–50; 63–70, where [...7....]s Achar[neus]

may be safely restored as [Pythokle]s Achar[neus] on the strength of lines 17–27 and 28–36). On the other hand, Alkibiades Thymaitades (ll. 51–62) and the unidentifiable Me[....9.....] (ll. 73–74) performed only one syntrierarchy each.

76. Euthykrates Kydathenaieus, syntrierarch on *Stephanephoria Hagnodemou,* [———]ia *Antandrou,* and [———] *Eudikou* (IG 2².1629.43–63, 91–110, 145–64); Diopeithes Phrearrhios, sole trierarch on *Hipparche Aristokratous,* and principal trierarch on [———]era *Chairionos* (ll. 64–75, 128–44); Demokles Meliteus, sole trierarch on *Axionike Lysikratou,* and principal trierarch on [———] *Eudikou* (ll. 76–90, 145–64).

77. *Urkunden* 180, 182–83, 189–94; *Staatsh.* 1³.661–69; Schaefer *Demosthenes* 2:527–28; Kahrstedt *Forschungen* 229. The spurious decree at Dem. 18.105, dating the enactment of the law in the archonship of Polykles (otherwise unknown), can be disregarded.

78. This is inferred from Dem. 18.107: "During the entire war [sc. against Philip], while the dispatches of squadrons were made in accordance with my own law," and from Aesch. 3.222. Cf. Schaefer *Demosthenes* 2:526–27, and 527 n. 2. Boeckh (*Staatsh.* 1³.668) held that Demosthenes' law was abrogated.

79. Schaefer *Demosthenes* 2:523; *Staatsh.* 1³.661; Jordan *AN* 82. Aesch. 3.222 says: "But what length of time could conceal your acts of plunder in the case of the triereis and the trierarchs? For when you had passed your law about the Three Hundred, and had persuaded the Athenians to appoint you superintendent of the navy, you were convicted by me of having made away with trierarchs of sixty-five fast-sailing ships." The order of events, as these are presented here, is first Demosthenes' law of 340, then his tenure as superintendent of the navy.

Although the precise meaning of Aeschines' claim (3.222) that Demosthenes had made away with trierarchs for sixty-five fast-sailing ships remains obscure (cf. Ruschenbusch [1990] 81 and Gabrielsen [1990] 94–97), it seems certain that the incident was the reason Aeschines brought legal charges against him. This attack should be exclusively associated with Demosthenes' office as *epistatēs tou nautikou,* not, as Thomsen (1964) 235 and others think, with the legal proceedings concerning his trierarchic legislation (Dem. 18.102–3) or any subsequent amendments to it (inferred from 312).

80. Cf. MacDowell (1986) 449. The only other naval legislation attested in the following period is the law of Diphilos, passed before 323/2. But all that is known of this law is that it ordered the epimeletai to hand money collected from defaulters over to the treasurer of the dockyards in the presence of the boule (*IG* 2².1631.509–11), and that it specified the terms on which hulls and equipment should be issued to trierarchs (1632.16–19).

81. This point is argued in detail in Gabrielsen (1990).

82. J. H. Lipsius, "Die attische Steuerverfassung und das attische Volksvermögen," *RhM* n.s. 71 (1916): 161–86, esp. 174–75; Strasburger "Trierarchie" 111–

12; Busolt-Swoboda *GS* 1203–4; Rhodes (1982) 6; Ruschenbusch (1978) 283, (1985d), (1987e); MacDowell (1986) 445–47, 49.

83. Davies *Wealth,* quotations from 20, 24; cf. also 19, 23, 33, and *APF* xxix.

84. *Urkunden* 177–84; *Staatsh.* 1³.661–69, esp. 664–65; Brillant "Trierarchia" 449; Kahrstedt *Forschungen* 228–29.

85. Kahrstedt (*Forschungen* 226) rightly stated: "Auf keinen Fall hat es eine Körperschaft der 300 an der Spitze der 1200 gegeben, was von "Ulpian" und vielen Neueren verkannt worden ist, ebensowenig ἡγεμόνες, δεύτεροι oder τρίτοι. Wo von den 300 die Rede ist, bezieht es sich allemal auf die finanziellen Symmorien seit 378." Cf. Thomsen (1964) 234.

86. Dem. 18.103, 312; Aesch. 3.222; Din. 1.42. Harpocration (s.v. "symmoria"), referring to a fragment from a speech of Hypereides (fr. 134 [Jensen/Kenyon]), says, inter alia, the following: "Demosthenes passed a law to the effect that the Three Hundred should perform trierarchies and [so] the trierarchic burdens became heavier." Cf. Schol. Dem. 21.155. But the exact meaning of this is far from crystal-clear. Another text assumed to support the prevailing view (Poll. 8.100, s.v. "chilioi kai diakosioi") erroneously implies that Demosthenes' law created three hundred (instead of the previous twelve hundred) *liturgists,* not trierarchs; cf. Gabrielsen (1989b) 148 and (1990) 93–94, against Ruschenbusch (1990) 80–81.

87. Gabrielsen (1989b); Ruschenbusch (1990) has objections, but cf. Gabrielsen (1990).

88. *IG* 2².1623.155; cf. Rhodes (1982) 6, 10; Gabrielsen (1989b) 151–52.

89. Jordan *AN* 77. Definition of the "middle class": Jones (1957) 8–10, 23–37, 80–93. But see now Strauss (1986) 42–43; Ober (1989) 27–31, and e.g., 129: "middling citizens."

90. Jones (1957) 35–37; E. Kluwe, "Die soziale Zusammensetzung der athenischen *Ekklesia* und ihr Einfluss auf politische Entscheidungen," *Klio* 58 (1976): 295–333; Kluwe, "Nochmals zum Problem: Die soziale Zusammensetzung der athenischen *Ekklesia* und ihr Einfluss auf politische Entscheidungen," *Klio* 59 (1977): 45–81; Markle (1985); Rhodes (1986); R. K. Sinclair, *Democracy and Participation in Athens* (Cambridge, 1988); Sinclair, "Lysias' Speeches and the Debate about Participation in Athenian Public Life," *Antichthon* 22 (1988) 54–66; Ober (1989) 134–38, 142–45; Hansen (1991) 125–27.

91. J. Sundwall, *Epigraphische Beiträge zur sozial-politischen Geschichte Athens im Zeitalter des Demosthenes,* Klio Beiheft 4 (Leipzig, 1906), is the first systematic attempt to document the representation of the rich among officeholders, but some of the methods used are questionable. See now Develin *AO* and *APF,* and specifically for the council, Rhodes *AB* 4–6.

92. Disregard of property qualifications: *Ath. Pol.* 7.4; 8.1. See generally Gabrielsen (1981), esp. 111–13, pace M. H. Hansen, "*Misthos* for Magistrates in Clas-

sical Athens," *SO* 54 (1979): 5–22, and Hansen, "Perquisites for Magistrates in Fourth-Century Athens," *C&M* 32 (1980): 105–25.

93. M. H. Hansen, "The Athenian 'Politicians,' 403–322 B.C.," in Hansen (1989), 1–23, esp. 1–3, quotation from 7; Hansen, "*Rhetores* and *Strategoi* in Fourth-Century Athens," in Hansen (1989), 25–72.

94. See now "Updated Inventory of *Rhetores* and *Strategoi* (1988)," in Hansen (1989), 34–72.

95. Hansen (1989) 11–12.

96. Lys. 21.1–5; *APF* xxi.

97. Dem. 10.37–38 (of 342/1?): "There was a time not long ago when the revenue of your state did not exceed a hundred and thirty talents, and yet of those able to discharge trierarchies or pay eisphorai there is not one that declined the duty that devolved on him in the absence of a surplus; but the triereis sailed out, and the money came in, and we did all that was required. Since then fortune has smiled on us and increased our revenues, and four hundred instead of one hundred talents are now coming into the treasury, though no property-owner suffers any loss but is rather the gainer, for all the rich citizens come up to receive their share of this increase, as indeed they have a perfect right to do."

## Epilogue

1. With the comments of Adkins (1960) 160–61.

2. *IG* 2².1953; 1629.190–204; Dem. 8.70; 18.257; [Dem.] 50.15; 51.22; Isae. 7.35–36; Isoc. 18.60–61.

3. [Dem.] 42.25: useful and philotimos with property and person. Cf. Dem. 21.189; Lys. 21.1–11.

4. *Epinoia Hierokleous:* payment of 882 drachmas for a complete set of equipment, normally valued at 2,169 drachmas: *IG* 2².1622.297–311; *Delias Timokleous:* 3,333 drachmas for replacing the ship with three others: 1623.124–34; 1628.396–418; 1629.915–39; 1631.10–15; payment of probably over 845 drachmas as guarantor of the ships for Chalkis (340): 1623.176; 1629.543; *Charis Archeneo:* 5,000 drachmas for the hull, and 1,084 drachmas for equipment: 1624.47–49; 1628.369–95; 1629.889–914; *Pasinike Archenikou:* 10,000 drachmas for the hull, and 2,299 drachmas for equipment: 1628.350–68; 1629.870–88, 577–84; *Kratousa Smikrionos:* payment of 3,024 drachmas for equipment: 1628.51–62; 1629.700–706; *Demokratia Chairestratou:* 5,000 drachmas for the hull: 1629.600–612, 839–40; 1631.192–94: *Ionike Smikrionos:* 2,169 drachmas for equipment: 1629.667–73.

5. *Hiera Demotelous: IG* 2².1628.43–50; *Iousa Archeneo:* 1628.109–18; *Eucharis Aleximachou:* 1629.755–57, 817–20; 1631.123–24, 178–81. Debt from rudders belonging to smaller vessels (akatoi): 1627.371–73; 1628.527–32; 1629.1004–9; 1631.325–27.

6. Demos son of Pyrilampes borrowed 1,600 drachmas and promised to pay an additional 400 drachmas in interest (2,000 drachmas in all), which sum he needed to meet the current expenses of his trierarchy (Lys. 19.25). His total expenditure presumably exceeded that sum by at least a further 1,000 drachmas.

7. Lys. 19.9; 21.16; 26.22; Isae. 7.38–40; Dem. 18.113; 21.189; 38.26; [Dem.] 49.46.

# Bibliography

ADKINS

1960     Adkins, A. W. H. *Merit and Responsibility: A Study in Greek Values.* Oxford.

1972     ————. *Moral Values and Political Behaviour in Ancient Greece from Homer to the End of the Fifth Century.* London.

AHLBERG

1971     Ahlberg, G. *Fighting on Land and Sea in Greek Geometric Art.* Acta Instituti Atheniensis Regni Suecie, no. 4.16. Stockholm.

ALEXANDRES

1950     Alexandres, K. Ἡ Θαλασσία Δύναμις εἰς τὴν Ἱστορίαν τῆς Ἀρχαίας Ἑλλάδος. Athens.

ANDERSON

1962     Anderson, R. *Oared Fighting Ships.* London.

ANDREADES

1933     Andreades, A. *A History of Greek Public Finance.* Vol. 1. Rev. and enl. trans. by C. N. Brown. Cambridge, Mass. (First published as Ἱστορία τῆς Ἑλληνικῆς Δημοσίας Οἰκονομίας. Athens, 1917.)

ANDREEV

1983        Andreev, V. N. "Zur Kontinuität der Vermögenselite Athens vom
            5. bis 3. Jahrhundert v. u. Z. Die Entstehung grosser Vermögen in
            Athen im 5./4. Jahrhundert v. u. Z." *JWG* 1:137–58.

ARMSTRONG

1949        Armstrong, J. I. "The Trierarchy and the Tribal Organization of
            the Athenian Navy." Ph.D. diss., Princeton University.

ASHERI

1963        Asheri, D. "Laws of Inheritance, Distribution of Land, and Political
            Constitutions in Ancient Greece." *Historia* 12:1–21.

ASHTON

1977        Ashton, N. G. "The Naumachia near Amorgos in 322 B.C." *BSA*
            72:1–11.

1979        ———. "How Many Pentereis?" *GRBS* 20:237–42.

BADIAN

1966        Badian, E., ed. *Ancient Society and Institutions: Studies Presented to
            Victor Ehrenberg.* Oxford.

BASCH

1969        Basch, L. "Phoenician Oared Ships." *MM* 55:139–62, 227–45.

1977        ———. "Trières grecques, phéniciennes et égyptiennes." *JHS* 97:
            1–10.

1980        ———. "M. le Professeur Lloyd et les trières: Quelques re-
            marques." *JHS* 100:198–99.

BERVE

1961        Berve, H. "Zur Themistokles-Inschrift von Troizen." *SBAW* 5:1–50.

BESCHI

1969–70     Beschi, L. "Il rilievo della trireme Paralos." *ASAA* n.s. 31–32:117–
            32.

BILLINGMEIER AND SUTHERLAND-DUSING

1981        Billingmeier, J.-C., and A. Sutherland-Dusing. "The Origin and
            Function of the Naukraroi at Athens: An Etymological and His-
            torical Explanation." *TAPhA* 111:11–16.

BISCARDI

1955     Biscardi, A. "Sul regime della comproprietà in diritto attico." In *Studi in onore di U. E. Paoli,* 105–43. Florence.

BLACKMAN

1969     Blackman, D. "The Athenian Navy and Allied Naval Contributions in the Pentecontaetia." *GRBS* 10:179–216.

BRAVO

1977     Bravo, B. "Remarques sur les assises sociales, les formes d'organisation et la terminologie du commerce maritime grec à l'époque archaïque." *DHA* 3:1–59.

BROCKMEYER

1971     Brockmeyer, N. "Athens maritime Strategie gegenüber dem Peloponnesischen Bund von Themistokles bis Perikles." *AU* 14:37–63.

BRUN

1983     Brun, P. *Eisphora—Syntaxis—Stratiotika. Recherches sur les finances militaires d'Athènes au IVe siècle av. J.-C.* Centre de recherches d'histoire ancienne, no. 50. Annales littéraires de l'Université de Besançon, no. 284. Paris.

1985     ————. "IG II² 1609 et le versement en nature de l'eisphora." *REG* 87:307–17.

BURFORD

1969     Burford, A. *The Greek Temple Builders of Epidaurus.* Liverpool.

BURKE

1985     Burke, E. M. "Lycurgan Finances." *GRBS* 26:251–64.

BURN

1984     Burn, A. R. *Persia and the Greeks: The Defence of the West, c. 546–478 B.C.* 2d ed. London.

CAPPS

1904     Capps, E. *The Introduction of Comedy into the City Dionysia.* Decennial publication of the University of Chicago, 1st ser., vol. 6, no. 11. Chicago.

CARGILL

1981     Cargill, J. *The Second Athenian League: Empire or Free Alliance?* Berkeley and Los Angeles.

CARTER

1986      Carter, L. B. *The Quiet Athenian.* Oxford.

CARTLEDGE AND HARVEY

1985      Cartledge, P. A., and F. D. Harvey, eds. *Crux: Essays Presented to G. E. M. de Ste. Croix on His Seventy-Fifth Birthday.* Exeter and London.

CASSON

1956      Casson, L. "The Size of the Ancient Merchant Ships." In *Studi in onore di A. Calderini e R. Paribeni,* 1:231–38. Milan.

1969      ———. "The Supper-Galleys of the Hellenistic World." *MM* 55: 185–93.

1976      ———. "The Athenian Upper Class and New Comedy." *TAPhA* 106:29–59.

1985      ———. "Greek and Roman Shipbuilding: New Findings." *American Neptune* 45:10–19.

CAWKWELL

1962      Cawkwell, G. L. "Notes on the Social War." *C&M* 23:34–49.

1963      ———. "Eubulus." *JHS* 83:47–67.

1973      ———. "The Date of I.G. II² 1609 Again!" *Historia* 22:759–61.

1981      ———. "Notes on the Failure of the Second Athenian Confederacy." *JHS* 101:40–55.

1984      ———. "Athenian Naval Power in the Fourth Century." *CQ* n.s. 34:334–45.

CECCHINI

1982–83   Cecchini, F. "Il problema naucraria e alcuni aspetti del mondo miceneo: Possibilità di connessione." *AFLPer* 6, no. 1:549–62.

CHAMBERS

1967      Chambers, M. H. "The Significance of the Themistocles Decree." *Philologus* 111:157–69.

CHARLES

1946      Charles, J. F. "The Anatomy of Athenian Sea Power." *CJ* 42:86–91.

CLARK

1990      Clark, M. "The Date of IG II² 1604." *BSA* 85:47–67.

COATES AND MCGRAIL

1985 Coates, J. F., and S. McGrail, eds. *The Greek Trireme of the Fifth Century B.C.: Discussion of a Projected Reconstruction*. London.

COATES, PLATIS, AND SHAW

1990 Coates, J. F., S. K. Platis, and J. T. Shaw. *The Trireme Trials, 1988: Report of the Anglo-Hellenic Sea Trials of "Olympias."* Oxford.

COZZOLI

1977 Cozzoli, U. "Le naucrarie clisteniche e l'entità della flotta ateniese alla Battaglia di Salamina." *MGR* 5:95–114.

DAIN

1931 Dain, A. "Inscriptions attiques trouvées dans les fouilles sous-marines de Mahdia." *REG* 44:290–303.

DAVIES

1967 Davies, J. K. "Demosthenes on Liturgies: A Note." *JHS* 87:33–40.
1969 ———. "The Date of IG ii² 1609." *Historia* 18:309–33.

DAVISON

1947 Davison, J. A. "The First Greek Triremes." *CQ* 41:18–24.

DE STE. CROIX

1953 de Ste. Croix, G. E. M. "Demosthenes' Τίμημα and the Athenian *Eisphora* in the Fourth Century B.C." *C&M* 14:30–70.
1966 ———. "The Estate of Phaenippus (Ps.-Dem., xlii)." In Badian (1966), 109–14.
1981 ———. *The Class Struggle in the Ancient Greek World from the Archaic Age to the Arab Conquests*. London.

DEUBNER

1966 Deubner, L. *Attische Feste*. 2d rev. ed., ed. B. Doer. Hildesheim.

DITTENBERGER

1872 Dittenberger, W. *Über den Vermögenstauch und die Trierarchie des Demosthenes*. Rudolfstadt.

DOW

1962 Dow, S. "The Purported Decree of Themistokles: Stele and Inscription." *AJA* 66:353–58.

EDDY

1968     Eddy, S. K. "Athens' Peacetime Navy in the Age of Perikles." *GRBS* 9:141–56.

ENGELS

1978     Engels, D. W. *Alexander the Great and the Logistics of the Macedonian Army.* Berkeley, Los Angeles, and London.

ÉTIENNE AND PIÉRART

1975     Étienne, R., and M. Piérart. "Un décret du Koinon des Hellènes à Platées en honneur de Glaucon, fils d'Étéoclès, d'Athènes." *BCH* 99:51–75.

FIGUEIRA

1981     Figueira, T. J. *Aegina: Society and Economy.* Monographs in Classical Studies. New York.

1986     ———. "Xanthippos, Father of Perikles, and the *Prutaneis* of the *Naukraroi.*" *Historia* 35:257–79.

FINLEY

1952     Finley, M. I. *Studies in Land and Credit in Ancient Athens, 500–200 B.C.: The Horos Inscriptions.* New Brunswick, N.J.

1973     ———, ed. *Problèmes de la terre en Grèce ancienne.* Paris.

1983     ———. *Politics in the Ancient World.* Cambridge.

FOXHALL AND FORBES

1982     Foxhall, L., and H. A. Forbes. "Σιτομετρεία: The Role of Grain as a Staple Food in Classical Antiquity." *Chiron* 12:41–90.

FROST

1968     Frost, F. J. "Themistocles' Place in Athenian Politics." *CSCA* 1: 105–24.

GABRIELSEN

1981     Gabrielsen, V. *Remuneration of State Officials in Fourth Century B.C. Athens.* Odense University Classical Studies, no. 11. Odense.

1985     ———. "The Naukrariai and the Athenian Navy." *C&M* 36:21–51.

1986     ———. "Φανερά and Ἀφανὴς Οὐσία in Classical Athens." *C&M* 37:99–114.

1987a     ———. "The *Antidosis* Procedure in Classical Athens." *C&M* 38: 7–38.

1987b     ———. "The *Diadikasia*-Documents." *C&M* 38:39–51.

1988        ———. "A Naval Debt and the Appointment of a Syntrierarch in *IG* II² 1623." *C&M* 39:63–87.

1989a       ———. "IG II² 1609 and Eisphora Payments in Kind?" *ZPE* 79: 93–99.

1989b       ———. "The Number of Athenian Trierarchs after ca. 340 B.C." *C&M* 40:145–59.

1990        ———. "Trierarchic Symmories." *C&M* 41:89–118.

1992        ———. "The Date of IG II² 1604 Again." *ZPE* 93:69–74.

GARLAN

1989        Garlan, Y. *Guerre et économie en Grèce ancienne.* Paris.

GARLAND

1987        Garland, R. *The Piraeus from the Fifth to the First Century B.C.* London.

GARNER

1987        Garner, R. *Law and Society in Classical Athens.* New York.

GARNSEY

1988        Garnsey, P. *Famine and Food Supply in the Graeco-Roman World: Responses to Risk and Crisis.* Cambridge.

1989        ———, ed. *Food, Health, and Culture in Classical Antiquity.* Cambridge Department of Classics Working Papers, no. 1. Cambridge.

GARNSEY, HOPKINS, AND WHITTAKER

1983        Garnsey, P., K. Hopkins, and C. R. Whittaker, eds. *Trade in the Ancient Economy.* London.

GAUTHIER

1976        Gauthier, P. *Un commentaire historique des "Poroi" de Xénophon.* Hautes études du monde gréco-romaine, no. 8. Geneva and Paris.

GLOTZ

1900        Glotz, G. "Les naucrares et les prytanes des naucrares dans la cité homérique." *REG* 13:137–57.

GOLIGHER

1907        Goligher, W. A. "Studies in Attic Law. II: The Antidosis." *Hermathena* 14:481–515.

GOMME

1933        Gomme, A. W. "A Forgotten Factor of Greek Naval Strategy." *JHS* 53:16–24.

GRAY

1974    Gray, D. "Seewesen." In *Archaeologia Homerica*, ed. F. Matz and
        G. H. Bucholtz, vol. 1, ch. G. Göttingen.

GRIFFITH

1935    Griffith, G. T. *The Mercenaries of the Hellenistic World*. Cambridge.

GUILMARTIN

1974    Guilmartin, J. F. *Gunpowder and Galleys: Changing Technology and
        Mediterranean Warfare at Sea in the Sixteenth Century*. Cambridge.

HAAS

1985    Haas, C. J. "Athenian Naval Power before Themistocles." *Historia*
        34:29–46.

HABICHT

1961    Habicht, C. "Falsche Urkunden zur Geschichte Athens im Zeitalter
        der Perserkriege." *Hermes* 89:1–35.

HAMMOND

1982    Hammond, N. L. G. "The Narrative of Herodotus VII and the
        Decree of Themistocles at Troezen." *JHS* 102:75–93.

1986    ———. "The Manning of the Fleet in the Decree of Themisto-
        kles." *Phoenix* 40:143–48.

HANSEN

1974    Hansen, M. H. *The Sovereignty of the People's Court in Athens in the
        Fourth Century B.C. and the Public Action against Unconstitutional Pro-
        posals*. Odense University Classical Studies, no. 4. Odense.

1975    ———. *Eisangelia*. Odense University Classical Studies, no. 6.
        Odense.

1976    ———. *Apagoge, Endeixis, and Ephegesis against Kakourgoi, Ati-
        moi, and Pheugontes*. Odense University Classical Studies, no. 8.
        Odense.

1985    ———. *Demography and Democracy: The Number of Athenian Citi-
        zens in the Fourth Century B.C.* Herning.

1989    ———. *The Athenian Ecclesia*. Vol. 2, *A Collection of Articles, 1983–
        1989*. Copenhagen.

1991    ———. *The Athenian Democracy in the Age of Demosthenes: Struc-
        ture, Principles, and Ideology*. Oxford.

HASEBROEK

1928    Hasebroek, J. *Staat und Handel im alten Griechenland: Untersuchungen zur antiken Wirtschaftsgeschichte.* Tübingen.

1931    ———. *Griechische Wirtschafts- und Gesellschaftsgeschichte bis zur Perserzeit.* Tübingen.

HEGYI

1969    Hegyi, D. "Athens and Aigina on the Eve of the Battle of Marathon." *AAntHung* 17:171–81.

HELBIG

1898    Helbig, N. "Les vases du Dipylon et les naucraries." *MAI* 36:387–421.

HEMELRIJK

1925    Hemelrijk, J. *Penia en Ploutos.* Amsterdam.

HIGNETT

1952    Hignett, C. *A History of the Athenian Constitution to the End of the Fifth Century B.C.* Oxford.

1963    ———. *Xerxes' Invasion of Greece.* Oxford.

HOLLADAY

1987    Holladay, A. J. "The Forethought of Themistocles." *JHS* 107:182–87.

HUMPHREYS

1978    Humphreys, S. C. *Anthropology and the Greeks.* London.

JAMESON

1960    Jameson, M. H. "A Decree of Themistokles from Troizen." *Hesperia* 29:198–223.

1962    ———. "A Revised Text of the Decree of Themistokles from Troizen." *Hesperia* 31:310–15.

1963    ———. "The Provisions for Mobilization in the Decree of Themistokles." *Historia* 12:385–404.

JEPPESEN

1961    Jeppesen, K. *Paradeigmata: Three Mid-Fourth Century Main Works of Hellenic Architecture Reconsidered.* Århus.

JOHNSON

1927    Johnson, A. C. "Ancient Forests and Navies." *TAPhA* 58:199–209.

JONES

1957        Jones, A. H. M. *Athenian Democracy.* Oxford.

JORDAN

1970        Jordan, B. "Herodotos 5.71.2 and the Naukraroi of Athens." *CSCA* 3:153–75.

KALINKA

1913        Kalinka, E. *Die Pseudoxenophontische* Ἀθηναίων Πολιτεία. Leipzig and Berlin.

KEIL

1902        Keil, B. *Anonymus Argentinensis: Fragmente zur Geschichte des Perikleischen Athen aus einem Strassburger Papyrus.* Strasbourg.

KIRCHHOFF

1865        Kirchhoff, U. "Über die Rede 'vom trierarchischen Kranze.'" *ADAW* 1:65–108.

KÖHLER

1879        Köhler, U. "Eine attische Marineurkunde." *AM* 4:79–89.

1883        ———. "Aus den attischen Marineinschriften." *AM* 8:165–80.

KOLBE

1901        Kolbe, W. "Zur athenische Marineverwaltung." *AM* 26:377–418.

KÖSTER

1923        Köster, A. *Das antike Seewesen.* Berlin.

KRÄNZLEIN

1963        Kränzlein, A. *Eigentum und Besitz im griechischen Recht des fünften und vierten Jahrhunderts v. Chr.* Berliner juristische Abhandlungen, no. 8. Berlin.

KUENZI

1923        Kuenzi, A. ΕΠΙΔΟΣΙΣ. Bern.

LAING

1965        Laing, D. R. "A New Interpretation of the Athenian Naval Catalogue IG II² 1951." Ph.D. diss., University of Cincinnati.

1968        ———. "A Reconstruction of I.G. II², 1628." *Hesperia* 37:244–54.

LAMBERT

1986          Lambert, S. D. "Herodotus, the Cylonian Conspiracy, and the ΠΡΥΤΑΝΙΕΣ ΤΩΝ ΝΑΥΚΡΑΡΩΝ." *Historia* 35:105–12.

LATTE

1968          Latte, K. "Kollektivbesitz und Staatsschatz in Griechenland." In *Kleine Schriften zu Religion, Recht, Literatur, und Sprache der Griechen und Römer,* ed. G. Gigon et al., 294–312. Munich.

LAUFFER

1974          Lauffer, S. "Die Liturgien in der Krisenperiode Athens." In *Hellenische Poleis,* ed. E. C. Welskopf, 1:147–59. Berlin.
1980          ———. "Die Bedeutung der Leiturgien für das Funktionieren der Demokratie." In *Die attische Demokratie,* ed. U. Margedant, 63–64. Frankfurt am Main.

LAZENBY

1987a         Lazenby, J. F. "The Diekplous." *G&R* 34:169–77.
1987b         ———. "Naval Warfare in the Ancient World: Myths and Realities." *IHR* 9:438–55.

LEHMANN

1968          Lehmann, G. A. "Bemerkungen zur Themistokles-Inschrift von Troizen." *Historia* 17:276–88.

LENARDON

1978          Lenardon, R. J. *The Saga of Themistocles.* London.

LEWIS, D. M.

1961          Lewis, D. M. "Notes on the Decree of Themistocles." *CQ* n.s. 11:61–66.
1973          ———. "The Athenian *Rationes Centesimarum.*" In Finley (1973), 187–214.

LEWIS, N.

1960          Lewis, N. "*Leitourgia* and Related Terms." *GRBS* 3:175–84.
1965          ———. "*Leitourgia* and Related Terms (II)." *GRBS* 6:227–30.

LIPSIUS

1878          Lipsius, J. H. "Die athenische Steuerreform im Jahr des Nausinikos." *JKP* 24:289–99.

LLOYD

1972      Lloyd, A. B. "Triremes and the Saïte Navy." *JEA* 58:268–79.

1975      ———. "Were Necho's Triremes Phoenician?" *JHS* 95:45–61.

1980      ———. "M. Basch on Triremes: Some Observations." *JHS* 100: 195–98.

LORENZEN

1964      Lorenzen, E. *The Arsenal at Piraeus.* Copenhagen.

MACDOWELL

1986      MacDowell, D. M. "The Law of Periandros about Symmories." *CQ* n.s. 36:438–49.

1990      ———. *Demosthenes against Meidias (Oration 21).* Oxford.

MAHAN

1890      Mahan, A. T. *The Influence of Sea Power upon History, 1660–1783.* Boston.

MARIDAKIS

1963      Maridakis, G. S. Ὁ Νόμος τοῦ Θεμιστοκλέους περὶ Θαλασσίου Ἐξοπλισμοῦ. Athens. (Also published as "La loi de Thémistocle sur l'armement naval," in *Studi in onore di Biondo Biondi,* 2:193–226. Milan, 1963.)

MARKLE

1985      Markle, M. M. "Jury Pay and Assembly Pay at Athens." In Cartledge and Harvey (1985), 265–97.

MARSTRAND

1922      Marstrand, V. *Arsenalet i Piraeus og Oldtidens Byggeregler.* Copenhagen.

MATTINGLY

1975      Mattingly, H. B. "Athens and Persia: Two Key Documents." *Philologus* 119:48–56.

1981      ———. "The Themistokles Decree from Troizen: Transmission and Status." In *Classical Contributions: Studies in Honour of Malcolm Francis McGregor,* ed. G. S. Shrimpton and D. J. McGargar, 79–87. Locust Valley, N.Y.

MEIGGS

1972        Meiggs, R. *The Athenian Empire*. Oxford.
1982        ————. *Trees and Timber in the Ancient Mediterranean World*. Oxford.

MERITT

1936        Meritt, B. D. "Archelaos and the Decelean War." In *Classical Studies Presented to Edward Capps on His Seventieth Birthday*, 246–52. Princeton, N.J.

MIGEOTTE

1982        Migeotte, L. "Épigraphie et littérature grecques: L'exemple des souscriptions publiques." *CEA* 14:47–51.
1983        ————. "Souscriptions athéniennes de la période classique." *Historia* 32:129–48.
1984        ————, ed. *L'emprunt public dans les cités grecques: Recueil des documents et analyse critique*. Quebec and Paris.

MILLETT

1991        Millett, P. *Lending and Borrowing in Ancient Athens*. Cambridge.

MOMIGLIANO

1944        Momigliano, A. "Sea Power in Greek Thought." *CR* 58:1–7.

MORRISON

1941        Morrison, J. S. "The Greek Trireme." *MM* 27:14–44.
1947        ————. "Notes on Certain Nautical Terms and on Three Passages in IG II² 1632." *CQ* 41:122–35.
1974        ————. "Greek Naval Tactics in the Fifth Century B.C." *IJNA* 3, no. 1:21–26.
1979        ————. "The First Triremes." *MM* 65:53–63.
1984        ————. "*Hyperesia* in Naval Contexts in the Fifth and Fourth Centuries B.C." *JHS* 104:48–59.
1987        ————. "Athenian Sea-Power in 323/2 B.C.: Dream and Reality." *JHS* 107:88–97.

MORRISON AND COATES

1986        Morrison, J. S., and J. F. Coates. *The Athenian Trireme: The History and Reconstruction of an Ancient Greek Warship*. Cambridge.
1989        ————, eds. *An Athenian Trireme Reconstructed: The British Sea Trials of "Olympias," 1987*. BAR International Series, no. 486. Oxford.

MOSSÉ

1979 Mossé, C. "Les symmories athéniennes." In *Points de vue sur la fiscalité antique,* ed. H. van Effenterre, 31–42. Publications de la Sorbonne, Études, no. 14. Paris.

MURRAY

1985 Murray, W. M. "The Weight of Trireme Rams and the Price of Bronze in Fourth-Century Athens." *GRBS* 26:141–50.

OBER

1978 Ober, J. "Views of Sea Power in the Fourth-Century Attic Orators." *AncW* 1:119–30.

1989 ———. *Mass and Elite in Democratic Athens: Rhetoric, Ideology, and the Power of the People.* Princeton, N.J.

OLIVER

1935 Oliver, J. H. "Greek Inscriptions." *Hesperia* 4:1–32.

ORMEROD

1924 Ormerod, H. A. *Piracy in the Ancient World.* Liverpool.

OSBORNE

1985a Osborne, R. *Demos: The Discovery of Classical Attika.* Cambridge.
1985b ———. "Law in Action in Classical Athens." *JHS* 105:40–58.
1988 ———. "Social and Economic Implications of the Leasing of Land and Property in Classical and Hellenistic Greece." *Chiron* 18:279–323.

PAPASTAVROU

1970 Papastavrou, I. S. Θεμιστοκλῆς Φρεάρριος: Ἱστορία τοῦ Τιτάνος καὶ τῆς Ἐποχῆς του. Athens. (Also published as *Themistokles.* Erträge der Forschung. Darmstadt, 1978.)

PICKARD-CAMBRIDGE

1968 Pickard-Cambridge, A. *The Dramatic Festivals of Athens.* 2d rev. ed., ed. J. Gould and D. M. Lewis. Oxford.

PODLECKI

1975 Podlecki, A. *The Life of Themistocles: A Critical Survey of the Literary and Archaeological Evidence.* Montreal and London.

RAUBITSCHEK

1949      Raubitschek, A. E. *Dedications from the Athenian Acropolis.* Cambridge, Mass.

RHODES

1980      Rhodes, P. J. "Athenian Democracy after 403 B.C." *CJ* 75:305–23.

1982      ———. "Problems in Athenian *Eisphora* and Liturgies." *AJAH* 7:1–19.

1986      ———. "Political Activity in Classical Athens." *JHS* 106:132–44.

RIHL

1987      Rihl, T. "The Attic ναυχραρίαι." *LCM* 12, no. 1:10.

ROBBINS

1918      Robbins, F. E. "The Cost to Athens of Her Second Empire." *CPh* 13:361–88.

ROBERTS

1986      Roberts, J. T. "Aristocratic Democracy: The Perseverance of Timocratic Principles in Athenian Government." *Athenaeum* 64:355–69.

ROBERTSON, D. S.

1927      Robertson, D. S. "The Duration of a Trierarchy." *CR* 41:114–16.

ROBERTSON, N.

1982      Robertson, N. "The Decree of Themistocles in Its Contemporary Setting." *Phoenix* 36:1–44.

ROBINSON

1937      Robinson, D. M. "A New Fragment of the Fifth-Century Athenian Naval Catalogues." *AJA* 41:292–99.

RODGERS

1937      Rodgers, W. L. *Greek and Roman Naval Warfare: A Study of Strategy, Tactics, and Ship Design from Salamis (480 B.C.) to Actium (31 B.C.).* Annapolis, Md.

RUSCHENBUSCH

1978      Ruschenbusch, E. "Die athenischen Symmorien des 4. Jh. v. Chr." *ZPE* 31:275–84.

1985a      ———. "Die Sozialstruktur der Bürgerschaft Athens im 4. Jh. v. Chr." *ZPE* 59:249–51.

1985b ————. "Die trierarchischen Syntelien und das Vermögen der Synteliemitglieder." *ZPE* 59:240–49.

1985c ————. "Ein Beitrag zur Leiturgie und zur Eisphora." *ZPE* 59: 237–40.

1985d ————. "Wechsel und Veränderungen im Kreis der 300 Leiturgepflichtigen und unsere Kenntnis der Oberschicht Athens in der Jahren 376 bis 322 v. Chr." *ZPE* 59:251–52.

1987a ————. "Das Datum von IG II/III² 1611 und der Bundengenossenkrieg." *ZPE* 67:160–63.

1987b ————. "Das Datum von IG II/III² 1612." *ZPE* 67:164.

1987c ————. "Demosthenes' erste freiwillige Trierarchie und die Datierung des Euböaunternehmens vom Jahre 357." *ZPE* 67:158–59.

1987d ————. "Der Endtermin in der Leiturgie des Trierarchen." *ZPE* 67:155–57.

1987e ————. "Symmorienprobleme." *ZPE* 69:75–81.

1990 ————. "Die Zahl der athenischen Trierarchen in der Zeit nach 340 v. Chr." *C&M* 41:79–88.

SCHACHERMEYR

1963 Schachermeyr, F. "Die Themistokles-Stele und ihre Bedeutung für die Vorgeschichte der Schlacht von Salamis." *JŒAI* 46:158–75.

SCHMIDT

1931 Schmidt, K. *Die Namen der attischen Kriegsschiffe.* Leipzig.

SCHMITT

1974 Schmitt, J.-M. "Les premières tétrères a Athènes." *REG* 87:80–90.

SCHWEIGERT

1939 Schweigert, E. "Fragments of the Naval Record of 357/6 B.C." *Hesperia* 8:17–25.

SEGRE

1936 Segre, M. "Una dedica votiva dell'equipaggio di una nave rodia." *Clara Rhodos* 8:227–44.

SEMPLE

1932 Semple, E. C. *The Geography of the Mediterranean Region: Its Relation to Ancient History.* London.

SIEWERT

1982 Siewert, P. *Die Trittyen Attikas und die Heeresreform des Kleisthenes.* Vestigia, no. 33. Munich.

SINCLAIR

1978     Sinclair, R. K. "The King's Peace and the Employment of Military and Naval Forces, 387–378." *Chiron* 8:29–54.

SNODGRASS

1983     Snodgrass, A. "Heavy Freight in Archaic Greece." In Garnsey, Hopkins, and Whittaker (1983), 16–26.

SOLMSEN

1898     Solmsen, F. "Ναύϰϱαϱος, ναύϰλαϱος, ναύϰληϱος." *RhM* 53:151–58.

SOMMERSTEIN

1981     Sommerstein, A. H., ed. *Aristophanes: Knights.* Warminster.

STARR

1989     Starr, C. G. *The Influence of Sea Power on Ancient History.* New York and Oxford.

STRAUSS

1986     Strauss, B. S. *Athens after the Peloponnesian War: Class, Faction, and Policy, 403–386 B.C.* London and Sydney.

SUNDWALL

1910     Sundwall, J. "Eine neue Seeurkunde." *AM* 35:37–60.
1915     ———. "Liste athenischer Marinebesatzungen." *AA* 3:124–37.

TÄNZER

1912     Tänzer, K. *Das Verpflegungswesens der griechischen Heere bis auf Alexander dem Grossen.* Jena.

TARN

1905     Tarn, W. W. "The Greek Warship." *JHS* 25:137–56, 204–24.
1930     ———. *Hellenistic Military and Naval Developments.* Cambridge.

THOMSEN

1964     Thomsen, R. *Eisphora: A Study of Direct Taxation in Ancient Athens.* Humanitas, no. 3. Copenhagen.
1977     ———. "War Taxes in Classical Athens." In *Armées et fiscalité dans le monde antique,* 135–47. Colloques nationaux du CNRS, no. 936. Paris.

TORR

1894     Torr, C. "Les navires sur les vases du Dipylon." *RA,* 3d ser., 25:14–28.

UNZ

1985        Unz, R. K. "The Surplus of the Athenian *Phoros*." *GRBS* 26:21–42.

VARTSOS

1978        Vartsos, J. A. "Class Divisions in Fifth Century Athens." *Platon* 30:226–44.

VÉLISSAROPOULOS

1980        Vélissaropoulos, J. *Les nauclères grecs.* Geneva and Paris.

VERNANT

1965        Vernant, J.-P. "Remarques sur la lutte de classe dans la Grèce ancienne." *Eirene* 4:5–19.

VEYNE

1976        Veyne, P. *Le pain et le cirque: Sociologie historique d'un pluralisme politique.* Paris.

WADE-GERY AND MERITT

1957        Wade-Gery, H. T., and B. D. Meritt. "Athenian Resources in 449 and 431 B.C." *Hesperia* 26:163–97.

WALLACE

1989        Wallace, R. W. "The Athenian *Proeispherontes*." *Hesperia* 58:473–90.

WALLINGA

1982        Wallinga, H. T. "The Trireme and Its Crew." In *Actus: Studies in Honour of H. L. M. Nelson,* ed. J. den Boeft and A. H. M. Kessels, 463–82. Utrecht.

1993        ———. *Ships and Sea-Power before the Great Persian War: The Ancestry of the Ancient Trireme.* Leiden.

WELWEI

1974        Welwei, K. W. *Unfreie im antiken Kriegsdienst.* Forschungen zur antiken Sklaverei, no. 5. Wiesbaden.

WHITEHEAD, D.

1983        Whitehead, D. "Competitive Outlay and Community Profit: Φιλοτιμία in Democratic Athens." *C&M* 34:55–74.

1986        ———. *The Demes of Attica 508/7–ca. 250 B.C.: A Political and Social Study.* Princeton, N.J.

WHITEHEAD, I.

1987        Whitehead, I. "The Periplous." *G&R* 34:178–85.

WILCKEN

1907       Wilcken, U. "Der Anonymus Argentinensis." *Hermes* 42:374–418.

WILLIAMS

1983       Williams, J. M. "Solon's Class System, the Manning of Athens' Fleet, and the Number of Athenian Thetes in the Late Fourth Century." *ZPE* 52:241–45.

WILSON

1970       Wilson, C. H. "Athenian Military Finances, 378/7 to the Peace of 375." *Athenaeum* 48:302–26.

WRIGHT

1892       Wright, J. H. "The Date of Cylon." *HSPh* 3:1–74.

WÜST

1957       Wüst, F. R. "Zu den πρυτάνιες τῶν ναυκράρων und zu den alten attischen Trittyen." *Historia* 6:176–91.

ZIEBARTH

1929       Ziebarth, E. *Beiträge zur Geschichte des Seeraubs und Seehandels im alten Griechenland.* Hamburg.

# Index

## General Index

*agathos*, distinguishing prowess, 7, 26

Aigina: fleet of, 27; war between Athens and, 32–33

*anepiklērōtos*, 80–82, 130, 180, 193, 224. *See also* ships, allocation of

*antidosis*, 51, 52, 53, 60, 66, 91–95, 188–89, 221; against Demosthenes, 52, 91–92, 95–96; against Isokrates, 65, 92, 95; against Meidias, 95; against Phainippos, 92; before expeditions, 76–77, 91–92; and democracy, 94–95; disliked by Isokrates, 9, 94–95, 221; exclusion of encumbered estates from, 90; function of, 94–95, 225; private settlement, 93, 246n. 22; property declared during, 93–94, 246n. 23. *See also diadikasia; skepsis*

*apodektai*, 128, 162, 254n. 23

*apographē*, 163–64, 169

*apostoleis*, 165, 258n. 27

archers, 37, 106, 107

*architheoria*, 7, 49

*archon eponymous*: appoints *choregoi*, 75; supervises estates of orphans, 89

*aretē*, distinguishing prowess, 7, 26, 219, 220

*arithmos* formulas, 15, 127–28

*arrhephoria*, 7

assembly: decides about shipbuilding, 134–36; determines the condition of hulls, 134

*aulētēs*, 106

boule, 35; doubles debts, 166; orders recovery of equipment, 159, 165; supervises shipbuilding, 133–35; tries cases against naval officials, 62

cavalry, exempt from trierarchies, 90, 96, 179, 261n. 13. *See also hipparchos*

*charis*, 56; and trierarchies, 10, 11, 226, 231n. 21. *See also* trierarchies, benefits from

*choregoi*, 7, 9, 50, 55, 58, 64, 177, 239n. 7; *antidoseis* for, 70, 75, 93, 95; exemption, 85; and *philotimia*, 48, 49; shortages, 180, 262n. 15; supplied by the tribes, 72, 75

crew: citizens, 72, 96, 107, 109; conscription of, 106–8, 248n. 6;

crew (*cont'd*)
food consumption by, 119–21;
foreigners, 96, 107, 112, 123;
maintenance, 4, 110–14, 115, 117;
minimum number per ship, 109–10;
provided by state, 1, 107–8, 110–14,
115, 117; provided by trierarchs, 1, 2,
107–9, 120–24, 201, 203 (*see also*
oarsmen; trierarchs); recruitment of,
28, 105–10; replacements, 119, 124;
slaves, 96, 100, 107, 108, 123; training,
110, 111, 249n. 13; water supply, 119,
120. *See also* desertion, by crews;
*epibatai; hyperēsia;* oarsmen

debts, trierarchic, 2, 52; clearance of, 15,
158, 160–69, 225; collection of, 84,
153, 157–62, 164–69, 225; difficulties
in recovering, 145, 155, 158, 162–69;
doubled, 162–63, 165–67, 222,
259nn. 33, 35, 38; taken over by heirs,
62–63, 66
demarchs, return oarsmen, 107, 124. *See
also naukraroi*
demes: liturgies of, 7, 47, 51, 93, 245n. 1;
trierarchs selected in, 57, 58, 60, 68,
72
Demosthenes' law, 182, 185, 191;
date, 209; and new patterns of
syntrierarchies, 207–8, 210, 212, 225;
and the Three Hundred, 192, 209–12,
225, 268n. 79, 269n. 86. *See also*
trierarchic expenditure, equal
distribution
desertion: by crews, 100, 113, 121–24; by
trierarchs, 80, 99
diadikasia: against naval officials, 62, 139;
for *antidoseis,* 73, 75, 76, 91–94; for
compensating equipment, 150, 160,
165, 226; for compensating ships,
138–39; documents, 69–71, 221; for
exemptions, 85. *See also antidosis;
skepsis*
diekplous, 39
dockyards: administration of, 14–15, 28,

150–51, 155, 164 (*see also* epimeletai
ton neorion); facilities, 28, 33, 148–49
(*see also skeuothēkē*); guards of,
257n. 4; personnel, 28, 133, 145;
treasurer of, 144, 151, 152, 163–64,
268n. 80. *See also* epimeletai ton
neorion
dokimastēs. *See* "tester"

eisphora, 7, 55, 184, 217: arrears, 117, 158;
to build ship-sheds and *skeuothēkē,*
257n. 10; the first, 116; number of
payers, 183–90, 262n. 21, 263n. 29;
paid by the Three Hundred, 64–65;
unwillingness to pay, 117; valuation of
properties for, 44, 52–54, 56–57,
184–85, 190. *See also proeisphora;
symmories, eisphora;* Thousand; Three
Hundred
epibatai: provided by the state, 106–7; in
Themistokles decree, 37. *See also*
hoplites
epidoseis, 73, 199–206, 225; compulsory,
200; definition, 143, 199–201; and
ship repairs, 143–44, 206; of 334/3,
267n. 71; of 340, 204–6; of 349/8, 204;
of 357, 203
epikleroi. *See* exemption from trierarchy,
of heiresses
epimeletai ton neorion: collect debts, 128,
156–57, 162; compile inventories,
14–15, 81, 232n. 32; diagrammata of,
14, 136, 232n. 32, 242n. 2, 256nn. 15,
17, 259n. 37; initiate legal action,
162–63, 165, 167, 258n. 27; inspect
ships, 137; issue hulls and equipment,
76, 136–37; replaced in 348/7–334/3,
150, 232n. 32; supervise naval
harbors, 14. *See also* dockyards,
administration of
equipment: on the Acropolis, 148, 157;
compensating, 2, 150, 152–53, 168,
176, 221–2; private, 82, 136, 153–56,
159, 163; shortages, 82–83, 146–49,
153, 182, 199, 224–5; storage of,

148–49, 157, 158 (*see also* dockyards,
facilities); transferred to other ships,
81–82, 154, 158; treasurer of hanging,
149, 257n. 11; value of, 136, 140,
152–53, 221–2, 270n. 4; withheld by
officials, 149–53, 163–64; withheld by
trierarchs, 83–84, 153–62, 164–65,
168–69. *See also tetrēreis; triēreis*
eutaxia, 50
exemption from trierarchy, 70, 85–95,
187; of *adynatoi*, 88, 186, 188–89; after
a liturgy, 85–87, 177, 224, 261n. 11; of
corporate property, 87–90, 186, 188;
disregarded, 72, 90, 179; of heiresses,
87–90, 186, 188, 242n. 4; of *klerouchs*,
87–90; of the nine *archons*, 90; of
orphans, 87–90, 186, 188; period of,
78, 86, 174, 177–78, 181, 195, 224;
while performing another liturgy,
87, 189, 224. *See also antidosis;*
cavalry

fleets: loans from sacred treasuries to
finance, 115–16; logistics of, 6, 111,
118–21, 218; maintenance, 4, 28,
110–14 (*see also triēreis,* maintenance)

generals, 39; appoint trierarchs, 37, 58,
68–70, 73–78, 167; carry *antidoseis* for
the Three Hundred, 192; in charge of
*symmories,* 69, 75–77, 92, 192, 193; in
charge of warship, 63; command
fleets, 23, 80; group *syntrierarchs,* 175;
introduce cases to court, 75, 76, 78, 92
(*see also antidosis*); and "politicians,"
214, 226; qualifications of, 5, 37,
229n. 8; supply pay, 78, 113–15, 117,
251nn. 26, 27
gymnasiarchy, 7, 9, 47, 64

helmsman, 39, 99, 106, 121–22,
238n. 54
hestiaseis, 7
hipparchos, 4, 96. *See also* cavalry
hippeis (Solonian class), 107

hoplitagōgoi, 106
hoplites, 68, 70; on *triēreis,* 106, 107. *See
also epibatai*
hulls: compensating, 2, 30, 80, 128,
136–39, 142, 145, 166, 167, 176, 216,
221–22; condition of, 79, 129–31; cost
of, 34, 136, 139, 141, 142, 145, 216,
221–22, 255n. 34; repairs, 142–45,
176, 198. *See also triēreis*
hypēresia, 106: availability in Athens, 39,
108; demands of higher pay by, 122;
hire by trierarchs, 107, 109, 121–22
(*see also* crews; trierarchs); in
Themistokles decree, 37

Kantharos, 13; pier at, 76, 109; ships of,
143, 147
keleustēs, 39, 106
Kleinias (son of Alkibiades), 1–3, 8, 26,
36, 201, 203, 226
kolakretai, 21
Konon (son of Timotheos), 2–3, 8, 62,
166–67, 222
Kybernetes. *See* helmsman

law courts: adjudicate ships, 138–39; treat
trierarchs leniently, 11, 162–64, 166,
182, 224–25. *See also diadikasia;*
skepsis
lēitourgia, definition, 6–7. *See also* liturgy
system
liturgical class: attitude of democracy
toward, 8–9, 11–12, 49, 59, 226,
231n. 26; contributes to national
revenue, 10, 215–17, 226; membership,
43–44, 51, 52; obligations, 7, 219; size,
177–80, 261n. 14. *See also* liturgy
system
liturgies, festival, 7, 48, 177–78:
exemption from, 52–53, 85–86, 89,
90, 177, 178, 180, 187; expenditure on,
47–48, 51, 216, 239n. 7; nominees
supplied by tribes, 72, 75; number of
persons needed for, 53, 71, 176–80.
*See also* metics

liturgy system, 27, 36; abolition of, 7, 12; attachment to democracy of, 7–8, 11–12, 219, 226; before 508/7, 20, 25; complaints against, 7, 9, 101, 221, 223; enlarged with trierarchy, 35–36, 38, 219; and fleet finance, 6, 36, 38, 101, 219; introduction of, 35. *See also* *lēitourgia*
metics: ineligible for trierarchies, 61, 240n. 25; in naval service, 107, 108, 122; perform festival liturgies, 7, 61, 179
Mounichia, 14; ships of, 130–31, 147

*naukrariai*, 30; each supplies a ship, 23, 29; fund of, 21, 23; likened to *symmories*, 22–23; local character of, 22; as precursor of trierarchy, 3, 19–24, 26, 219; *prytanes* of, 20; reorganized by Kleisthenes, 20, 22–23, 29; subdivisions of tribes, 20, 21, 22. *See also* *naukraroi*
*naukraroi*: etymology, 23–24; financial duties of, 21; officials, 21; *prytanies* of, 21, 233n. 6; religious duties of, 24, 233n. 8; supply and command warships, 20; surrender duties to *demarchs*, 20, 22–23. *See also* *naukrariai*
naval architects, 142, 143. *See also* shipwrights
Naval law, 137, 160
naval pay: given in full, 111, 112, 114, 122 (*see also* oarsmen); irregularity of, 112–13, 114, 117, 122–23; purchase power of, 110, 120; rates of, 111–14, 122, 124; terminology, 110–11; withheld, 111, 113, 123, 250n. 17. *See also* generals; oarsmen; *thranitai*; trierarchs
naval warfare: in antiquity, 5–6, 230n. 11; and piracy, 25, 114
navy, Athenian: funds for, 115–16, 216, 218; organization before 480, 24–26, 36, 219, 234n. 19; size: — in 4th

century, 127–29, 194; — in 431, 74, 126, 176–77, 187; — before 480, 19–20, 25, 27, 29, 32–34, 236n. 31; — in 480, 29, 31, 37, 38, 127

oarsmen: energy requirements of, 118–19, 120; fighting, 119; fully paid, 122; hired by trierarchs, 107–8, 121–24 (*see also* crews); insufficient number on ship, 107–8, 109; 170 on *triērēs*, 6, 106; slaves, 100, 107, 108, 123; trierarch's outlays for, 48, 108, 112, 121–22 (*see also* trierarchs). *See also* *thalamioi*; *thranitai*; *zygioi*

*Paralos*, 20, 73; all-citizen crew, 109; Paraloi supply commander, 88
*pentēkontarchos*, 39, 106; hires oarsmen, 251n. 33
*pentēkontors*, 27, 127, 229n. 3; use in warfare and commerce, 25, 234n. 21
*pentereis*, 128, 229n. 3; complement of, 106; number of, 127
Periandros's law, 182–99; creates *symmories*, 182–90, 197, 224; criticisms of, 182, 199, 264n. 44; date, 182; increases number of trierarchs, 180, 182, 199, 224; introduces *epimelētai* of *symmories*, 192–93; provisions about equipment, 159–60, 166, 198, 225. *See also* *symmories*, trierarchic
*periplous*, 39
*philotimia*: and liturgies, 48, 49, 55, 56, 90, 92; and usefulness to community, 101, 220
*proeisphora*, 7, 217, 264n. 39; *antidoseis* for, 70; definition, 179; exemption from, 58, 87, 189, 245n. 5; introduction, 179, 240n. 22; of 362, 57–58, 72, 116–17, 189, 240n. 21; to pay crews, 116. *See also* *eisphora*; *symmories*, *eisphora*; Three Hundred
property: concealment of, 9, 10, 46–47, 53, 58–59, 60–61, 67, 223; exchange of, 92–93 (*see also* *antidosis*);

inheritance of, 44, 60–67; invisible,
53–60, 223, 240n. 16; put to public
utility, 10–12, 35, 48–50, 55, 56, 226,
231n. 21; qualifying for trierarchies,
43, 45–53, 56, 59, 64, 66, 71, 187,
220–21, 223, 238n. 3, 239nn. 4–5, 95;
visible, 53–60, 73, 223, 240n. 16
*prōratēs*, 39, 106

*Salaminia*, 73
shipbuilding, 131–36; annual, 133–36;
before 483/2, 29, 32, 33; in foreign
shipyards, 34, 131; and institutional
developments, 29–30, 31–38, 219;
materials, 27–28, 139–42, 153, 155,
256n. 37; timber, 6, 28, 132, 137,
140–42, 155. *See also* Themistokles
ships: adjudicated, 138–39; allocation of,
37, 80–84, 130, 180, 193, 224 (*see also
anepiklērōtos*); donations of, 34, 131;
fully manned, 79, 109–10, 118;
guarantors of, 205–6, 270n. 4; lacking
equipment, 82, 83–84, 146–49,
257n. 2; private, 1, 2, 24–25, 26, 36,
201–3, 219, 229n. 4, 235n. 23;
purchased from Corinth, 29, 33–34,
36. *See also pentēkontors; pentereis;
tetrērēis; triakontors; triēreis*
ship-sheds: built by Themistokles, 33;
increase of, 131, 257n. 10
ships' ratings, 193; "first," 129–30; "new,"
80, 82, 129, 130; "old," 80, 81, 129,
130; "second," 129–30; "select,"
129–30, 135, 193; "third," 130–31
shipwrights, 28, 39, 106, 133, 137, 142. *See
also* naval architects
*skepsis*: for *antidoseis*, 75, 76, 92; for
compensating ships, 138–39; for
exemptions, 85, 92. *See also antidosis;
diadikasia*
*skeuothēkē*, 147, 148; Philon's, 149, 157,
257n. 10. *See also* dockyards, facilities
*stratiōtides*, 106
*symmories, eisphora*, 22, 211; *hēgēmon*
(leader) of, 88, 185, 191–92, 211,

269n. 85; introduction, 183; number
of, 22, 57, 58, 77, 190. *See also
eisphora; proeisphora;* Three Hundred
*symmories*, trierarchic, 4, 167; allocation
of ships to, 81, 82, 84, 193, 199,
211–12, 224; attempt of 354 to reform,
22, 186, 188, 190–91; distribution of
trierarchs in, 75, 77–78; epimeletai of,
159–62, 164–65, 167, 169, 191–93;
introduction, 77, 84, 182–90, 220;
·members share liabilities, 145, 157,
160, 167–69, 194–95, 225 (*see also
synteleis*); prepare ships, 195–97;
Twenty, the, 22, 81, 167, 182, 186, 188,
190–91, 212, 224. *See also* Periandros's
law
symmory debate, 22, 183–90, 194
*synchoregy*, 174, 177, 178
*syntaxeis*, 117
*synteleis*, 182, 193, 209, 212, 220; assist
active trierarchs, 194–98, 223, 225;
share expenditure, 69, 168–69
syntrierarchies, 173–82, 260n. 3; cost of,
49–50, 52, 125, 215–16; definition,
168, 174; division of responsibility,
175–76, 195, 207–8, 224, 26Inn. 7, 8;
introduction, 173–74, 220, 224,
260n. 1; nominal, 63, 167, 212;
number of persons performing one,
175, 260n. 4, 264n. 45; option to
perform, 175, 223; temporary
suspension of, 180–81

*tamias trieropoiikon:* and embezzlement,
152; owes equipment, 150, 151–52
"tester," 137, 143
*tetrērēis*, 222, 229n. 3; built annually, 135,
152, 255n. 27; complement of, 106;
number of, 127, 133; standard set of
equipment, 228
*thalamioi*, 106. *See also* oarsmen
Themistokles: builds ships in 483/2,
27–35, 218; creator of trierarchy, 20,
26, 30, 31, 34; fortifies Piraeus, 33,
336n. 39

Themistokles' decree, 3, 218; and
  allotment of ships, 37, 244n. 25;
  authenticity of, 37–38, 237nn. 48, 50;
  and qualifications of trierarchs, 37
Thousand, the, 70–71
thranitai, 106; bonuses to, 112, 122. See
  also oarsmen
Three Hundred, the, 185, 191–92,
  264n. 39; antidoseis for, 192. See also
  Demosthenes' law; eisphora
timēma. See eisphora, valuation of
  properties for
triakontors, 127–28, 229n. 3; use in
  warfare and commerce, 25
tribute, imperial, 116, 125. See also Navy,
  Athenian, funds for
triērarchia, definition, 4, 77. See also
  trierarchies
trierarchic expenditure: equal distribution, 69, 209, 211, 225; unequal
  distribution, 8, 196–97, 199, 209,
  264n. 44. See also Demosthenes' law
trierarchies: benefits from, 8, 10, 11, 50,
  99–101, 215, 248n. 31 (see also charis);
  compulsory, 8, 60, 62, 65, 72–73, 95,
  206, 220–21, 225–26; dodging, 9, 10,
  53, 54, 67, 77, 92, 94, 182, 220, 223,
  225; inherited, 60–67, 73, 221; involve
  danger, 10, 97, 101–2; justify property
  rights, 10–11, 59, 73, 226; length of,
  48, 77, 78–80, 223; oppressiveness of,
  8–9, 12, 173, 209, 221–23; outside
  Athens, 6, 230n. 12; shared by
  relatives, 66, 174, 175; registers of
  those eligible, 44, 68–73, 75, 77, 221;
  running cost of, 2, 49–50, 88, 98–99,
  118, 120–21, 124–25, 215–16, 222,
  271n. 6; voluntarism in undertaking,
  8, 10, 11, 36, 44, 48, 50, 59–60, 65, 68,
  71–73, 199–200, 203, 205, 221, 226.
  See also triērarchia; trierarchs
triērarchos, definition, 4–5. See also
  trierarchs
trierarchs: as debt collectors, 81, 159–61,
  164–65, 166, 198, 225, 226; hire

substitutes, 72, 78, 91, 95–102, 181,
  188, 220, 223; honors received by, 11,
  36, 59, 83, 101, 220, 226;
  imprisonment of, 225, 244n. 21;
  influence on politics by, 213–15, 226;
  introduce equipment, 154, 156;
  number of, 37, 53, 69–71, 74–75, 77,
  84, 87, 157–58, 176–88, 210–12,
  262n. 22; pay crews, 48, 78, 108, 112,
  113, 120–25 (see also crews; oarsmen);
  personal service by, 37, 39, 96, 97;
  raise loans, 52, 56, 124, 198, 271n. 6;
  receive public funds, 113, 115, 143,
  197–98, 252n. 47; of sacred ships, 73;
  seek asylum, 92; shortages, 83–84,
  101, 158, 176, 180–82, 186, 193–94,
  198–99, 211, 224–25; 60-year long
  existence, 87, 88, 97; spend more than
  required, 10, 86, 187; state control of,
  12, 53, 84, 95, 199, 225. See also
  trierarchies; triērarchos
triēreis: average life, 135; complement of,
  1, 6, 28, 106, 109–10, 218 (see also
  crews; epibatai; hypēresia; oarsmen);
  dependence on bases, 6, 119;
  emergence of, 27, 235n. 25; horse
  transports, 113, 127–28; limited
  capacity to take provisions, 6, 119,
  251n. 30; maintenance, 6, 36, 126, 129,
  131, 135–37, 218; replica, 4, 27, 34;
  size, 6; speed, 118; standard set of
  equipment, 227–28; tactical
  capabilities, 5–6, 118–19, 218; use by
  privateers, 100, 201, 202. See also
  hulls; ships
trieropoioi, 132, 137, 254n. 73
Twelve Hundred, the, 71, 183–90,
  194–96; hire out their duty, 97, 197;
  retained by Demosthenes' law,
  210–12, 225. See also Periandros's law
Twenty, the, 167, 192. See also symmories,
  trierarchic

Zea, 14; ships of, 130–31, 147
zygioi, 106. See also oarsmen

# Literary Texts Cited

Aelianus, *Varia Historia*, *13.12*, 77

Aeschines

1. *Against Timarchus: 11*, 85; *101*, 59, 240nn. 16, 18; *105*, 248n. 34

2. *On the False Embassy: 133*, 249n. 6; *148*, 244n. 23; *175*, 253n. 1

3. *Against Ctesiphon: 19*, 137, 248n. 33; *25*, 232n. 32, 257n. 10; *30*, 133; *89–105*, 267n. 72; *222*, 192, 209, 264n. 39, 268nn. 78, 79, 269n. 86

Aeschylus, *Psychagogoi, fr. 274*, 148

Ammianus Marcellinus, *14.8.14*, 256n. 37

Ammonios, naukleroi kai naukraroi, 234n. 14

Andocides

1. *On the Mysteries: 73–74*, 259n. 35, 244n. 23; *92–93*, 259n. 35; *118*, 240n. 16; *132*, 72

2. *On his Return: 11*, 140

3. *On the Peace: 3–5*, 132, 254n. 24; *6–7*, 132; *9*, 253n. 1

Androtion (*FGrH*, 324), *F 36*, 233n. 8

Anonymus Argentinensis (P. Strassburg 84), 254n. 24; *9–11*, 132, 134–35

Antiphanes, *fr. 204*, 9

Antiphon, *Tetralogies, 2.2.12*, 231n. 22

Aristides, *46.186*, 235n. 26

Aristophanes

*Acharnenses: 161–62*, 122; *544–45*, 119, 126; *916ff.*, 257n. 4

*Aves, 108*, 131

*Ecclesiazousai: 197–98*, 98; *597–601*, 59; *601–2*, 240n. 16

*Equites: 541–44*, 252n. 42; *912–18*, 74; *1300–1310*, 140; *1366–67*, 250n. 17

*Ranae: 190–92*, 249n. 9; *364*, 140; *1063–68*, 9, 54

Aristotle

*Athenaion Politeia: 4.2*, 229n. 8; *7.4*, 269n. 92; *8.1*, 5, 269n. 92; *8.3*, 21–23; *20.1–22.1*, 236n. 41; *21.5*, 22; *22.5*, 236n. 41; *22.7*, 28, 30–31, 235nn. 26, 29; *42.5*, 245n. 4; *43.5*, 266n. 56; *46.1*, 134, 137, 254n. 21; *48.1*, 259n. 35; *48.3*,

163; *56.3*, 75, 85, 92, 243n. 9, 244n. 19, 261n. 12; *56.6–7*, 89; *61.1*, 69, 75, 92, 192, 262n. 19; *61.2*, 244n. 21; *61.7*, 243n. 12; *63.3*, 259n. 35

*Ethica Nicomachea: 1120a6–8*, 48; *1120a21–23*, 49; *1122a19–1123a*, 45, 49; *1122b19–27*, 49

*Oeconomica: 2.2.4*, 26; *2.2.7*, 251n. 33

*Politica: 1279b17–1280a4*, 44; *1291a33–34*, 43, 213; *1291b24*, 109; *1304a22*, 109; *1304b20–1305a7*, 12; *1304b29*, 230n. 12; *1305a4–5*, 12; *1309a14–20*, 12; *1321a31–42*, 7; *1322b2–6*, 5

*Rhetorica: 1387a15ff.*, 60; *1399a35ff.*, 72, 245n. 4; *1411a9–10*, 251n. 25

Athenaeus: *1.27E–F*, 140; *3.103F*, 9; *4.168F*, 265n. 54; *5.208A*, 251n. 32

Demosthenes

1. *First Olynthiac: 6*, 250n. 24; *20*, 250n. 24

2. *Second Olynthiac: 24ff.*, 250n. 24; *28*, 250n. 25; *29*, 185, 190, 264n. 42

3. *Third Olynthiac: 4*, 249n. 6; *5*, 108; *11*, 244n. 23; *20*, 250n. 24; *30*, 250n. 25

4. *First Philippic: 7*, 248n. 34; *16*, 113; *22–24*, 113–14, 250n. 25, 252n. 46; *28*, 120; *29*, 114; *36*, 76, 91, 249n. 6; *43*, 108

8. *On the Chersonese:* 250n. 27; *8ff.*, 252n. 27; *21–23*, 250n. 24; *24–26*, 250n. 25; *28*, 117; *70–71*, 231n. 23, 248n. 33, 270n. 2

9. *Third Philippic: 15*, 250n. 27

10. *Fourth Philippic, 37–38*, 250n. 25, 270n. 97

13. *On Financial Organization, 20*, 185

14. *On the Symmories: 13*; *16–21*, 22, 70, 75, 81, 87, 130, 184, 186, 187, 188, 189, 190, 191, 193, 194, 199, 234n. 12, 239n. 14, 242n. 35, 258n. 15, 262nn. 18, 19, 263nn. 25, 26, 264n. 44, 267n. 70; *22–23*, 239n. 12, 243n. 10; *24–29*, 185; *25–28*, 231n. 26

15. *On the Liberty of the Rhodians, 32*, 244n. 23

17. *On the Treaty with Alexander, 28*, 140

Demosthenes (*cont'd*)

18. *On the Crown: 87,* 267n. 72; *99,* 195;
*102–8,* 69, 92, 185, 191, 192, 194, 195,
196, 197, 199, 209, 211, 212, 223,
242n. 1, 244n. 21, 245n. 3, 252n. 41,
259n. 35, 262n. 18, 263n. 25,
264nn. 39, 44, 265n. 47, 268nn. 77,
78, 79, 269n. 86; *113,* 271n. 7; *132,*
257n. 4; *171,* 192, 264n. 39; *257,*
248n. 33, 270n. 2; *312,* 185, 269n. 86
19. *On the False Embassy: 60,* 134;
*281–82,* 248n. 34; *303,* 38
20. *Against Leptines,* 177; *8,* 86; *10,*
248n. 34; *18–20,* 61, 179, 261n. 11; *23,*
262n. 18; *26,* 189; *28,* 75, 187, 189,
243n. 9, 261n. 12; *31ff.,* 196, 246n. 14;
*40,* 246n. 21; *44,* 90; *75,* 246n. 15;
*84–85,* 246n. 15; *100,* 266n. 56; *103,* 101;
*130,* 75, 243n. 9, 261n. 12; *135,* 266n. 56
21. *Against Meidias: 13,* 75, 261n. 12,
262n. 15; *64,* 246n. 15; *78–80,* 49, 52,
88, 91, 95, 96, 246n. 19, 246n. 21;
*152–57,* 263n. 27, 264n. 39; *154–55,* 87,
97, 98, 108, 194, 195, 196, 197, 213, 215,
223, 245n. 6, 246n. 16, 247n. 29,
252n. 47, 260n. 3, 262n. 18, 265nn. 47,
53; *156–58,* 48, 95, 239n. 14, 240n. 25,
246n. 8; *159–67,* 175, 195, 203, 204,
220, 248n. 34, 247n. 29, 266n. 66,
267n. 67; *163–67,* 96, 99, 100, 155, 188,
195; *165,* 247n. 28, 263n. 33; *171–74,*
243n. 12; *189,* 270n. 3, 271n. 7
22. *Against Androtion: 8,* 134; *13,*
255n. 24; *17,* 152; *44–45,* 117, 158; *60,*
162; *63,* 156, 162
23. *Against Aristocrates: 171,* 250n. 25;
*209,* 250n. 25
24. *Against Timocrates: 11–14,* 100, 176,
259n. 31; *39–40,* 259n. 35
25. *Against Aristogeiton I,* 164
27. *Against Aphobus I: 7,* 239n. 14,
246n. 8; *37,* 88; *64,* 51, 60
28. *Against Aphobus II: 2–4,* 239n. 14,
58, 223, 240n. 18, 246n. 8; *7–8,* 56,
239n. 14, 240nn. 18, 19; *17,* 49, 91, 92,

95, 96, 246nn. 19, 21, 23; *19–20,* 61,
231n. 24; *24,* 58, 231n. 24, 240n. 18,
248n. 34
29. *Against Aphobus III, 59–60,*
239n. 14, 246n. 8
30. *Against Onetor I, 15–17,* 246n. 16
35. *Against Lacritus, 48,* 75, 264n. 42
36. *For Phormio, 58,* 248n. 34
38. *Against Nausimachus and Xenopeithes:*
*2ff.,* 66; *7,* 240n. 16; *26,* 271n. 7; *36,* 56
39. *Against Boeotus I, 7–8,* 75, 77, 92,
243n. 9, 261n. 12, 263n. 25, 264n. 42
42. *Against Phaenippus,* 246nn. 19, 23,
247n. 24; *1,* 94; *3–5,* 90, 192, 231n. 22,
239n. 12, 264nn. 39, 42; *9,* 90; *11,* 93;
*12ff.,* 246n. 22; *17–19,* 89, 246n. 21;
*21–23,* 51, 53, 240n. 18, 264n. 39; *25,*
248nn. 33, 34, 264n. 39, 270n. 3; *28,*
90
45. *Against Stephanus I: 66,* 50, 55,
240n. 16; *78,* 240n. 25; *85,* 108, 203,
240n. 25
47. *Against Euergus and Mnesibulus,* 13,
226; *20ff.,* 81, 141, 147, 154, 158,
159–60, 161, 162, 164–66, 183,
232n. 31, 243n. 17, 244n. 28, 255n. 30,
260n. 43, 262n. 19, 264n. 43, 265n. 47;
*23,* 151, 154, 155, 258n. 28; *24–26,* 155,
259n. 34; *28,* 155; *29–32,* 65, 193,
244n. 22, 258n. 15, 262n. 19; *36,* 136,
258n. 15; *43–44,* 136, 154, 244n. 28,
258n. 15, 259n. 37; *53–61,* 56, 98; *67,*
98
48. *Against Olympiodorus: 12,* 240nn. 16,
17; *33–35,* 61, 240n. 17
49. *Against Timotheus: 6–8,* 117,
262n. 16; *11–12,* 52, 117, 121, 262n. 16;
*15,* 117, 122; *29,* 155; *34–36,* 140, 155; *44,*
117; *46,* 271n. 7; *67,* 266n. 56
50. *Against Polycles,* 13, 50, 52, 78–80,
100, 110, 121, 231n. 22, 243n. 17; *4–9,*
87, 107, 153, 252n. 48; *8–10,* 48, 57,
116, 179, 189, 240n. 16, 264n. 39; *10ff.,*
122, 123, 244n. 19, 248n. 3; *14–16,* 15,
48, 76, 117, 123, 124, 248n. 33,

252nn. 43, 44, 270n. 2; *17–19*, 122,
   251n. 33, 252n. 48; *22–24*, 76, 119, 123,
   248n. 33, 252n. 48; *26*, 258n. 15; *30ff.*,
   261n. 7; *39–40*, 175, 261n. 7; *41–42*, 76,
   82, 96, 99, 153, 244nn. 20; *46–48*,
   238n. 54, 244n. 21; *48–50*, 122,
   237n. 46; *52–53*, 96, 247n. 26,
   266n. 62; *56*, 252n. 48; *59–63*, 98,
   247n. 28; *66*, 76; *68*, 176
   51. *On the Trierarchic Crown*, 13; *5–9*, 92,
   96, 97, 99, 108, 109, 122, 153, 244n. 20,
   248n. 3; *11*, 113, 197, 252n. 47; *13*, 100;
   *17*, 109; *22*, 270n. 2
   53. *Against Nicostratus*, 4, 98
   59. *Against Neaera*, 6, 259n. 35
   *Epistulae*, *3.41*, 240n. 16
   *Exordia*, *41.2*, 250n. 24
Digest, *47.22.4*, 234n. 21
Dinarchus
   1. *Against Demosthenes*: *42*, 192, 210,
   264n. 39, 269n. 86; *70–71*, 59, 229n. 8,
   240nn. 16, 18, 19; *96*, 133, 257n. 10
Diodorus Siculus: *8.19.1*, 235n. 23; *11.41.2*,
   236n. 39; *11.43.3*, 135, 235n. 30; *12.40.4*,
   126; *14.94.2*, 251n. 26; *14.99.4*, 251n. 26;
   *15.47.7*, 251n. 26; *16.21.1*, 253n. 8;
   *16.57.2–3*, 251n. 26; *18.10.2*, 133,
   249n. 6; *18.15.8*, 253n. 8; *18.18.5*, 190
Diogenes Laertius, *7.12*, 265n. 54
Dionysius Halicarnassensis, *De Lysia*,
   *526*, 189
Douris (*FGrH*, 76), F *10*, 230n. 15
Harpocration: aphanes ousia kai phanera,
   54; chilioi diakosioi, 242n. 6,
   262n. 18; diagramma, 211, 242n. 2;
   diagrapheus, 211; hegemon
   symmorias, 185; koinonikon,
   242n. 35; symmoria, 211, 269n. 86;
   synteleis, 262n. 18
Hellanikos (*FGrH*, 323a), F *25* [*171*],
   249n. 9
*Hellenica Oxyrhynchia*: *1.1–3*, 201; *2.1*, 108;
   *3.1–2*, 201; *14.1–2*, 123; *15.1*, 123,
   248n. 3, 250n. 17
Hermippos, *fr. 63*, 140

Herodotus: *1.63.2*, 235n. 21; *3.57.2*,
   235n. 27; *5.47*, 229n. 4; *5.68–69*,
   337n. 41; *5.71.2*, 21, 233n. 5; *5.81*, 33;
   *5.84–89*, 234n. 19; *5.94–95*, 234n. 19,
   236n. 34; *5.97.3*, 32; *6.14*, 230n. 12;
   *6.36–41*, 235n. 23, 236n. 34; *6.87–93*,
   32, 33, 236n. 31; *6.116*, 33; *6.132–33*, 33,
   236n. 31; *6.138–40*, 236n. 34; *7.44.3*,
   237n. 50; *7.144.1–2*, 28, 29, 32, 38, 135,
   235nn. 26, 30, 238n. 50; *7.173–75*, 38;
   *7.181–82*, 39, 230n. 12; *8.1.1–2*, 29, 38;
   *8.11*, 39; *8.14.1*, 29, 238n. 50; *8.17*, 1,
   229n. 1, 249n. 11; *8.19*, 110; *8.41*, 38;
   *8.46–47*, 229n. 4, 230n. 12; *8.85*,
   230n. 12; *8.87*, 39; *8.90*, 230n. 12; *8.93*,
   39, 230n. 12
Hesiod, *Opera et Dies*, *663–65*, 238n. 52
Hesychius: nauklaroi, 22; naisteres,
   234n. 18
Hipponax, *fr. 45*, 235n. 25
Hypereides: *fr. 102*, 242n. 2; *fr. 134*, 192,
   196, 264n. 39, 265n. 47, 269n. 86; *fr.
   152*, 242n. 2; *fr. 159*, 185, 211, 262n. 19
Isaeus
   2. *On the Estate of Menecles*: *42*, 47, 51,
   53; *34–35*, 47
   3. *On the Estate of Pyrrhus*, 80, 47, 51
   4. *On the Estate of Nicostratus*, 27,
   248n. 34
   5. *On the Estate of Dicaeogenes*: 6,
   243n. 12; *35–36*, 45, 46–47, 50, 53,
   175, 247n. 29; *37–38*, 200; *41–42*,
   86–87, 231nn. 22, 23; *43*, 56, 240n. 18;
   *45*, 56
   6. *On the Estate of Philoctemon*: *1*, 176; *16*,
   246n. 18; *27*, 64; *30*, 240n. 16; *38*, 64;
   *60*, 64, 240n. 22, 243n. 18, 261n. 11,
   264n. 39
   7. *On the Estate of Apollodorus*: *5*, 77, 86;
   *32*, 46; *35–36*, 248n. 33, 270n. 2; *37–38*,
   73, 86, 195, 196, 244n. 19, 245n. 3,
   262n. 19, 271n. 7; *39–40*, 48, 49, 57,
   240n. 18; *41–42*, 46, 51, 57, 226,
   248n. 34; *47*, 240n. 18
   8. *On the Estate of Ciron*, *35*, 240n. 16

Isaeus (*cont'd*)

11. *On the Estate of Hagnias: 42, 52,*
263n. 35; *44,* 46; *48,* 155, 201, 202; *50,*
248n. 34

Fragments: *15, 55,* 240n. 16; *18,* 262n. 18;
*33,* 71, 242n. 6

Isocrates

7. *Areopagiticus: 35,* 240n. 18; *42,*
248n. 32; *54,* 96, 109

8. *On the Peace: 48,* 96, 248n. 6; *79,*
249n. 6; *128,* 9, 94, 221, 262n. 19; *143,*
244n. 23

15. *Antidosis: 4–5,* 92, 95, 188; *133,*
250n. 20; *145,* 65, 95, 187, 190,
262n. 18; *154,* 241n. 33; *156–58,* 46,
241n. 33

17. *Trapeziticus, 2–11,* 240n. 17

18. *Against Callimachus: 48,* 240n. 18; *50,*
122; *58–61,* 174, 175, 179, 199,
231n. 22, 240n. 18, 248n. 33, 270n. 2;
*63,* 231n. 22

Justinus, *Epitome, 2.12.12,* 235n. 26

Kleidemos (*FGrH,* 323): F 8, 22, 29, 191,
233n. 9, 234n. 12; *F 21,* 111

*Lexica Segueriana: 236.13,* 242n. 2; *257,* 22;
*283,* 23

Libanius

*Declamationes: 9.38,* 235nn. 26, 28;
*32.1.37,* 262n. 18

Lycurgus, *Against Leocrates, 139–40,* 178,
231n. 21

Lysias

3. *Against Simon: 20,* 95; *47,* 95

4. *On a Wound by Premeditation, 1–3,*
246n. 22

6. *Against Andocides, 46–47,* 247n. 28

7. *On the Olive Stump, 31,* 231n. 22

9. *For the Soldier, 4,* 243n. 15

12. *Against Eratosthenes, 83,* 240n. 16

14. *Against Alcibiades I, 5–9,* 244n. 23

15. *Against Alcibiades II, 11,* 244n. 23

18. *On the Confiscation of the Property of
the Brother of Nicias: 6,* 241n. 32; *20–21,*
65; *23,* 231n. 21

19. *On the Property of Aristophanes,*

258n. 20; *9,* 46, 271n. 7; *21–22,*
241n. 32, 267n. 72; *25–26,* 52, 271n. 6;
*29,* 86, 125, 215, 241n. 30; *42,* 125, 215,
241n. 30; *45,* 57; *47,* 241n. 32; *55–58,*
62, 243n. 18, 241n. 28, 248n. 33; *58ff.,*
46, 62, 247n. 29; *61–62,* 46, 61, 62,
226, 231n. 24

20. *For Polystratus: 23, 55, 59; 33,*
240n. 16

21. *Against a Charge of Taking Bribes:
1–11,* 10, 50, 77, 86, 90, 125, 179,
245n. 4, 270nn. 3; *96; 2,* 215, 244n. 19;
*6,* 77, 266n. 62; *10–15,* 10, 11, 59, 73,
108, 121, 231n. 24, 238n. 54; *16,*
271n. 7; *25,* 231n. 21

22. *Against the Grain Dealers, 13,*
240n. 19

24. *For the Invalid, 9,* 246n. 21

25. *Against a Charge of Subverting the
Democracy, 12–13,* 231nn. 21, 23

26. *On the Scrutiny of Euandros: 3,*
248n. 33; *22,* 271n. 7

27. *Against Epicrates,* 258n. 20

28. *Against Ergocles,* 248n. 31, 251n. 26,
258n. 20; *3–4,* 250n. 24

29. *Against Philocrates,* 248n. 31,
258n. 20, 259n. 35; *3–4,* 78, 101,
250n. 24; *9,* 250n. 24

32. *Against Diogeiton: 14,* 50; *24,* 61, 98,
174, 245n. 4, 261n. 7; *26–27,* 50, 98,
125, 174, 216, 243n. 17

Fragments: *35,* 188; *54,* 71, 242n. 6; *79:*
240n. 16

Nepos, *Themistocles, 2.2,* 234nn. 26, 28

Nicolaus, *Progymnasmata, 8.7,* 235nn. 26,
28

*Oxyrhynchus Papyri, 1804,* 262n. 19,
264n. 37

Pausanias: *10.9.8–9,* 238n. 54, 252n. 42;
*10.15.5,* 234n. 12

Philochoros (*FGrH,* 328): F 41, 183; *F 45,*
262n. 18; *F 46,* 239n. 14; *F 49,* 204,
249n. 6; *F 56a,* 257n. 10; *F 158,*
251n. 27

Photios, naukraria, 233n. 9, 234n. 14

Pindar
  *Olympian Odes: 5.15*, 219; *6.9*, 26; *10.91*,
    26
Plato
  *Gorgias, 455D–E*, 257n. 5
  *Respublica: 341C–D*, 252n. 42; *488C–D*,
    238n. 54
Plutarch
  *Moralia: 303C*, 251n. 32; *349A*, 120;
    *349B*, 239n. 7; *841D*, 257n. 10; *848E*,
    204; *849F*, 267n. 68
  *Alcibiades: 1*, 229n. 1; *10.1*, 265n. 54
  *Alexander, 34.2*, 229n. 4
  *Cimon: 8.6*, 266n. 60; *9.2–4*, 111
  *Pericles: 11.4*, 111; *26.3–4*, 235n. 21; *35.1*,
    202
  *Phocion: 9.1–2*, 265n. 54; *28.7*, 263n. 34
  *Solon: 8.10*, 32; *12.1–11*, 233n. 5
  *Themistocles: 4.1–3*, 235nn. 26, 28; *4.10*,
    32; *7.5*, 243n. 12; *19.2*, 236n. 39
Pollux
  *Onomasticon: 8.40*, 244n. 23; *8.43*,
    244n. 23; *8.100*, 262n. 18, 269n. 86;
    *8.108*, 23, 29, 234n. 15; *8.134*, 246n. 10;
    *10.10*, 148
Polyaenus: *1.30.5*, 235n. 26, 238n. 50;
    *3.9.51*, 250n. 17; *3.9.55*, 251n. 26
Polybius, *2.62.6–7*, 127, 190, 239n. 14
Pseudo-Xenophon
  *Athenaion Politeia: 1.2*, 39, 108; *1.13*, 9,
    39, 86, 173; *1.19–20*, 249n. 13; *2.11–12*,
    141; *3.2*, 232n. 32; *3.4*, 74, 87, 176, 187
Scholia: in Ar. *Av.* 1541, 233n. 8; in Ar.
    *Eq.* 445, 233n. 5; in Ar. *Nub. 37*,
    233n. 8, 234n. 14; in Ar. *Ran. 404*,
    174; in Dem. *18.105–6*, 262n. 18; in
    Dem. *21.80*, 100, 262n. 18; in Dem.
    *21.154*, 262n. 18; in Dem. *21.155*,
    269n. 86
Stesimbrotos (*FGrH*, 107), F *2*, 235n. 26
Strabo, *13.1.38 (C 599)*, 236n. 34
Suda: anaumachiou, 244n. 23;
    demarchos, demarchoi, 234n. 14;
    diagramma, 242n. 2; synteleis,
    262n. 18

Theophrastus
  *Characters: 22.2–3*, 265n. 54; *26.6*, 7
  *Historia Plantarum, 4.8.4*, 140
Thucydides: *1.10.4*, 25; *1.13.1*, 27; *1.13–14*,
    19; *1.14.1–2*, 27, 29, 235n. 26; *1.26.3–12*,
    233n. 5; *1.27.2*, 108; *1.31.1*, 252n. 44;
    *1.45*, 115; *1.49.1–3*, 249n. 11; *1.50–51*, 115;
    *1.91.1*, 248n. 3; *1.93.3–4*, 33, 236n. 39;
    *1.98.1*, 256n. 39; *1.104*, 254n. 18;
    *1.109–10*, 254n. 18; *1.117.2–3*, 115; *1.121.3*,
    116; *1.126.8*, 21; *1.138.3*, 32; *1.141.3–5*,
    116; *1.142.9*, 249n. 13; *1.143.1–5*, 5, 39,
    108, 116, 252n. 44; *2.13.3–8*, 116, 126;
    *2.24.2*, 75, 116, 132; *2.42.2*, 126, 252n. 1;
    *2.70.2*, 250n. 20; *2.87*, 238n. 54; *2.90.6*,
    108; *2.103.1*, 254n. 15; *3.16.1*, 107;
    *3.17.1–4*, 107, 110, 111; *3.19.1*, 116; *3.49.3*,
    120; *3.50.1*, 254n. 15; *3.88.1*, 119;
    *3.115.7–8*, 249n. 13; *4.11.4–12.1*,
    230n. 12; *4.14.1*, 108; *4.16.1–3*, 254n. 15;
    *4.75.1*, 238n. 54; *4.108.1*, 256n. 39; *6.8.1*,
    112; *6.16.1–4*, 231n. 21; *6.31.1–3*, 108,
    112, 122, 248n. 3; *6.39.1*, 231n. 26;
    *6.42–44*, 119, 249n. 11; *6.50.1*, 202; *6.61.1*,
    202; *6.61.6*, 266n. 60; *6.62.3*, 100;
    *6.93–94*, 115; *7.9–15*, 118; *7.13.1–3*, 100,
    123, 251n. 31; 252n. 44; *7.14.1*, 119;
    *7.24.2*, 254n. 15; *7.38.2–3*, 143,
    238n. 54, 256n. 43; *7.39.2*, 238n. 54,
    252n. 42; *7.47.2*, 119; *7.62.1*, 39,
    252n. 42; *7.69–70*, 238n. 54, 243n. 10;
    *7.74–75*, 132; *8.1.2–3*, 108, 132, 248n. 3;
    *8.5.5*, 112; *8.17*, 119; *8.19.3*, 108, 254n. 15;
    *8.24.2*, 106; *8.29.1–2*, 112; *8.30.2*,
    254n. 19; *8.45.2–3*, 113, 230n. 12,
    250n. 17; *8.47.2–48*, 12, 173; *8.57.1*, 123;
    *8.63.4*, 12, 173; *8.73.5*, 109; *8.74.2*,
    249n. 11; *8.78–79*, 123, 254n. 19;
    *8.83.1–3*, 123; *8.86.9*, 249n. 11
Tyrtaeus, *fr. 12*, 26
Xenophon
  *Anabasis, 7.1.27*, 116, 253n. 1
  *Hellenica: 1.5.4–7*, 113, 252n. 44;
    *1.5.11–12*, 202, 238n. 54, 252n. 42;
    *1.6.23–24*, 107, 133, 266n. 63;

Xenophon, *Hellenica (cont'd)*
    *1.7.4–35*, 39, 237n. 46; *2.1.19–21*, 228,
    251n. 33; *2.2.20*, 133; *2.3.40*, 203; *4.2.14*,
    181; *4.8.25–31*, 251n. 26; *5.1.13*,
    252n. 46; *5.1.14*, 115; *5.1.19*, 127; *5.2.10*,
    240n. 16; *5.4.34*, 133; *5.4.61*, 248n. 6;
    *6.2.11–12*, 108, 117, 262n. 16; *6.2.27–30*,
    249n. 13; *6.2.35–38*, 251n. 26
  *Oeconomicus*, 98; *2.3ff.*, 45, 221, 260n. 1;
    *8.8*, 118; *20.27–28*, 101
  *De Vectigalibus: 3.14*, 203; *6.1*,
    257n. 10

## Epigraphic Texts Cited

Behrend *Pachturkunden* no. 35. *See IG*
  $2^2$.2496
Dain (1931), 243n. 12
*Hesperia: 2 (1933)*, 393, no. 12: 248n. 1; *4
  (1935)*, 164, no. 24: 248n. 1; *7 (1938)*,
  277, no. 12: 242n. 5; *7 (1938)*, 306, no.
  29: 242n. 5; *9 (1940)*, 343, no. 43:
  253n. 6, 257n. 11; *12 (1943)*, 1, no. 1:
  237n. 42; *15 (1946)*, 160, no. 17:
  242n. 5; *37 (1968)*, 374, no. 51:
  247n. 29
IG $I^2$: *73* (see IG $I^3$.153); *74* (see IG $I^3$.154);
  *212*, 108; *342* (see IG $I^3$.493); *373–74* (see
  IG $I^3$.474–79); *897–901*, 243n. 10; *948*,
  236n. 34
IG $I^3$: *18*, 127; *60*, 106; *89*, 140; *117*, 133, 140,
  254nn. 21, 23; *127*, 108, 232n. 32,
  255n. 28; *153*, 109–10, 134, 232n. 32,
  254n. 21; *182*, 140, 254n. 21; *236*, 108,
  137, 160, 232n. 32, 247n. 29, 259n. 34;
  *254*, 93, 245n. 1; *363*, 115; *364*, 115;
  *366*, 132, 254n. 21; *369*, 250n. 22;
  *370.134–35*, 115; *375.34–37*, 115; *474–79*,
  216; *493*, 132; *498*, 231n. 29; *499*,
  231n. 29; *500*, 231n. 29
IG $2^2$: *1* (see IG $I^3$.127); *31*, 253n. 2; *40*,
  241n. 25; *120*, 232n. 31; *158*, 240n. 19;
  *212*, 246n. 14; *213*, 243n. 12, 247n. 29;
  *417*, 239n. 8; *505 and add. 661*, 149,
  249n. 9; *1138*, 247n. 29; *1147*, 246n. 14;

*1214*, 57; *1241*, 246n. 9; *1254*, 243n. 12;
  *1424A*, 240n. 25; *1443*, 258n. 16; *1471B*,
  257n. 12; *1479B*, 257n. 12; *1481B*,
  257n. 12; *1491*, 241n. 25; *1492*, 241n. 25;
  *1604★* (see IG $I^3$.498); *1604★a* (see IG
  $I^3$.499); *1604*, 127, 130, 133, 178, 180,
  253n. 10, 254n. 20
    *.15*, 81; *.20*, 80; *.26–27*, 81; *.32*, 80;
    *.56*, 137; *.64–65*, 130, 254n. 22;
    *.79–82*, 81, 82, 241n. 25; *.87–88*, 82,
    247n. 29; *.90–93*, 80, 82, 247n. 29
  *1605*, 253n. 10; *.38–39*, 175; *1606*,
  253n. 10, 254n. 15; *.7–10*, 244n. 26;
  *1607*, 180, 181, 253n. 10, 254n. 15
    *.26–27*, 81, 244n. 26; *.74–96*, 129;
    *.101–14*, 244n. 26; *.136–38*, 244n. 26
  *1608*, 81, 180, 181, 253n. 10; *.52–4*,
  244n. 26; *1609*, 232n. 31, 253n. 10,
  260n. 3
    *.21*, 257n. 6; *.27*, 240n. 25; *.57*,
    258n. 22; *.64*, 156; *.68–70*, 154,
    261n. 5; *.76–77*, 175; *.84–87*, 156,
    240n. 25; *.91–94*, 82; *.112*, 247n. 29
  *1610*, 253n. 10
    *.6–7*, 148; *.23–24*, 254n. 15;
    *.26–27*, 136
  *1611*, 129, 264n. 41
    *.3–9*, 256n. 1, 253n. 4; *.10–18*, 149,
    257nn. 2, 6; *.19–22*, 146, 257n. 2;
    *.33–37*, 147; *.42–64*, 232n. 31;
    *.65–134*, 129; *.73–96*, 135, 254n. 13;
    *.97–103*, 254n. 13; *.106–33*, 130, 133,
    135, 254n. 13; *.135–40*, 254n. 13;
    *.157–70*, 254n. 13; *.185–99*, 147,
    254n. 13; *.268–70*, 147, 257n. 6;
    *.283–373*, 83, 244n. 29; *.374ff.*, 161;
    *.434–48*, 156, 259n. 32
  *1612*, 264n. 41
    *.47–84*, 148, 232n. 31; *.91–99*, 143,
    256n. 36; *.114*, 247n. 29; *.132–38*, 66,
    80, 175, 243n. 17; *.145–50*, 143,
    256n. 36; *.218–35*, 137, 143; *.241–49*,
    143, 175; *.262ff.*, 161; *.271–78*, 66, 175;
    *.301–16*, 175, 203, 259n. 37; *.352–59*,
    261n. 5

*1613*

.*41–43*, 130, 147; .*60–71*, 130;
.*210–14*, 253n. 5, 260n. 4; .*224–26*,
253n. 5; .*241–42*, 257n. 6; .*257–70*,
135, 148; .*282–310*, 147, 253nn. 4, 5,
256n. 1, 257n. 6, 267n. 70
*1614*, .*140–65*, 147, 148, 256n. 1
*1615*, 191, 193, 260n. 43, 262n. 19,
264n. 43; .*88–104*, 63, 161
*1616*, 161, 193, 260n. 43, 262n. 19,
264n. 43
.*8*, 265n. 48; .*117–30*, 63, 162,
259n. 30
*1617*, 149, 161, 191, 193, 260n. 43,
262n. 19, 264n. 43
*1618*, 161, 191, 193, 260n. 43, 262n. 19,
264n. 43
.*6*, 263n. 33; .*83–91*, 156; .*106–7*,
259n. 30
*1619*, 161, 191, 193, 260n. 43, 262n. 19,
264n. 43
*1620*, 62, 241n. 26
.*32–55*, 139; .*65–73*, 258n. 15
*1621*
.*7*, 257n. 6; .*28*, 257n. 6; .*68*, 109;
.*101*, 257n. 6
*1622*, 243n. 10
.*45*, 261n. 8; .*115*, 261n. 8; .*130–45*,
261nn. 5, 8; .*165–84*, 162, 261n. 8;
.*196–200*, 245n. 4, 261n. 8; .*244–70*,
156, 175, 259n. 32, 261n. 8; .*294–311*,
261n. 8, 270n. 4; .*328–50*, 156,
259n. 32, 261n. 8; .*351–63*, 162,
260n. 4, 261n. 8; .*373–75*, 261n. 8;
.*420–31*, 151, 153; .*446–77*, 154, 171,
240n. 25; .*580–783*, 264n. 45;
.*587–610*, 69, 241n. 29; .*656–65*, 66;
.*715–40*, 162, 255n. 30; .*769–83*, 156
*1623*
.*6–34*, 138, 232n. 32, 244n. 22,
255n. 33, 256n. 36, 259n. 39,
260n. 4; .*35–49*, 258n. 16; .*57–71*,
259n. 33, 260n. 44; .*87–123*,
241n. 29, 256n. 36, 259n. 33;
.*124–49*, 256n. 36, 258n. 22,

259nn. 33, 39, 260nn. 4, 44,
270n. 4; .*144–59*, 63, 167, 193,
255n. 29, 258n. 15, 259n. 33,
264nn. 42, 43, 269n. 88; .*160–99*,
205, 267n. 72, 270n. 4; .*202–17*, 164,
241n. 25, 258n. 15; .*218–24*, 163,
259n. 33; .*225–36*, 243n. 12,
244n. 22, 247n. 29; .*245–59*,
240n. 25, 244n. 22, 258n. 22,
260n. 4; .*268–75*, 241n. 25, 258n. 16;
.*286–99*, 129; .*301–33*, 63, 244n. 22,
254n. 22, 267n. 71; .*368–75*,
258n. 17
*1624*, 232n. 31
.*42–49*, 228, 258n. 16, 270n. 4;
.*63–70*, 258n. 16; .*77–83*, 63,
247n. 29; .*95*, 261n. 8
*1625*, 161, 193, 260n. 43, 262n. 19,
264n. 43
*1627*, 257n. 12
.*17–34*, 127, 152; .*50*, 109; .*73–75*, 152;
.*155–71*, 152; .*194–233*, 66, 162, 164,
241n. 29, 258n. 16, 261n. 8,
263n. 33, 265n. 48; .*234–48*, 151,
254n. 22, 255n. 32; .*266–81*, 127,
253n. 4, 257n. 8, 267n. 70, 270n. 5;
.*288–317*, 255n. 30, 257n. 10;
.*320–21*, 149; .*353–59*, 133, 148, 155,
257n. 10; .*371–75*, 128, 151; .*398–407*,
254n. 14, 257n. 10; .*416–20*, 148,
257n. 10; .*421–35*, 143–44
*1628*, 257n. 12
.*8–16*, 155, 243n. 12; .*17–27*, 260n. 4,
267n. 75; .*28–42*, 254n. 22,
267n. 75; .*43–78*, 63, 260n. 4,
267n. 75, 270nn. 4, 5; .*79–88*,
243n. 12, 253n. 9; .*100–18*, 63,
270n. 5; .*136–46*, 63, 260n. 4;
.*207–12*, 128; .*228–49*, 166, 257n. 10,
259n. 39; .*350–68*, 166, 254n. 14,
259n. 41, 270n. 4; .*369–76*, 62, 128,
228, 247n. 29, 258n. 16, 259n. 41,
270n. 4; .*396–418*, 259nn. 39, 41,
260n. 44; .*460–65*, 254n. 22,
255n. 32; .*481–500*, 128, 253nn. 4, 6;

IG 2²: *1628* (cont'd)
.*501–32*, 257n. 8, 270n. 5; .*562–70*,
144, 256n. 36; .*609–18*, 255n. 33;
.*634–36*, 259n. 33
*1629*
.*3–15*, 254n. 22, 260n. 4; .*32–36*,
254n. 22; .*43–75*, 260n. 4, 268n. 76;
.*76–144*, 70, 128, 268n. 76; .*128–75*,
204, 254nn. 15, 22, 268n. 76;
.*165–271*, 76, 92; .*190–210*, 192,
248n. 33, 262n. 19, 270n. 2; .*272–78*,
208; .*330–51*, 128, 142, 152, 155;
.*475–99*, 128, 263n. 33, 265n. 48;
.*500–508*, 63; .*516–43*, 205, 267n. 72,
270n. 4; .*544–68*, 243n. 7, 261n. 7,
263n. 33, 265n. 48; .*572–99*, 162,
261n. 8, 270n. 4; .*600–656*, 240n. 25,
258n. 19, 270n. 4; .*647–64*, 258n. 15,
258n. 22; .*667–99*, 142, 155, 162,
243n. 12, 258nn. 16, 17, 270n. 4;
.*700–715*, 63, 270n. 4; .*722–57*, 128,
138, 254n. 22, 255n. 32, 270n. 5;
.*771–80*, 138, 247n. 29; .*783–812*, 128,
138, 253n. 4, 267n. 75; .*817–20*,
270n. 5; .*826–58*, 255n. 33,
263n. 33, 265n. 48, 270n. 4;
.*870–914*, 62, 228, 247n. 29,
258n. 16, 270n. 4; .*915–56*, 259n. 39,
260n. 44, 270n. 4; .*1004–9*, 270n. 5;
.*1030–36*, 254n. 14; .*1039–44*, 144;
.*1085–92*, 255n. 33; .*1151–52*, 255n. 30
*1630*, 253n. 6
*1631*
.*10–15*, 128, 260n. 44, 270n. 4;
.*44–48*, 128, 258n. 18; .*100–124*,
254n. 22, 255n. 32, 270n. 5;
.*148–74*, 100, 128, 255nn. 4, 33;
.*176–99*, 255n. 33, 263n. 33,
265n. 48, 270nn. 4, 5; .*199–216*,
254n. 22, 255n. 33, 257n. 8;
.*257–65*, 228, 259n. 33; .*279–83*, 228,
255n. 33; .*288–327*, 163, 270n. 5;
.*336*, 255n. 30; .*350–403*, 152,
163–64, 258n. 23, 259n. 34; .*404–29*,
119, 151, 258nn. 15, 17; .*429–48*, 164,
241n. 25, 256n. 36; .*442–503*, 144,

212; .*442–654*, 168; .*448–62*,
260n. 45, 265n. 48; .*466–73*,
247n. 29, 260nn. 45, 46, 265n. 48;
.*496–99*, 247n. 29, 260n. 46;
.*499–520*, 106, 144, 247n. 29,
268n. 80; .*517–30*, 139, 152, 212,
247n. 29, 256n. 36; .*551–62*,
260n. 46, 263n. 33, 265n. 48;
.*582–91*, 260nn. 45, 46, 263n. 33,
265n. 48; .*592–601*, 260n. 45;
.*635–59*, 168, 258n. 15, 260nn. 4, 45;
.*678–79*, 260n. 45
*1632*
.*14–19*, 152, 268n. 80; .*25–35*,
243n. 13, 260n. 4; .*56–89*, 247n. 29,
260n. 4, 264n. 45; .*151–52*, 247n. 29;
.*186*, 247n. 29; .*189–90*, 100; .*233–39*,
243n. 13; .*307–12*, 247n. 29, 260n. 4;
.*329*, 247n. 29; .*342*, 247n. 29
*1635*, 252n. 47; *1648*, 257n. 12; *1649*,
257n. 12; *1668*, 149; *1672–73*, 216;
*1924.16*, 247n. 29; *1925.16–17*, 247n. 29;
*1928*, 242n. 5; *1929*, 71, 242n. 5; *1930*,
71, 242n. 5; *1931*, 71, 242n. 5; *1932*,
242n. 5; *1951*, 69, 106, 174, 248n. 1,
249n. 9; *1953*, 83, 244n. 29, 270n. 2;
*2318*, 237n. 42, 260n. 2; *2409*,
247n. 29; *2492*, 246n. 9; *2496*, 57,
246n. 9, 263n. 35; *2497*, 246n. 9; *2498*,
246n. 9; *2499*, 246n. 9; *2966*, 88,
243n. 12; *3073–88*, 230n. 16; *3095*, 174
Laing (1968) 246, 253n. 6, 257n. 11
ML: no. 14 (= *IG* 1³.1), 32; no. 23,
37–38, 237n. 45, 238n. 50, 244n. 25,
249n. 11; no. 55 (see *IG* 1³.363); no. 61
(see *IG* 1³.364); no. 91 (see *IG* 1³.117);
no. 94 (see *IG* 1³.127)
Oliver (1935) no. 1 (see *IG* 1³.236)
Raubitschek (1949) no. 27, 49
Robinson (1937). See *IG* 1³.500
Schweigert (1939) no. 5, 232n. 31,
260n. 4
SEG: *10.226* (see *IG* 1³.366); *10.384*, 48
Segre (1936) 228, 248n. 35
Tod: no. 111, 141; no. 117, 253n. 2; no.
139.35–36, 90; no. 126, 140

Library of Congress Cataloging-in-Publication Data

Gabrielsen, Vincent.
    Financing the Athenian fleet : public taxation and social
relations / Vincent Gabrielsen.
        p.   cm.
    Includes bibliographical references and index.
    ISBN 0-8018-4692-7 (alk. paper)
        1. Trierarchy (Athens)  2. Naval art and science—Greece—Athens—
History.  I.  Title.
VA521.G33   1994
336.2'7—dc20                                                93-44414